Constructing the Pluriverse

Constructing the

Duke University Press · Durham and London · 2018

Pluriverse

BERND REITER,
EDITOR

The Geopolitics of Knowledge

© 2018 DUKE UNIVERSITY PRESS
Printed in the United States of America on acid-free paper ∞
Designed by Courtney Leigh Baker
Typeset in Garamond Premier Pro and DIN
by Westchester Publishing Services.

Library of Congress Cataloging-in-Publication Data
Names: Reiter, Bernd, [date–] editor.
Title: Constructing the pluriverse: The Geopolitics
of Knowledge / Bernd Reiter, editor.
Description: Durham : Duke University Press, 2018. |
Includes bibliographical references and index.
Identifiers: LCCN 2017060938 (print) | LCCN 2018000304 (ebook)
ISBN 9781478002017 (ebook)
ISBN 9781478000013 (hardcover : alk. paper)
ISBN 9781478000167 (pbk. : alk. paper)
Subjects: LCSH: Civilization, Western. |
Civilization, Modern. | Decolonization. |
Postcolonialism. | Imperialism. | Knowledge, Theory of. |
Science—Philosophy. | Social sciences—Philosophy.
Classification: LCC CB245 (ebook) |
LCC CB245 .C66 2018 (print) | DDC 909/.09821—dc23
LC record available at https://lccn.loc.gov/2017060938

COVER ART: *Soft Geometry*, Marta Minujín. Courtesy of Marta
Minujín Archives.

Contents

Part IV. Rethinking Politics, Democracy, and Markets

Foreword. On Pluriversality and Multipolarity

Over a fourteen- to fifteen-year span starting in 1995, I used the concept of pluriversality in many instances in my work.[1] I first heard of the concept during the early years of the Zapatista uprising. Franz Hinkelammert introduced the concept, as far as I know, and Enrique Dussel was using it during that period, and it fit perfectly well with the idea of pluritopic hermeneutics that I had borrowed from Raymundo Pannikar—an idea that became central to my argument in *The Darker Side of the Renaissance* (Mignolo 1995). But it was the Zapatistas' own decolonial political vision of a world in which many worlds would coexist that announced the pluriverse. The ontology of the pluriverse could not be obtained without the epistemology of pluriversity.

Epistemology and hermeneutics, in the Western genealogy of thought, investigate and regulate the principles of knowledge, on the one hand, and the principles of interpretation, on the other. Both strains are embedded in the self-proclaimed universality of Western cosmology and act as its gatekeepers. Together, epistemology and hermeneutics prevent the possibility of pluriversality, with all its internal diversity, and close off ways of thinking and doing that are not grounded in Western cosmology. The way out is the decolonial restoration of gnoseology fueling the march toward pluriversality.

When you—scholar, intellectual, journalist, or some such, trained in Western epistemology—have to navigate two or more cosmologies, as I had to while writing *The Darker Side of the Renaissance*, you need a point of reference that is contained in neither epistemology nor hermeneutics. I had recourse to the concept of pluritopic hermeneutics, which I adapted from Raimon Panikkar's (2017) diatopical hermeneutics. Although hermeneutics is retained, it is also reduced to size and to its restricted domain: namely, the provincial, universal assumptions sustaining Western cosmology. Gnoseology came to the rescue and I introduced it later on in *Local Histories/Global Designs* (Mignolo 2012c).

Why did Panikkar need diatopical hemeneutics, and why did I need pluritopic hermeneutics? Because I was dealing with a pluriverse of meaning. Pluriversality became my key argument for calling into question the concept of universality, so dear to Western cosmology. How so? Western epistemology and hermeneutics (meaning the Greek and Latin languages, translated into the six modern European and imperial languages) managed to universalize their own concept of universality, dismissing the fact that all known civilizations have been founded on the universality of their cosmologies. The West's universalizing tendency was nothing new, but it claimed a superior position for itself. The pluriverse consists in seeing beyond this claim to superiority, and sensing the world as pluriversally constituted. Or, if you wish, pluriversality becomes the decolonial way of dealing with forms of knowledge and meaning exceeding the limited regulations of epistemology and hermeneutics. Consequently, pluriversality names the principles and assumptions upon which pluriverses of meaning are constructed.

There is no reason to believe that the Bible is universal and the Popol Vuh is not. However, delinking from the Western universal is nonetheless a difficult decolonial task. The universalization of Western universality was part of its imperial project. Accordingly, a key idea in *Local Histories/Global Designs: Coloniality, Subaltern Knowledges, and Border Thinking* (Mignolo 2000a) was to argue for pluriversality as a universal project. Pluriversality as a universal project is aimed not at changing the world (ontology) but at changing the beliefs and the understanding of the world (gnoseology), which would lead to changing our (all) praxis of living in the world. Renouncing the conviction that the world must be conceived as a unified totality (Christian, Liberal, or Marxist, with their respective *neos*) in order for it to make sense, and viewing the world as an interconnected diversity instead, sets us free to inhabit the pluriverse rather than the universe. And it sets us free to think decolonially about the pluriversality of the world rather than its universality.

Consequently, pluriversality as a universal project means that the universal cannot have one single owner: the universal can only be pluriversal, which also corresponds with the Zapatistas' vision of a world in which many worlds coexist. All of us on the planet have arrived at the end of the era of abstract, disembodied universals—of universal universality. Western universalism has the right to coexist in the pluriverse of meaning. Stripped of its pretended universality, Western cosmology would be one of many cosmologies, no longer the one that subsumes and regulates all the others.

Thus conceived, pluriversality is not cultural relativism, but the entanglement of several cosmologies connected today in a power differential. That power differential, in my way of thinking and doing, is the logic of coloniality covered up by the rhetorical narrative of modernity. Modernity—the Trojan horse of Western cosmology—is a successful fiction that carries in it the seed of the Western pretense to universality. Expanding on this line of reasoning, it was necessary to introduce a concept that could capture the "/" of modernity/

coloniality, that is, the "/" between the entanglement and the power differential. And that concept was rendered as border thinking, border epistemology, border gnosis.

If a pluriverse is not a world of independent units (as is the case with cultural relativism) but a world entangled through and by the colonial matrix of power, then a way of thinking and understanding that dwells in the interstices of the entanglement, at its borders, is needed. So the point is not to study the borders while still dwelling in a territorial epistemology you are comfortable with. Such an approach would imply that you accept that there is a pluriverse someplace out there, but that you observe it from someplace else, somewhere outside the pluriverse.

To do so is necessarily to maintain the territoriality of the disciplines, grounded in the imperial epistemology of modernity. To think pluritopically means, instead, to dwell in the border. Dwelling in the border is not border crossing, even less looking at and studying the borders from the territorial gaze of the disciplines. Today border studies have become fashionable, even in Europe. Scholars studying borders are for the most part not dwelling in them. The people who dwell in the border are the migrants from Africa, west Asia (the so-called Middle East), and Latin America, predominantly. That's what I learned from Gloria Anzaldúa. Like migrants and queers, Chicanos and Chicanas are always dwelling in the border, whether they are actual migrants or not.

I think the impact that *Local Histories/Global Designs* had was owed to the fact that it was written while inhabiting the border. I did not observe the border; I inhabited it. As a matter of fact, it was my awareness of inhabiting the border that prompted the book. I needed to write from inside the border rather than write about the border while inhabiting the territory (be it a nationality or a discipline).

In the preface to the second edition of the book (Mignolo 2012c), I revealed a secret: that the argument was a rewriting of Hegel's philosophy of history from the position of inhabiting the border. Hegel—as I read him—was well grounded in the territory. For him, there was nothing else but the territory. But I was not there. So border thinking and doing (or, in this case, writing) became the way (as in Buddhism) or the method (as in Western sciences, social or not) of decolonial thinking and doing—a way and a method with infinite possibilities and permutations, to be sure, not constrained or prescriptive in its direction.

This combination of border thinking and border doing was a key point in moving away from the ideological trap that distinguishes theory from praxis. Reflexive praxis is, instead, the founding principle of Amawtay Wasi (Universidad Intercultural de las Nacionalidades y Pueblos Indígenas Amawtay Wasi). Why? Because its very educational project is built on border epistemology. It relies on indigenous and Andean cosmology—not rejecting indigenous European cosmology but embodying it within Andean cosmology—thus a cosmovivencia (Huarachi 2011).[2]

I learned from indigenous cosmology what I couldn't learn from Hegel and Western cosmology. However, I was trained (in body and mind) in the latter. Learning from what Western modernity had disavowed, and not observing and describing what modernity disavowed, opened up new dimensions of the border to me. Sensing that border is not a mental or rational experience, I sensed it, and sensing is something that invades your emotions, and your body responds to it, dictating to the mind what the mind must start thinking, changing its direction, shifting the geography of reasoning. Pluriversality for me goes in tandem with the enactment of border thinking, and not with the description of border thinking that happens not in yourself but someplace else.

In *The Darker Side of Western Modernity* (Mignolo 2011), I returned to pluriversality and the pluriverse of meaning, connecting it with the idea of the multiverse in Humberto Maturana's epistemology. The multiverse is for Maturana a world of truth in parentheses, while the universe is a world built on truth without parentheses—unqualified, unconditional. Universality is always imperial and war driven. Pluri- and multiverses are convivial, dialogical, or plurilogical. Pluri- and multiverses exist independently of the state and corporations. It is the work of the emerging global political society—that is, the sector of society organizing itself around specific projects, having realized that neither the state nor the corporation has room for multi- or pluriverses.

While multi- and pluriverses characterize the essence of the global political society, in the realm of the state and the corporations the vocabulary is that of a multipolar world. The multipolar world of today has been opened up by the economic growth and political confidence of China's interstate politics, together with the BRICS (Brazil, Russia, India, China, South Africa) nations, the growing economics and politics of Indonesia and Turkey, and the Latin American states in Mercosur, following the leadership of Brazil. When Vladimir Putin "stole" Barack Obama's threat of invading Syria, it was evident that the unipolar world that made the invasion of Iraq possible was no longer in place. And it seems obvious, too, that Putin's chess move was enabled by the support of the BRICS alliance, of which he is the current chair. Thus, I would like to use *pluriversity* in the sphere of the decolonial projects emerging out of the global political society (deracializing and depatriarchizing projects, food sovereignty, reciprocal economic organization and the definancialization of money, decolonization of knowledge and of being, decolonization of religion as a way to liberate spirituality, decolonization of aesthetics as a way to liberate esthesis, etc.) and *multipolarity* in the sphere of politico-economic dewesternization, led by state projects.

Despite their different spheres of reference, these two expressions—pluriversity and multipolarity—are today both used to underscore the disintegration of Eurocentrism. Eurocentrism is synonymous with Westernization (Latouche 1982). Eurocentrism was the partition of the globe by European institutions and actors to the benefit of Europe and the core Western states. The United States followed suit after World War II. By 2000, the signs marking the end of Westernization were no longer possible to ignore. It is not only that there were no more places to expand into: the reemergence of the disavowed was also becoming loud and clear. Indeed, the multipronged struggle for decolonization during the Cold War (and the Bandung Conference of 1955) had been an especially eloquent sign of the end of an era—an era that can be traced from 1500 all the way to 2000, roughly speaking. On the other hand, China's millennial comeback after the humiliation it suffered during and after the Opium Wars was sending strong signs to whoever was paying attention.

Now we, on the planet, are experiencing the consequences of decoloniality after decolonization and the consequences of dewesternization after the Cold War (Mignolo 2012b). Dewesternization (led by BRICS, Iran) has already mapped the multipolar world of the twenty-first century. This multipolar world is capitalist and decentered. As a result of this decentering, the United States, seconded by the European Union, is having more and more difficulty imposing its will and desires on the rest of the planet. Strong states have emerged whose leaders refuse to have bosses and receive orders (e.g., Ukraine, West Asia, the China Development Bank and the BRICS bank, and China and Russia's military affirmation). Therefore, the multipolar world arises out of the conflicts between dewesternization and the response to it being mounted by the West: namely, rewesternization, the effort to not lose the privileges acquired over the past five hundred years.

Westernization was defined by a coherent set of global designs. Intramural wars (the Thirty Years' War, World War I, and World War II) emerge from intramural conflicts in the process of Westernization. Dewesternization, on the other hand, is a heterogeneous set of responses disputing the unipolar management of the world's population and natural resources. If Westernization was unipolar, dewesternization is multipolar. Unipolarity was successful in enacting the global designs associated with Westernization. Multipolarity, on the other hand, can no longer be controlled by global designs; it fractures them, by definition. Indeed, multipolar processes are processes of de-designing. Dewesternization is the de-designing of Westernization.

Decoloniality, on the other hand, does not compete with dewesternization and rewesternization, but rather aims to delink from both—that is, to delink from state forms of governance, from the economy of accumulation, and from the ego-centered personalities that both enacted and reproduced Westernization: the modern subject forcing the formation of colonial subjects. Crucially, decoloniality is not a master plan or a global design. It is, above all, a diverse horizon of liberation for colonial subjects, constructed by the colonial subjects themselves. There cannot be a decolonial global design, for if that were the case, it would merely be the reproduction of ego-centered personalities who claim to hold the master key of decoloniality. Decoloniality starts with the transformations and liberations of subjectivities controlled by the promises of the state, the fantasies of the market, and the fears of armed forces, all tied together by the messages of mainstream media.

While ego-centered personalities and modern subjects are subjectivities formed in and by the processes of Westernization and Eurocentrism, decolonial processes emerge from an analysis and awareness of the promises of modernity and the disenchantments of coloniality. If, then, state-led dewesternization is forcing the formation of a multipolar world order, decoloniality is opening the horizon of a pluriversal world. Pluriversality, contrary to de- and rewesternization, focuses not on the state, the economy, or the armed forces, but on delinking from all of these forces. Decolonial delinking, however, should benefit from and draw on dewesternization, to the extent that dewesternization is fracturing the ambitions of Westernization—of which the process of neoliberalism was its last desperate attempt (Mignolo 2002).

Modern ego-centered personalities are driven by competition; decolonial and communal personalities are driven by the search for love, conviviality, and harmony (Mignolo 2000b). For this reason, decoloniality cannot aim to take the state, as was the aim of the decolonization movements during the Cold War. And so decoloniality also delinks from Marxism. Indeed, it withstands alignment with any school or institution that would divert its pluriverse back into a universe, its heterogeneity back into a totality.

NOTES

1. The first time I introduced *pluriversity* into my argument was in a series of lectures delivered between 1996 and 1998. Later, in 2002, I published an essay on the subject in Binghamton University's *Review: A Journal of the Fernand Braudel Center*, under the title "The Zapatistas' Theoretical Revolution: Its Historical, Political, and Epistemological Consequences." The essay appeared, slightly revised, as a chapter in *The Darker Side of Western Modernity* (Mignolo 2011).

2. In a similar strain, Oyeronke Oyewumi (1997) rejects the idea of a world "view" as a European way of favoring the visual. Oyewumi instead proposes the concept "world-sense."

REFERENCES

Huarachi, Simon Yampara. 2011. "Andean Cosmovivencia: Living and Living Together in Integral Harmony—Suma Qamaña." *Bolivian Studies Journal* 18:1–22.

Latouche, Serge. 1982. *L'occidentalization du monde*. Paris: La Découverte.

Mignolo, Walter D. 1995. *The Darker Side of the Renaissance: Literacy, Territoriality, and Colonization*. Ann Arbor: University of Michigan Press.

Mignolo, Walter D. 2000a. *Local Histories/Global Designs: Coloniality, Subaltern Knowledges, and Border Thinking*. Princeton, NJ: Princeton University Press.

Mignolo, Walter D. 2000b. "The Many Faces of Cosmo-polis: Border Thinking and Critical Cosmopolitanism." *Public Culture* 12 (3): 721–48.

Mignolo, Walter D. 2002a. "The Enduring Enchantment: (Or the Epistemic Privilege of Modernity and Where to Go from Here)." *South Atlantic Quarterly* 101 (4): 927–54. http://waltermignolo.com/wp-content/uploads/2013/03/enchantment.pdf.

Mignolo, Walter D. 2002b. "The Zapatistas' Theoretical Revolution: Its Historical, Political, and Epistemological Consequences." *Review: A Journal of the Fernand Braudel Center* 25 (3): 245–75.

Mignolo, Walter D. 2011. *The Darker Side of Western Modernity: Global Futures, Decolonial Options*. Durham, NC: Duke University Press.

Mignolo, Walter D. 2012a. *The Darker Side of the Renaissance: Literacy, Territoriality, and Colonization*, 2nd ed. Ann Arbor: University of Michigan Press.

Mignolo, Walter D. 2012b. "Delinking, Decoloniality and Dewesternization: Interview with Walter Mignolo (Part II)." *Critical Legal Thinking*, May 2. http://criticallegalthinking.com/2012/05/02/delinking-decoloniality-dewesternization-interview-with-walter-mignolo-part-ii/.

Mignolo, Walter D. 2012c. *Local Histories/Global Designs: Coloniality, Subaltern Knowledges, and Border Thinking*, 2nd ed. Princeton, NJ: Princeton University Press.

Oyewumi, Oyeronke. 1997. *The Invention of Women: Making and African Sense of Western Gender Discourses*. Minneapolis: University of Minnesota Press.

Panikkar, Raimon. 2017. "Diatopical Hermeneutics." http://www.raimon-panikkar.org/english/gloss-diatopic.html.

Acknowledgments

Thank you to Sandra Harding, whose work has inspired me and who has been a mentor over the past years, always ready to offer advice, insight, and help. Academic work would be so much more fun and so much more relevant at the same time could it count on more scholars like you!

Thank you to Arturo Escobar for his generosity, brilliance, kindness, and support.

Thank you to Ulrich Oslender for standing with me in this project and others.

Thank you to my students, many of whom have long seen through the universalist claims of the white European males we read in our seminars and demanded more diverse and pluriversal approaches.

Thank you to my department and chair for supporting this project.

I received a small grant from the University of South Florida's Publishing Council. Thank you!

I want to dedicate this book to my wife, Miranda.

—Bernd Reiter

Introduction

Sooner or later, the time will have to come to draw attention to the manner in which the exclusion of other traditions of knowledge by reductionist science is itself part of the problem that has led to myriad failed development initiatives all around the world. —ODORA HOPPERS, *Indigenous Knowledge and the Integration of Knowledge Systems*

This book seeks to move beyond the critique of colonialism and Western (thought) hegemony toward the construction of what Raewyn Connell calls a "mosaic epistemology" (chapter 1, this volume). While it is still necessary to first offer a thorough critique of Western, or Northern, domination, it is equally pressing to move beyond the critique of such "paradogma" (chapter 9, this volume) as *development*. It is high time to elaborate different ways to perceive and explain the world and find solutions for the many pressing problems of the Global South, many of which, after all, were created by adhering to the development recipes sold wholesale by Western and Northern development specialists and their organizations. The common thread that brings all the contributions assembled here together is the effort to move beyond one-dimensional solutions to diverse problems and the imposition of universalist claims about the very nature of humanity toward the construction of the pluriverse. Given the centrality of pluriversality in the endeavor, the foreword allows for an extended definition and short genealogy of this term.

Escaping colonial mind-sets and frameworks is difficult (Mbembe 1992). It seems even more difficult to construct different, that is, counterhegemonic, analytical frameworks and approaches for the social sciences. Authors such as Jìmí Adésínà (2002) and Paulin Hountondji (1997) have already engaged in the presentation and critical evaluation of "endogenous knowledge" (the title of Hountondji's 1997 edited volume) with important contributions in the fields of non-Western ontologies, epistemologies, and technologies. Both of these authors write from a West African (Nigerian and Beninese) standpoint, introducing non-Western ways to think about, analyze, and manipulate the world. Given that the central critique of Western, colonial epistemologies and analytical frameworks is that they claim to be universalist and explain it all while in fact being biased and limited, the approaches discussed by Adésínà and Hountondji self-consciously avoid making such sweeping claims. They instead offer partial knowledge that is context specific and limited. If we take the critique of the coloniality of knowledge and power seriously (Quijano 2000), then all knowledge production must henceforth be partial, context specific, and limited, leading us away from parsimonious schemata that explain the (social) world toward a much more complex and mosaic construction of the bases of different and competing scientific knowledges. This is what Raewyn Connell refers to in chapter 1—and it is also what guides this volume. The consequence of embracing such a mosaic epistemology is that the search for alternative and place-bound epistemologies and approaches is potentially endless, and it opens the doors to a sort of epistemological relativism, where one approach to explaining the world is as good as the next. Adding random non-Western epistemologies from different places of the world is, however, not what this volume seeks to achieve. Instead, I follow Sandra Harding, who has argued that "we need realistic reassessments of both Western and non-Western knowledge systems" (2008: 6). For Harding this means that "if we are to take seriously the achievements of another culture, we have to talk about it in our terms, rather than theirs" (2008: 16).

The ontologies, epistemologies, and alternative, non-Western approaches to democracy presented in this volume all live up to this claim in that they talk directly to the current canon of accepted approaches in the social sciences. All of them explicitly offer a new and different way to approach questions that are at the core of most social sciences: development, economic growth, identity, democracy, political power, and self-rule. While some contributions focus on highlighting the problems and pitfalls created by the coloniality of power and knowledge (Quijano 2000), the majority of contributions assembled here point at ways to conceptualize the core questions and answers of the social sciences differently. By doing so, this volume proposes a recalibration of the Western compass that so far is providing guidance to most of the social sciences in most places of the world. We all need to rethink what development, growth, political power, democracy, nationalism, and self-rule mean and can mean—but the traditional, Western approaches of European science do not contain the tools to ask different questions and find new and different answers. The chapters assembled here do.

Feminism and a Successor Science

During the 1970s, American feminist scholars started calling for a successor science. For Sandra Harding (1986), one of the central proponents of this claim, such a science needs to recognize its own standpoints and limitations, thus embracing partiality. All knowledge production is embodied and conditioned by the researcher's situatedness. We cannot see it all, and we cannot know it all. However, most traditional scientific production has pretended just that, thus "playing the God trick," as Donna Haraway (1988) argued so eloquently. Those who played the God trick were mostly metropolitan male intellectuals. They relied on the concepts and categories of their own, limited, world—and yet they applied them to explain the whole world (Connell 2007).

These intellectuals were also involved, directly or indirectly, in the construction and institutionalization of academic departments and associations, and their journals and annual meetings and conferences. As a result of such limitlessness, European ontologies, epistemologies, and research programs have thoroughly conquered the world, suffocating all other approaches to make sense of, explain, and control the natural and social environment (Chakrabarty 2007). Science, however, is the structured and systematic production of knowledge—and by that account, all societies and all groups, everywhere and anytime, are engaged in scientific endeavors, even if not all of them are institutionalized to the same degree (chapters 1 and 2, this volume).

Colonialism, however, erased many local scientific traditions by declassifying them as primitive and folklore and substituting what was perceived as Southern superstition with Northern science. To some authors, the very power of colonialism rested on its ability to name and categorize the world according to its own heuristic schemata and interest, thus inventing, and enforcing, such binaries as modern/traditional, progressive/backward, and civilized/primitive (Escobar 2011; Oyewumi, 1997; Lugones 2007).

In postcolonial times, this situation of Western, or Northern, colonial hegemony lived on as political elites from the Global South continued to send their offspring to be educated in London, Paris, Leiden, Brussels, Berlin—and, after World War II, in New York, Boston, or Los Angeles. The educational meccas erected in these places continued to reproduce the colonial traditions they inherited from the former colonizers, and the students trained there returned to their homelands—if they returned at all—with European, and later American, mind-sets. The theories and methods they learned made many of them strangers in their native lands. Even worse, the concepts, categories, and approaches they learned abroad did not help them in the analysis of their own countries or in the solving of the very specific problems they encountered once they returned and assumed positions of influence.

It is indeed high time for a postcolonial successor science, particularly in the social sciences and the humanities, where academic prestige is construed on the knowledge of a broadly accepted canon of thought. When I write these lines, this canon can no longer consist of the Western tradition alone. The analytical toolboxes created by Weber, Marx, and Durkheim do not contain the tools that are necessary to understand the whole world. Neither do those of Beck, Coleman, Bourdieu, Foucault, or Latour—as Sandra Harding (2008) and Raewyn Connell (2007) have made abundantly clear. If we are seriously interested in understanding the different problems of the Global South, we need much larger and more specific toolboxes.

Beyond Eurocentrism

Walter Mignolo (2015) argues that the time is ripe to debunk the idea that there is one truth and one law to be discovered, able to capture and explain all human behavior and culture. In the foreword to Luisetti, Pickles, and Kaiser's *The Anomie of the Earth*, Mignolo dwells on the work of Carl Schmitt (2003), who argued that the current *nomos* of the world was preceded by a previous, first nomos. Instead, argues Mignolo (2015), the universalist claims of today were preceded by many different nomoi, each one responding to different, place-bound environments and challenges. These nomoi were destroyed by colonialism.

Ramón Grosfoguel (2013) has made a similar claim, showing, in more detail, how European colonization has destroyed not only people and their cultures, but also their diverse knowledge systems. Genocide thus went hand in hand with "epistemicide" (Santos 2014). Grosfoguel's (2013) analysis, which relies on the extensive work of Enrique Dussel, shows how the universalist truth claims of white European males from five countries (Germany, France, Italy, the United Kingdom, and the United States) were made possible only after conquest and extermination—first of Jews and Muslims during the Spanish Reconquista, the enslavement of indigenous people and Africans, and finally the genocide/epistemicide of women. For Grosfoguel, quoting Dussel, "the arrogant and idolatric God-like pretention of Cartesian philosophy is coming from the perspective of someone who thinks of himself as the center of the world because he has already conquered the world" (Grosfoguel 2013: 77).

The claim that the time is ripe to abandon the search for universal laws guiding human behavior resonates strongly with Immanuel Wallerstein's (1991, 1998) assessment that the twenty-first century is a century of crisis, leading either to a consolidation of U.S. imperialism and the corresponding hegemony of Western thought or to a breakdown of this system, which has lasted for some five hundred years, and its replacement with a plurality of fairer and more egalitarian local systems.

Ramón Grosfoguel, Nelson Maldonado-Torres, and José Saldávar (2005) argue that if Wallerstein is correct, then we face an urgent need to search for new and different utopias, able to inform our thoughts and actions toward constructing better, fairer, and more equitable democracies and economies. This book is dedicated to contributing to precisely this effort.

Jìmí Adésínà (2002) has offered an example, and an explanation, of how exactly this search for new utopias can be conducted. First, Adésínà takes on the idea that the social sciences need to produce nomothetic knowledge, showing that all knowledge is bound by the place, time, and positionality of the knowledge producer and hence ideographic. He then sets out to elaborate a different epistemology, based on the work of Nigerian sociologist Akinsola Akiwowo (1922–2014), who grounded his epistemological proposals on Yoruba ontology. Adésínà shows that Yoruba ontology and cosmology contain an element of "mutual self-embeddedness of contradictory states of being" (Adésínà 2002: 105), which is fundamentally different from the Aristotelian logic of discrete and exclusive binaries. As such, the Yoruba logic of multivalence, which Adésínà calls "fuzzy logic," allows for the construction of an entirely different analytical apparatus and, it demands a different kind of research methodology. Adésínà's efforts thus resemble those of Raewyn Connell (2007) to construct Southern theory. It is also in tune with Oyeronke Oyewumi's (1997) recognition that the binary categories of male/female, modern/premodern, and human/nonhuman were invented and enforced by colonial power, constituting, to this day, a "coloniality of power" (Quijano 2000).

The call for decolonization, issued by such authors as Silvia Rivera Cusican-qui (2010, 2012), Janet Conway and Jakeet Singh (2011), Cristina Rojas (2015), Sylvia Wynter (2003), Wiebke Keim (2008), Rhoda Reddock (2014), and Sujata Patel (2014), to name but a few, thus points to the need to move beyond the critique of colonialism and toward the active construction of the pluriverse through the systematic elaboration of different ontologies and corresponding epistemologies. The efforts by Jìmí Adésínà (2002), Raewyn Connell (2007), Silvia Cusicanqui (2010), Gyan Prakash (1994), Sharmila Rege (2003), and many others already provide a map others can use and follow in this effort. This map points at the need to discuss different, non-Western epistemologies in connection to their corresponding ontologies and to embrace partial, place-bound knowledges. These authors also highlight the need to operationalize these epistemologies so they can be applied in concrete research projects and become research questions and designs. One immediate consequence of doing this is the question of what kinds of research methods correspond to this project. Once the legitimacy of nomothetic research is lost, the question of what a decolonial research project, design, and corresponding methodology look like emerges with urgency. From the onset, it seems clear that statistics is the method par excellence linked to the project of binary categorizing and thus is deeply implicated in the colonial construction of Western, male superiority (Harding 2008). It is also worth noting that Adésínà's proposal to consider the fuzzy logic of Yoruba cosmology as an epistemological anchor for analyzing social realities outside of binary and mutually exclusive categories resonates strongly with fuzzy-set qualitative comparative analysis (fsQCA), as proposed and elaborated by the American sociologist Charles Ragin (2008).

While it is beyond the scope of this book and the capacity of the editor to address all these issues, this book nevertheless is firmly committed to constructing the pluriverse by highlighting some different, non-Western, and non-Western-centric ontologies and epistemologies. Some of the authors assembled here have also taken steps to outline the analytical and methodological consequences of decolonizing the social sciences, but much more needs to be done in this regard.

The contributors represent the very diversity I seek to achieve. They are writing from their specific standpoints and are aware of the partiality of their views—but embrace limitation as a positive contribution to theory development and the construction of itinerary research programs. The proposals, theories, models, questions, frameworks, concepts, and analytical tools they develop and propose are introduced so they can be applied to the examination of restricted local realities—but they also allow for a critical evaluation and reassessment of traditional and hegemonic viewpoints, worldviews, and ideologies, and the research programs connected to them. I believe that such new ideas and frameworks not only allow for a better understanding of poor countries, North-South relations, and the world system. I also believe that an intensive engagement with the countries of the South will produce new insight into the interactions of agency, institutions, and structure. To be sure: instead of working out the contradictions of universalism and coloniality, I propose, in this volume, to take an initial step from analyzing problems to their solution, where I perceive the solution to be the consideration of other approaches to the world and to science, that is, other ontologies, epistemologies, and political ideologies.

All authors writing for this volume have responded to calls sent out by the editor in 2014 and thereafter. I have asked them: What would an Indian/(West)

African/Colombian/Brazilian/Islamic/Malaysian/Iranian political philosophy look like? What sort of questions would it ask? What kinds of ontologies and epistemologies would it be based on? What kinds of research questions could be developed from it and what sorts of research programs or designs? How could it be operationalized? The answers were, as expected, as broad and diverse as they should be. Some authors have also given their own interpretation to this call and focused on what they perceive as the most relevant aspect of this call and the political philosophy they wanted to write about.

The World Reified according to Colonial Knowledge

Reification might be the biggest hindrance to scientific advancement. Reification refers to the act of attributing ontological status to epistemological and analytical tools. Put simply: we cannot know with certainty that the world truly is the way we think it is. Even worse: what we think is real certainly is not the only reality out there, as different people access the same reality from different places and thus either see, or experience, a different slot of the same reality, or they perceive a different reality altogether.

The problems do not end here, unfortunately. There is a well-founded suspicion that not only do different people perceive different realities, or at least different facets of the same reality—but different people create different realities through their different, discursive interactions with it and with each other. This is not to say that the material world exists only in our minds. This just says that we cannot know anything about how the world really is, as it is our own naming, categorizing, and ordering that gives it meaning—to us. Hence, as an inevitable consequence, our perception of the world is influenced by us, who we are, and what we know. Or, put even simpler: who we are will influence what we know, and what we know will influence what is real to us.

Any theory, model, or explanation is thus underdetermining, and this world has space for many different ways of explaining it and making sense out of it. It has no space for fixed recipes for the future. To think that the Western way of thinking about and explaining the world is the only one is ignorant. To think that the European way of explaining the world is somehow closer to the way the world really is is naive. To explain the world without unveiling, or even being aware of, the purpose for this explanation makes for an incomplete and biased explanation, often dressed as universal. There simply are no universally valid explanations of and about the world. Offering Western recipes to the entire world achieves first and foremost a further spreading of Western ideology and a delegitimization of non-Western thought.

All of this highlights the urgent need to do a better job, produce "stronger objectivity" (Harding 1993) and a more sympathetic and engaged science that is less pretentious about knowing the truth and more aware of its own limitations, its partiality, its interests and motivations, and its positionality (Henderson 2011). This need becomes apparent every time a class is taught, anywhere in the world, on world ideologies, globalization, or development, as even most first-semester students intuitively know that there must be more to world ideology than capitalism, socialism, and fascism. Classes on globalization and development do not fare much better, as the costs of these growth strategies have become all too clear to almost everyone, so that no longer can we argue that pollution is simply a side effect of economic development, or that progress consists of the ability to buy more stuff. Consumerism cannot be the only goal of development.

This book presents the kind of answer we, as academics, are able to provide. It seeks to present different voices, speaking from different locations and different positionalities about their conceptions of the world, of development, of progress, and the role science can and should play in it. The emphasis is on constructing the pluriverse, as I agree with the assessment of such authors as Immanuel Wallerstein (1998) and Ramón Grosfoguel (2013) that the knowledge produced by white males from only five countries has lost its legitimacy to explain the whole world by formulating universal statements about human behavior and interaction. Such authors as Enrique Dussel (2002) and Anibal Quijano (2000) have long pointed at the coloniality of power that made this knowledge production possible—and demanded a thorough decolonization of the social sciences and the construction of a "transmodernity" (Dussel 2002).

While most authors writing in the decolonization tradition agree that the time to move beyond the critique of colonialism and offer new and different ways to make sense and explain diverse (social) worlds has arrived, the endeavor to actually do so has proven difficult. While book titles such as Gyan Prakash's (1994) *After Colonialism* promise to do just that, most contributions in that book and similar others still focus mostly on critique. This is so, I suspect, because colonialism has so thoroughly destroyed and delegitimized non-Western thought and has committed not just genocide, but epistemicide (Chakrabarty 2007; Santos 2014). The institutional requirements to produce knowledge outside of the world's capitalist metropolitan centers are precarious at best, thus suffering today from the very marginalization colonial rule has cast them into (Adésínà 2005; Cusicanqui 2012). In addition, academic traditions, particularly in the social sciences and humanities, are built on critique and critical exegesis, thus making it difficult, even for those of us working in metropolitan universities, to venture into the unknown and not yet accepted. The disciplinary power of zealous academics, exercised in the form of blind peer review, tends to punish anything perceived as transgressing the boundaries of the already accepted canon—even if this canon is decolonization itself (Kuhn 2012).

The contribution this books seeks to make is to actively engage in such a transgression by showcasing academic work that does not fit neatly into the established canon of thought and approaches in the social sciences. It is a book written for social science students and researchers in that it proposes texts that might be helpful when analyzing specific problems of different non-Western and nonmetropolitan societies and cultures. Each chapter is written with a clear commitment to producing situated and partial knowledge and as such they all offer ideographic knowledge, grounded in specific ontologies and lifeworlds. The epistemological possibilities each contribution contains are elaborated more by some authors than by others, and the same is true for the methodological implications each contribution contains.

This is reflective, I think, of the early stages where we find ourselves in this effort to decolonize the social sciences. Much more work needs to be done here so that we can all move beyond the patchwork efforts this book and similar others are currently able to provide. This is particularly true for elaborating the operational steps that can be taken to transform non-Western ontologies and epistemologies into research programs, with corresponding designs and methodologies.

However, this book is not trying to identify and promote a new Karl Marx, Max Weber, or Emile Durkheim, simply because I believe that the universalist claims these authors formulated are part of the problem we face today. Instead of searching for the Indian Foucault, I suggest reining in the analytical reach of the French Foucault and putting him in conversation with the Indian Mohandas Karamchand Gandhi. It is worth reading the fourteenth-century Muslim scholar Ibn Khaldun, not because he can substitute for the German philosopher Immanuel Kant, but because both Kant and Khaldun offer epistemologies and analytical tools worth considering when seeking to understand different, place-bound phenomena. I do think, however, that we have to carefully reevaluate the reach of the universalist claims someone like Kant has formulated—so that Ibn Khaldun might work as a remedy for the universalism of Immanuel Kant.

This book locates itself as a postcolonial contribution to the production of knowledge and the conditions, as well as the consequences, of such knowledge production. The authors showcased here represent a narrow sliver of what is out there—and they reflect, to a great extent, my own positionality and cultural context as a political science professor working, and trained, mostly in Northern, metropolitan universities. As someone who has lived, worked, studied, and taught in Brazil and Colombia, I am fully aware that each country has its own intellectual and academic traditions that have not been entirely wiped out, but rather suppressed and transformed, by colonialism. As Sujata Patel (2014) has argued, colonialism imposed a format to which local thinking and theorizing had to—and still has to—conform. It also imposed a language—English—as the only language able to reach broad circulation. As a result, the great contributions by such Brazilian authors as Jacob Gorender (2001), who elaborated a (neo-Marxist) theoretical framework for colonial slaveholding societies claiming and demonstrating that slave societies represent a different, sui generis, type of society, do not fit into the available societal categories developed by Max Weber and Karl Marx. Similarly, the important work of Colombian sociologist Orlando Fals Borda is known to a broader audience only insofar it has been translated into English, whereas the pioneering contributions by his colleague, cultural anthropologist Manuel Zapata Olivella, remain largely unknown outside Colombia. Every colonized country can count on a series of native intellectuals whose contributions remain unknown and unused. Jìmí Adésínà (2005) has explained in detail how difficult it is to overcome the coloniality of power and create, in his case, an African university.

This book is the direct result of my own frustration when teaching university seminars on such topics as development, modernization, world ideologies, and globalization, as the available textbooks are all unduly narrow, biased, and Eurocentric, while claiming to cover and explain the whole world. This frustration is shared by most of my students, who wonder, ask, and at times demand the inclusion of Muslim thinkers, Indian philosophers, and Native American conceptions of markets, democracy, and development in the syllabi. This book represents my effort as a comparative political scientist, who is not a postcolonial scholar and yet teaches classes about the world, to learn about, and from, different ways of making sense of the world and with that diversify my own teaching. Engaging with the texts I have been able to assemble has allowed me to question my own positionality as a comparativist and Latin Americanist, making me more aware of the unconscious assumptions and biases that underlie my own thinking and analysis. It is my hope that the texts I have been able to assemble achieve the same for each reader.

This volume only presents a start for many possibilities for pluralizing the social sciences and humanities.

Chapter Overview

In the foreword, Walter Mignolo provides a genealogy of the term *pluriverse*, from how he has first used it to how it continues to influence his work today.

In part I of this book, all five authors provide the foundations for what is to come. First, Raewyn Connell identifies the problem of epistemic violence caused by the global economy of knowledge. She explains how other knowledges were, and continue to be, marginalized by colonialism and imperialism—and she offers ways out of this marginalization based on feminist theory. She thus locates the problem this book seeks to tackle and initiates the search for solutions by introducing different Southern theoretical approaches. In her assessment, moving toward a feminist democracy of theory, which relies on a mosaic epistemology and tackles the issues of power and the state, identity, methodology, and land, offers a way to realize the full potential of gender analysis.

Sandra Harding revisits her long-standing efforts to make feminist standpoint theory an integral part of scientific endeavors; then she elaborates on her second scholarly contribution to this field—the recognition of different, non-European scientific traditions and their importance for creating a better, more just, and more inclusive successor science.

Arturo Escobar, like Walter Mignolo and Sandra Harding, is a pioneer in the effort to decolonize the Western scientific tradition and its underlying ontologies and epistemologies. In chapter 3, Escobar lays out the foundations for a more relational approach to reality, which is inspired by his knowledge, and research, in the Colombian Pacific.

In chapter 4, Walter Mignolo first elaborates on the crises of hegemonic, Western models of thought, science, and technology—and proposes a new and different way to approach the world, inspired by Humberto Maturana's philosophy of cognition and his politics of love. Chapter 5, by Aram Ziai, elaborates a critique of development understood in its traditional way and argues for free cooperation, based on the recognition that most social problems are specific and local in nature and thus cannot be solved with recipes conceived in different, Northern or Western contexts.

Part II takes us to other ontologies. In chapter 6, Ulrich Oslender launches the effort of detecting, describing, capturing, and understanding other ontologies by introducing the aquatic epistemologies of the Colombian Pacific. These are based on a peculiar and local perception and understanding of the world—hence a local, Colombian Pacific aquatic ontology.

Issiaka Ouattara takes us deep into the reality of West Africa and its oral traditions. Writing from his vantage point as an educator and researcher in the Ivory

Coast, Ouattara is able to highlight and explain the importance of the West African griots and pinpoint their centrality in the making of West African modernity.

In chapter 8, Manu Samnotra elaborates the ontology of Mahatma Gandhi—particularly his thoughts and writings on autonomy, self-rule, and village democracy (*Hind Swaraj*). Chapter 9, by Catherine Walsh, is the final contribution to this section and introduces the concept of *buen vivir*, which was anchored in the new Ecuadorian and Bolivian constitutions. While buen vivir offers an alternative and more holistic way to conceptualize development, it is still wedded to the core tenets of development and economic growth, as Walsh demonstrates.

Part III focuses more directly on science and epistemology. Manuela Boatcǎ, in chapter 10, proposes to conceptualize Europe without excluding the European overseas department in the Caribbean. A conceptualization of Caribbean Europe allows for a creolization of the very notion of Europe, which includes its colonial dimensions. Hans-Jürgen Burchardt argues in chapter 11 that an approach to politics that focuses narrowly on rational action cannot capture all the irrational, emotional, and group-oriented actions that characterize all our lives, particularly in the realm of politics. To move beyond this analytical dead end, Burchardt rereads the writings of Baruch Spinoza and Norbert Elias, both of whom have proposed systematic ways to take emotions and irrational behavior into analytical account.

Chapter 12, by Zaid Ahmad, then advances this critique by probing into the epistemology of Ibn Khaldun, a Muslim scholar and traveler of the fourteenth century, and his writings about the centrality of religion in human affairs.

Venu Mehta, in chapter 13, introduces Jain epistemology, particularly the Jain concept of *anekāntavāda*, and demonstrates how closely Jain philosophy is related to feminist standpoint theory and decolonial literature, thus highlighting once more that much of what is broadly perceived and claimed as Western has deep and old roots in non-Western thought and religious practice.

Part IV of this book pushes this effort further by offering different, that is, nonhegemonic and noncolonial, ways of thinking about and analyzing politics, democracy, and markets.

In chapter 14, I highlight the crises of democracy, citizenship, and politics that are so widely bemoaned everywhere today—and introduce solutions elaborated by some Native American groups over the past centuries. This chapter argues that Native Americans have long understood the epistemic thread coming from colonial European approaches to explaining the world for the sake of ruling it—and they have formulated very clear formulas for breaking away from colonial domination.

In chapter 15, finally, Ehsan Kashfi shows how the Iranian prerevolutionary intellectuals Ali Shariati and Abdolkarim Soroush elaborated ways to break away from Western domination and formulate an independent path of development and modernity, based on their interpretation of Islam.

In the conclusion, I revisit this book's achievements and shortcomings. I end with a call for more research into the plentiful and heterogeneous efforts to explain the world, politics, democracy, and science that are present and alive among different societies and groups all over the world.

REFERENCES

Adésínà, Jìmí. 2002. "Sociology and Yorùbá Studies: Epistemic Intervention or Doing Sociology in the 'Vernacular'?" *African Sociological Review* 6 (1): 91–114.

Adésínà, Jìmí. 2005. "Realizing the Vision: The Discursive and Institutional Challenges of Becoming an African University." *African Sociological Review* 9 (1): 23–39.

Ahmed, Sara. 2014. *The Cultural Politics of Emotion*. Edinburgh: Edinburgh University Press.

Chakrabarty, Dipesh. 2007. *Provincializing Europe*. Princeton, NJ: Princeton University Press.

Chatterjee, Partha. 1998. *A Possible India*. Oxford: Oxford University Press.

Chatterjee, Partha. 2001. "On Civil and Political Society in Post-colonial Democracies." In *Civil Society*, edited by Sudipta Kaviraj and Sunil Khilnani, 165–78. Cambridge: Cambridge University Press.

Connell, Raewyn. 2007. *Southern Theory*. Cambridge: Polity.

Conway, Janet, and Jakeet Singh. 2011. "Radical Democracy in Global Perspective: Notes from the Pluriverse." *Third World Quarterly* 32 (2): 689–706.

Cusicanqui, Silvia. 2010. "The Notion of 'Rights' and the Paradoxes of Postcolonial Modernity: Indigenous Peoples and Women in Bolivia." *Qui Parle* 18 (2): 29–54.

Cusicanqui, Silvia. 2012. "Ch'ixinakax utixiwa: A Reflection on the Practices and Discourses of Decolonization." *South Atlantic Quarterly* 111 (1): 95–109.

Dussel, Enrique. 2002. "World System and 'Trans'-Modernity." *Nepantla: Views from the South* 3 (2): 221–44.

Easterly, William. 2015. *The Tyranny of Experts*. New York: Basic Books.

Eisenstadt, S. N. 2000. "Multiple Modernities." *Daedalus* 129 (1): 1–29.

Escobar, Arturo. 2011. *Encountering Development*. Princeton, NJ: Princeton University Press.

Gorender. Jacob. 2001. *O Escravismo Colonial*. São Paulo: Atica.

Grosfoguel, Ramón. 2013. "The Structure of Knowledge in Westernized Universities." *Human Architecture* 11 (1): 73–90.

Grosfoguel, Ramón, Nelson Maldonado-Torres, and José Saldávar, eds. 2005. *Latin@s in the World-System: Decolonization Struggles in the 21st Century U.S. Empire*. New York: Routledge.

Haraway, Donna. 1988. "Situated Knowledges." *Feminist Studies* 14 (3): 575–99.

Harding, Sandra. 1986. *The Science Question in Feminism*. New York: Open University Press.

Harding, Sandra. 1993. *The Racial Economy of Science*. Bloomington: Indiana University Press.

Harding, Sandra. 2008. *Sciences from Below*. Durham, NC: Duke University Press.

Henderson, Hazel. 2011. "Real Economies and the Illusions of Abstraction." CADMUS 1 (3): 60–65.

Hoppers, Catherine Odora, ed. 2002. *Indigenous Knowledge and the Integration of Knowledge Systems*. Cape Town: New Africa.

Hountondji, Paulin, ed. 1997. *Endogenous Knowledge: Research Trails*. Oxford: CODESRIA.

Keim, Wiebke. 2008. "Distorted Universality—Internationalization and Its Implications for the Epistemological Foundations of the Discipline." *Canadian Journal of Sociology* 33 (3): 555–74.

Kuhn, Thomas. 2012. *The Structure of Scientific Revolutions*. Chicago: University of Chicago Press.

Lugones, Maria. 2007. "Heterosexualism and the Colonial/Modern Gender System." *Hypatia* 22 (1): 186–209.

Lugones, Maria. 2014. "Rumo a um feminism descolonial." *Estudos Feministas* 22 (3): 935–52.

Mbembe, Achille. 1992. "Provisional Notes on the Postcolony." *Africa* 62 (1): 3–37.

Mignolo, Walter D. 2015. Foreword to *The Anomie of the Earth*, edited by Federico Luisetti, John Pickles, and Wilson Kaiser. Durham, NC: Duke University Press.

Oyewumi, Oyeronke. 1997. *The Invention of Women: Making and African Sense of Western Gender Discourses*. Minneapolis: University of Minnesota Press.

Patel, Sujata. 2014. "Afterword: Doing Global Sociology: Issues, Problems, and Challenges." *Current Sociology Monograph* 62 (4): 603–13.

Prakash, Gyan, ed. 1994. *After Colonialism*. Princeton, NJ: Princeton University Press.

Quijano, Anibal. 2000. "Coloniality of Power, Eurocentrism, and Latin America." *Nepantla* 1 (3): 533–80.

Ragin, Charles. 2008. *Redesigning Social Inquiry: Fuzzy Sets and Beyond*. Chicago: University of Chicago Press.

Reddock, Rhoda. 2014. "Radical Caribbean Social Thought: Race, Class Identity and the Postcolonial Nation." *Current Sociology Monograph* 62 (4): 493–511.

Rege, Sharmila. 2003. "More Than Just Tacking Women on to the 'Macropicture': Feminist Contributions to Globalization Discourses." *Economic and Political Weekly* 38 (43): 4555–63.

Rojas, Cristina. 2015. "Ciudadania Indigena: Luchas historicas por la igualdad y la diferencia colonial en Bolivia." *Cuadernos de Antropologia Social* 42:19–34.

Sachs, Wolfgang. 2010. *The Development Dictionary*. London: Zed.

Santos, Boaventura de Sousa. 2014. *Epistemologies of the South: Justice against Epistemicide*. New York: Routledge.

Sayer, Andrew. 1992. *Method in the Social Sciences*. New York: Routledge.

Schmitt, Carl. 2003. *The Nomos of the Earth in the International Law of the Jus Publicum Europaeum*. New York: Telos.

Wallerstein, Immanuel. 1991. *Unthinking Social Science*. London: Polity.

Wallerstein, Immanuel. 1998. *Utopistics: Or Historical Choices of the Twenty-First Century.* New York: New Press.

Wynter, Sylvia. 2003. "Unsettling the Coloniality of Being/Power/Truth/Freedom: Towards the Human, after Man, Its Overrepresentation—an Argument." *New Centennial Review* 3 (3): 257–337.

Part I. **Toward the Pluriverse**

1 · Meeting at the Edge of Fear

Theory on a World Scale

The evening will be under my disposal · and the meeting at the edge of fear is mine ·
I am another Buthayna · perfume springs from me · as well as love and diaspora
—SALEHA OBEID GHABESH, "Who Will Secure a Safe Haven for Buthayn?"

"A Significant Error in Feminist Scholarship": The Problem

A quarter of a century ago, in a powerful essay called "Feminism and Difference," Marnia Lazreg wrote of the treatment of women in colonized societies
as "a significant error in feminist scholarship" (1988: 100). A split vision of the
world, derived from colonialism and preoccupied with cultural difference,
meant that women in Arab countries not only had to contest oppressive gender relations; they also had to break with the prevailing paradigm of feminist
knowledge.

In an essay much better known to Anglophone feminists, "Under Western
Eyes," Chandra Talpade Mohanty (1991) also called attention to the colonial
gaze in Northern gender scholarship. A decade after Lazreg's article, the Australian sociologist Chilla Bulbeck (1998) published *Re-orienting Western Feminisms*, tracing the vast diversity of women's experience and political struggles
across the postcolonial world, and arguing for a "braiding" of multiple feminisms on a world scale.

Another decade on, reflecting on the importation of U.S. feminist ideas into
China in translations bankrolled by the Ford Foundation, Min Dongchao
argued that "the power relation behind this global flow of feminist ideas,
publications and activism should be revealed" (2007). Mara Viveros (2007)
in Colombia argued for a decolonizing perspective on race, and South-South
links, as essential for feminist theory. Shailaja Fennell and Madeleine Arnot
in Britain criticized the way global research on gender and education was

dominated by Anglo-American concepts, and offered examples of Southern feminist challenges to "hegemonic gender theory" (2008: 525). Reviewing scholarship on African women and gender relations, Akosua Adomako Ampofo, Josephine Beoku-Betts, and Mary Johnson Osirim cautioned about the importation of both postmodernist and Marxist theory, since both "produce biased and borrowed knowledge that mask[s] existing gender subordination" (2008: 334). Sondra Hale (2009), examining the "migrating concept of gender" in the Arab world, questioned North/South hierarchy in gender studies and especially the idea that gender studies in the South should be all about practical matters, not theory.

Why this continuing unease? Feminist scholarship is often interested in the majority world. There is now a large research literature on globalization and gender, and a whole library about gender and development. We have collections of global gender research (e.g., Bose and Kim 2009). Northern feminist journals regularly publish issues about Latin American feminism, Arab feminism, and so on, and seek out contributions from the Global South. Thanks to scholars such as Mohanty (1991) and Spivak (1988), and the rise of black and Latina feminism, postcolonial feminism has become a fixture in North American curricula and is now debated in Europe too (Reuter and Villa 2009). Prominent feminist thinkers often now formulate their ideas taking global issues and postcolonial perspectives into account: a notable example is Sandra Harding's (2008) reformulation of feminist epistemology in *Sciences from Below*.

There is, nevertheless, a striking imbalance in this large literature. The great bulk of feminist writing that circulates internationally and discusses the Global South is empirical, descriptive, or policy writing. If there is theory in it— conceptualization, methodology, or explanatory frameworks—the theory almost always comes from the Global North.

There is a good sociological reason for this. Feminist scholarship, whether in universities, state agencies, or nongovernmental agencies (NGOs), is produced by a workforce embedded in a global economy. The Beninese philosopher Paulin Hountondji (1997, 2002), who has provided the best analysis of this issue, identifies a global division of labor in the production of knowledge, with its roots in imperialism. The colonial world served as a rich source of data as well as material goods. Information and specimens were shipped back to the metropole (the French term for the imperial center, the colonizers' homeland), which became the site of the theoretical moment in science. In the era of neoliberal globalization, the metropole continues to be the main site of theoretical processing, now including corporate research institutes and databanks.

Intellectual workers in the periphery are pushed toward a stance that Houn-tondji calls "extraversion." To function successfully as a scientist, one must read the leading journals published in the metropole, learn the research techniques taught there, and gain recognition there. Career paths include advanced training in the metropole, attending conferences in the metropole, and, for the more successful, getting jobs in the metropole. The theoretical hegemony of the North is simply the normal functioning of this economy of knowledge.

This global economy of knowledge is startlingly at odds with the political history of gender relations. In fact, the intellectuals of colonized societies and settler populations have a rich history of thought and debate about gender inequality, going as far back as Sor Juana in seventeenth-century Mexico. Contemporary with first-wave feminism in the metropole were women like Aisha Taymour in Egypt, author of *The Mirror of Contemplating Affairs* (1892), which examined Qur'anic texts concerning women (Elbendary 2002); and Raden Adjeng Kartini, author of the classic *Letters of a Javanese Princess* (Kartini 2005), who despite her early death became the inspiration for generations of Indonesian feminists (Robinson 2009). A close contemporary of Kartini, He-Yin Zhen, wrote remarkable analyses of men's power, women's labor, and feminist politics in the radical intellectual ferment of late Qing China (Liu, Karl, and Ko 2013).

The women of the May Fourth movement in China launched new writing projects on women's experience in the 1920s that represented a major cultural breakthrough (Ng and Wickeri 1996). Huda Sharawi and other Arab women launched the Egyptian Feminist Union in 1923 (Badran 1988). There were also men in the colonized and semicolonial world who thought about gender reform. They included Qasim Amin in Egypt, author of *The Emancipation of Women* (1899), Jin Tianhe in China, author of *The Women's Bell* (1903), and Bankimchandra Chatterjee, famous as a novelist but also an advocate of gender equality and one of a number of nineteenth-century Bengali intellectual men who took up this cause.

Gender analysis of originality and power has continued to come from the Global South. One example is Heleieth Saffioti's great pioneering work *A Mulher na Sociedade de Classes* (*Women in Class Society*, published in São Paulo in 1969, before the famous texts of the Northern women's liberation movement). Another is the Moroccan sociologist Fatima Mernissi's ([1975] 1985) *Beyond the Veil*, a notable statement of a social-relations view of gender (contemporary with Gayle Rubin's [1975] "The Traffic in Women" but more historically sensitive) and a pathbreaking feminist analysis of the situation of men and patterns of masculinity. A third is Bina Agarwal's (1994) *A Field of One's Own*, which in depth of empirical knowledge, combined with integrative and imaginative power, is one of the greatest achievements of feminist scholarship in our time.

A striking proof of the fecundity of thought in the periphery has been provided by Francesca Gargallo Celentani (2012) in *Feminismos desde Abya Yala: Ideas y Proposiciones de las Mujeres de 607 Pueblos en Nuestra America*. This book documents discussions with the women of indigenous communities from Mexico to Chile, exploring local feminist ideas about coloniality, patriarchy, violence, religion, racism, internal colonialism, identity, environment, and more.

Saffioti's work is very well known in Brazil, and is known in other parts of Latin America. It is little known elsewhere and is very rarely mentioned in discussions of gender theory in the metropole. Mernissi's work is regarded in Anglophone gender studies as an exotic ethnography and is never cited as theory. Agarwal's work is well known in development economics and increasingly in environmental debates, but I have never seen it discussed in a Northern text of feminist theory. Little of the output from movements or NGOs, or official reports, gets read in the global metropole. Even the output of universities has limited presence in metropolitan forums.[1]

The problem is not a deficit of ideas from the global periphery—it is a deficit of recognition and circulation. This is a structural problem in feminist thought on a world scale. If the only versions of theory that circulate globally and hold authority are those that arise from the social experience of a regional minority, there is a drastic impoverishment of gender studies as a form of knowledge.

Some scholars who recognize these patterns picture a stark dichotomy of South versus North, indigenous knowledge versus Western knowledge. While the decolonizing anger driving these images is understandable, the empirical picture of gender studies is more complicated. Migration to the North may lead to critique as well as assimilation; hence the expatriate feminism subtly analyzed by Josephine Beoku-Betts and Wairimu Ngaruiya Njambi (2005). Some expatriates travel back and forth, sponsor others in intellectual chain migrations, and organize joint projects and publications. Some intellectuals from the North spend time in the colonial world and are influenced by it. Maria Mies's (1986) pioneering *Patriarchy and Accumulation on a World Scale* came out of this experience, as she notes in her autobiography.

And there is no question that Northern ideas can be used in new ways by Southern thinkers. Heleieth Saffioti made highly creative use of Marxist structuralism, and Bina Agarwal has made highly creative use of bargaining models. Kathy Davis's (2007: 175–83) history of the circulation of *Our Bodies, Ourselves* notes the changes in themes and political assumptions made in the Latin American edition, *Nuestros Corpos, Nuestras Vidas.* Across the Pacific, the Northern categories of political economy were reworked for Philippine history in Elizabeth Uy Eviota's (1992: 172) *The Political Economy of Gender,* emphasizing the "structural coercion" that defines women's collective situation in the neocolonial economy. A more recent example is the critique of the Northern canon and the reworking of concepts of difference by Colombian feminists in *El Genero: Una Categoria util para las Ciencias Sociales* (Arango and Viveros 2011).

Yet with all these qualifications, metropolitan thought still provides the dominant theoretical framing for gender knowledge globally, and intellectual dependence is still the usual situation around the periphery. This is not good enough. The social experience of the colonized world is historically different, and the practical work of feminism, in the settings where the majority of the world's people live, requires theory that responds to this history. We need to conceive gender theory itself in new and globally inclusive ways.

This is a huge and complex task. What follows is a reconnaissance of three issues that immediately arise. First, recognizing the global patterning of knowledge raises questions about the concept that underlies the whole field of knowledge—the idea of gender itself. Second, giving priority to the South requires us to think about the tasks undertaken by feminist intellectual workers, potentially rewriting the agenda of feminist theory. Third, we need to reconsider the epistemological and practical character of the knowledge project launched by feminism and find a relevant shape for knowledge formation on a world scale.

The discussion that follows moves rapidly across a large terrain, and I apologize if it is sometimes rather breathless. I have grouped examples and citations by problem, not by place or period (which would be more usual). In doing this, I emphasize points of contact between the experience of different parts of the world and encourage readers to think about the issues on a world, not just a regional, scale.

"At the Imperial Source": The Coloniality of Gender

In a powerful argument, Amina Mama shows that to understand violence against women in postcolonial Africa we must understand the violence of colonialism; and to understand that, we must start with "gender relations and gender violence at the imperial source" (1997: 48). The Christian societies of Europe that launched the global conquest of the last five hundred years were already patriarchal and warlike. What Sarah Radcliffe, Nina Laurie, and Robert Andolina (2004) have called "the transnationalization of gender" has a very long history, and it is more illuminating to speak of the coloniality of gender. This term has been introduced by the philosopher Maria Lugones (2007, 2010). Though her account is very abstract, it provides a useful point of entry to the problem.

Lugones's argument draws on two schools of thought. One is the Latin American school of decolonial thought, which has developed a powerful critique of Eurocentrism in the culture of the region. Lugones draws particularly on the Peruvian sociologist Aníbal Quijano's (2000) account of the coloniality of power, which has continued to structure South American realities in the centuries since direct colonial rule was replaced by new forms of global power. The other is a long-running African discussion of indigenous knowledge and African philosophy (Hountondji 2002). Some scholars, especially in the African diaspora, have argued that precolonial societies were not patriarchal or were not structured by gender, that feminism involves cultural colonization, and that a distinctive African perspective on women is required (for example, Nnaemeka 2005; Oyewumi 1997). Lugones, making a sharp contrast between the colonial and the indigenous, speaks of gender as "a colonial imposition" (2010: 748).

Such formulations are refreshing. They contest the mental habits that see the non-European world as the home of primitive gender dichotomy and unreconstructed patriarchy. However, the empirical grounds are debatable. The benign view of indigenous society has attracted strong criticism within Africa, with other feminists challenging the factual claims, the cultural essentialism, and the implicit conservatism of the politics (Bakare-Yusuf 2004; Hendricks and Lewis 1994). It is difficult to deny the presence of gender and the existence of gender inequalities in most of the world's regions at the time when Western colonization began, East Asia, India, North Africa, Australia, and the Pacific among them. We have to recognize the vigor of precolonial gender orders; the complex structures of gender relations as theorized by Agarwal, Mernissi, Saffioti, and others; and the turbulent gendered history of colonization.

Lugones's picture, then, is too stark; but the dynamic she has named is of great importance. It leads toward a profoundly historical concept of gender. Concrete evidence of gender divisions of labor and the cultural recognition of gender goes back about forty thousand years (Balme and Bowdler 2006). Human reproductive distinctions became enmeshed with social structure as anatomically modern humans spread around the planet. Plainly, gender relations have gone through many transformations in different environments in the millennia since. The idea of the coloniality of gender concerns the most recent global upheaval of power and populations, the five hundred years of European empire and the global capitalist economy.

As Valentine Mudimbe observes in *The Idea of Africa*, "To establish itself, the new power was obliged to construct a new society" (1994: 140). A crucial part of this was the disordering of gender relations. The widespread rape of indigenous women by the men of colonizing forces both was an immediate violation of bodies, and broke down existing structures of sexuality, family, and inheritance. Populations that survived conquest might be relocated in forced migrations, with families torn apart (the taking of indigenous children continued far into the twentieth century). Structures of gender authority were always rebuilt, often by missionaries. Workforces for colonial industries were sometimes taken over as they stood, but often were assembled by force, expropriation of land, or economic pressure. Rulers and settlers created systems of inheritance and tried to project their power through time. As soon as plunder turned into colonization, then, reproductive bodies and gender relations were at the heart of the imperial project.

Mara Viveros (2007) in Colombia notes how colonialism wove together gender and racial hierarchies with peculiar intensity. In colonial situations, gender and race can hardly be regarded as separate variables. The meaning of race was constituted in gender dynamics—for instance, the rules against intermarriage between colonizers and colonized that hardened in most European empires in the second half of the nineteenth century. Conversely, meanings of gender were defined by beliefs about race, such as the hierarchies of masculinity that the British colonists defined among their Indian subjects (Sinha 1995).

The creation of a colonial gender order was never a simple transplantation. Ashis Nandy (1983) points out in his classic study of the psychology of British rule in India that colonial conquest created new patterns of masculinity, both for the colonized and for the colonizer. Robert Morrell's (2001) remarkable history of settler masculinity in colonial Natal traces the institution building, the harsh and insistent definitions of gender, and the continuing violence against indigenous people that was required.

In the contemporary world, direct imperial rule has been replaced by financial power, corporate investment, differential trade relations, frequent but dispersed military interventions, development aid programs, and the multilateral state structure of the United Nations. Gender relations are embedded in, and constituted by, all of these structures. This is documented in many ways, including the extensive literatures on gender in development (Harcourt 2009) and in the globalized economy (Gottfried 2013). For instance, gender hierarchies have underpinned exploitation in the factories of the "south China miracle" and among the *baomu*, migrant domestic workers, of neoliberal Chinese cities (Hairong 2008; Kwan 1998). The changes may also be highly contradictory: as Sonia Montecino (2001) observes in neoliberal Chile, the modernization of gender relations in privileged classes may be achieved by demanding archaic feminized labor from the popular classes.

The transition to a postcolonial world involved gender dynamics as intimately as the creation of colonialism did. Decolonization is often presented as a combat between groups of men, but women's presence in anticolonial struggles has been shown by persistent feminist research (Ghoussoub 1987; Mama 1997; Mies 1986; Robinson 2009). Sexism and violence within independence movements was a frequent part of the women's experience (Bennett 2010), and most postcolonial regimes reneged fairly soon on the promise of equality. Some, like General Suharto's New Order in Indonesia, constructed very regressive places for women (Robinson 2009). Nevertheless, Marnia Lazreg, whose analysis of this process in Algeria is classic, notes that "the very fact that women entered the war willingly was in and of itself a radical break in gender relations" (1990: 768). Shahnaz Rouse (2004) makes a similar argument about Pakistan, where women had been active in decolonization struggles, and where a repressive patriarchy was not a given at the start.

In these analyses, violence does not appear as a consequence of preexisting gender arrangements, that is, a dependent variable as in most Northern research on gender-based violence (European Commission 2010). Rather, violence is treated as an important part of the historical process that makes the gender order; violence is in that sense constitutive. In an issue of *Feminist Africa*, Jane Bennett discusses homophobic and transphobic violence and muses that in such cases the connection between gender and violence changes shape: "gender, as practiced conventionally despite diversity of contexts, is violence" (2010: 35, emphasis in original). Recognizing constitutive violence as a general feature of the coloniality of gender may give us some grip on situations of extreme gender violence today.

In a long historical perspective, then, feminism in the colonial and postcolonial world signifies far more than ethnographic diversity to be added to Northern gender studies. It documents a great historical transformation in the social processes through which gender is constituted. It offers a path to rethinking gender itself, on a scale commensurate with the world we live in. If one side of the coloniality of gender is the gender dynamic within imperialism and contemporary globalization, the other side is the significance of imperialism and neoliberal globalization, and the world they have brought into being, for the constitution of gender.

"Like Bamboo Shoots after a Spring Rain":
Changing the Agenda

In an eloquent article called "Awakening Again," about the resurgence of feminism in 1980s China, Min Dongchao (2005) observes that despite the importance of activists' contact with U.S. feminists, there was a gulf between the historical experiences from which the two groups were working. The coloniality of gender implies a changed problematic for gender theory, an expansion and reshaping of intellectual agendas.

This is not easy to specify, for a "new and heterogeneous" field of knowledge marked by multiple tensions, as Magdalena Leon (2007: 23) puts it. However, thematic surveys of regional literatures, such as Leon's in Latin America, Arnfred's (2003) in Africa, or Agnihotri and Mazumdar's (1995) in India, provide starting points. The issue of indigenous knowledge and its relation to Northern knowledge systems, mentioned in the previous section, is one direction where the agenda has to be expanded. Four others are easy to see in gender literatures from the South.

The first is power and the state. Under the influence of post-structuralism, recent Northern feminist thought has de-emphasized the concept of the state—to the point where, in one textbook of gender theory, *state* does not even appear in the index. It is now much more common across the postcolonial world than in the metropole to meet definitions of gender as "a specific form of domination," to quote the prospectus of the gender studies school at the Universidad Nacional de Colombia (2010). The attention to large-scale violence in the picture of power has already been mentioned.

Debates about the state and its role in gender relations are vigorous in postcolonial contexts, and it is not hard to see why: state power was the central issue in decolonizing struggles, and postcolonial states have had their own gender trajectories. Peripheral industrialization created new privileged sites of men's employment, such as the oil-funded industries of Algeria (Lazreg 1990) or the fragile motor industry in Australia. Dictatorships in Southern countries such as the Indonesian New Order created new configurations of masculinized power. Yet development strategies in the same countries might invest in girls' education on a large scale (Lazreg 1990). Mernissi (1985) noted this, and ironically suggested that the state, as sponsor of economic development, had become the main threat to men's supremacy in Morocco.

The second issue concerns the concept of identity, so important in metropolitan feminism in the last generation. There are critics in the South who argue that identity questions matter little compared with poverty, power, and violence (El Saadawi 1997: 117–33). To others, identity does matter, but in a different way. Both Sonia Montecino (2001) in Chile and Elisa Nascimento (2007) in Brazil place collective identities at the center. This concept is the core of a modern classic of feminism, Julieta Kirkwood's (1986) *Ser Política en Chile*, which treats the problem of identity as the problem of transforming the group into a historical subject capable of contesting the specific oppression produced by patriarchy. This radically historicizes the issue of identity rather than treating it as a philosophical or psychological problem.

This approach has been criticized. Nelly Richard (2004) argues that Kirkwood missed the diversity of sexuality and the importance of cultural contestation. Feminist discussions of identity and subjectivity in Latin America have changed under the influence of Northern post-structuralism (de Lima Costa 2002, 2006). Yet the issue Kirkwood explored is widely relevant. Transforming collective consciousness and forming collective agency was beautifully described by Lu Yin in the May Fourth movement in China, when new ideas sprouted up "like bamboo shoots after a spring rain" (Ng and Wickeri 1996: 112).

A third issue is methodology, a field impacted by postcolonial debates outside gender studies, notably Linda Tuhiwai Smith's (1999) *Decolonizing Methodologies*. Feminist research too offers new departures in methodology. A notable example is the work by Chilean feminists to create a method for measuring progress (or lack of it) toward gender equality, the Indice de Compromiso Cumplido (index of achieved commitments). This index escapes the top-down logic of international league tables and is explicitly tied to a politics of citizen control (Valdes 2001). Another is the use of international online discussions sponsored by UNIFEM, with hundreds of participants from both North and South, as a methodology of theory. This approach to theorizing grows out of activist experience and addresses exclusion and coercion as well as cultural differences (Ackerly 2001).

Perhaps the most striking methodological model has come from Islamic feminists. In *Le Harem Politique*, Fatima Mernissi (1991) attempted a full-scale reinterpretation of the religious position of women. She looked critically at the way the tradition of Hadith (attested statements of the Prophet) had been constructed by male scholars, and at their selective interpretations of the Qur'an. Islamic scholarship has long worked by critical scrutiny of canonical texts. Islamic feminism argues that Qur'anic principles include gender justice, and that patriarchal customs in Muslim communities are non-Islamic intrusions. Engaging in *ijtihad*, interpretation, is not a scholastic irrelevance. It is a form of theorizing central to Islamic intellectual life and therefore a significant part of the global picture of gender theory.

The fourth issue is the land: a topic almost completely absent from Northern gender theory. Taking land is a central process in colonization, with enormous consequences for the colonized. For instance, a sharp loss of women's authority accompanied the Great Mahele, the division of communal lands in Hawai'i in 1846–55 (Stauffer 2004). Australian indigenous societies too were profoundly structured through their relations with the land, and that structuring included gender relations. Kinship and descent, gender divisions of labor, women's and men's ritual and art, all involved—and still involve—relations with the land, such as rights of use, environmental knowledge, routes of travel, and symbolic meanings of the landscape. An important collection of Aboriginal writing on land rights is named *Our Land Is Our Life*. Marcia Langton (1997), one of the contributors, argues in a chapter called "Grandmothers' Law" that women's system of law and ties to place were crucial, under the pressure of colonizing violence.

The connection between gender and land is central to the work of Bina Agarwal. In her famous book *A Field of One's Own: Gender and Land Rights in South Asia* (Agarwal 1994), and in a research agenda stretching over four decades (Agarwal 2000, 2010), Agarwal provides a multistranded but remarkably clear account of how gender relations work in agricultural society—where nearly half the world's people, and a majority of the world's poor people, live. Her synthesis embraces gender divisions of labor, poverty, household bargaining, local political processes, patriarchal norms and their contestation, women's networks and activism, state strategies, and changing technologies in agriculture and forestry. It is perhaps the fullest contemporary demonstration of the multidimensional and dynamic character of gender relations.

Though based on close-focus research in South Asian communities, Agarwal's approach is easily adapted to other sites. Her work provides a powerful demonstration of the importance of land rights for change in gender relations and has led to important contributions to environmental thinking. It shows— as dramatically as the rise of deconstructionist feminism in the Global North— how a change of agenda can have far-reaching consequences for gender theory and feminist strategy.

The combination of these themes—and others emerging from postcolonial transformations—makes the case for a comprehensive rethinking of theory. This is important for the metropole too. Analyses from the South are already valuable for understanding gender dynamics in the North. The historical experience of massive disruption of gender orders helps in understanding the twenty-first-century impact of economic crisis and neoliberal politics within the metropole. Enriched feminist repertoires of methods and ideas help in understanding increasingly mobile and plural populations. The main thing metropolitan feminism stands to gain, however, is the same that feminism around the Global South does. It is the vision of a wider world, the dramatic expansion in what gender analysis can be.

Toward a Feminist Democracy of Theory

To realize this possibility, we need both an idea of the shape that feminist knowledge on a world scale could take, and practices capable of moving toward it. Here my argument draws on current debates about the coloniality of knowledge, Southern theory, and indigenous knowledge (Connell 2007; Odora Hoppers 2002). Three main images of the shape of global knowledge are revealed in these discussions.

The first is the pyramidal model implicit in the mainstream economy of knowledge. Theory is universal; it is mostly generated at the apex of the global system, sometimes with data input from the rest. Once formed, it trickles down to the rest. Scholars in the Global South, and in marginal institutions of the Global North, can participate in theory making if they migrate to the apex, or learn its language and contribute from a distance. The difficulties in this model have already been mentioned in this chapter. It discards much of the actual wealth of knowledge formation, forces Southern experience into Northern molds, and legitimizes stark inequalities within the world's intellectual workforce.

The second image might be called mosaic epistemology. Separate knowledge systems sit beside each other like tiles in a mosaic, each based on a specific culture or historical experience, and each having its own claims to validity. Mosaic epistemology offers a clear alternative to Northern hegemony and global inequality, replacing the priority of one knowledge system with respectful relations among many.

However, a mosaic approach also faces major difficulties, pointed out by Bibi Bakare-Yusuf (2004) in her careful critique of a well-known Afrocentric text. Cultures and societies are dynamic, not fixed in one posture. Precolonial societies were not silos, but interacted with each other over long periods of time, absorbed outside influences, and had internal diversity. Uma Narayan (1998) similarly reflects on the problem of essentialist treatments of culture that use iconic gender practices such as sati and assume uniformity within a culture. These arguments are reinforced when we recognize the massive disruption of existing gender orders. As Jane Bennett (2008: 7) in South Africa points out, much feminist research is done in conditions where "relative chaos, gross economic disparities, displacement, uncertainty and surprise" are the norm, not the exception.

Theory adequate to what Teresa Valdes (2007) calls the emancipatory interest in knowledge on a world scale requires a more interactive epistemology. Such an approach has to recognize both the diversity of local gender orders and the coloniality of gender.

The third image of knowledge emphasizes horizontal interactions and might be called a solidarity-based epistemology. The picture is one of mutual learning on a world scale, in which different formations of knowledge are respected but enter into educational relations with each other. These relations include critique, since education always requires active engagement and evaluation. Solidarity, like education, implies a concern with social justice—the principle that prioritizes the interests of the least advantaged. While unequal gender orders dominate the world, while new forms of gender exploitation and gender violence are still coming into existence, that principle alone will provide energy for solidarity-based knowledge projects.

Such a view of knowledge is implicit in many current discussions, including Bulbeck's (1998) idea of "braiding" feminisms and Bennett's (2008) observations on methodology for feminist research in Africa. In this perspective, the continuing unpredictable interweaving of ideas and experience around the majority world is an asset, not a difficulty. This is not to say that building solidarity is ever easy, given the history of colonization and constitutive violence, and the huge inequalities of the contemporary world. Aileen Moreton-Robinson (2000) shows some of the reasons in her critique of white feminism in Australia from an Aboriginal viewpoint: institutional orthodoxies, entrenched racisms, and social distance.

Making a solidarity-based epistemology work requires a practice of seeing gender fundamentally in the perspective of coloniality. Within Northern knowledge institutions, this means far-reaching changes in curricula. How many gender studies programs now get by with just one course, or even one lecture, on postcolonial feminisms? It means changes in the definition of scholarly competence, toward a model of world competence. In the periphery, it means displacing ingrained habits of deference to the metropole. It means new projects of building South-South links—never easy, though attempts are under way (e.g., Wieringa and Sivori 2013). It is not enough to have work from India, South Africa, the Maghreb, Brazil, Mexico, and Australasia separately. It is by seeing this work together that we become conscious of a body of knowledge with a scope and sophistication comparable to the output of the metropole.

Much of the knowledge about gender arising in the majority world is activist knowledge (Conway 2011), rather than the product of academic reflection. To give one example: in the early 1990s a retired accountant, Esther Chavez, was dismayed at the number of women whose dead and often mutilated bodies were being found in the desert around Ciudad Juarez, near the Mexico-U.S. border. She launched a personal research project to document the murders and demand action. In the face of growing violence and official indifference this became a movement, eventually an international campaign, to stop the femicide (Chavez 2010). Such change projects demand more than the categorical formulas and statistics that pass for a gender perspective in official development programs, the "technification of knowledges of gender" identified by Teresa Valdes (2007).

The relation between academic and activist knowledge is an old issue in feminist politics, which takes a more hopeful shape when imagined globally. Regional and global networks have some capacity to hold different arenas together, and have attracted increasing interest from feminist thinkers. Valentine Moghadam, Millie Thayer, and others have documented counterpublics and networks that address issues ranging from structural adjustment and trade to lesbian and gay rights, the position of women in Muslim-majority countries, and men's involvement in gender equity (Moghadam 2005; Tambe and Trotz 2010; Thayer 2010; the MenEngage Alliance, www.menengage.org). Mara Viveros (2007) suggests the growing importance of South-South links for feminist theory; Ashwini Tambe (2010) offers a model of transnational feminist studies and notes that even locally based feminisms may have distant links.

The workforce of gender research in the majority world, plus South-South linkages across this workforce, plus the heterogeneous counterpublics that need and use this knowledge, represent an alternative to the global economy of knowledge dominated by the metropole. This alternative is still developing. It is not yet strongly institutionalized, and its resources are far less than the mainstream's. Many parts are vulnerable to violence and dispersal. But it is important to say that this alternative exists, even in limited forms.

To dramatize the issue a little, I suggest that we are moving from a Northern-centered global economy of knowledge with a pyramidal epistemology to a Southern-centered global democracy of knowledge with a solidarity-based epistemology, where theory is produced and recognized at many sites, and thus brought closer to popular struggles and everyday life.

As this structure develops, it will certainly produce multiple types of feminist theory. Brazilian universities with journals such as *Estudos Feministas* and *Cadernos Pagu* will produce one kind of theory; Muslim feminisms engaged in the contestation of ijtihad will produce another; Indian engagements with land and environment yet another. There cannot be a uniform Southern theory of gender. What is possible is a differently structured world process of producing and circulating knowledge. To make this happen, a shared doctrine is not needed. It needs overlapping visions of gender justice, arenas of connection and mutual learning, and enough sense of solidarity to make these arenas work.

This brings me to the poem with which this chapter began. In 2002, Saleha Obeid Ghabesh, a poet from the Gulf states, published "Who Will Secure a Safe Haven for Buthayn?" based on the story of a medieval poet. The princess Buthayna bint al-Mutamed was enslaved during the collapse of the Muslim kingdom of Andalusia; she then negotiated with her suitor and her father a new path in life. The modern poet, in a complex act of solidarity, reaches across thousands of kilometers and centuries of time to find parallels with the subjugation of women and the position of Arab societies now. She uses the rich resources of the Arabic poetic tradition to suggest both the need for new departures and the fear and hesitation involved (Gohar 2008). The symbolism has wide relevance. The meeting at the edge of fear is ours, as well.

ACKNOWLEDGMENTS

This chapter was made possible by the writing, advice, hospitality, and support of many colleagues in Brazil, South Africa, Costa Rica, Indonesia, Chile, India, China, Senegal, Taiwan, Aotearoa/New Zealand, Australia, Mexico, and Colombia as well as in the global metropole. My thanks to them all. Rebecca Pearse contributed immensely as research assistant. Deep gratitude goes to my far-flung support team, especially Barrie Thorne, Robert Morrell, and Kylie Benton-Connell.

NOTES

This chapter was first published as an article with the same title in *Feminist Theory* 16 (1): 49–66. It is reprinted here with permission of the author.

1. To take just one example, see the last five years of *Feminist Theory*: the majority of articles come from institutions in North America and Europe.

REFERENCES

Ackerly, Brooke A. 2001. "Women's Human Rights Activists as Cross-Cultural Theorists." *International Feminist Journal of Politics* 3 (3): 311–46.

Agarwal, Bina. 1994. *A Field of One's Own: Gender and Land Rights in South Asia.* Cambridge: Cambridge University Press.

Agarwal, Bina. 2000. "Conceptualising Environmental Collective Action: Why Gender Matters." *Cambridge Journal of Economics* 24 (3): 283–310.

Agarwal, Bina. 2010. *Gender and Green Governance: The Political Economy of Women's Presence within and beyond Community Forestry*. Oxford: Oxford University Press.

Agnihotri, Indu, and Vina Mazumdar. 1995. "Changing Terms of Political Discourse: Women's Movement in India, 1970s–1990s." *Economic and Political Weekly* 30 (29): 1869–78.

Ampofo, Akosua Adomako, Josephine Beoku-Betts, and Mary J. Osirim. 2008. "Researching African Women and Gender Studies: New Social Science Perspectives." *African and Asian Studies* 7 (4): 327–41.

Arango, Luz Gabriela, and Mara Viveros, eds. 2011. *El Genero: Una Categoria util para las Ciencias Sociales*. Sede Bogotá: Universidad Nacional de Colombia.

Arnfred, Signe. 2003. "African Gender Research: A View from the North." CODESRIA *Bulletin* 1:6–9.

Badran, Margot. 1988. "The Feminist Vision in the Writings of Three Turn-of-the-Century Egyptian Women." *British Journal of Middle Eastern Studies* 15 (1/2): 11–20.

Bakare-Yusuf, Bibi. 2004. "'Yorubas Don't Do Gender': A Critical Review of Oyeronke Oyewumi's *The Invention of Women: Making an African Sense of Western Gender Discourses*." *African Identities* 1:121–43.

Balme, Jane, and Sandra Bowdler. 2006. "Spear and Digging Stick: The Origin of Gender and Its Implications for the Colonization of New Continents." *Journal of Social Archaeology* 6 (3): 379–401.

Bennett, Jane. 2008. "Editorial. Researching for Life: Paradigms and Power." *Feminist Africa* 11:1–12.

Bennett, Jane. 2010. "'Circles and Circles': Notes on African Feminist Debates around Gender and Violence in the C21." *Feminist Africa* 14:21–47.

Beoku-Betts, Josephine, and Wairimu Ngaruiya Njambi. 2005. "African Feminist Scholars in Women's Studies: Negotiating Spaces of Dislocation and Transformation in the Study of Women." *Meridians: Feminism, Race, Transnationalism* 6 (1): 113–32.

Bose, Christine E., and Minjeong Kim, eds. 2009. *Global Gender Research: Transnational Perspectives*. New York: Routledge.

Bulbeck, Chilla. 1998. *Re-orienting Western Feminisms: Women's Diversity in a Postcolonial World*. Cambridge: Cambridge University Press.

Celentani, Francesca Gargallo. 2012. *Feminismos desde Abya Yala: Ideas y Proposiciones de las Mujeres de 607 Pueblos en Nuestra America*. Bogotá: Desde Abajo.

Chavez, Esther. 2010. *Construyendo Caminos y Esperanzas*. Ciudad Juarez: Casa Amiga Centro de Crisis.

Connell, Raewyn. 2007. *Southern Theory: The Global Dynamics of Knowledge in Social Science*. Cambridge: Polity.

Conway, Janet. 2011. "Activist Knowledges on the Anti-globalization Terrain: Transnational Feminisms at the World Social Forum." *Interface* 3 (2): 33–64.

Davis, Kathy. 2007. *The Making of "Our Bodies, Ourselves": How Feminism Travels across Borders*. Durham, NC: Duke University Press.

de Lima Costa, Claudia. 2002. "O Sujeito no Feminismo: Revisitando os Debates." *Cadernos Pagu* 19:59–90.

de Lima Costa, Claudia. 2006. "Lost (and Found?) in Translation: Feminisms in Hemispheric Dialogue." *Latino Studies* 4:62–78.

Elbendary, Amina. 2002. "Reintroducing Aisha." *Al-Ahram Weekly On-line*, no. 586 (May 16–22). http://weekly.ahram.org.eg/Archive/2002/586/cu4.htm.

El Saadawi, Nawal. 1997. *The Nawal el Saadawi Reader*. London: Zed.

European Commission. 2010. *Feasibility Study to Assess the Possibilities, Opportunities and Needs to Standardize National Legislation on Violence against Women, Violence against Children and Sexual Orientation Violence*. Luxembourg: Publications Office of the European Union.

Eviota, Elizabeth Uy. 1992. *The Political Economy of Gender: Women and the Sexual Division of Labour in the Philippines*. London: Zed.

Fennell, Shailaja, and Madeleine Arnot. 2008. "Decentering Hegemonic Gender Theory: The Implications for Educational Research." *Compare: A Journal of Comparative and International Education* 38 (5): 525–38.

Ghoussoub, Mai. 1987. "Feminism—or the Eternal Masculine—in the Arab World." *New Left Review* 161 (1): 3–18.

Gohar, Saddik M. 2008. "Toward a Revolutionary Emirati Poetics: Ghabesh's Beman ya Buthayn Taluthin?" *Nebula* 5 (1/2): 74–87.

Gottfried, Heidi. 2013. *Gender, Work, and Economy: Unpacking the Global Economy*. Cambridge: Polity.

Hairong, Yan. 2008. *New Masters, New Servants: Migration, Development, and Women Workers in China*. Durham, NC: Duke University Press.

Hale, Sondra. 2009. "Transnational Gender Studies and the Migrating Concept of Gender in the Middle East and North Africa." *Cultural Dynamics* 21 (2): 133–52.

Harcourt, Wendy. 2009. *Body Politics in Development: Critical Debates in Gender and Development*. London: Zed.

Harding, Sandra. 2008. *Sciences from Below: Feminisms, Postcolonialities and Modernities*. Durham, NC: Duke University Press.

Hendricks, Cheryl, and Desiree Lewis. 1994. "Voices from the Margins." *Agenda* 10 (20): 61–75.

Hountondji, Paulin J. 1997. "Introduction: Recentering Africa." In *Endogenous Knowledge: Research Trails*, edited by Paulin J. Hountondji, 1–39. Dakar: CODESRIA.

Hountondji, Paulin J. 2002. "Knowledge Appropriation in a Post-colonial Context." In *Indigenous Knowledge and the Integration of Knowledge Systems*, edited by Catherine Alum Odora Hoppers, 23–38. Claremont: New Africa.

Kartini, Raden Adjeng. 2005. *On Feminism and Nationalism: Kartini's Letters to Stella Zeehandelaar, 1899–1903*. Clayton, Australia: Monash University Press.

Kirkwood, Julieta. 1986. *Ser Politica en Chile: Las Feministas y los Partidos*. Santiago: FLACSO.

Kwan, Lee Ching. 1998. *Gender and the South China Miracle: Two Worlds of Factory Women*. Berkeley: University of California Press.

Langton, Marcia. 1997. "Grandmothers' Law, Company Business and Succession in Changing Aboriginal Land Tenure Systems." In *Our Land Is Our Life*, edited by Galarrwuy Yunupingu, 84–116. St. Lucia: University of Queensland Press.

Lazreg, Marnia. 1988. "Feminism and Difference: The Perils of Writing as a Woman on Women in Algeria." *Feminist Studies* 14 (1): 81–107.

Lazreg, Marnia. 1990. "Gender and Politics in Algeria: Unraveling the Religious Paradigm." *Signs* 15 (4): 755–80.

Leon, Magdalena. 2007. "Tensiones presentes en los estudios de genero." In *Genero, Mujeres y Saberes en America Latina*, edited by Luz Gabriela Arango and Yolanda Puyana, 23–46. Bogotá: Universidad Nacional de Colombia.

Liu, Lydia H., Rebecca E. Karl, and Dorothy Ko, eds. 2013. *The Birth of Chinese Feminism: Essential Texts in Transnational Theory.* New York: Columbia University Press.

Lugones, Maria. 2007. "Heterosexualism and the Colonial/Modern Gender System." *Hypatia* 22 (1): 186–219.

Lugones, Maria. 2010. "Toward a Decolonial Feminism." *Hypatia* 25 (4): 742–59.

Mama, Amina. 1997. "Sheroes and Villains: Conceptualizing Colonial and Contemporary Violence against Women in Africa." In *Feminist Genealogies, Colonial Legacies, Democratic Futures*, edited by M. Jacqui Alexander and Chandra Talpade Mohanty, 46–62. New York: Routledge.

Mernissi, Fatima. [1975] 1985. *Beyond the Veil: Male-Female Dynamics in Modern Muslim Society.* London: Saqi.

Mernissi, Fatima. 1991. *Le Harem Politique: Le Prophete et les Femmes.* Paris: Albin Michel.

Mies, Maria. 1986. *Patriarchy and Accumulation on a World Scale: Women in the International Division of Labour.* London: Zed.

Min Dongchao. 2005. "Awakening Again: Travelling Feminism in China in the 1980s." *Women's Studies International Forum* 28 (4): 274–88.

Min Dongchao. 2007. "Translation as Crossing Borders: A Case Study of the Translations of the Word 'Feminism' into Chinese by the CSWS." *Transversal* 4. http://eipcp.net/transversal/1107/min/en.

Moghadam, Valentine. 2005. *Globalizing Women: Transnational Feminist Networks.* Baltimore: Johns Hopkins University Press.

Mohanty, Chandra Talpade. 1991. "Under Western Eyes: Feminist Scholarship and Colonial Discourses." In *Third World Women and the Politics of Feminism*, edited by Chandra Talpade Mohanty, Ann Russo, and Lourdes Torres, 51–80. Bloomington: Indiana University Press.

Montecino, Sonia. 2001. "Identidades y diversidades en Chile." In *Cultura y Desarrollo en Chile*, edited by Manuel Antonio Garreton, 65–98. Santiago: Andres Bello.

Moreton-Robinson, Aileen. 2000. *Talkin' Up to the White Woman: Indigenous Women and Feminism.* St. Lucia: University of Queensland Press.

Morrell, Robert. 2001. *From Boys to Gentlemen: Settler Masculinity in Colonial Natal, 1880–1920.* Pretoria: University of South Africa.

Mudimbe, V. Y. 1994. *The Idea of Africa: African Systems of Thought.* Bloomington: Indiana University Press.

Nandy, Ashis. 1983. *The Intimate Enemy: Loss and Recovery of Self under Colonialism.* New Delhi: Oxford University Press.

Narayan, Uma. 1998. "Essence of Culture and a Sense of History: A Feminist Critique of Cultural Essentialism." *Hypatia* 13 (2): 86–106.

Nascimento, Elisa Larkin. 2007. *The Sorcery of Color: Identity, Race, and Gender in Brazil*. Philadelphia: Temple University Press.

Ng, Janet, and Janice Wickeri, eds. 1996. *May Fourth Women Writers: Memoirs*. Hong Kong: Chinese University of Hong Kong.

Nnaemeka, Obioma. 2005. "Mapping African Feminisms." In *Readings in Gender in Africa*, edited by Andrea Cornwall, 31–40. London: International African Institute, James Currey and Indiana University Press.

Odora Hoppers, Catherine A., ed. 2002. *Indigenous Knowledge and the Integration of Knowledge Systems*. Claremont, South Africa: New Africa.

Oyewumi, Oyeronke. 1997. *The Invention of Women: Making an African Sense of Western Gender Discourses*. Minneapolis: University of Minnesota Press.

Quijano, Aníbal. 2000. "Coloniality of Power and Eurocentrism in Latin America." *International Sociology* 15 (2): 215–32.

Radcliffe, Sarah A., Nina Laurie, and Robert Andolina. 2004. "The Transnationalization of Gender and Reimagining Andean Indigenous Development." *Signs* 29 (2): 387–416.

Reuter, Julia, and Paula-Irene Villa, eds. 2009. *Postkoloniale Soziologie: Empirische Befunde, theoretische Anschluesse, Politische Intervention*. Bielefeld: Transcript.

Richard, Nelly. 2004. *Masculine/Feminine: Practices of Difference(s)*. Durham, NC: Duke University Press.

Robinson, Kathryn M. 2009. *Gender, Islam, and Democracy in Indonesia*. Abingdon, UK: Routledge.

Rouse, Shahnaz. 2004. *Shifting Body Politics: Gender, Nation, State in Pakistan*. New Delhi: Women Unlimited.

Rubin, Gayle. 1975. "The Traffic in Women: Notes on the 'Political Economy' of Sex." In *Toward an Anthropology of Women*, edited by Rayna R. Reiter, 157–210. New York: Monthly Review Press.

Saffioti, Heleieth I. B. 1978. *Women in Class Society [A mulher na sociedade de classes]*. New York: Monthly Review Press.

Sinha, Mrinalini. 1995. *Colonial Masculinity: The "Manly Englishman" and the "Effeminate Bengali" in the Late Nineteenth Century*. Manchester: Manchester University Press.

Smith, Linda Tuhiwai. 1999. *Decolonizing Methodologies: Research and Indigenous Peoples*. London: Zed.

Spivak, Gayatri Chakravorty. 1988. *In Other Worlds: Essays in Cultural Politics*. New York: Routledge.

Stauffer, Robert H. 2004. *Kahana: How the Land Was Lost*. Honolulu: University of Hawai'i Press.

Tambe, Ashwini. 2010. "Transnational Feminist Studies: A Brief Sketch." *New Global Studies* 4 (1): article 7.

Tambe, Ashwini, and Alissa Trotz. 2010. "Historical Reflections on DAWN: An Interview with Gita Sen." *Comparative Studies of South Asia, Africa and the Middle East* 30 (2): 214–17.

Thayer, Millie. 2010. "Translations and Refusals: Resignifying Meanings as Feminist Political Practice." *Feminist Studies* 36 (1): 200–230.

Universidad Nacional de Colombia. 2010. *Escuela de Estudios de Genero*. Bogotá: Universidad Nacional de Colombia.

Valdes, Teresa, ed. 2001. *El indice de Compromiso Cumplido—ICC: Una Estrategia Para el Control Ciudadano de la Equidad de Genero*. Santiago de Chile: FLACSO.

Valdes, Teresa. 2007. "Estudios de genero: Una mirada evaluativa desde el cono sur." In *Genero, Mujeres y Saberes en America Latina*, edited by Luz Gabriela Arango and Yolanda Puyana, 47–62. Bogotá: Universidad Nacional de Colombia.

Viveros, Mara. 2007. "De diferencia y diferencias. Algunos debates desde las teorias feministas y de genero." In *Genero, Mujeres y Saberes en America Latina*, edited by Luz Gabriela Arango and Yolanda Puyana, 175–90. Bogotá: Universidad Nacional de Colombia.

Wieringa, Saskia, and Horacio Sivori, eds. 2013. *The Sexual History of the Global South: Sexual Politics in Africa, Asia and Latin America*. London: Zed.

2 · One Planet, Many Sciences

The indigenous knowledge systems of non-Western cultures have served those cultures well in the past. As the British anthropologist Bronislaw Malinowski (1948) noted some seventy years ago, awareness of nature's causal relations was necessary for every culture's survival. Could such multiple knowledge systems flourish again today, continually transforming themselves to engage effectively with their changing natural and social environments as they have in the past? It is hard to imagine how such projects could succeed. They would have to proceed in the face of increasing poverty in the Global South created by today's forms of Western expansion. For example, Western development policies, implemented through agencies such as the International Monetary Fund and the World Bank as well as by national organizations and transnational corporations, initially were intended to eliminate poverty around the globe. Instead, they have created the "dedevelopment" and "maldevelopment" of so many non-Western societies, and the weakening and even disappearance of their indigenous knowledge traditions. Yet such indigenous traditions persist in sometimes impoverished and other times robust forms around the world, including in immigrant communities in Northern countries. Probably many of these traditions are too fragile to survive the continuing onslaughts of Western expansion. Consequently, valuable achievements of human inquiry about nature and social relations are disappearing from sight on a daily basis (Maffi 2001).[1]

Modern Western natural and social sciences have played a major role in helping to disempower other knowledge traditions. Yet the days are over when knowledgeable observers can continue to believe that there is or could be exactly one real science. Modern Western sciences certainly are international, but that is not the same as being culture free or the only possible effective and rational knowledge system. Indeed, the unity of science thesis no longer looks reasonable if one is considering only modern Western sciences, quite apart from the multitude of ontologically, methodologically, and epistemologically mutually incompatible knowledge systems still to be found in other cultures (Galison and Stump 1996; Kellert, Longino, and Waters 2006; Harding 2015).

Yet the appeal of the unity ideal is difficult to resist when it is advanced by such well-known and powerful contemporary scientists as, for example, the influential author of *Consilience: The Unity of Knowledge*, Edward O. Wilson. He believes "in the unity of the sciences—a conviction, far deeper than a mere working proposition, that the world is orderly and can be explained by a small number of natural laws" (Wilson 1998, 5). Moreover, some science intellectuals from other parts of the world have become alarmed at what they see as the increasing popularity of the science studies critiques of familiar Western philosophies of science, and especially of arguments supporting indigenous knowledge systems (Nanda 2004). Most people in the West as well as many educated people elsewhere cannot imagine how alternatives to modern Western sciences could ever be effective or gain widespread legitimacy. The unity of science appears to be the only reasonable response to what is claimed to be the power of modern Western sciences (Goonatilake 1998). How could any other organization of natural and social scientific knowledge and practice possibly even be intelligible?

Underlying this unity of science thesis are Western stances of exceptionalism and triumphalism. Exceptionalism holds that there is one empirical world. It has a distinctive order that keeps it functioning. The truest and most effective knowledge system must seek to mirror nature's unique order. There is one and only one such system, our modern Western one. The triumphalist stance attributes all the successes of modern science to its rigorous method, its disenchanted ontology, the distinctive organization of scientific communities, the skeptical attitude of scientists, or some other such internal feature of scientific inquiry. All the unfortunate events in the world that critics claim are caused at least in part by modern sciences and their technologies, such as environmental destruction, successful European colonization of hostile environments, the atomic bomb, the deskilling of labor, the genetic theory and engineering that informed and enabled the Holocaust—these are the consequence of bad politics, not of modern sciences' pure inquiry method, according to this view. Thus Western scientific exceptionalism and triumphalism internalize all the benefits of modern Western sciences and externalize their costs to social, political, and economic forces conceptualized as completely outside science itself. It is going to take a lot of intellectual and political work to dislodge these powerful cognitive and moral positions.

In light of this situation, it would be useful to begin to envision alternatives to the unity of science thesis. Of course, we can look at the historical record and see that many other effective knowledge traditions existed before the emergence of modern Western sciences. And, to be sure, remnants and residues of these traditions exist even into the present day. So the project here is not simply to imagine ourselves in another knowledge tradition that is conceptualized as isolated from the rest of the world, especially from modern Western natural and social sciences. Instead, the project here will be to envision keeping both eyes open—one on contemporary Western sciences and their philosophies and the other on other cultures' scientific practices and legacies.[2] What kinds of future relations can we imagine between modern Western natural and social sciences and these other still existing fragile science and technology traditions? What possibilities appear if we open both eyes, not just the one that has been fixated on the modern West? Such an exercise can help us to think more creatively about the possibilities and the value for everyone of living in a world of multiple knowledge systems.[3]

We live on one planet. The scientific choices made by each culture have effects on other cultures and their knowledge systems as one culture's choices bring about changes in the environment, in animal and human bodies, and in the economies, favored political forms, educational systems, media concerns, and other features of societies. Of course, these days it is the choices made by the Global North that have the most powerful effects on other cultures' conditions and opportunities. Moreover, class, gender, ethnicity, religion, and history produce different and conflicting approaches to natural and social science issues in the metropolitan centers, as they do in the cultures at the global peripheries. The vast majority of the world's peoples who were already economically and politically most vulnerable have had to bear most of the costs and have received the fewest benefits of the advance of modern Western natural and social sciences and their applications.

To be sure, it would be a mistake to hold that all of the difficulties Third World cultures face at this moment in history are the doing of the Global North or its sciences. These cultures, too, have indigenous legacies of inequality and exploitation. They, too, have followed science and technology policies that turned out to be unwise. They, too, have suffered from natural and social processes that they could not figure out how to escape. The point here is that the balance sheet for both modern sciences and other knowledge traditions looks different from the perspective of the lives of the world's citizens who are economically and politically most vulnerable than it does from that of the lives of advantaged groups in the Global North and elsewhere. Moreover, there are good reasons to think that in some respects the perspectives of the elites are less objective.[4] After all, elite perspectives tend to discount the value of the vast majority of the world's human experience interacting with their natural and social environments. How could such a waste of human experience be reasonable? (Santos 2014). We can start off thinking about the strengths and limitations of unified or disunified sciences from the perspective of the daily lives of economically and politically vulnerable groups around the globe. This was the kind of argument developed in standpoint theories.

After the Unity of Science Thesis: Standpoint Methodology

Already, in the nineteenth century, Karl Marx argued that if one wanted to understand how economic and political relations in industrial societies actually worked, one should start out thinking about them from the perspective of those who benefited least from such relations. Marx's focus was on the industrial workers of his day, the proletariat. As wealth accumulated for factory owners and others of their social class, so did poverty and misery accumulate for workers who were not paid what their labor was actually worth. Yet the prevailing social theories could not recognize this as a problem and as a threat to the legitimacy of their supposedly just institutions and fair practices. Nor, at first, could the workers themselves. *The Communist Manifesto* was written to convince factory workers that they could actually organize to resist their exploitation. The emergence of labor unions and subsequent history of labor relations was justified in terms of this kind of argument about the standpoint of the proletariat.

The demands of the new social justice movements of the 1960s and 1970s, such as the civil rights movement, poor people's movements, the women's movement, and gay and lesbian rights movements, invariably made this kind of argument on behalf of their constituencies. Standpoint theory turned out to be a kind of organic epistemology and methodology, tending to arise whenever a new group of exploited people stepped onto the stage of history. For example, feminists argued that the stereotypical relationship between men and women was something like that between bosses and workers. If one wanted to understand how gender relations shaped the organization of society, one should start off asking questions about those social relations from women's daily lives, not from the perspective of members of Congress, the Supreme Court, the World Bank, the medical-industrial complex, or the social theorists at elite institutions whose thinking, intentionally or not, served such dominant institutions. Women had been excluded from the design and subsequent management of those institutions. Starting off from the perspective of their daily lives enabled a more objective understanding not only of women's lives, but also of men's, and of the dominant institutions that men designed and directed. It was good science that was the problem, not just the more obvious bad science. Thus, standpoint methodology was not supposed to produce merely more accurate ethnographies of how women and other oppressed groups understood themselves and their worlds. Instead, it was to enable anyone and everyone to gain empirically more reliable and comprehensive accounts of dominant social structures—of national and global structural social relations (Harding 2004; Hartsock 1983; Rose 1983; Smith 1974, 1990).

Standpoint approaches are also a useful way to think about the benefits of postcolonial and indigenous ways of knowing. Indeed, some of the most powerful criticisms of modern Western natural and social sciences have come from such perspectives.[5] Though each standpoint analysis or argument always draws on perspectives and insights that are distinctive to the particular geographical, historical, and cultural sites from which they arise, these also tend to focus on familiar targets, namely the central Enlightenment (and older) assumptions and practices of which the modern West is most proud. In the case of research ideals, these are the standards for objectivity, rationality, good method, the proper scientific self, and the supposedly admirable fit of these standards with ideals of multicultural secular democracy, fairness, and social progress. Virtually every new social justice movement has focused in a distinctive way on such features of modern Western natural and social sciences. Yet while criticizing such standards, they are and must also be deployed by the critics. Consequently, there are fascinating overlaps, dissonances, and contradictions between as well as within different social justice movement analyses emerging from particular culturally shaped ways of interacting with global political contexts even today.[6] After all, the ability to function productively in the context of inconsistent and conflicting ideals and concepts is itself considered a mark of maturity in individual human development. And in this work are hints and beginnings of explorations of what might be the possible future relations between modern Western sciences and other knowledge traditions.

Surely, such relations actually will be more complex than the following schema suggests, and other possibilities not considered here may turn into realities. Yet considering as many possible models as we can will illuminate the history of modern Western and other cultures' inquiries about nature and social relations. It can give rise to more fruitful questions about what kinds of inquiries we could and should want in the future. Let us begin by noting just why it is that context-focused research is both so inevitable and valuable.

Keeping a Focus on Both the Challenges and Resources of Dynamic Histories, Geographies, and Cultures

Of course, peoples around the world share certain needs and desires—for example, for adequate food, clean water, shelter, good health, community, and protection from dangers, natural and social—though one must take care not to attribute to others those needs and desires that are in fact only characteristic of privileged groups, as Northerners all too often have done. Social justice movements have criticized the tendency of elites to take as universally desirable those kinds of projects that in fact benefit only those elites.

While some basic needs and desires are widely shared, cultures' locations in local and global environmental and social relations make different ways of satisfying such needs and desires important and give different groups access to different resources. This is so in at least five respects. Different cultures occupy different locations in nature's heterogeneous order: prairies or islands, in cold or tropical climates. They can expect to encounter monsoons, droughts, hurricanes, earthquakes, avalanches, sandstorms, or tornadoes. Moreover, they have different interests in nature even in the same geographical location. On the borders of the Atlantic, some societies will be interested in fishing, others in using the ocean as a coastal trading route, a military highway, or a refuse dump. Still others will be interested in mining the oil and minerals beneath the ocean's floor. Furthermore, different cultures can draw on different cultural narratives and their distinctive metaphors, analogies, and models to understand nature and their relation to it—conceptualizing the earth as a living body, as God's gift to his people, as a mechanism, or, in environmental sciences, as a lifeboat or spaceship. Each such narrative draws attention to different features of nature's order and appropriate ways to interact with it. And different societies tend to organize the production of knowledge about nature in much the same way that they organize the production of other social products. In the West, both craft and factory production models are used. Finally, a culture's location in global social, economic, and political geographies and histories shapes the way it will understand each of the other distinctive relations to the production of knowledge mentioned (Harding 1998, chapter 4).

No one would deny that there are aspects of modern Western sciences and their cultures and practices that can and should be used to benefit all peoples living in every society. What is at issue is not that claim, but a host of others having to do with which aspects these are, how they should be used in different cultures, how the benefits and costs of their production and use are to be distributed, which achievements of other cultures' knowledge systems should also become international, how cultures should act when they encounter conflicts between their own and other knowledge systems, and who will make those decisions.

Answers to those questions will be controversial. For instance, for the small middle classes in most Global South societies, modern sciences often represent desirable resources for the ways that these groups participate in industry, agriculture, medicine, the state organization of social life, and global conversations about such topics. As Third World feminists have taken the lead in pointing out, indigenous and non-Western cultures and their knowledge systems often legitimate cruel and oppressive social relations (Narayan 1989). Modern sciences and their philosophies provide attractive alternatives to such traditional knowledge systems. The value placed on empirical evidence, on high standards for objectivity, and the impersonal, fair assessment of knowledge claims is a precious, hard-won gain, they argue, when compared with many traditional ways of arriving at legitimate belief in those cultures (no less than in the Global North). Moreover, participating in modern science brings the kind of higher status and increased power in important local as well as international contexts that are awarded to many things of Northern origin. Additionally, modern scientific assumptions and practices are demanded as a condition of economic aid by such international organizations as the World Bank and the International Monetary Fund. Thus, many citizens of the Global South whose voices reach the Global North are no more critical of modern sciences than are many Northerners. The attempt to nourish the ideal of a world of many well-functioning sciences would seem to face serious obstacles in the Global South no less than in the Global North.

It can help in thinking about such obstacles to recognize that modern Western scientific assumptions and practices never can be adopted wholesale, so to speak, by non-Western cultures. Rather, whatever is adopted must be linked into existing material infrastructures, knowledge systems, and ethical and moral assumptions and practices. The new must always be sutured into the old (to use a surgical metaphor), as observers of such processes report (Gupta 1998; Medina, Marques, and Holmes 2014; Murata 2003). All scientific and technical projects are always already hybrid, one could say, as they have continually had to be adjusted and readjusted to the changing needs and desires of societies that are always transforming themselves. For example, we can currently observe such processes in the ways that sustainable energy sources are developed to replace high reliance on fossil fuels. It takes a lot of suturing work to make giant electric batteries, solar panels, and windmills reasonable alternatives to fossil fuel energy sources.[7]

Moreover, we should also keep in mind that great social changes have often been stimulated by the farsighted projects of a few visionaries. Think, for example, of the good effects of the work of people recently regarded as kooks, such as environmental whistle-blower Rachel Carson, the activists who have been slowly forcing the U.S. Food and Drug Administration to require more accurate labeling of our foods and drugs, and the gay health activists who brought about changes in the standards of the National Institutes of Health for research on AIDS. Many features of the postcolonial critical analyses already express perspectives that appear in virtually every Global South culture and are rapidly gathering support in the North. Certainly, many Northerners are beginning to recognize that we greatly benefit from more extensive and respectful discussions of the issues raised in and by these writings.

So what could be appropriate relations between other cultures' knowledge systems and modern Northern sciences if we give up the goal of unified science? As I have been arguing, we do not have to think these goals up all by ourselves, for we can start with suggestions that have appeared in the postcolonial and decolonial science studies literatures.

Projects Starting in the Global South

Integrate Other Sciences into Western Sciences

One proposal is to integrate endangered indigenous knowledge systems into the sciences originating in the Global North.[8] The continued expansion of Northern economic, political, social, and cultural relations is rapidly causing the extinction of many indigenous cultures, from the rain forests of the Amazon to the ice-bound lands where the Inuit traditionally hunted and fished, to the urban centers where many American Indians now live. These processes threaten to lose for humanity the unique and valuable kinds of knowledge that such cultures have achieved.

> Just as forest peoples possess much knowledge of plants and animals that is valid and useful, regional civilizations possess stores of elaborate knowledge on a wide variety of topics. These stores, the results of millennia of human enquiry, were lost from view because of the consequences of the European "discovery." But now it appears they will be increasingly opened up, foraged for valid uses, and what is worthy opportunistically used. The operative word should be "opportunistically," to guard against a mere romantic and reactionary return to assumed past golden ages of these civilizations. (Goonatilake 1992, 242)

Just as modernization pressures are reducing the diversity of plant, animal, and even human genetic pools, so, too, they are reducing the diversity of cultures and their languages and the valuable human ideas developed in them (Maffi 2001). These scientific legacies are interesting and valuable to preserve for their own sake. But they can also make important contributions to modern research.

Such projects raise important questions. Of course, it can seem to be a good thing to preserve in any way possible scientific legacies that are about to be lost (Goonatilake 1998). Yet if this were the only strategy for doing so, it would offer no resistance to the eventual extinction of all non-Northern scientific traditions. As indicated, modern Northern sciences have always appropriated ideas, techniques, and raw materials from other cultures. So this proposal would please Northern pharmaceutical companies, for example, which are already busy integrating knowledge of plant remedies developed by Amazonian rain forest Indians into modern medicines that can be sold for profit.

Philosophically, if this were the only relation between Western and non-Western knowledge systems, it would lend misleading support to the assumptions of unified science. It would reinforce the ideal of one authoritative knowledge system, secure in its triumphalism and exceptionalism. This project would incorporate only those non-Northern elements that could be incorporated without dissonance into Northern sciences. Other kinds of valuable knowledge, which Northern science cannot recognize either as knowledge or as valuable, would have to be abandoned. This project would leave us with one global science that is predominantly the product of the Northern civilization tradition and that lacks much of the knowledge that other cultures have produced and need, and that could become valuable to many others. Moreover, in abandoning the rich local cultural traditions that have given birth to and sustained other cultures' knowledge projects, such a process would lose resources for future scientific discoveries and inventions, and for human flourishing. This project fails to recognize the importance for everyone of preserving cultural difference—of at least some of the concepts, commitments, and practices of cultures around the globe that are in conflict with Western assumptions and practices (Chakrabarty 2000).

Finally, this criticism illuminates who have been the beneficiaries and who have had to bear the costs of modernization and development projects that supposedly were to benefit the world's already least-advantaged peoples. How should Northerners feel about extracting for the benefit of the already most advantaged societies the resources that become available to them from cultures that are dying as a consequence of Northern expansionist policies and practices?

Another proposal argues that scientific projects in the Global South should be "delinked" from Northern ones (Amin 1990). This is thought to be necessary if societies in the South are to construct fully modern sciences within their indigenous scientific traditions. Otherwise, capitalism inevitably succeeds in turning Southern cultures into markets that can increase profits for elites in the North (just as it continually extends into more and more aspects of daily life in the North). The Third World Network puts the issue this way: "Only when science and technology evolve from the ethos and cultural milieu of Third World societies will it become meaningful for our needs and requirements, and express our true creativity and genius. Third World science and technology can only evolve through a reliance on indigenous categories, idioms and traditions in all spheres of thought and action.... A major plank of any such strategy should be the delinking of the Third World from the secular dynamic which institutionalizes the hegemony of the West" (1993, 487, 495).

It makes sense at least to consider this strategy when one recognizes that there are many more universal laws of nature that such delinked sciences could discover if they were permitted to develop out of civilizational settings different from those that have been directed by Northern projects. Such a delinking program could make a world of different but interrelated culturally diverse sciences.

Yet it is hard to imagine how this kind of delinking could occur. We live in a continually shrinking world, where policies and practices of one country inevitably have effects on their neighbors and on distant countries. This is especially the case for policies and practices of the most powerful countries. For example, water use, fishing practices, and military projects of one country often have great effects on others. Transnational corporations can operate outside of any nation's policies and remain relatively unfettered by weak international laws and enforcement resources. Moreover, so many contemporary problems are global in nature, refusing to recognize national borders. Asian bird flu, AIDS, and SARS quickly spread around the globe. Atomic radiation and the effects of pesticides, acid rain, and other environmental pollutants quickly spread. Legal and illegal migrations, forced and voluntary, transport one country's problems and resources to others. Global media, the Internet, and cell phones are not blocked by border controls. How delinked could any culture become in this kind of ever more densely linked world?

Of course, some cultures—in Africa, New Guinea, and elsewhere—are so very impoverished and powerless that they are already delinked in important respects from Northern scientific and technological traditions. If they do not offer the North either natural or human resources or markets, they have become de facto delinked in important ways from the global political economy. Yet in other ways nature and culture converge to ensure that they are not permitted to completely delink; they must still suffer the effects of such global economies and their technologies on their environments, as well as on their health, life, and well-being. For example, impoverished African, Asian, and Latin American cultures are not delinked from the effects of global pandemics, environmental destruction, or their neighbors' well-armed expansionist agendas. Nor are the poorest people in rural and urban parts of the United States.

However, even if no one can completely delink from the global political economy, attempting to delink as much as possible—even just daring to think about it—enables more critical thinking in the North and more creative strategizing elsewhere (Chakrabarty 2000; Escobar 1995; Mignolo 2011; Santos 2014). For example, we in the North can begin to try to recognize what scientific culture and practices in the North would or should be if the South no longer provided so many needed extractable resources such as fieldwork laboratories, workers, or markets, voluntary or involuntary, for modern sciences and the kinds of so-called development they have advanced. What if we could not export to the least-developed cultures the North's environmentally polluting industries and toxic wastes, and extract sweatshop labor? We in the North would be forced to change the ways we live that produce such undesirable practices. What would a sustainable North look like in these respects?

There are alternatives to the world in which we live. Considering delinking enables more critical thought about just what can be practical and desirable forms of resistance to continued European and U.S. expansion.

Integrate Northern Sciences into Other Sciences

A third proposal is to integrate in the other direction, where other cultures so desire. Thus, indigenous scientific traditions around the world would be strengthened through adopting those parts of Northern sciences that they desired to integrate into their own indigenous traditions, leaving relatively intact the distinctive local identities of such traditions, as the Third World Network (1993) proposed.

This is not a new idea or practice. This kind of process has already occurred continuously during encounters between peoples of European descent and those encountered by them around the globe. Other cultures selectively borrowed scientific and technological resources from the Europeans they encountered, transforming those resources as they were relocated into local cultures, just as the Europeans were doing in borrowing from them. One report describes how elements of Western medicine were integrated into local knowledges in China (Hsu 1992). Another charts how elements of Western sciences and technologies were sutured into Japanese contexts (Murata 2003). The Japanese selectively borrowed from the European sciences and technologies that they encountered, always retaining the distinctive national identity of their project while modernizing it with the assistance of European resources. Similar processes have been described for Latin America (Medina, Marques, and Holmes 2014).

Indian science theorist Ashis Nandy argues for this kind of "reverse dissemination" to become a comprehensive program. He points out that India

> is truly bicultural. It has had six hundred years of exposure to the West and at least two hundred years of experience in incorporating and internalizing not merely the West but specifically Western systems of knowledge. It need not necessarily exercise the option that it has of defensively rejecting modern science *in toto* and falling back upon the purity of traditional systems of knowledge. It can, instead, choose the option of creatively assessing the modern system of knowledge, and then integrating important segments of it within the frame of its traditional visions of knowledge. In other words, the Indic civilization today, because it straddles two cultures, has the capacity to reverse the usual one-way procedure of enriching modern science by integrating within it significant elements from all other sciences—pre-modern, non-modern and postmodern—as a proof of the universality and syncretism of modern science. (Nandy 1990, 11)

If this kind of scenario were to become a widespread model, there would be many culturally distinctive scientific traditions that shared some common elements with modern Western sciences and, no doubt, each other (Selin 2007). Two forms of multiculturalism would be advanced: culturally diverse sciences around the globe and diverse cultural origins (recognized as such) within each local science.

Is this proposal possible? To some extent it is already a fact, as the reports above indicate. Moreover, it is an increasingly prevalent one as other cultures reassert the desirability and legitimacy of their own traditions in the context of decolonization projects. Additionally, there is increasing Northern appreciation and respect for social justice forms of multiculturalism in general, and for an end to Northern imperialism and colonialism. Of course, such tendencies still appear controversial to advocates for the unity of science or for delinking. Yet these days there are regularly occurring conferences around the globe focused on indigenous knowledge traditions and their legal rights. There are journals devoted to ethnobotany, ethnomathematics, and similar topics and an online journal, the *Indigenous Knowledge and Development Monitor*.[9] Moreover, at least some prestigious Northern institutions have become more hospitable to recognizing other scientific and technological traditions both at home and around the globe. For example, the University of California at Los Angeles hospital has for almost two decades featured a Center for East-West Medicine, directed by a physician with medical degrees from both UCLA and a Hong Kong medical school. This center champions "a new health model that blends the best of Chinese medicine with modern biomedicine" (*Vital Signs* 2003). In cities with large immigrant populations, such arrangements have become increasingly welcome. An exploration of other cultures' knowledge traditions occurred in a traveling exhibit originating in the mid-1990s at the Ontario Museum of Science and Technology (1997) in Toronto. Titled *A Question of Truth*, it presented some thirty-eight interactive exhibits for children and adults that presented the scientific and technological systems of other cultures.

These transformations in policy and institutional practice suggest that modern Northern sciences will probably not succeed in completely eliminating other knowledge traditions, as in the older ideal of philosophies of science. At least some of the others seem able to thrive in close proximity to Northern sciences and technologies, borrowing from the latter when it is regarded as desirable and relying on their own traditions otherwise. Yet many of the marginalized cultures are not strong enough to resist the continued expansion of Northern-originated modernization. The global cognitive diversity that is such a potential resource for each and every culture will suffer as such cultures, their scientific and technological traditions, and the physical and social environments upon which they depend disappear. It could be a gift to Northern sciences as well as to those of other cultures if Northern societies even more vigorously found their own reasons to want a more democratic balance of their own and other cultures' scientific and technological projects.

Transform Northern Sciences on Southern Model

A fourth proposal goes even further in revaluing Southern scientific traditions. It argues that Southern sciences and their cultures can provide useful models for global sciences of the future in a number of respects, as several of the examples above already suggest. Many elements of the distinctively modern scientific ethic are unsuitable not only for economically and politically vulnerable peoples in the South and elsewhere but also for any future human or nonhuman cultures at all. For example, modern sciences' commitments to a utilitarian approach to nature, to externalizing the costs and internalizing the benefits of scientific advances, and to an ethic of increasing consumption (development) are not ones that can support future life on earth.[10] "Modern science has become the major source of active violence against human beings and all other living organisms in our times. Third World and other citizens have come to know that there is a fundamental irreconcilability between modern science and the stability and maintenance of all living systems, between modern science and democracy" (Third World Network 1993, 496). Thus, Southern scientific traditions that do not share such problematic commitments can provide models for the kinds of global sciences that our species must have in order for it and the rest of nature to survive. As two biologists put the point three decades ago, Northern sciences should realistically be assessed as a transitional stage in scientific development since they destroy both the natural world and fair social relations upon which the flourishing and even survival of all cultures and their sciences depend (Levins and Lewontin 1988).

The point here is not that Southern cultures and their scientific traditions are all good and Northern ones all bad. Southern cultures, no less than Northern ones, have developed patterns of erroneous belief and systematic ignorance about aspects of nature that have left them unnecessarily vulnerable to life's vicissitudes. They, too, have supported entrenched patterns of social injustice. Rather, the point here is that all of us can learn from Southern knowledge traditions.

Moreover, we can learn from the particular skills and insights that they have developed under imperial and colonial regimes. For example, some Southern societies have learned to negotiate effectively with a powerful North, as Nandy (1990) argued about Indian elites in the colonial era. The forms of multiculturalism that they have chosen or have been forced to adopt give them valuable knowledge about how to live in a world different from that of elites in the North. They cannot afford the illusion that they are dependent on no other culture. They cannot get away with imagining that they can take what they wish from nature and other peoples. Nor can they expect respect beyond their borders for the idea that they are the one model of the uniquely and admirably human or that their ideas are uniquely and universally valid. Southern scientific traditions can offer valuable models for global sciences here, too.

In this scenario, Northern groups would take into their sciences and cultures precisely those Southern cultural elements that would transform modern sciences into more effective ones for the flourishing of both better sciences and of social justice tendencies in the North. In contrast to the first proposal, it would be precisely some of the elements of Southern cultures most incompatible with modern sciences and their philosophies that would be valued: the Southern forms of democratic, pacific, life-maintaining, and communal tendencies, where they exist, that are so at odds with the imperialistic, violent, consuming, and possessively individualistic ones that critics identify in Northern sciences and culture. To be sure, the former are not always well practiced in Southern cultures. Nor are they absent from Northern cultures, as the postcolonial critics are perfectly aware and always caution. In this fourth scenario, there would be many culturally different sciences, each with culturally diverse origins. But central among the elements most valued in each case would be those that advance cooperation, democracy, the richness of indigenous achievements, and sustainable development.

Is this a real possibility? Will people of European descent be able to accept the idea that our democratic traditions, in which (our forms of) scientific rationality and technical expertise play a central role, are not the only viable ones? What would greater intellectual inclusivity mean in this context? Certain kinds of preparation for such a practice can be encouraged in the North.

Projects Starting in the Global North

Unique contributions to viable future sciences can be made by those of us who value many features of the European tradition but are opposed to the history of modern sciences' service to militarism, profiteering, and social injustice. As critics from both the North and South note, it is unimaginable how one could advance social justice anywhere without recourse to so many basic concepts and practices of Northern democracies (e.g., Chakrabarty 2000). So the project here cannot be to abandon Northern modern sciences, but rather to figure out how to retain valuable elements of them while abandoning the ones that do not contribute to democracy understood as requiring egalitarian inclusivity. Progressives in the North do not have to retreat to stoicism when the topic of non-Western science and criticisms of Western science is raised. There are alternatives to fight or flight. We do not have to regard our only appropriate responses to criticisms of Eurocentrism as aggressive or defensive ones. Instead, we can recognize the opportunities and challenges in critically retrieving and modernizing the best in European and U.S. cultural traditions for sciences that are suitable participants in an emerging postcolonial world in which respect for many of the achievements of many cultures is the only legitimate ethic.

Indeed, the last half-century has brought about vast changes in global social relations, for both better and worse from the perspective of the antiauthoritarian social justice movements that began to emerge around the globe in the 1960s and 1970s. Anticolonial movements, the U.S. civil rights movement, women's movements, poor people's movements—these and many subsequent other social movements have refused the exceptionalist and triumphalist stances of Northern societies and the kinds of knowledge on which they depend and that they produce. Even in the last few years new such movements have arisen, such as those of Occupy and the Arab Spring. As sociologist David Hess has observed, there is no doubt that globalization has had hideous effects in many parts of the globe as it ever more smoothly enables and encourages expansion of capitalist forms of economic control of the poor by the already rich, often with the assistance of scientific and technical resources. Yet it also has opened doors for progressive forms of research (Hess 2011). We can actively continue to encourage and expand such practices. Several have already been encountered in earlier discussions here.

Southern Voices

One important project is to continue to add to our local environments—our classrooms, faculties, conferences, syllabi, footnotes, policy circles, television interviewees and interviewers, newspaper reports, and the like—the voices and presences of peoples whose cultures have borne more of the costs and received fewer of the benefits of Northern research practices. Of course simply adding diverse peoples to scientific sites has never in itself been sufficient to exert the kind of transformation called for in the North by postcolonial science studies. "Add diversity and stir," to paraphrase a feminist saying about adding women, will be insufficient to eliminate Eurocentric sciences and their philosophies. But it is certainly an important action in itself, and can become transformative if larger social justice movements are actively drawing on the diversity of experiences that diverse groups can bring to everyone's projects.

New Geographical and Historical Maps: "Science Crit"?

We can relocate the projects of sciences and science studies that originate in the Global North and those originating in other cultures on the more accurate geographical and historical maps created by the new feminist, indigenous, postcolonial, and decolonizing studies. We can abandon the familiar map charted by Eurocentric and androcentric accounts of the mainly European and U.S. history of science, and by anthropological accounts of other cultures' superstitions and false beliefs. This project will require rethinking what it is that sciences and science studies should be describing and explaining, and how they should do so. In what ways have the existing projects in physics, chemistry, engineering, biology, geology, medicine, and environmental and other sciences been excessively contained by Eurocentric assumptions and goals? What about economics, political science, international relations, sociology, and anthropology (cf. Tickner and Blaney 2013)? How have the conceptual frameworks and practices of Eurocentric philosophies of these natural and social sciences guided and made them appear not only reasonable but also the only such reasonable kinds of sciences?

We are not used to keeping a clear focus on both Northern sciences and those of other cultures. The natural sciences have lacked the kinds of critical historical, philosophical, sociological, and ethnographic resources necessary for them to identify Eurocentric beliefs that limit their understanding of the natural world and the history of modern Northern sciences and other cultures' knowledge systems. Simply reporting other cultures' achievements will not provide these resources. As many contemporary observers of Northern sciences and their philosophies put the point, these Northern sciences and their philosophies are epistemologically and—even more importantly—ontologically underdeveloped.[11] The modern Western scientific imagination lacks the critical social sciences and, in particular, critical social sciences of science and technology. These latter are a kind of science of science, mapping the relations between the social and intellectual features of scientific institutions and their practices and cultures. We need science criticism in the way we need the fields of literary or art criticism. The post-Kuhnian social studies of science and technology provide many of the resources for such a field (e.g., Hackett et al. 2007; Jasanoff et al. 1995).

Strategically Positioned Research

We can think of these kinds of tasks as a progressive project for constructing the fully modern Northern sciences that creatively develop key elements of the Northern cultural legacy—that, one could say, modernize them.[12] Our Northern sciences today are not, it turns out, quite as modern as they could be insofar as they entrench traditional Eurocentric superstitions and false beliefs about the achievements of both Western sciences and other cultures' knowledge systems. One striking feature noted earlier in some of the Third World analyses is that they propose what we can think of as principled ethnosciences when they contemplate constructing fully modern sciences that conscientiously and critically use their indigenous cultural legacies, rather than—as they point out—only European ones.[13] Those of us who value some of the conceptual features of the Northern tradition can similarly strengthen notions of objectivity, rationality, and scientific method—notions central not only to our scientific tradition but also to such other Northern institutions as the law and public policy.

Collaborative Research

Missing from the above lists are methodological guidelines for cooperative science and technology projects, ones where communities and scientists from the North work with partners from the South. Of course many of the most obnoxious so-called development projects have conceptualized their work as cooperations or collaborations with Southern partners—sometimes governmental or corporate partners, but in other cases progressive nongovernmental organizations. But it is a different kind of collaboration that is proposed here. One could think of this kind of collaborative research as at the radical end of the well-known continuum of participatory action research (PAR) projects in the social sciences. The point of PAR has been to position research projects in already existing progressive social movement projects. Initially, PAR emerged as part of efforts in the 1970s to conduct research that was for poor people, not just about them. Its inspiration lay in the work of Paulo Freire, liberation theology, New Left politics, and various kinds of "people's science" that were emerging around the globe at that time (Park et al. 1993). Of course, what counts as significant participation of, for example, poor people can be a controversial question. There are plenty of records of such controversies (e.g., Cooke and Kathari 2001). Our interest here is in that radical end of the PAR spectrum that is exemplified by the collaborative research projects that have been emerging in the field of archaeology especially, and also in some development projects in Latin America focused on health, environmental, and agricultural issues (Colwell-Chanthaphonh and Ferguson 2008; Fortmann 2008).

The significant move in this kind of research is that the modern Northern scientists must give up intellectual control of their research projects. Instead, the design and management of the research is to be jointly achieved by Northern scientists and their indigenous or Southern partners. The latter must be equally empowered-in-the-project partners with the Westerners. In one of the more ambitious statements of such radical PAR goals, the new research was to combine education, research, and activism in order to enable economically, politically, or socially vulnerable communities to learn how to figure out the kind of information they needed, figure out what the required research would be to obtain that information, and to conduct the community relations necessary so that they could themselves transform their own lives (Park et al. 1993).[14] In a

2008 speech to the American Archaeology Association, philosopher of archaeology Alison Wylie spelled out the deep transformations in how researchers could think about their work. "Consultation and reciprocity turn into collaborative practice when descendant communities get directly involved in the intellectual work of archeology. It is a matter of according control to collaborative partners in areas traditionally reserved exclusively to disciplinary authority: setting the research agenda and shaping both the process and the products of archaeology inquiry" (Wylie 2008, 5).

Though this proposal is for collaboration between Northern and Southern researchers, I categorize it here as starting in the North only because it requires a preliminary transformation by Northerners of fundamental and dominant intellectual and ethical conceptions of what a proper scientific self is and should be in a truly democratically inclusive multicultural research relation.[15]

With Both Eyes Open

Much more can be said about what is involved in starting in the South and in the North to develop a world of sciences with both eyes open. Envisioning future relations between, and projects for, both modern Northern sciences and other cultures' scientific and technological traditions can lead to far more accurate and valuable understandings, not only of other cultures' scientific legacies but also of fruitful but unexplored possibilities in Northern cultures and practices. Moreover, it can provide resources for the greatly expanded accountability practices for which so many critics have called. Eurocentric philosophies of modern Northern sciences assume there is no reason to explore or reflect on any scientific traditions but their own. They leave us blind in one eye that could be critically examining other traditions. And they leave us with distorted vision in the other eye, which can see only the Global North and only from within its own self-serving mythologies.

NOTES

This essay is an updated and revised version of chapter 3, "With Both Eyes Open: A World of Sciences" in *Science and Social Inequality* (Harding 2006).

1. Readers may find it confusing that I sometimes refer to the West, at other times the North versus the South, and at yet other times the First versus Third World or industrialized versus unindustrialized societies. Wouldn't it be better to use just one set of terms throughout? No, alas! Each of these contrasts came into use in a specific era of global politics. While none has subsequently completely disappeared, their use can be misleading or irrelevant with reference to other eras. West versus East describes the direction of

travel to Europe's imperial and colonial projects from European homelands. (The United States, as well as much of Europe itself, has at least in the last couple of centuries identified itself with this West.) First versus Third World is a Cold War contrast marking when the unaligned nations (unaligned with either the Soviet Union's Second World or the West's First World) organized themselves as a distinctive force in global politics of the day. North versus South came into use by representatives from Southern countries at the 1992 Rio de Janeiro United Nations conference on the environment. Industrialized or not can be important in the history of so-called development projects, but not in other contexts. And civilized versus savage or backward was a favored contrast of the colonizers. It will not be invoked here. I shall tend to use the contrast most appropriate for the particular historical context at issue. Of course use of any such contrasts can be problematic as they tend to homogenize both sides and obscure the often widespread hybrid or mixed contexts. Yet we need to be able to refer to powerful and widespread social forces and their resistors, yet without further empowering them. We are stuck with only contradictory options. And that is itself in part the topic of this essay.

2. Laura Nader (1996) recommends "both eyes open" in "Anthropological Inquiry into Boundaries, Power, and Knowledge."

3. For just a few of the important geographies of knowledge produced in the social sciences, see Gieryn (1999), Livingstone (2003), and Powell (2007).

4. This chapter focuses primarily on what the North thinks of as natural sciences. Yet the arguments here are applicable to social sciences in several ways. Social science methods have all either modeled themselves upon those preferred in the natural sciences or have been designed against those preferred in the natural sciences. So to focus on problems with the supposed value freedom of the natural sciences undermines both the purportedly unproblematic nature of natural science models and also the contrast with such models. Indeed, indigenous knowledge systems tend to perceive the nature versus culture binary that underlies natural versus social sciences as a distinctive and Northern invention that obscures how what we think of as nature and culture are always already suffused with the other. That binary appears to have been invented as a mirror image of typical indigenous ontologies (Viveiros de Castro 2004). Of course, the entire field of science studies—the sociologies, ethnographies, politics, and economics of scientific theory and practice—is grounded in the assumption that sciences and their societies coproduce and coconstitute each other. There can be no natural science free of specific cultural, social, and historical values and interests, just as the nature studied by sciences is itself thereby already constituted in distinctive ways by the social context in which it is found interesting to study (e.g., Jasanoff 2005).

5. For useful reviews of this postcolonial science studies literature and its relation to the postcolonial studies that has become institutionalized in U.S. literature departments, see Anderson (2009), Anderson and Adams (2007), and Seth (2009). Yet the related but distinct Latin American decolonial perspectives tend to be missing from postcolonial studies and from its focus on knowledge systems. For the latter, see, for example, Coronil (1997), Dussel (1995), Medina, Marques, and Holmes (2014), Mignolo (2000, 2008), Mignolo and Escobar (2010), Morana, Dussel, and Jauregui (2008), and Santos (2014).

6. See Chakrabarty's (2000) illuminating reflections on just these necessary contradictions in the project of criticizing fundamental Western Enlightenment concepts and practices while simultaneously needing to make use of them.

7. Note that this kind of argument does not assume that any science is a coherent whole. Rather, sciences are always collections of disparate elements, "assemblages" (Watson-Verran and Turnbull 1995).

8. Of course, our Northern sciences contain many elements that already originated in the other cultures that Northerners have encountered (Goonatilake 1992; Harding 1998).

9. *Indigenous Knowledge and Development Monitor*, https://app.iss.nl/ikdm/ikdm/.

10. Recollect that it was the exceptionalist and triumphalist stance of modern Western sciences that claimed those sciences responsible for all their achievements, but only bad politics that was responsible for the huge disasters that many critics wanted to attribute at least in part to modern Western sciences. Modern Western sciences only do pure or basic research, according to this account. Thus they are free of any particular social, economic, or political values and interests. For discussions of how this kind of claim became important to the U.S. scientific establishment at precisely the moment when the U.S. government began massive funding of scientific research through the Manhattan Project, which created the atomic bomb, and the founding of the National Science Foundation in the late 1940s, see Hollinger (1996). For the important role of the Cold War in making necessary this claim to the value of freedom of scientific research, see Reisch (2005). See also chapter 5 of Harding (2015) for discussion of these issues.

11. For the ontological issues, see Blaney and Tickner (2017) and Viveiros de Castro (2004).

12. Beck (1992) has made a similar argument for the development of a "second, reflexive modernity" to complete the tasks that the "first, industrial modernity" has left undone.

13. Fredric Jameson (2003) makes a similar point about the value of the "principled relativism" of feminist standpoint theory.

14. It is questionable whether graduate students should be permitted to do such collaborative projects before they have been fully trained in how to design and manage a conventional empirically successful research project, and then invited to examine just how to function honestly in a collaborative research relation. These collaborative projects are extremely difficult to achieve even by the most seasoned researchers, as the sources cited describe.

15. I discuss this issue further in chapter 7, "After Mr. Nowhere: New Proper Scientific Selves," in *Objectivity and Diversity* (Harding 2015).

REFERENCES

Amin, Samir. 1989. *Eurocentrism*. New York: Monthly Review Press.

Amin, Samir. 1990. *Delinking: Toward a Polycentric World*. New York: Zed.

Anderson, Warwick. 2009. "From Subjugated Knowledge to Conjugated Subjects: Science and Globalization, or, Postcolonial Studies of Science?" *Postcolonial*.

Anderson, Warwick, and Vincanne Adams. 2007. "Pramoedya's Chickens: Postcolonial Studies of Technoscience." In *The Handbook of Science and Technology Studies*, 3rd ed., edited by Edward J. Hackett, Olga Amsterdam, Michael E. Lynch, and Judy Wajcman, 181–207. Cambridge, MA: MIT Press.

Beck, Ulrich. 1992. *Risk Society: Towards a New Modernity*. London: SAGE.

Blaney, David L., and Arlene B. Tickner. 2017. "Worlding, Ontological Politics and the Possibility of a Decolonial IR." *Millennium* 45 (3): 293–311.

Chakrabarty, Dipesh. 2000. *Provincializing Europe: Postcolonial Thought and Historical Difference*. Princeton, NJ: Princeton University Press.

Colwell-Chanthaphonh, Chip, and T. J. Ferguson, eds. 2008. *Collaboration in Archaeological Practice: Engaging Descendant Communities*. New York: Altamira.

Cooke, Bill, and Uma Kathari, eds. 2001. *Participation: The New Tyranny?* London: Zed.

Coronil, Fernando. 1997. *The Magical State: Nature, Money, and Modernity in Venezuela*. Chicago: University of Chicago Press.

Dussel, Enrique. 1995. *The Invention of the Americas: Eclipse of the "Other" and the Myth of Modernity*. Translated by Michael Barber. New York: Continuum.

Escobar, Arturo. 1995. *Encountering Development: The Making and Unmaking of the Third World*. Princeton, NJ: Princeton University Press.

Fortmann, Louise, ed. 2008. *Participatory Research in Conservation and Rural Livelihoods: Doing Science Together*. Hoboken, NJ: Wiley-Blackwell.

Galison, Peter, and David J. Stump, eds. 1996. *The Disunity of Science: Boundaries, Contexts, and Power*. Stanford, CA: Stanford University Press.

Gieryn, Thomas F. 1999. *Cultural Boundaries of Science*. Chicago: University of Chicago Press.

Goonatilake, Susantha. 1992. "The Voyages of Discovery and the Loss and Rediscovery of the 'Other's' Knowledge." *Impact of Science on Society*, no. 167: 241–64.

Goonatilake, Susantha. 1998. *Toward a Global Science: Mining Civilizational Knowledge*. Bloomington: Indiana University Press.

Gupta, Akhil. 1998. *Postcolonial Developments: Agriculture in the Making of Modern India*. Durham, NC: Duke University Press.

Hackett, Edward J., Olga Amsterdamska, Michael E. Lynch, and Judy Wajcman, eds. 2007. *The Handbook of Science and Technology Studies*, 3rd ed. Cambridge, MA: MIT Press.

Harding, Sandra. 1986. *The Science Question in Feminism*. Ithaca, NY: Cornell University Press.

Harding, Sandra, ed. 1993. *The "Racial" Economy of Science: Toward a Democratic Future*. Bloomington: Indiana University Press.

Harding, Sandra. 1998. *Is Science Multicultural? Postcolonialisms, Feminisms, and Epistemologies*. Bloomington: Indiana University Press.

Harding, Sandra, ed. 2004. *The Feminist Standpoint Theory Reader: Intellectual and Political Controversies*. New York: Routledge.

Harding, Sandra. 2006. *Science and Social Inequality: Feminist and Postcolonial Issues*. Chicago: University of Illinois Press.

Harding, Sandra. 2008. *Sciences from Below: Feminisms, Postcolonialities and Modernities*. Durham, NC: Duke University Press.

Harding, Sandra, ed. 2011. *The Postcolonial Science and Technology Studies Reader*. Durham, NC: Duke University Press.

Harding, Sandra. 2015. *Objectivity and Diversity: Another Logic of Scientific Research*. Chicago: University of Chicago Press.

Hartsock, Nancy. 1983. "The Feminist Standpoint." In *Discovering Reality*, edited by Sandra Harding and Merrill Hintikka, 283–310. The Netherlands: Kluwer.

Hess, David J. 2011. "Science in an Era of Globalization: Alternative Pathways." In *The Postcolonial Science and Technology Studies Reader*, edited by Sandra Harding. Durham, NC: Duke University Press.

Hollinger, David. 1996. *Science, Jews, and Secular Culture*. Princeton, NJ: Princeton University Press.

Hsu, Elizabeth. 1992. "The Reception of Western Medicine in China: Examples from Yunnan." In *Science and Empires: Historical Studies about Scientific Development and European Expansion*, edited by Patrick Petitjean, Catherine Jami, and Anne Marie Moulin. Dordrecht: Kluwer.

Jameson, Fredric. 2004. "'History and Class Consciousness' as an Unfinished Project." *The Feminist Standpoint Theory Reader*, edited by Sandra Harding. New York: Routledge.

Jasanoff, Sheila, ed. 2007. *Designs on Nature: Science and Democracy in Europe and the United States*. Princeton, NJ: Princeton University Press.

Jasanoff, Sheila, Gerald E. Markle, James C. Petersen, and Trevor Pinch, eds. 1995. *Handbook of Science and Technology Studies*. Thousand Oaks, CA: SAGE.

Kellert, Stephen H., Helen Longino, and C. Kenneth Waters, eds. 2006. *Scientific Pluralism*. Minnesota Studies in the Philosophy of Science, 19. Minneapolis: University of Minnesota Press.

Latour, Bruno. 1993. *We Have Never Been Modern*. Translated by Catherine Porter. Cambridge, MA: Harvard University Press.

Levins, Richard, and Richard Lewontin. 1988. "Applied Biology in the Third World." In *The Dialectical Biologist*. Cambridge, MA: Harvard University Press.

Livingstone, David N. 2003. *Putting Science in Its Place: Geographies of Scientific Knowledge*. Chicago: University of Chicago Press.

Maffi, Luisa, ed. 2001. *On Biocultural Diversity: Linking Language, Knowledge, and the Environment*. Washington, DC: Smithsonian Institution Press.

Maffie, James. 2005a. "The Consequence of Ideas." *Social Epistemology* 19 (1): 63–76.

Maffie, James, ed. 2005b. "Science, Modernity, Critique." *Social Epistemology* 19 (1).

Malinowski, Bronislaw. 1948. *Magic, Science, and Religion, and Other Essays*. Garden City, NY: Doubleday Anchor.

Medina, Eden, Ivan da Costa Marques, and Christina Holmes, eds. 2014. *Beyond Imported Magic: Essays on Science, Technology, and Society in Latin America*. Cambridge, MA: MIT Press.

Mignolo, Walter D. 2000. *Local Histories/Global Designs: Coloniality, Subaltern Knowledges and Border Thinking*. Princeton, NJ: Princeton University Press.

Mignolo, Walter D. 2011. *The Darker Side of Western Modernity: Global Futures, Decolonial Options*. Durham, NC: Duke University Press.

Mignolo, Walter D., and Arturo Escobar, eds. 2010. *Globalization and the Decolonial Option*. London: Routledge.

Morana, Mabel, Enrique Dussel, and Carlos A. Jauregui, eds. 2008. *Coloniality at Large: Latin America and the Postcolonial Debate*. Durham, NC: Duke University Press.

Murata, Junichi. 2003. "Creativity of Technology and the Modernization Process of Japan." In *Science and Other Cultures: Issues in Philosophies of Science and Technology*, edited by Robert Figueroa and Sandra Harding. New York: Routledge.

Nader, Laura, ed. 1996. *Naked Science: Anthropological Inquiry into Boundaries, Power, and Knowledge*. New York: Routledge.

Nanda, Meera. 2004. *Prophets Facing Backward: Postmodern Critiques of Science and Hindu Nationalism in India*. New Brunswick, NJ: Rutgers University Press.

Nandy, Ashis, ed. 1990. *Science, Hegemony, and Violence: A Requiem for Modernity.* New Delhi: Oxford University Press.

Narayan, Uma. 1989. "The Project of a Feminist Epistemology: Perspectives from a Nonwestern Feminist." In *Gender/Body/Knowledge,* edited by Susan Bordo and Alison Jaggar. New Brunswick, NJ: Rutgers University Press.

Ontario Museum of Science and Technology. 1997. *A Question of Truth* [museum catalog]. Toronto: Ontario Science Centre.

Park, Peter, Mary Brydon-Miller, Budd Hall, and Ted Jackson, eds. 1993. *Voices of Change: Participatory Research in the United States and Canada.* Westport, CT: Bergin and Garvey.

Powell, Richard C. 2007. "Geographies of Science: Histories, Localities, Practices, Futures." *Progress in Human Geography* 31:309–29.

Reisch, George A. 2005. *How the Cold War Transformed Philosophy of Science: To the Icy Slopes of Logic.* Cambridge: Cambridge University Press.

Rodney, Walter. 1982. *How Europe Underdeveloped Africa.* Washington, DC: Howard University Press.

Rose, Hilary. 1983. "Hand, Brain and Heart: A Feminist Epistemology for the Natural Sciences." *Signs: Journal of Women in Culture and Society* 9 (1): 73–90.

Santos, Boaventura de Sousa. 2014. *Epistemologies of the South: Justice against Epistemicide.* Boulder, CO: Paradigm.

Selin, Helaine, ed. 2008. *Encyclopedia of the History of Science, Technology and Medicine in Non-Western Cultures.* 2nd ed. Dordrecht: Kluwer.

Seth, Suman 2009. "Putting Knowledge in Its Place: Science, Colonialism, and the Postcolonial." *Postcolonial Studies* 12, no. 4.

Smith, Dorothy. 1974. "Women's Perspective as a Radical Critique of Sociology." *Sociological Inquiry* 44.

Smith, Dorothy. 1990. *The Conceptual Practices of Power: A Feminist Sociology of Knowledge.* Toronto: University of Toronto Press.

Snow, C. P. 1964. *The Two Cultures: And a Second Look.* Cambridge: Cambridge University Press.

Third World Network. 1993. "Modern Science in Crisis." In *The "Racial" Economy of Science,* edited by Sandra Harding. Bloomington: Indiana University Press.

Tickner, Arlene B., and David L. Blaney, eds. 2013. *Claiming the International.* London: Routledge.

Turnbull, David. 2005. "Multiplicity, Criticism and Knowing What to Do Next." *Social Epistemology* 19 (1): 19–32.

Vital Signs. 2003. UCLA Healthcare 29 (5).

Viveiros de Castro, Eduardo. 2004. "Exchanging Perspectives: The Transformation of Objects into Subjects in Amerindian Ontologies." *Common Knowledge* 10 (3): 463–84.

Watson-Verran, Helen, and David Turnbull. 1995. "Science and Other Indigenous Knowledge Systems." In *Handbook of Science and Technology Studies,* edited by Sheila Jasanoff, Gerald E. Markle, James C. Petersen, and Trevor Pinch. Thousand Oaks, CA: SAGE.

Wilson, Edward O. 1998. *Consilience: The Unity of Knowledge.* New York: Knopf.

Wylie, Alison. 2008. "Legacies of Collaboration: Transformative Criticism in Archaeology." Patty Jo Watson Distinguished Lecture, Archaeology Division, American Anthropological Association, San Francisco, November 21.

3 · Transition Discourses and the Politics of Relationality

Toward Designs for the Pluriverse

It should come as no surprise that from an epistemic and ontological perspective, globalization, whatever it means, has taken place at the expense of relational worlds. Whatever concept we use to refer to the system of domination that has been in place and in continued expansion for the past few hundred years—modern/colonial world system, capitalist world economy, integrated world capitalism, neoliberal capitalist globalization, or what have you—that much is clear. Epistemic and ontological analyses thus emerge as a necessary dimension of analysis for understanding the current conjuncture of crises, domination, and attempts at transformation.

In terms of crises, besides the threefold crisis Marxist theory of capitalism (accumulation, fiscal, and legitimation crises), one needs to add the ecological crisis of reason (Leff 2002; Plumwood 2002; Shiva 2005, 2008), the crisis of meaning (Dreyfus and Kelly 2011), and the epistemic crisis of knowledge, cogently stated by Santos's (2007) diagnosis that what most characterizes our present moment is that we are facing modern problems for which there are no longer sufficient modern solutions. If one thinks about domination, second, one can say that to the accumulation by dispossession happening today with the brutal expansion of the corporate mining and agrofuels production frontier, one has to add the fact that these processes constitute a clear attack on relational worlds; it is no coincidence that land grabbing and massive displacement hit particularly hard territories customarily inhabited by ethnic and peasant groups worldwide.[1] Today, in other words, we are witnessing a renewed attack on anything collective (well beyond the collective demands and organizing of peasants and the working classes) and the destruction of nondualist worlds. As the *indignados* mobilizations in southern Europe evidence, even the middle classes are not immune to these pressures; their subjectivities, too, are territories to be conquered by the "ratiogenic monster" (Plumwood 2002) that is market-driven accumulation; and these middle classes have even fewer cultural and social resources at their disposal to resist the attack and to even consider seriously other ways of being, hence the wave of desperation, suicides, confusion, and of course protests witnessed over the past few years in many parts of the world, particularly led by youth and the unemployed.

This is the merciless world of the infamous 1 percent, foisted upon the 99 percent (and the natural world) with a seemingly ever-increasing degree of virulence, cynicism, and illegality, since more than ever *legal* only signals what conforms to a self-serving set of rules, whether these rules legitimize who the powerful countries can invade, or how the economy needs to be run (World Trade Organization, so-called free-trade agreements); under these rules, paradoxically, the more the powerful intervene, the more their intervention is legitimated, all in the name of freedom, democracy, reason, progress, development, and so on. This is why in terms of attempts at transformation, it is necessary to come up with ways of thinking about change that go beyond, or complement, those from the recent past (individual or collective action within a liberal framework, or resistance, revolution, even social movements within a Marxist framework). *Transition* is emerging as one such attempt to point at a type of transformation that embraces more than the economic, social, and cultural aspects of change as commonly understood; indeed, one that tries to weave these aspects, plus the ecological, together into a proposal for the planet as a whole. This takes us beyond globalization understood as the universalization of modernity into an understanding of planetarization as the creation of better conditions for the pluriverse.

This chapter is devoted to this proposition. The first section reviews succinctly the main discourses of transition emerging from both the Global North and the Global South. A main argument here is that the conversations between these two sets of transition narratives need to be taken up in earnest as a strategy toward a more effective politics of transition. The second part looks at some of the social and political transformations taking place in Latin America since the late 1990s; it purports to complement the usual discussion of these trends in terms of a turn to the left with an ontological reading of the social movements that in many ways are behind the state-level transformations as an important example of what we may call the political activation of relationality. To anticipate the argument, Latin America today is likely the clearest case of a struggle between neoliberal globalization (the project of the right), alternative modernizations (the leftist project at the level of the state), and the creation of post/noncapitalist and post/nonliberal worlds. This latter project relies primarily on the political mobilization of relational worlds by communities and social movements. The last segment suggests a further reinterpretation of these trends in terms of the reemergence of the pluriverse and argues for the constitution of a field of pluriversal studies.

Discourses of Transition: Emerging Trends

Arguments about the need for a profound, epochal transition are a sign of the times; they reflect the depth of the contemporary crises. To be sure, crisis and transitions have a long genealogy in the West, whether in the guise of civilizational crisis, transitions to and from capitalism, apocalyptic visions of the end of the world, sudden religious or technological transformations, or science fiction narratives. This is not the place to analyze this genealogy; however, it seems to me that it is possible to argue that transition discourses (TDs) are emerging today with particular richness, diversity, and intensity to the point that a veritable field of transition studies can be posited as an emergent scholarly-political domain. Transition studies and transition activism have come of age. Notably, as even a cursory mapping of TDs would suggest, those writing on the subject are not limited to the academy; in fact, the most visionary TD thinkers are located outside of it, even if in most cases they engage with critical currents in the academy. TDs are emerging from a multiplicity of sites, principally social movements worldwide, from some civil society NGOs, from some emerging scientific paradigms and academic theories in the social and human sciences, and from intellectuals with significant connections to environmental and cultural struggles. Several fields have prominent TDs, including culture, ecology, religion and spirituality, alternative science (e.g., complexity), political economy, and new digital and biological technologies. Only the first three are touched upon in what follows.

As Mezzadra has pointed out, "the problem of transition reemerges in each historical moment when the conditions of translation have to be established anew" (2007, 4). What he means by *translation* is the process by which different, often contrasting, cultural-historical experiences are rendered mutually intelligible and commensurable; this has happened in recent history through the imposition of the cultural codes of capitalist modernity on an increasingly global scale. This process, as he goes on to suggest, is no longer acceptable; rather, a new type of heterolingual translation, in which new commonalities are built precisely out of incommensurable differences, is needed. As I argue here, there are some radical differences in the current wave of TDs when compared with those of the most recent past. Two of these differences, underscored by Boaventura de Sousa Santos (2007), are that the transition/translation process cannot be led by, nor lead to, a general theory; in fact, the only general theory possible, as he puts it to the dismay of much leftist theorizing, is the impossibility of any general theory. The second, and related, aspect is that today more clearly than ever translation involves complex epistemological processes—intercultural and interepistemic—which require in turn a type of cognitive justice that has yet to be recognized. A third element is that transition/translation entails multiple ontologies; in other words, when radically envisioned, transition involves moving from the one-world Euro-American metaphysic (Law 2011) to the world as pluriverse, that is, without preexisting universals (Blaser, de la Cadena, and Escobar 2009). Transition toward the pluriverse thus calls for an expanded concept of translation that involves ontological and epistemic dimensions.

One additional element needs to be considered. This is the unevenness and differential character of TDs in the Global North and the Global South—the geoepistemopolitics of TDs. It is important both to consider the entire ensemble of TDs and to establish conversations between Northern and Southern TDs, not only in order to gain perspective but to come up with a clear politics for the transition movement. Those engaged in transition activism and theorizing in the North rarely delve seriously into those being proposed in the South, and those in the South tend to dismiss too easily Northern proposals, or to consider them inapplicable to the South. There is little concerted effort to bringing these two sets of discourses and strategies into dialogue; this dialogue would be not only mutually enriching but perhaps essential for an effective politics of transformation. The range of discourses can only be hinted at here; in the North, the most prominent include degrowth; a variety of transition initiatives; the end of the Anthropocene; forecasting trends toward 2050 or 2052 (e.g., Club of Rome; see Randers 2012); some approaches involving interreligious dialogues; and some developments in conjunction with UN processes, particularly within the Stakeholders Forum. Among the explicit transition initiatives are the transition town initiative (TTI, UK), the Great Transition Initiative (GTI, Tellus Institute, U.S.), the Great Turning (Macy 2007, 2012), and the Great Work or transition to an Ecozoic era (Berry 1999). In the Global South, TDs include postdevelopment and alternatives to development, communal logics (relational, feminist, autonomous), crisis of civilization model, and transition to postextractivism. While the features of the new age to come are postgrowth, postmaterialist, posteconomic, and postcapitalist, those for the South are expressed in terms of postdevelopment, post/nonliberal, post/noncapitalist, and postextractivist (see Escobar [2012a, 2012b] for further treatment, and figure 3.1).

A hallmark of most contemporary TDs is that they posit a radical cultural and institutional transformation—indeed, a transition to an altogether different world. This is variously conceptualized in terms of a paradigm shift (e.g.,

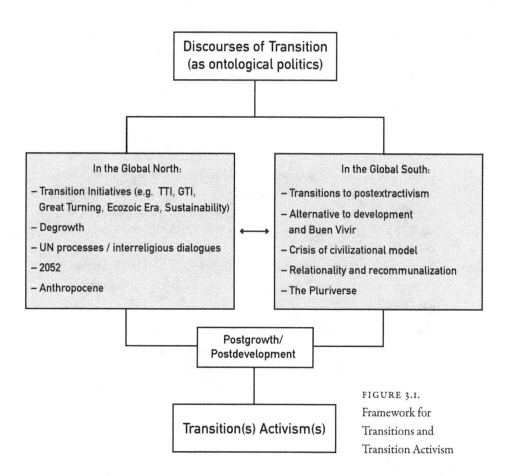

FIGURE 3.1.
Framework for
Transitions and
Transition Activism

Raskin et al. 2002); a change of civilizational model (e.g., Shiva 2008; Latin
American indigenous movements); the emergence of a new order; a quantum
shift (Laszlo 2008); the rise of a new, holistic culture; or even the coming of
an entirely new era beyond the modern dualist (e.g., Goodwin 2007; Macy
2007), reductionist (e.g., Kauffman 2008), and economic (e.g., Schafer 2008)
age. This change is often seen as impending or as already happening, although
most TDs warn that the results are by no means guaranteed. Let us listen to a
few statements on the transition:

> The global transition has begun—a planetary society will take shape over
> the coming decades. But its outcome is in question.... Depending on
> how environmental and social conflicts are resolved, global development
> can branch into dramatically different pathways. On the dark side, it is all
> too easy to envision a dismal future of impoverished people, cultures and

nature. Indeed, to many, this ominous possibility seems the most likely. But it is *not* inevitable. Humanity has the power to foresee, to choose and to act. While it may seem improbable, a transition to a future of enriched lives, human solidarity and a healthy planet is possible. (Raskin et al. 2002, ix)

Life on our planet is in trouble. It is hard to go anywhere without being confronted by the wounding of our world, the tearing of the very fabric of life. . . . Our planet is sending us signals of distress that are so continual now they seem almost normal. . . . These are warning signals that we live in a world that can end, at least as a home of conscious life. This is not to say that it *will* end, but it *can* end. That very possibility changes everything for us. . . . This is happening now in ways that converge to bring into question the very foundation and direction of our civilization. A global revolution is occurring. . . . Many are calling it the Great Turning. (Macy 2007, 17, 140)

If we accept the death of our own human bodily form, we can perhaps begin to accept the eventual death of our own civilization. . . . Global warming is an early symptom of the death of our current civilization. . . . We can slow this process by stopping [overconsumption] and being mindful, but the only way to do this is to accept the eventual death of this civilization. (Nhat Hanh 2008, 57)

While what these authors mean by civilization is not necessarily the same, these statements broadly refer to the cultural model that has prevailed in the West over the past centuries: its industrial growth model (Macy 2007), a way of life centered on consumption (Nhat Hanh 2008), with its reigning ideologies of materialism, market capitalism, and progress (Raskin et al. 2002). And whereas it is striking to find a revered Buddhist teacher (Thich Nhat Hanh) calling on us to meditate on the death of the current civilization, even many of the most secular visions emphasize a deep transformation of values. Indeed, the most imaginative TDs link together aspects of reality that have remained separate in previous imaginings of social transformation: ontological, cultural, politico-economic, ecological, and spiritual. These are brought together by a profound concern with human suffering and with the fate of life itself; it could not be otherwise, given that they are triggered by, and respond to, the interrelated crises of energy, food, climate, and poverty.

Thomas Berry's notion of the Great Work—a transition "from the period when humans were a disruptive force on the planet Earth to the period when humans become present to the planet in a manner that is mutually enhancing" (1999, 11)—has been influential in TDs. Berry calls the new era Ecozoic.[2] For Berry, "the deepest cause of the present devastation is found in the mode of consciousness that has established a radical discontinuity between the humans and other modes of being and the bestowal of all rights on the humans" (1999, 4). The divide between the human and the nonhuman domains is at the basis of many of the critiques, along with the idea of a separate self. Macy (2007, 2012) speaks of a cognitive and spiritual revolution, which involves the disappearance of the modern self and its replacement with an ecological, nondualist self that reconnects with all beings and recovers a sense of evolutionary time, effaced by the linear time of capitalist modernity.

Common to many TDs, and perhaps best exemplified by the GTI, is the idea that humanity is at a branching point and entering a planetary phase of civilization as a result of the accelerating expansion of the modern era of the past few decades; a global system is taking shape with fundamental differences from previous historical phases. The character of the transition will depend on which worldview prevails. The key is to anticipate unfolding crises, envision alternative futures, and make appropriate choices. The GTI distinguishes among three worldviews or mind-sets—evolutionary, catastrophic, and transformational—with their corresponding global scenarios: conventional worlds, barbarization, and the Great Transition (GT).[3] Only the last promises lasting solutions to sustainability challenges, but it requires fundamental changes in values as well as novel socioeconomic and institutional arrangements. As with some of the degrowth narratives, the GT paradigm redefines progress in terms of nonmaterial human fulfillment. It highlights interconnectedness and envisions a dematerialized production, the decoupling of well-being from growth and consumption, and the cultivation of new values (e.g., solidarity, ethics, community, meaning). It seeks to bring about an era of renewable energy and so forth. The GT involves, above all, a values-led shift toward an alternative global vision, one that replaces industrial capitalism with a civilizing globalization.

Many TDs are keyed into the need to move to postcarbon or post–fossil fuel economies. Vandana Shiva has brought this point home with special insight and force (see especially Shiva 2005, 2008). For Shiva, the key to the transition "from oil to soil"—from a mechanical-industrial paradigm centered on globalized markets to a people- and planet-centered one, which she calls Earth democracy—lies in strategies of relocalization, that is, the construction of decentralized, biodiversity-based organic food and energy systems that operate on the basis of grassroots democracy, place-based knowledge, local economies, and the preservation of soils and ecological integrity. Such TDs exhibit an acute consciousness of the rights of communities to their territories and resources, of the tremendously uneven patterns of global consumption, environmental impact, and structures of exploitation maintained by capitalism, and of the concomitant need for social and environmental justice. This is why their insistence on "the imperative that we change the way we live" if we want to "move beyond oil" is coupled with a view of the "need to reinvent society, technology, and economy" (Shiva 2008, 1). In other words, critiques of capitalism, cultural change (sometimes including spirituality), and ecology are systematically connected to each other in the various diagnoses of the problem and possible ways forward (see also, e.g., Korten 2006; Mooney, ETC Group, and What Next Project 2006; Sachs and Santarius 2007; Santos 2007; Schafer 2008). The proposed "ecology of transformation" (Hathaway and Boff 2009) is seen as the route to counteract the ravages of global capitalism and for constructing sustainable communities. In Hathaway and Boff's vision, the main components of the strategy are ecological justice, biological and cultural diversity, bioregionalism, rootedness in place, self-reliance and openness, participatory democracy, and cooperative self-organization. Although these visions certainly have roots in, say, anarchism and ecology, they presuppose a cosmology of liberation that is attuned to a kind of spirituality appropriate to current planetary conjectures and threats and to an Ecozoic era.

One of the most concrete proposals for a transition to a post–fossil fuel society that responds adequately to peak oil and climate change is the TTI devised for towns and communities to engage in their own transition visions, scenarios, and practices (see Hopkins 2008, 2011). This compelling vision, already a movement involving more than a hundred towns in the North, includes both the outline of a long-term post–peak oil scenario and a primer for towns and communities to move along the transition timeline. The relocalization of food, energy, and decision making are crucial elements of the TTI. The TTI also contemplates the reinvigoration of communities so that they become more localized and self-reliant, with lower-energy infrastructures (energy descent or powerdown), and, very importantly, tools and processes for rebuilding the resilience of ecosystems and communities eroded by centuries of delocalized, expert-driven economic and political systems. Resilience is actually the TTI approach's response to conventional notions of sustainability; it requires seeding communities with diversity, increasing reliance on social and ecological self-organization, strengthening the capability to produce locally, and so forth. As currently stated, however, the TTI is closer to alternative development than to alternatives to development. There is thus an important bridge that needs to be built between the TTI vision and postdevelopment.[4]

Transition discourses thus posit a profound cultural, economic, scientific, and political transformation of dominant institutions and practices. Emphasizing relocalization and the rebuilding of local communities go directly against most globalization discourses; they bet on the fact that small is not only possible but perhaps inevitable (e.g., Estill 2008; Hopkins 2008, 68–77). By making visible the damaging effects of the cultural institutions of the individual and the market, they direct our attention to the need to reconstruct identity and economy, oftentimes in tandem with those communities where the regimes of the individual and the market have not yet taken a complete hold on socionatural life. They advocate for a diverse economy with a strong basis in communities, even if of course not bound to the local (Gibson-Graham 2006). The consideration of spirituality in many TDs is a reminder of the systemic exclusion of this important area from our secular academies. In emphasizing the continuity between nature and culture, finally, TDs bring to the fore one of the crucial imperatives of our time: the need to reconnect with each other and with the nonhuman world. This latter is also a call for the ascendancy of the pluriverse, as we shall see in the next section.[5]

América Latina/Abya Yala:
The Political Activation of Relationality?

The Question of Development Reconsidered:
Buen Vivir *and the Rights of Nature*

Some Latin American movement and intellectual debates envision feasible steps for moving away from the civilizational model of modernization and globalized development.[6] In gathering after gathering of indigenous peoples, Afro-descendants, women, and peasants, the crisis of the Western *modelo civilizatorio* is invoked as the single most important cause of the current global/energy/climate and poverty crisis. A shift to a new cultural and economic paradigm is recognized both as needed and as actively under construction.[7] While the emphasis on a transition at the level of the entire model of society is strongest among some indigenous movements, it is also found, for instance, in agroecological networks for which only a shift toward localized, agroecological food production systems can lead us out of the climate and food crises. The agroecological proposals resonate with Shiva's, and are echoed partially by the global network Via Campesina, centered on food sovereignty based on peasant agriculture. The meaning of transition and postdevelopment can be ascertained clearly in the most recent debates on the definition of development and the rights of nature taking place in countries such as Ecuador and Bolivia. A new wave of movements and struggles in these countries and elsewhere in the continent is taking place, which can be interpreted in terms of two inter-related processes, namely, the activation of relational ontologies and a redefini-tion of political autonomy. While these trends are contradictory and deeply contested, they point toward the relevance of postdevelopment and make tan-gible the notion of post/nonliberal/capitalist socionatural configurations.

The Ecuadorian and Bolivian constitutions, issued in 2008, have garnered well-deserved international attention because of their pioneering treatments of development and, in the Ecuadorian case, of the rights of nature. It should be emphasized that these constitutions are the result of complex social, cul-tural, and political struggles that peaked over the past decade. The constitu-tions introduced a novel notion of development centered on the concept of *sumak kawsay* (in Quechua), *suma qamaña* (in Aymara), or *buen vivir* (BV, in Spanish), or "living well." As Alberto Acosta, one of the foremost architects of the Ecuadorian constitution states, sumak kawsay entails a conceptual rupture with the conceptions of development of the previous six decades. More than a constitutional declaration, "*Buen Vivir* constitutes an opportunity to con-struct collectively a new development regime" (Acosta 2009, 6). Although a number of sources are cited as the basis for this conception—including critical analyses of development and postdevelopment, as well as feminist, ecological, and human development frameworks—the larger share of the credit goes to indigenous organizations. For Catherine Walsh, "the integral vision and the basic condition of the Buen Vivir have been at the basis of the cosmovisions, life philosophies and practices of the peoples of Abya Yala and the descendants of the African diaspora for centuries; they are now re-apprehended as guides for the re-founding of the Bolivian and Ecuadorian state and society" (2009, 5). It can indeed be said that sumak kawsay and suma qamaña stem "from the social periphery of the global periphery," as Spanish development critic José María Tortosa put it (cited in Acosta 2010).

Very succinctly, and following Acosta and Gudynas, BV grew out of several decades of indigenous struggles as they articulated with social change agen-das by peasants, Afro-descendants, environmentalists, students, women, and youth.[8] Crystallized in ninety-nine articles of the Constitution (out of 444), BV "presents itself as an opportunity for the collective construction of a new form of living" (Acosta 2010, 7). Rather than an isolated intervention, BV should be seen in the context of a panoply of pioneering constitutional innova-tions, including the rethinking of the state in terms of plurinationality, of soci-ety in terms of interculturality, an expanded and integral notion of rights, and a revisioned development model, the goal of which is precisely the realization of BV. All of these innovations, in addition, should be seen as multicultural, multiepistemic, and in terms of deeply negotiated and often contradictory political construction processes. It is clear, however, that BV constitutes a challenge to long-standing notions of development.

Indigenous ontologies or cosmovisions do not entail a linear notion of development, nor a state of underdevelopment to be overcome; neither are they based on scarcity or the primacy of material goods. Echoing these tenets, BV purports to introduce a different philosophy of life into the vision of society. This makes possible an ethics of development that subordinates economic objectives to ecological criteria, human dignity, and social justice. Development as BV seeks to articulate economics, environment, society, and culture in new ways, calling for mixed social and solidarity economies; it introduces issues of social and intergenerational justice as spaces for development principles; acknowledges cultural and gender differences, positioning interculturality as a guiding principle; and enables new political-economic emphases, such as food sovereignty, the control of natural resources, and a human right to water.

It would be a mistake, however, to see BV as a purely Andean cultural-political project, a point that Acosta (2010) adamantly argues. As already mentioned, BV is also influenced by critical currents within Western thought; conversely, it aims to influence global debates. That said, there is ample recognition that indigenous and Afro knowledges have been subjected to long-standing processes of marginalization. In this way, BV seeks to reverse the coloniality of power, knowledge, and being that has characterized the modern/colonial world system since the Conquest (Quijano 2010). For Peruvian sociologist Aníbal Quijano (2010), BV constitutes a new horizon of historical meaning, emerging from the long history of indigenous resistance against the Eurocentric modern/colonial world system. In some debates in Andean countries, this is referred to as epistemic decolonization.

Many of the arguments about BV can also be made regarding another prominent idea heatedly discussed in South America, that of the rights of Nature; the two aspects are closely interrelated. For Uruguayan social ecologist Eduardo Gudynas (2009a, 2009b), the rights of Nature, or *pachamama*, recognized in the Ecuadorian constitution, represent an unprecedented "biocentric turn," away from the anthropocentrism of modernity. For Gudynas, this move resonates as much with the cosmovisions of ethnic groups as with the principles of ecology. To endow Nature with rights means to shift from a conception of nature as object for exploitation to Nature as subject; indeed, in this conception the idea of rights of Nature is intimately linked with humans' right to exist.

This notion implies an expanded ecological notion of the self that, unlike the liberal notion, sees the self as deeply interconnected with all other living beings and, ultimately, with the planet as a whole. For Gudynas, this amounts to a sort of "meta-ecological citizenship," a plural kind of citizenship involving cultural and ecological dimensions, and which requires both environmental justice and ecological justice for the protection of people and nature, respectively.[9] This biocentric turn represents a concrete example of the civilizational transformation imagined by the transition discourses discussed earlier.

Social Movements as Ontological Struggles:
Toward Post/Noncapitalist and Post/Nonliberal Worlds?

The recognition of the rights of Nature is closely related to the last aspect of the Latin American transformations I want to discuss, albeit all too briefly; this is the notion and practice of relationality. There is an interesting convergence between certain philosophical, biological, and indigenous peoples' narratives in asserting that life entails the creation of form (difference, morphogenesis) out of the dynamics of matter and energy.[10] In these views, the world is a pluriverse, ceaselessly in movement, an ever-changing web of interrelations involving humans and nonhumans. It is important to point out, however, that the pluriverse gives rise to coherences and crystallizes in practices and structures through processes that have a lot to do with meanings and power—perhaps what John Law has called "coherence without consistency" (2004, 139), or provisionally stable realities; in this way it can be seen in terms of a multiplicity of worlds. Notwithstanding, the worlds and knowledges constructed on the basis of modernist ontological commitments became a One World, a universe. This universe has acquired certain coherence in socionatural forms such as capitalism, the state, the individual, industrial agriculture, macrodevelopment projects, and so forth.[11]

It is precisely this set of assumptions that discussions about BV and rights of Nature unsettle. Although I cannot discuss this point here at length, the unsettling of modern constructs points to the existence of nonliberal or postliberal social orders; these are worlds that go beyond the foundational liberal notions of the individual, private property, and representative democracy. Stated in anthropological and philosophical terms, these nonliberal worlds are place based and can be characterized as instances of relational worldviews or ontologies. As already stated, relational ontologies are those which eschew the divisions between nature and culture, between individual and community, and between us and them that are central to modern ontology. This is to say that some of the struggles in Ecuador and Bolivia, and in other parts of the continent, including struggles for autonomy in Chiapas and Oaxaca, as well as indigenous and Afro struggles and some peasant struggles in Colombia (Oslender 2004, 2016), Peru, and Guatemala, can be read as ontological struggles; they have the potential to denaturalize the hegemonic dualisms on which the liberal order is founded (Blaser 2010; de la Cadena 2010; Escobar 2010; Povinelli 2001). The universal and homolingual thrust of modernity dictates that it should attempt to tame those different worlds, that is, to efface the pluriverse. Bringing the pluriverse into visibility by focusing on ontological conflicts—that is, conflicts that arise from the unequal encounter between worlds, as in so many conflicts involving resource exploitation today—can be said to constitute a particular field of study, which Blaser (2010) refers to as political ontology.[12]

The emergence of relational ontologies challenges the epistemic foundation of modern politics. That identification of Nature with pachamama, and the fact that it is endowed with rights, goes beyond environmental political correctness given that pachamama cannot be easily fitted into the philosophical structure of a modern constitution, within which nature is seen as an inert object for humans to appropriate. Its inclusion in the Ecuadorian Constitution thus contributes to disrupting the modern political and epistemic space because it occurs outside such space (de la Cadena 2010). Something similar can be said of the notion of buen vivir. Both notions are based on ontological assumptions in which all beings exist always in relation and never as objects or individuals. At stake in many cultural-political mobilizations in Latin America at present, in this way, is the political activation of relational ontologies; these mobilizations thus refer to a different way of imagining life, to another mode of existence (Quijano 2010); they point toward the pluriverse. In the successful formula of the Zapatistas, the pluriverse can be described as "a world where many worlds fit." More abstractly perhaps, the pluriverse signals struggles for bringing about "worlds and knowledges otherwise"—that is, worlds and knowledges constructed on the basis of different ontological commitments, epistemic configurations, and practices of being, knowing, doing.

The notions of nonliberal and noncapitalist practices are actively being developed in Latin America, particularly in relation to both rural and urban forms of popular mobilization in Oaxaca, Chiapas, Ecuador, Bolivia, and southwest Colombia.[13] These are not just theoretical notions but the outcome of grounded political analyses, particularly in terms of the development of forms of *autonomía* that involve nonstate forms of power stemming from communal cultural, economic, and political practices. In some cases, such as the Zapatista communities of Chiapas or the indigenous communities in Oaxaca, contemporary autonomous forms of communal government are seen as rooted in several centuries of indigenous resistance (Esteva 2005; Subcomandante Marcos and the Zapatistas 2006). In other cases, such as the Aymara urban communities of El Alto, Bolivia, what takes place is a creative reconstitution of communal logics on the basis of novel forms of territoriality. Yet most cases of autonomous organization involve certain key practices, such as communal assemblies, the rotation of obligations, and horizontal, dispersed forms of power. Emerging from this interpretation is a fundamental question, that of "*being able to stabilize in time* a mode of regulation outside of, *against and beyond* the social order imposed by capitalist production and the liberal state" (Gutiérrez Aguilar 2008, 46, emphasis in original).

This proposal implies three basic points: the steady decentering and displacement of the capitalist economy with the concomitant expansion of diverse forms of economy, including communal and noncapitalist forms; the decentering of representative democracy and the setting into place of direct, autonomous, and communal forms of democracy; and the establishment of mechanisms of epistemic and cultural pluralism (interculturality) among various ontologies and cultural worlds. From a post-structuralist perspective, it is thus possible to speak of the emergence of postliberal and postcapitalist forms of social organization. It is important to make clear once again what the *post* means. Postdevelopment signaled the possibility of visualizing an era when development ceased to be a central organizing principle of social life; even more, it visualized such a displacement as happening in the present. The same is true for postliberalism, as a space-time under construction when social life is no longer so thoroughly determined by the constructs of economy, the individual, instrumental rationality, private property, and so forth. *Postcapitalist* similarly means looking at the economy as made up of a diversity of capitalist, alternative capitalist, and noncapitalist practices (Gibson-Graham 2006). *Post*, succinctly, means a decentering of capitalism in the definition of the economy, of liberalism in the definition of society, and of state forms of power as the defining matrix of social organization. This does not mean that capitalism, liberalism, and state forms cease to exist; it means that their discursive and social centrality have been displaced somewhat, so that the range of existing social experiences that are considered valid and credible alternatives to what exist is significantly enlarged (Santos 2007).

As proponents of BV and the rights of Nature emphasize, these notions should be seen as processes under construction rather than as finished concepts. This is more strongly the case when considering that the bulk of the policies of the progressive governments in Latin America at present undermine the very conditions for their realization. Despite their break with many of the main tenets of neoliberal economic models, most of these governments maintain development strategies based on the export of natural resources, such as agricultural and mineral commodities, including oil and gas, but also new rubrics such as soy in Argentina and Brazil. The main difference in these government policies lies in that revenues are appropriated somewhat differently, with particular emphasis on poverty reduction through redistributive policies. But the neo-extractivist orientation of the model poses a tremendous challenge and is the main source of tension between states and civil society sectors (Gudynas 2009a, 2015). This model affects greatly the possibilities for the implementation of the rights of Nature, as the neo-extractivism of the progressive governments (the dramatic expansion of mining and agrofuels such as soy in many countries, as well as macro infrastructures such as ports and highways) not only tolerates but coexists easily with environmental destruction (Gudynas 2009b, 2014).

It is also clear, however, that the concepts of BV and rights of Nature have succeeded in placing the question of development on the agenda again with particular acuity; this has in turn implied broaching the issue of a transition to a postextractivist society head on. In Ecuador and Bolivia in particular, postextractivism and postdevelopment thus bring together the state, NGOs, social movements, and intellectuals into a crucial and intense debate (Gudynas 2015). There is the sense of an impasse created by the tense coexistence of progressive yet economistic and developmentalist policies at the level of the state, and the ability of movements to problematize such policies from below—a sort of promiscuous mixture of capitalist hegemony and movement counterpowers, of radical demands for change and the reconstitution of ruling (Colectivo Situaciones 2006). How this dynamic plays out in each country cannot be decided in advance, and will be of significance beyond the region given the worldwide intensification of extractivism by global colonial capitalism.

Emerging Trends in the Latin American Debates

The current moment in South America is thus characterized by a significant renovation of the debates on development (Gudynas and Acosta 2011). While state social and economic policies continue to be developmentalist, the critical perspectives have been gaining some ground and resonance at all levels. Critical positions "agglutinate a diversity of tendencies with decolonizing ambitions, pointing through a series of categories and limit-concepts at the dismantling of the apparatuses of power, the imaginaries, and the myths at the basis of the current developmentalist model" (Svampa 2012, 51). Taken as a whole, it is possible to identify five major areas of work in this regard; these can only be identified here without much elaboration (see Escobar 2014 for a discussion of each area):

1. EPISTEMIC DECOLONIZATION. This area stems from the limited but perhaps growing influence in academic and activist circles of the research program on decolonial thought. The value of this perspective lies in going beyond critical intra-European perspectives on modernity in its reinterpretation of modernity as modernity/coloniality and in identifying the epistemic dimension as key to the transformation of the world. Over the past few years, a group of students and activists has appropriated this framework and taken it in new directions (e.g., gender, nature, interculturality, urban situations), thus partially redressing some of the critiques directed against the first wave of decolonial thought of the late 1990s and early 2000s.

2. ALTERNATIVES *TO* DEVELOPMENT. Buen vivir and the rights of Nature have doubtlessly been the trigger in the rearticulation of the critiques of the fundamental ideas underlying development (e.g., growth, progress, market reforms, extractivism, material consumption, etc.). This has brought about "a return to the problematic of alternatives *to* development" (Gudynas and Acosta 2011, 75), in other words, a more profound sense of alternatives than simply development alternatives. In Ecuador and Bolivia in particular, alternatives *to* development find their sources in past and current academic critiques but especially in the proposals and struggles of indigenous movements. What is emerging, no matter how precariously, is a political platform for the construction of alternatives *to* development, in both theory and practice.

3. TRANSITIONS TO POSTEXTRACTIVISM. Of recent origin in the current decade, the framework of transitions to postextractivism is a significant conceptual development with important methodological advances in political and policy debates, particularly in Peru but increasingly in other Andean countries. The point of departure is the extractivist nature of the development model of both the neoliberal and progressive regimes, what in South America is called the commodity consensus. The framework includes a conceptualization of different types of extractivism (predatory, sensible, and indispensable); a workshop methodology with diverse groups about the options for postextractivism; and concrete actions and campaigns to create the conviction that "there is life after extractivism" (Gudynas 2012). This line of work has a decided ecological orientation, and has been largely proposed and developed by the Centro Latinoamericano de Ecología Social, CLAES (Gudynas 2011b, 2012, 2014, 2015).

4. DISCOURSES ON THE MODEL OF CIVILIZATIONAL CRISIS. This discourse is prominent among some indigenous, black, and peasant movements and intellectuals. The basic argument is that the contemporary ecological and

food crisis is a crisis of the Western civilizational model, and that a shift toward a new ecological, cultural, and economic paradigm is needed. The new models have to be anti- or postcapitalist, but, not only that, they have to reaffirm the value of life in all of its dimensions, which involves plural conceptions of nation, nature, economy, time, citizenship, and so forth. This is an area that will likely experience more compelling articulations, although it is not without precedent, for instance, in Mexican anthropologist Bonfil Battalla's (1991) interesting work on *Mexico profundo* as a "negated civilization" or in Ashis Nandy's work of the 1980s on the dialogue of civilizations (e.g., Nandy 1987). Contrary to what many in the academy might fear, the thrust of the discourses on civilizational transition in recent years has been decidedly antiessentialist, historical, and pluralistic.

5. COMMUNAL LOGICS AND RELATIONALITY. This last area actually constitutes several lines of work. As with the concepts of system and civilization, the concept of community has been considered problematic in constructivist social theory for similar reasons, yet it is having a resurgence within various epistemic-political spaces. A main conceptual intervention is the distinction between state and communal logics. As two observers of the indigenous-popular insurrections in Bolivia in 2000–2005—which led to the election of Evo Morales as the first indigenous president of the country—put it, the concept of communal logics attempts to make visible forms of "self-regulation of social co-existence beyond the modern state and capital," a type of society set into movement during the insurrection "characterized by non-capitalist and non-liberal social relations, labor forms, and forms of organization" (Gutiérrez 2008, 18; see also Zibechi 2006, 52). For Aymara sociologist Felix Patzi Paco (2004, 2012), the communal form of politics occurs precisely because of the existence of an entire cultural background organized in terms of communal systems; these systems embrace all aspects of life. What he proposes is that the communal system is an alternative to the liberal one, based on private property and representative democracy. "By communal or communitarian concept we mean the collective property of resources combined with their private management and utilization. . . . In contradistinction to modern societies, indigenous societies have not reproduced the patterns of differentiation nor *the separation among domains* (political, economic, cultural, etc.). . . . The communal system thus presents itself as opposed to the liberal system" (Patzi Paco 2004, 171, 172).

The communal has been the subject of retheorization by a loosely interconnected group of intellectual activists focusing on key political mobilizations in Bolivia and southern Mexico. The Mexican sociologist Raquel Gutiérrez Aguilar (2008, 2012) has coined the term *entramados comunitarios* (communitarian entanglements), in contradistinction with "transnational corporate coalitions." By the first term she means "the multiplicity of human worlds that inhabit and generate the world under guidelines of respect, collaboration, dignity, affect, and reciprocity and which are not completely subjected to the logic of capital accumulation even if affected and sometimes overwhelmed by such a logic" (Gutiérrez Aguilar 2012, 3). These logics are found among many kinds of social groups, rural and urban. This view echoes Esteva's (2012), who sees the autonomous movements of Chiapas and Oaxaca as fostering a reorganization of society but from the "communal condition" that constitutes the autonomous weave (*tejido*) of society and which he sees as having been at play in rural and urban popular neighborhoods since time immemorial.

The final important elaboration of this concept is the framework of *feminismo comunitario* proposed by a feminist group from La Paz, Comunidad Mujeres Creando Comunidad; this framework starts by constructing the community "as an inclusive principle for the caring of life" (Paredes 2012, 27). A second important component of the framework is the notion of *entronque patriarcal*, which refers to the intersection of various forms of precolonial, colonial, and contemporary patriarchy. The framework constitutes a radical critique of neoliberal capitalism, patriarchalism, and liberal feminisms as it develops a reinterpretation of gender (including gender complementarity) along relational, communal lines. This proposal is not directed solely at indigenous people, women, or even Bolivians but, as Paredes explains, is intended for all living beings—women, men, intersexuals, and nature. This is a compelling and cogent proposal that deserves much attention.

It is important to mention that the thought of community is heterogeneous, with important differences among various authors.[14] They are characterized, however, by a serious attempt at generalizing the concept (that is, not restricting it to indigenous, ethnic, or gender minorities) and by being careful not to idealize or homogenize the communal. There is rather an emphasis on the creation of new spheres of the communal (Esteva 2012) and on broaching the entire gamut of forms the communal takes, old and new. More than a preconstituted entity, the community is "the name given to a specific organizational and political code, to a singular political technology. . . . Contrary to common sense, the community produces dispersion" (Colectivo Situaciones 2006, 212), and hence becomes essential for the invention of nonstate, noncapitalist forms of coexistence. The concept implies a nondualist ontology.

Underlying many of the mobilizations of indigenous, Afro-descendant, women's, land-based and popular groups are relational worldviews that are coming to the forefront as viable alternatives to modern social and political arrangements. These mobilizations might thus be seen as ontological-political projects. They push for nonrepresentational politics and nondualist understandings of socionatural worlds. Their politics of difference often entail a political ontology (Blaser 2010; de la Cadena 2010). In many of these mobilizations, for instance, against mining, the activation of relational ontologies politicizes modern binaries by mobilizing nonhumans (e.g., mountains, water) as sentient entities and as actors in the political arena. Struggles against the destruction of life are thus conjuring up the entire range of the living.[15]

Given what has been said, the argument about the ongoing transformations in Latin America can be summarized as follows. These transformations suggest two potentially complementary but also competing projects: alternative modernizations, based on anti-neoliberal development models, possibly leading to postcapitalist economies and alternative forms of modernity (*una modernidad satisfactoria*), which is the project of the progressive regimes; and transition projects, based on nondominant sets of practices (e.g., communal, indigenous, ecological, relational) and forms of autonomous politics, potentially leading to a multiplicity of post/nonliberal and post/noncapitalist socionatural configurations (a pluriverse). The question becomes: is it possible to go beyond capital (as the dominant form of economy), Euro-modernity (as dominant cultural construction of socionatural life), and the state (as central form of institutionalization of the social)? Three scenarios: postcapitalist, postliberal, and post-statist.

The notion of postdevelopment continues to be useful in the articulation of critiques of existing tendencies (e.g., neo-extractivism), to orient inquiry toward noneconomistic possibilities, and to keep alive the imaginaries of beyond development and of alternatives *to* development (e.g., postextractivism and cultural and ecological transitions). Postdevelopment remains an apt concept to rekindle, and contribute to articulate, many of the crucial questions of the day. As Acosta (2010) put it, more than a development alternative, buen vivir constitutes an alternative to development, and to this extent it can be seen as moving along "the road to postdevelopment." The challenges to moving along this road are manifold, including heightened productivism; dependent insertion into global capitalism via export of primary commodities (neo-extractivism); *las nuevas derechos* (the new rights); and old and new imperialisms. The main challenges for social movements include how to keep spaces for autonomous thought and politics open while engaging with state and global forces; how to promote new forms of cooperation and social organization; and how to develop forms of power at a broader scale based on communal/nonliberal logics that might contribute to the collective appropriation of the production of socionatural life. A key question suggests itself: can the emergent cultural-political subjects in Latin America reach a dynamic condition of alterity capable of reconstituting socionatural structures, along the lines of relationality, pluralism, and pluriversality?

Designs for the Pluriverse?

Discourses of globalization, whether mainstream or leftist, more often than not see the global as a space that is naturally and fully occupied by forms of socionatural life that are in fact an extension of Western-style modernity. No matter how qualified, globalization in these discourses always amounts to a deepening and universalization of capitalist modernity. There is something terribly wrong with this imaginary if we are to take seriously the transition discourses and notions of buen vivir and rights of Nature, let alone if we are to confront the ever-worsening ecological and social crisis. To paraphrase, scratch a globalization discourse and you will find homo economicus at large, alleged individuals fighting to become miniature capitalist clones (e.g., microfinance, modernizing rural development), assumptions of linear rationality as the default mode of thinking of those wanting to make it in a competitive world, a view of nature as resource to be extracted at any cost, or groups and movements struggling to recapture the modernist project for allegedly liberating purposes (leftist versions). These discourses reflect a view of the world as seen by those who rule it—a world from above. They deploy pervasive apparatuses of power that organize people's perceptions and experiences.

It bears repeating that this view of globalization as universal, fully economistic, delocalized, and multicultural (yet with dominant Euro-American cultures as the preeminent model), where (affluent) individuals are endowed with rights and nations have to accept the dictates of the same global rationality or risk becoming failed states, is increasingly made possible by the immense power of corporations and maintained within manageable levels of dis/order by military might. The underside of globalization, in this way, is none other than global coloniality. From its very global conditions are emerging, however, responses and forms of creativity and resistance that make increasingly visible the poverty, perniciousness, and destructiveness of this imaginary.

As Blaser (2010) put it, the present moment can be seen as one of intense struggle between two visions of globality: globality defined as modernity writ large (the one-world world); or globality as a pluriverse. Rather than as globalization, the latter possibility might be more appropriately described as a process of planetarization articulated around a vision of the Earth as a living whole that is always emerging out of the manifold biophysical, human, and spiritual elements and relations that make up the pluriverse, from the biosphere to the noosphere. Many of the features envisioned in the transition discourses—from strategies of relocalization to the rise of an ecological civilization—will find a more auspicious home in this notion. We need to stop burdening the Earth with the dualisms of the past centuries and acknowledge the radical interrelatedness, openness, and plurality that inhabit it. To accomplish this goal, it might be useful to start thinking about human practice in terms of ontological design (Winograd and Flores 1986), or the design of worlds and knowledges otherwise (decolonial thought). As in the case of ecological design, ontological design would seed designs with diversity or build on already existing diversity; this is a principle for the pluriverse. Design would no longer involve the taming of the world for (some) human purposes, but, to summon again Berry's (1999, 11) words, building worlds in which humans and the Earth can coexist in mutually enhancing manners. More politically perhaps, "in this way the defense of human life, and conditions for life on the planet, may become the new horizon of meaning of the struggles of resistance by the majority of the world's people" (Quijano 2010, 7).

It should be stressed that different ontologies do not mean separate worlds. Worlds are multiple and different but not disconnected (Law 2004); they overlap and interact with one another, hence the importance of looking at the articulations that divergent worlds might be capable of among themselves while maintaining their autonomy (via structural coupling). If the pluriverse is made up of multiple worlds and partial connections, a key question becomes, how do they relate to each other? At this level, questions of in/commensurability and translation, of zones of contact and partial common ground, become important. It is important to keep in mind that struggles related to postliberalism are susceptible to being both overlooked and reinscribed as fully comprehensible through modern categories. As Povinelli (2001) well put it, there is always an unwillingness of the liberals/moderns to let themselves "be undone," and this unwillingness finds its way even into the critical academies of the Global North. What is called for is a new wave of dialogical engagements with non/postliberal forms and relational ways of knowing, in all of their cultural and political richness, troubling aspects, and unevenness; how would these dialogues recast the analysis of the conjuncture and our very frameworks? What conceptual tools do the social and human sciences have for engaging with relational ways of knowing? How might academic theories be refurbished to meet this challenge?

Going well beyond critique, a nascent field of pluriversal studies would—and already does, as I tried to show here—discover the forms adopted by the multiple worlds that make up the pluriverse, without trying to reduce them to manifestations of known principles. Pluriversal studies will focus on those processes that can no longer be easily accommodated in the epistemic table of the modern social sciences. This is why pluriversal studies cannot be defined in opposition to globalization studies, nor as its complement, but needs to be outlined as an altogether different intellectual and political project. No single notion of the world, the human, civilization, the future, or even the natural can fully occupy the space of pluriversal studies. Even if partly building on the critical traditions of the modern natural, human and social sciences, pluriversal studies will travel its own paths as it discovers worlds and knowledges that the sciences have effaced or only gleaned obliquely.

NOTES

1. Marxist geographer David Harvey (2003, 137–82) elaborates on the concept of accumulation by dispossession in his book *The New Imperialism*, where he draws on Karl Marx's and, notably, Rosa Luxemburg's writings on primitive accumulation.

2. See the work of the Center for Ecozoic Societies in Chapel Hill, North Carolina, directed by Herman Greene (http://www.ecozoicsocieties.org/).

3. Briefly, the conventional worlds scenario relies on either market forces (global markets driving global development) or policy reform (comprehensive government and international action for poverty reduction and environmental sustainability), or a combination of both. These scenarios might achieve some moderation of current trends, yet they cannot muster the political will to make their avowed goals feasible. Similarly, the second scenario, barbarization, has two variants: breakdown (institutional collapse) and fortress world (global apartheid with the vast majority of the world outside). Writings on GTI include ideas about how to work toward the transition through concrete institutional and cultural changes. The GTI, based on the influential analysis of branch points and scenario building by Argentinean ecologist Gilberto Gallopín, is currently housed at the Tellus Institute; see GTI (2002) and the project's website, Great Transition Initiative (http://www.greattransition.org/). Some of the transition visions are based on a framework of interacting complex socionatural systems from the community to the planetary level. While the more conventional scenarios imply a clear teleology, GTI-type scenarios actually build on nonlinear dynamic principles as part of the transition concept. This includes the concepts of bifurcation and macroshifts (see, e.g., Goodwin 2007; Laszlo 2008). It should be said that despite their global character, most TDs still take the Western modern experience as point of reference and driver for change. While this makes sense given modern hegemonies, critical TDs need to more explicitly incorporate experiences and dynamics from socionatures in the Global South.

4. The transition approach is a remarkable concept and set of tools. Initiated in the town of Totnes, Devon, UK (also home to Schumacher College), it has spread rapidly. Over one hundred communities worldwide are engaged in transition plans inspired by

the handbook. The primer for transition initiatives is detailed and feasible. See also the related website, Transition Network (https://transitionnetwork.org/).

5. I do not discuss here further the politics of these TDs, which is left implicit in most of them. This politics can be fruitfully theorized from leftist and academic approaches (e.g., autonomist anticapitalist imaginaries, Deleuzian/Guattarian postcapitalist politics, Foucauldian and feminist biopolitical and posthumanist analyses, anarchism, Latin American autonomía, critical geography, etc.), but these will need to meet the epistemic and ontological challenges of non-Eurocentric and biocentric transition discourses.

6. For a lengthy treatment of the Latin American transformations during the past decade, including the argument made here, and full set of references, see Escobar (2010).

7. See issue no. 453 of *América Latina en Movimiento* (March 2010) called "Alternativas civilizatorias" (https://www.alainet.org/es/revistas/453) (http://alainet.org/publica /453.phtml). A forum called "Perspectives on the 'Crisis of Civilization' as the Focus of Movements" was held at the World Social Forum in Dakar (February 6–11, 2011), coordinated by Roberto Espinoza, Janet Conway, Jai Sen, and Carlos Torres. It included participants from several continents.

8. The literature on BV and the rights of Nature is already vast, although almost exclusively in Spanish. This is perhaps the most interesting intellectual and political debate in South America at present. See the useful short volumes by Acosta and Martínez (2009a, 2009b), Acosta (2010), and Gudynas (2009a, 2009b; Gudynas [2011a] for an English summary of his thoughts on BV).

9. In both Gudynas and Macy, this transformed notion of the self is based on Arne Naess's deep ecology framework and its pioneering view of the ecological self.

10. In some indigenous narratives, the creation of form is seen as the passage from indistinctive to distinctive (see, e.g., Blaser [2010] for the case of the Yshiro of Paraguay).

11. This is a very incomplete statement on what is a complex debate involving four positions on modernity: (1) modernity as a universal process of European origin (intra-Euro/ American discourses); (2) alternative modernities (locally specific variations of the same universal modernity); (3) multiple modernities, that is, modernity as multiplicity without a single origin or cultural home (Grossberg 2010); and (4) modernity/coloniality, which points out the inextricable entanglement of modernity with the colonial classification of peoples into hierarchies, and the possibility of alternatives to modernity or transmodernity. See Escobar (2008, chap. 4) for a fuller treatment.

12. The ontological conflicts involved in neo-extractivist economies in Latin America and other world regions are the subject of an ongoing collaborative research project by Mario Blaser, Marisol de la Cadena, and me. The project's general goal is to theorize the pluriverse as a space of ontological-political practices (see, e.g., Blaser, de la Cadena, and Escobar 2014).

13. Some of the main texts include Esteva (2005), Gutiérrez Aguilar (2008), Mamani (2005), Patzi Paco (2004, 2012), and Zibechi (2006).

14. Not only that, there are disagreements among some of these authors about the usefulness of the term. Since the early 1980s, for instance, the Taller de Historia Oral Andina (THOA) in Bolivia has emphasized the reconstitution of the *ayllu*, which is not conceived in terms of community. The Bolivian discussions on these issues are amazingly

rich and diverse, involving well-known Aymara intellectuals such as Simon Yampara, Pablo Mamani, Felix Patzi, Julieta Paredes, and Marcelo Fernández Osco, and academics and intellectuals such as Silvia Rivera Cusicanqui, Javier Tapia, and Gustavo Soto, among many others. See Escobar (2014) for additional discussion and references.

15. Many of these environmental struggles are documented in the Barcelona-based Environmental Justice Atlas (https://ejatlas.org/). My argument is that many of these situations also involve ontological conflicts.

REFERENCES

Acosta, Alberto. 2009. "El Buen Vivir, una oportunidad por Construir." *Ecuador Debate*, no. 75, 33–48.

Acosta, Alberto. 2010. *El Buen Vivir en el camino del post-desarrollo: Una lectura desde la Constitución de Montecristi*. Quito: Fundación Friedrich Eber, FES-ILDIS.

Acosta, Alberto. 2012. "El buen vivir en la senda del posdesarrollo." In *Renunciar al bien común: Extractivismo y (pos)desarrollo en América Latina*, edited by Gabrila Massuh, 283–305. Buenos Aires: Mardulce.

Acosta, Alberto, and Esperanza Martínez, eds. 2009a. *Derechos de la naturaleza: El futuro es ahora*. Quito: Abya-Yala.

Acosta, Alberto, and Esperanza Martínez, eds. 2009b. *El buen vivir: Una vía para el desarrollo*. Quito: Abya-Yala.

Berry, Thomas. 1999. *The Great Work: Our Way into the Future*. New York: Bell Tower.

Blaser, Mario. 2010. *Storytelling Globalization from the Chaco and Beyond*. Durham, NC: Duke University Press.

Blaser, Mario, Marisol de la Cadena, and Arturo Escobar. 2014. "Introduction: The Anthropocene and the One-World." Unpublished manuscript.

Colectivo Situaciones. 2006. "Epílogo: Notas sobre la noción de 'comunidad' a propósito de *Dispersar el poder*." In *Dispersar el poder*, edited by R. Zibechi, 211–20. Buenos Aires: Tinta Limón.

de la Cadena, Marisol. 2010. "Indigenous Cosmopolitics in the Andes: Conceptual Reflections beyond Politics." *Cultural Anthropology* 25 (2): 334–70.

Dreyfus, Hubert, and Sean Kelly. 2011. *All Things Shining: Reading the Western Classics to Find Meaning in a Secular Age*. New York: Free Press.

Escobar, Arturo. 2008. *Territories of Difference: Place, Movements, Life, Redes*. Durham, NC: Duke University Press.

Escobar, Arturo. 2010. "Postconstructivist Political Ecologies." In *International Handbook of Environmental Sociology*, 2nd ed., edited by Michael Redclift and Graham Woodgate, 91–105. Cheltenham, UK: Elgar.

Escobar, Arturo. 2012a. *Encountering Development: The Making and Unmaking of the Third World*, 2nd ed. Princeton, NJ: Princeton University Press.

Escobar, Arturo. 2012b. "Linking 'Degrowth' and 'Alternatives *to* Development': Elements for a *Transition Politics* across Movements." Presented at the Third International Conference of Degrowth, Ecological Sustainability and Social Equity. University of Architecture and Design (IUAV), Venice, September 19–23.

Escobar, Arturo. 2014. *Sentipensar con la Tierra: Nuevas lecturas sobre desarrollo, territorio, y diferencia*. Medellín: UNAULA.

Esteva, Gustavo. 2005. "Celebration of Zapatismo." *Humboldt Journal of Social Relations* 29 (1): 127–67.

Esteva, Gustavo. 2012. "Los quehaceres del día." In *Renunciar al bien común: Extractivismo y (pos)desarrollo en América Latina*, edited by Gabriela Massuh, 237–83. Buenos Aires: Mardulce.

Esteva, Gustavo, and Madhu Suri Prakas. 1998. *Grassroots Post-modernism: Remaking the Soil of Cultures*. London: Zed.

Estill, Lyle. 2008. *Small Is Possible: Life in a Local Economy*. Gabriola Island, BC: New Society.

Gibson-Graham, J. K. 2006. *A Postcapitalist Politics*. Minneapolis: University of Minnesota Press.

Goodwin, Brian. 2007. *Nature's Due: Healing Our Fragmented Culture*. Edinburgh: Floris.

Grossberg, Lawrence. 2010. *Cultural Studies in the Future Tense*. Durham, NC: Duke University Press.

Gudynas, Eduardo. 2009a. *El Mandato Ecológico: Derechos de la Naturaleza y Políticas Ambientales en la Nueva Constitución*. Quito: Abya-Yala.

Gudynas, Eduardo. 2009b. "La Ecología Política del Giro Biocéntrico en la Nueva Constitución de Ecuador." *Revista Estudios Sociales* 32:34–47.

Gudynas, Eduardo. 2011a. "Buen Vivir: Today's Tomorrow." *Development* 54 (4): 441–47.

Gudynas, Eduardo. 2011b. "Más allá del nuevo extractivismo: Transiciones sostenibles y alternativas al desarrollo." In *El desarrollo en cuestión: Reflexiones desde América Latina*, edited by Ivonne Farah and Fernanda Wanderley, 379–410. La Paz: CIDES UMSA. http://www.gudynas.com/publicaciones/GudynasExtractivismoTransiciones Cides11.pdf.

Gudynas, Eduardo. 2012. "Hay vida después del extractivismo: Alternativas a la sobreexplotación de los recursos naturales." In *Pobreza, desigualdad y desarrollo en el Perú/ Informe Oxfam Perú 20122/2012*, 45–53. Lima: Oxfam.

Gudynas, Eduardo. 2014. *Derechos de la naturaleza/Etica bicentrica y políticas ambientales*. Lima: PDTG/redGE/CLAES.

Gudynas, Eduardo. 2015. *Extractivismos: Economía, ecología y política de un modo de entender el desarrollo y la naturaleza*. Cochabamba: CEDIB/CLAES.

Gudynas, Eduardo, and Alberto Acosta. 2011. "La renovación de la crítica al desarrollo y el buen vivir como alternativa." *Utopía y Praxis Latinoamericana* 16 (53): 71–83. http:// www.gudynas.com/publicaciones/GudynasAcostaCriticaDesarrolloBVivirUtopia11.pdf.

Gutiérrez Aguilar, R. 2008. *Los ritmos del Pachakuti: Movilización y levantamiento indígena-popular en Bolivia*. Buenos Aires: Tinta Limón.

Gutiérrez Aguilar, Raquel. 2012. "Pistas reflexivas para orientarnos en una turbulenta época de peligro." In *Palabras para tejernos, resistir, y transformar en la época que estamos viviendo*, edited by R. Gutiérrez Aguilar, 9–34. Oaxaca: Pez en el Árbol.

Harvey, David. 2003. *The New Imperialism*. Oxford: Oxford University Press.

Hathaway, Mark, and Leonardo Boff. 2009. *The Tao of Liberation: Exploring the Ecology of Transformation*. Maryknoll, NY: Orbis.

Hopkins, Rob. 2008. *The Transition Handbook: From Oil Dependency to Local Resilience.* White River Junction, VT: Chelsea Green.

Hopkins, Rob. 2011. *The Transition Companion: Making Your Community More Resilient in Uncertain Times.* White River Junction, VT: Chelsea Green.

Kauffman, Stuart. 2008. *Reinventing the Sacred.* New York: Basic Books.

Korten, David. 2006. *The Great Turning: From Empire to Earth Community.* Bloomfield, CT: Kumarian.

Laszlo, Ervin. 2008. *Quantum Shift in the Global Brain: How the New Scientific Reality Can Change Us and Our World.* Rochester, VT: Inner Traditions.

Law, John. 2004. *After Method: Mess in Social Science Research.* London: Routledge.

Law, John. 2011. "What's Wrong with a One-World World." Presented to the Center for the Humanities, Wesleyan University, September 19. *heterogeneities*, September 25, http://www.heterogeneities.net/publications/Law2011WhatsWrongWithAOneWorld World.pdf.

Leff, Enrique. 2002. *Saber Ambiental.* Mexico City: Siglo XXI.

Macy, Joanna. 2007. *World as Lover, World as Self: Courage for Global Justice and Ecological Renewal.* Berkeley, CA: Parallax.

Macy, Joanna. 2012. *Active Hope: How to Face the Mess We're in without Going Crazy.* Novato, CA: New World Library.

Mamani, Pablo. 2005. *Geopolíticas indígenas.* El Alto, Bolivia: CADES.

Mezzadra, Sandro. 2007. "Living in Transition: Toward a Heterolingual Theory of the Multitude." *Transversal*, June. http://eipcp.net/transversal/1107/mezzadra/en.

Mooney, Pat, ETC Group, and What Next Project. 2006. *The What Next Report 2005–2035: Trendlines and Alternatives.* Stockholm: Dag Hammarskjöld Foundation.

Nandy, Ashis. 1987. *Tradition, Tyranny, and Utopias.* Delhi: Oxford University Press.

Nhat Hanh, Thich. 2008. *The World We Have.* Berkeley, CA: Parallax.

Oslender, Ulrich. 2004. "Fleshing Out the Geographies of Social Movements: Colombia's Pacific Coast Black Communities and the Aquatic Space." *Political Geography* 23 (8): 957–85.

Oslender, Ulrich. 2016. *The Geographies of Social Movements: Black Communities on Colombia's Pacific Coast and the Aquatic Space.* Durham, NC: Duke University Press.

Paredes, Julieta. 2012. *Hilando fino desde el feminismo comunitario.* La Paz: DED (Deutscher Entwicklungsdienst).

Patzi Paco, F. 2004. *Sistema Comunal: Una Propuesta Alternativa al Sistema Liberal.* La Paz: CEA.

Patzi Paco, Félix. 2012. *Tercer sistema. Modelo Comunal: Propuesta alternativa para salid del capitalismo y el socialismo.* La Paz: Author.

Plumwood, Val. 2002. *Environmental Culture: The Ecological Crisis of Reason.* New York: Routledge.

Povinelli, Elizabeth. 2001. "Radical Worlds: The Anthropology of Incommensurability and Inconceivability." *Annual Review of Anthropology* 30:319–34.

Quijano, Aníbal. 2010. "Buen Vivir: Entre el 'desarrollo' y la des/colonialidad del poder." Unpublished manuscript, Lima.

Randers, Jorgen. 2012. *2052: A Global Forecast for the Next Forty Years*. White River Junction, VT: Chelsea Green.

Raskin, Paul, Tariq Banuri, Gilberto Gallopín, Pablo Gutman, Al Hammond, Robert Kates, and Rob Swart. 2002. *Great Transition: The Promise and the Lure of Times Ahead*. Boston: Stockholm Environment Institute.

Sachs, Wolfgang, and Tilman Santarius, eds. 2007. *Fair Futures: Resource Conflicts, Security, and Global Justice*. London: Zed.

Santos, Boaventura. 2007. *The Rise of the Global Left: The World Social Forum and Beyond*. London: Zed.

Schafer, Paul. 2008. *Revolution or Renaissance: Making the Transition from an Economic Age to a Cultural Age*. Ottawa: University of Ottawa Press.

Shiva, Vandana. 2005. *Earth Democracy*. Cambridge, MA: South End.

Shiva, Vandana. 2008. *Soil, Not Oil: Environmental Justice in an Age of Climate Crisis*. Cambridge, MA: South End.

Subcomandante Marcos and the Zapatistas. 2006. *The Other Campaign/La Otra Campaña*. San Franciso: City Lights.

Suchman, Lucy. 2007. *Human-Machine Reconfigurations: Plans and Situated Actions*. Cambridge: Cambridge University Press.

Svampa, Maristella. 2012. "Pensar el desarrollo desde América Latina." In *Renunciar al bien común: Extractivismo y (pos)desarrollo en América Latina*, edited by Gabrila Massuh, 17–58. Buenos Aires: Mardulce.

Walsh, Catherine. 2009. *Interculturalidad, estado, sociedad: Luchas (de)coloniales de nuestra época*. Quito: Abya Yala.

Winograd, Terry, and Fernando Flores. 1986. *Understanding Computers and Cognition*, 163–79. Norwood, NJ: Ablex.

Zibechi, R. 2006. *Dispersar el poder: Los movimientos como poderes anti-estatales*. Buenos Aires: Tinta Limón.

4 · On Pluriversality and Multipolar World Order

Decoloniality after Decolonization;
Dewesternization after the Cold War

But to rely on benevolence alone to influence the Europeans in Asia to relinquish the privileges they have acquired in China would be an impossible dream. If we want to regain our rights we must resort to force. —SUN-YAT SEN, 1924

Europe undertook the leadership of the world with ardor, cynicism and violence. Look at how the shadow of her palaces stretches out ever farther! Every one of her movements has burst the bounds of space and thought. Europe has declined all humility and all modesty; but she has also set her face against all solicitude and all tenderness. . . .

Come, then, comrades, the European game has finally ended; we must find something different. We today can do everything, so long as we do not imitate Europe, so long as we are not obsessed by the desire to catch up with Europe. —FRANTZ FANON, 1961

Monocentrism after Pluricentrism

I have argued in several places that the world order before 1500 was pluricentric and noncapitalist. There were by then around the world and after the axial age, hundreds of centers of complex organizations that today we call civilizations. In the Old World (according to the Western semantic of world order in the sixteenth century), civilizations and cultures were connected from Fez and Timbuktu to Beijing going through Baghdad. There were inequalities within each culture or civilization, but no one single civilization imposed itself over the others religiously, economically, politically, and cognitively (that is, imposing one way of knowing as the right one and disavowing the rest). It was an interconnected Old World, noncapitalist and pluricentric.

By 1500, radical changes began to take place in the history of humankind. A New World emerged in the European consciousness that prompted Renaissance men of letters to set up the foundation of the current world order: the planet was divided between the Old World and the New World and, by the seventeenth century, into Western and Eastern hemispheres. The Global South was unimaginable at that point. There was no such division before 1500, and not one single locus of enunciation that could have established it as the ontology of the globe for five hundred years. And here was the trick, a magic trick and trap that still effectively narcotizes the imaginary and the feelings of many people: while Europe, Asia, and Africa were classified as the Old World and the Americas as the New World, Eastern and Western hemispheres were a superimposed distinction. Asia was in the East and the Americas in the West.

East and West are obviously not ontological places on a round planet. They are fictions invented by someone who placed himself in the middle, between East and West. Furthermore, that instance of enunciation has the privilege of placing himself at the center. The center (be it Rome or the Greenwich Meridian) is the invention of the actors and institutions that are telling the stories that the planet is divided into Eastern and Western hemispheres. To understand what I mean, suppose that someone is in Beijing and believes that he is at the center of the world—which was the case until the Jesuits arrived toward 1580 and showed them Abraham Ortelius's world map and realized that in European cartography China was in the upper left corner of the map. However, Chinese did not change their belief in being at the center. The Western *mapamundi* at the time was changed: the Pacific was placed at the center and so China occupied the place it was expected.[1] And that is still what the world looks like in East Asian cartography, placing the Pacific at the center of a flat, rectangular map. Maps are powerful cognitive instruments that control your imaginary and your feelings. In Western cartography the West began to be built as the location of a superior civilization, Christian first and secular later. Geographically, Europe was both the center from which East and West were determined and also located in the West. Western Christians (located in the territories that will become Europe) located themselves in the West: not to the west of the East, but to the west of Jerusalem.

To understand the meaning and consequences of a pluriversal imaginary and multipolar interstate world order today, it is imperative to understand how and when the polycentric world order before 1500 was overruled by the coming into being of the monopolar world order that lasted until 2000.

Whether 1500 shall be earmarked as the beginning of the era of the Anthropos is a matter of dispute. However, and seen in retrospect, it was at that moment that the world order became increasingly cognitively monocentric (Christian theology and secular science and philosophy), economically capitalist, and politically regulated by monarchical statehood (e.g., the Spanish viceroyalties and the thirteen early British colonies in North America) and later on by the exportation of the secular nation-state, first to the Americas (the so-called American Revolution, the Haitian Revolution, the independence of Spanish and Portuguese colonies), and second to Asia and Africa. The monocentric world order is today exploding. Out of the explosion and the debris of the crashing monocentric world order, two trajectories emerge in coexistence: one is being called a multipolar world order, and the second is pluriversality as a universal project. The first is a state-led project of dewesternization. The second is the project of the emerging political society of decoloniality.

I would like to stress that I see no single winner in the short and perhaps also long run. It is imperative to understand the coexistence of the multipolar world order and pluriversality as a universal project. No single option at this point can eliminate the other. Thus, to understand where pluriversality as a universal project stands and what are the possibilities and the limits, it is imperative to understand the strength of the multipolar world order in which decoloniality coexists. Let's begin by describing the meaning of multipolarity today.

By 1500, the emergence of the Atlantic commercial circuits and the conquest and colonization of the Americas were material events in need of firsthand conceptual narratives (or, better yet, storytelling). Remember also that in the fourteenth century Europe was not yet what it would become. It was the land of Western Christians, one culture on a planet populated by long-lasting civilizations in Asia, Africa, and the Americas. The overarching frame available at that point was Christian theology mixed with the seed of Renaissance humanism, the seed of secular philosophy and science that erupted in the eighteenth century and did not stop growing until today's fourth industrial revolution,[2] complemented by narratives of the posthuman and the Anthropocene. Westernization of the world between 1500 and 2000 was not limited to politics and economy but, above all, included knowledge. Without knowledge that builds an image of the world and invents its ontology, there is no world order. The order is created by the instances of enunciation (actors, languages, institutions) that control and manage knowledge. Knowledge shapes sensing, and sensing provokes and engenders knowledge. The heart dominates the brain. Thus, the firsthand narratives that erupted in the sixteenth century, told by Europeans (Spanish, Portuguese, French, British, Dutch, and no less Italians and Germans), appropriated the world cognitively.

Universalism was the cognitive philosophy (theological and secular) that justified the monocentric world order, the privileges of Western civilization, and the idea of modernity, to drive the rest of the planet in that direction. Universals were and are fictions. Michel-Rolph Trouillot[3] masterfully demonstrated the formation and power of North Atlantic universal fictions from 1492 to

1945. North Atlantic universal fictions were built on four basic pillars erected during the Renaissance, and it was out of these pillars that universalism and the monopolar world order were built. The crashing of the fictions that maintained both monocentric world order and universalism gave rise to an innovative narrative emerging from awareness and the need to delink from monopolarity and universalism. Thus, storytelling (or if you prefer, theories and ethnographies) of multipolarity and pluriversalism emerge. But that is not all.

The attitudes, beliefs, doing, thinking, and sensing that conform the political, economic, and cognitive delinking in the formation of a multipolar world engender responses from the beneficiaries, and obviously from the defenders, of monopolarity and universalism. Thus, if the instantiation and installation of North Atlantic universal fictions encompassed the long and variegated process of Westernizing the world (with the collaboration, of course, of the locals), the moment in which universal fictions began to be disbelieved and contested forced the articulation of new strategies to maintain alive the success of Westernization. Thus, rewesternization consists of the political, economic, and cognitive efforts (e.g., storytelling of posthuman and Anthropocene, as well as optimistic narratives such as that of the fourth industrial revolution and the magnificent promises that biotechnology brings to human existence) to maintain the privileges that Westernization provided.[4]

The multipolar world order was in the making before the collapse of the Soviet Union, but no one was paying attention to it. The Cold War was ingrained in the monopolar world order. The dispute was within Western political philosophies on managing the state and the economy. It was a dispute for the control of monopolarity and in no way an opening toward multipolarity. The opening to multipolarity was taking place in East Asia, away from the Western memories in which liberalism and Marxism were both embedded. The seed was Singapore and the carrier the China of Deng Xiaoping. Later came the slow recovery of Russia under Vladimir Putin, the formation of BRICS (Brazil, Russia, India, China, and South Africa) and the increasing political affirmation of China and Russia in the global political arena. The multipolar world order arises, enacting the politics of dewesternization. What makes multipolarity possible is the appropriation of capitalism to enact a divergent politics. Without a strong economy like China's, Russia's military revival (Trenin 2016), and the formation of the BRICS bank, the politics of dewesternization and multipolarity would not have been possible. Now it is irreversible in spite of efforts by the Obama administration (chiefly the TPP, canceled by the Trump administration) and the moving of NATO troops to the frontiers of Russia.

Multipolarity is an interstate world order that is possible because the five hundred years of unipolar Westernization ended. Neoliberalism was the last prospective story promoting monopolarity, a homogenization of the world under Western aegis. However, it is not easy to renounce five hundred years of privilege. And thus rewesternization, the effort to maintain Western leadership under the new circumstances, was the response to dewesternization. Thus, the conflict is no longer a cold war, for the Cold War was framed entirely under Western political theory and political economy. Dewesternization is enacted economically under capitalist economics and culturally under the revival of memories that Westernization disavowed—thus the meaning of reviving China's millenarian praxis of living and thinking and the weight Russia is placing on remembering Russia's imperial past. Western media take pleasure in joking about both, more about Russia under Putin. I take these jokes as evidence, on the one hand, that dewesternization is working and, on the other, of the difficulties of Western media but also sometimes scholars in understanding that Western memories and its glorious pasts grounded in ancient Greece and Rome are not universal and cannot be the pillars of a world order under a single memory: Western memory. The Cold War was fought within those parameters. Soviet secularism sided the Orthodox Church, which was consistent with secularism but also with the attempt to incorporate Russia in the Western orbit. Both ideologies, liberalism and socialism, were well grounded on Western cognitive frames. Soviet leaders repressed their own sensibilities and projected them into the universality of the Western ideological frame. Thus, the scenario I depicted at the beginning of this essay (the pluricentric and noncapitalist world order) is being enacted by capitalist dewesternization and reactivating local memories, knowledge, ways of being and of inhabiting the world. On the other hand, it is being enacted at the margin of capitalism, at the margin of the interstate system, by the emerging global political society. Pluriversality is the name and the horizon of all decolonial trajectories today, on the planet, arising from the awareness of repressive forces of coloniality.

But where, then, is pluriversality in this scheme? This is the argument I am making. First, multipolarity is an interstate project prompted by the emergence of dewesternizing politics and culture, for there is a cultural reemergence and recovery of dignity that shall not be overlooked. You can blame China's Communist Party leaders and Vladimir Putin, but you shall not forget that the blamers are blaming from the assumption of a self-serving universality that China and Russia are violating. Or China and Russia cannot be blamed without blaming at the same time Western Europe and the United States, where the actors, institutions, and languages (notice that Mandarin Chinese and Russian were not languages in which universal fictions were invented and promoted) that engendered dewesternizing responses appropriating capitalist economy and delinking politically from Western institutions and expectations.

Second, pluriversality names the visions of hundreds of thousands of organizations arising from the moment people realize that they cannot expect much if anything from either the states or the corporations recognizing, however, that China lifted significantly the line of extreme poverty and created a consumerist middle-class. Pluriversality comes from the emerging global political society, to give it a name. Political society is a connector, explicit or implicit, between the hundreds of thousands of projects that configure the global political society. The global political society has this in common: delinking from the state, corporations, and financial institutions. Delinking means here that while living under state regulations and capitalist economics, it is possible to engage in autonomous communal organization that secures well-being and harmony among the people engaged in such acting, doing, and thinking. Pluriversality cannot be designed and universally managed; it just happens in multiple locations and from multiple memories and praxis of living locally entangled with coloniality.

Now the question arises: where are we (scholars, intellectuals, artists, journalists, intellectuals, activists, and artivists [artists + activists]) in this scheme? Are we just reporting, analyzing, arguing, performing, and creating installations to make the reader or the audience aware of the political society? Are we (all of us mentioned in the previous parentheses) to imagine ourselves storytellers and reporters or shall we also imagine ourselves as one sector of the global political society? I cannot respond for the millions of people in the roles mentioned above. But I could say that I see myself (my work and the people I work with in academia and outside of it) advancing the global political society. Our work is located in the cultural sphere (the disciplines in which we are inscribed, the institutions where we work: universities, museums, newspapers, television, radio, all sorts of cultural and pedagogical institutions) where knowledge and understanding are created, transformed, contested, reified, and so on. At this point it is necessary to bring *coloniality of knowledge* into the picture.

A pluriverse cannot be obtained just by the efforts of the political society to delink from the state, the corporations, the financial sector, and the repressive side of religious institutions. For the pluriverse to materialize it is necessary to *relink* with whatever is relevant in each specific project and to *connect* with coexisting decolonial projects in different areas (sexuality, racism, religion, economic, art, knowledge) and in different parts of the planet.[5] Otherwise, the variegated organizations of the political society would remain disconnected activities holding each of them together by the local storytelling of their members, conceiving themselves as an organization confronted with the state, the corporations, the financial sector, and repressive religious institutions but not as part of a global linkage, decolonially constructing the pluriverse.

And here is where we (scholars, intellectuals, artists, curators, journalists, etc.) who engage in conversations on the pluriverse run into difficulties. For we are at once members of a particular organization of the political society and the ones who are engaged in conceptualizing and propagating (through books, conferences, articles, workshops, lectures, courses, and seminars), the idea of the pluriverse. The ontology of the pluriverse, in other words, cannot be obtained without the epistemology enacted by storytelling exploring the meaning and significance of pluriversality as a universal project.

At this point, a couple of clarifications are in order. First, I am using the expression *political society* (which I borrow from Partha Chatterjee's [2004] *The Politics of the Governed*) instead of *social movements*. And I am using Chatterjee's expression in a larger sense—not referring only to popular politics, which presupposes that the governed are only the lower classes in relation to the middle class, to which, in general, scholars, intellectuals, journalists, artists, and so on belong. When I state that I see myself and the people I work with, in academia and outside of it, as sectors of the political society, I make clear that we (those mentioned in the parenthesis) are governed and our politics move in two directions. One is in describing and contributing to the visibility of the popular politics of the governed and the other is our own intellectual politics of the governed. Or if you prefer the other terminology: we shall see and constitute ourselves as a social movement. That is what I mean by saying that I consider the work I do with others, in and out of academia, part of the global political society.

The second clarifying point is why I prefer *political society* to *social movements*. Around 2005, a weeklong seminar took place in Spain (El Escorial) organized by Heriberto Cairo Carau. Among the noted participants was Nina Pacari, a Kichwa politician and lawyer from Ecuador. In one of her oral presentations, of which there is no record, she refuted scholars who refer to social or indigenous movements. "We are not movements"—she said, as it was imprinted in my memory the moment Pacari said it—"We do not move. We are a nation and have been always there from time immemorial."[6] The fact that Kichwas and other nations of Ecuador do not move doesn't mean that they are not politically active, organizing themselves and confronting from their cosmologies the cosmologies that permeate the government, religious, pedagogical, and

economic institutions of the Ecuadorian state. We (scholars, intellectuals, journalists, artists, etc.) do not move and are not a nation.

We (those in parentheses) are connected by our professional lives, by racial/
ethnic and gender/sexual concerns, and by the political commitments among
all of us who share decolonial visions and pluriversality as a universal project.
There are also many of us who are equally politically and ethically committed
to the struggle for justice, for equity, toward noncapitalist economies (uncou-
pling economy from capitalism), and for balance and harmony in the all-
encompassing living planet and cosmos, pachamama, Umma, Tianxia, and so
on. After all, the Greek word *cosmopolis* is one among many, and not the one
and only. In my own way of thinking, I connect pluriversality with decoloniality, and decoloniality as one way to walk and build pluriversality; that is, the
multiplication of storytelling promoting the pluriverse.

Let's move to a more specific argument to better understand, on the one
hand, multipolarity and dewesternization and, on the other, pluriversity and
decoloniality. But before entering that territory, it is necessary to understand
the historical foundation of the colonial matrix of power (CMP) since, in my
argument, multipolarity and pluriversity, as well as the roads to them, dewesternization and decoloniality, respectively, both are the outcome of the foundation and mutations of CMP.

The Colonial Matrix of Power: The
Historical Foundation of Western Civilization

Let's start by making more explicit what I mean by *coloniality*. Coloniality is
shorthand for the coloniality of power, and both are stand-ins for the CMP. The
use of one term or the other depends on how much detail we want to invoke
with the expression.

The colonial matrix of power (CMP) is a complex structure of management
and control composed of domains, levels, and flows. Like the unconscious in
Sigmund Freud or surplus value in Karl Marx, the CMP is a theoretical concept
that helps make visible what is invisible to the naked (or rather the nontheoret-
ical) eye. Unlike Freud's unconscious or Marx's surplus value, though, the CMP
is a concept created in the Third World, in the South American Andes. That is,
it is not a concept created in the conceptual history or in the academy of Europe
or the United States. The concept was born out of theoretical-political struggles
in South America, at the intersection between the academic and the public
spheres. Driven by local critics of development, the CMP bears the impulse of
liberation theology and emerged out of the limits of dependency theory in the

1970s. These, of course, were also the years of the struggle for decolonization in Asia and Africa.

In order to understand the CMP, it must first be understood that coloniality is constitutive and not derivative of modernity.[7] For this reason, we (in the collective project) write "modernity/coloniality." The slash that divides and unites modernity with coloniality means that coloniality is constitutive of modernity: there is no modernity without coloniality. Highlighting global coloniality means that global modernity is only half of the story, the visible one. The other half—hidden—is global coloniality.[8]

But the question now is, what holds all the domains of the CMP together? To answer this question, we need to introduce the levels of the CMP. Within each domain are different levels of management and control. The rhetoric of modernity is heavily utilized within these levels, in order to convince the population that such-and-such a decision or public policy is for the betterment (i.e., the happiness and salvation) of everyone. While theological principles and philosophical-scientific truths have historically sustained the domains of the CMP, the mainstream media today play an equally crucial role in disseminating the rhetoric of modernity and salvation in the face of ever-changing enemies.

The actors and institutions that create, pronounce, and transform the ideals that drive the idea of modernity are the same actors and institutions that (intentionally or not) keep all the domains interrelated and also keep these interrelations invisible. It is within this context that we must understand the recent creation of the figure of the expert, who appears often in the mainstream media to explain this or that aspect of a news story, and who knows a great deal about one domain but is ignorant of the others and of how all the domains are connected.

Outside the domains and their levels of management and control is a broader level where the domains themselves are defined, their interrelations legislated and authorized. We might call the domains themselves the content of the conversation, or that which is enunciated, talked about, studied, and debated. Conversely, the broader level where the domains are defined and interrelated relates to the terms (rules, assumptions, principles) of the conversation, or enunciation proper.

This broader level is also the level of knowledge in the deep sense of the word. It is composed of actors, languages, and institutions. The institutions involved are mainly colleges, universities, museums, research centers (think tanks), institutes, foundations, and religious organizations. At the same time, the enormous visibility of generous donors hides the fact that generosity is a fact of life for billions of people in the world, beyond the smaller areas of elite institutions and the actors that sustain them.

As for the languages in which the content of the conversation has been established and maintained, these have been and still are the six modern European imperial languages: Italian, Spanish, and Portuguese during the Renaissance; German, English, and French since the Enlightenment. For Russia and China to enter the conversation, the conversation has to be in English, French, or German. The reverse does not hold: leaders of the core European Union (of which Poland and Hungary are not part) can maintain their French, English, or German without needing to learn Russian or Chinese.

The essential feature to take notice of within the CMP's domains is the domain of knowledge. Knowledge has a privileged position: it occupies the level of the enunciated, where the content of the conversation is established, and it occupies the level of the enunciation, which regulates the terms of the conversation. A pedagogical metaphor would help clarify the point I am making here. Think of a puppeteer. You do not see the puppeteer; you only see the puppets. You are drawn by the puppets; by their movements and dialogues. What you see and hear is the content of the conversation. In order to see the terms of the conversation, you would have to disengage from the illusion and focus on the puppeteer behind the scenes who is regulating the terms of the conversation.

Knowledge in the CMP occupies two positions: it is one of the puppets (the content of the conversation), and it also denotes the designs that the puppeteer creates to enchant the audience. The decoloniality of knowledge involves changing the terms of the conversations: decoloniality aims at altering the principles and assumptions of knowledge creation, transformation, and dissemination (Smith 1999). Dewesternization, by contrast, disputes the content of the conversation. The apparent paradox is that the domains of the CMP seem to be isolated and independent of one another. The CMP, then, needs experts within a given domain. These experts are unknowingly not simply of other domains but of the logic (the terms of the conversation) that keeps all the domains interlinked.

Consequently, the CMP is held together by the flows that emanate from the enunciation (from the terms of the conversation, the rhetoric of modernity). These flows interconnect all the domains and connect the domains with the actors and institutions, in the major languages of the European idea of modernity. Inevitably, the question of subjectivity and subject formation emerges: the CMP is involved in the creation of particular persons/subjects and institutions, but it also takes on a life of its own, shaping and contorting the subjectivity (the reasoning and emotions) of the person managing it. Because of coloniality, control of the terms of enunciation (that is, control of knowledge) is necessary for controlling the domains, and controlling the domains means managing the people whose lives are shaped by the domains. The flows, finally, are moved by the triple plays of forces and power differential of domination/exploitation/ conflicts. Decoloniality is one manifestation of the conflicts that emerge in every domain and above all, in the domain of knowledge: the knowledge constituting the domains (the content) and the knowing constituted and managed in and by the mobile and ever changing enunciation.

Closing the Cycle of Western Hegemony

Now that we have a general understanding of the promises announced by the rhetoric of modernity (the promises of salvation by conversion, progress, civilization, development, defeating terrorism, or ending the drug economy in order to finally live in a developed and happy world) and the consequences of enacting what these salvation discourses promise, we can look at the present world (dis)order and speculate on the underlying causes of the prevailing chaos.

I have stated already that the underlying causes can be found within global coloniality. By global coloniality, I mean that the specificities of the CMP that were put in place in the sixteenth century—through the appropriation of massive amounts of land in Anahuac, Tawantinsuyu, Mayab, Abya Yala, the Turtle Islands, and other places, the arrival of uninvited Europeans, and their initiation of a massive slave trade—have now permeated most of the planet through the dominant form of governance (the modern nation-state), the type of economy (economic coloniality), universities and museums, and the media and entertainment industry.

To make short the very long story that connects the sixteenth century with the twenty-first: If we look closely at the European invasion of Tawantinsuyu (the name the Incas gave to their territory) from approximately 1532 to 1580, we find that the United States' invasion of Iraq in 2003 is almost an exact replica, carried out some five hundred years later by the last imperial state in a long history of the consolidation of Western civilization and expansion. In short, these are two moments in the long history of the Westernization of the world (Latouche 1989).[9]

This replication is not happenstance. It is inscribed in the salvationist logic of modernity and the irrepressible need of coloniality to enact the promises of modernity. In other words, the replication has to do with the persistence of the

CMP, with its rhetoric of modernity as salvation and its legitimization of the logic of coloniality as domination, dispossession, and oppression. The history of the CMP is not a linear one. On the contrary, it is a heterogeneous historic-structural set of nodes connecting different places and moments within the historical foundation of Western civilization and its trajectory of Westerniza-tion. It is a set of global designs (economic, religious, political, aesthetic, racial, sexual, epistemic, subjective) for creating a homogeneous world order. It has failed, and it couldn't have been otherwise. The failure of Westernization is the major reason and cause of the world disorder we are living through.

During this historical period, Western imperial states did practically what-ever they pleased in the rest of the world, beginning, it is important to remember, with their historical foundation in the Atlantic in the sixteenth century. Western imperial states went through a series of conflicts and wars, fighting among them-selves. First, England and France disputed the primacy of the Spanish Empire; then there was the religious war that ended in the Peace of Westphalia and the foundation of the modern secular bourgeois state; then came World War I, thirty years after the Berlin Treaty, by which European states had distributed among themselves the entire African continent. The prelude to World War I witnessed two new contenders for the control of CMP: Japan, after victories over China (1905) and Russia (1905); and the United States, after the final de-feat of the old Spanish Empire in the Hispano-American War (1898–1901). The Hispano-American war was a signpost for the entry of the United States into the global arena, and it saw the United States claiming its rights to CMP globalism.

In addition, and returning to my quest for the underlying causes of the cur-rent prevailing chaos, globalism as I use it here is a process that must again be traced back to the sixteenth century and that is inextricably tied up with the CMP. There are several sources I could draw on to illustrate this point. I refer to just one: Carl Schmitt's (2006) crucial notion of "global linear thinking." Schmitt connects global linear thinking with the emergence, in the sixteenth century, of international law, and the emergence of international law with his conception of the "second *nomos* of the earth."

The second nomos means, for Schmitt, that since the sixteenth century the planet has been mapped by European actors and institutions aligned with European interests.[10] During the period in which the first nomoi predominated, there was no single nomos that interfered with the others or was imposed on the others. By contrast, the second nomos was the first in the history of human-ity that was implemented to manage and control other nomoi. This implemen-tation began in the sixteenth century. Importantly, the second nomos of the earth manifested itself in the creation of international law.

To be sure, the story here has to go through the rise and fall of the Soviet Union and Russia's reemergence after a humiliating defeat. But it must also take into account the role of international law. The Berlin Congress was yet another chapter in the march of international law that emerged in the sixteenth century and went uncontested until recently.[11] Russia's reclaiming of Crimea meant that the unfolding of the Western imperial nomos (global linear thinking constitutive of CMP) escaped the exclusive control of Western institutions. Beyond the pros and cons of the Russian intervention in Ukraine, there is a history of the second nomos of the earth reaching its limits: the limits imposed by dewesternization. The current prevailing chaos seems to have its roots in globalism and the Eurocentric building of international law. Needless to say, international law is a crucial component of the CMP: it is the flow that connects the CMP with the actors and institutions involved in controlling land and trade regulations.

Unilinear assumptions are common to (neo)liberal and (neo-)Marxist worldviews. Giovanni Arrighi, a Marxist sociologist, has surmised that China will be the next hegemon, based on Western imperial history from its foundation in Spain and Portugal and the instauration of the Atlantic commercial circuits, to the United States, going through the Netherlands, France, and England. If, however, we take into account the complex, diffuse ways the CMP was formed, transformed, and managed by overlapping Western empires, we would conclude that neither Russia nor China could be the next hegemon, even if either country wanted to be, for the simple reason that such an outcome is not possible today and won't be possible for a long time hence.

All of this is to say that, while the Westernization of the world was carried out without any major challenges (beyond the ones among the very same Westernizers—e.g., World War I and World War II) from the non-European spheres, dewesternization has halted that immutable process and challenged the West's control and management of the CMP. Dewesternization means that the control and management of CMP is now in dispute—and it is precisely this dispute that engenders not a new unipolar order (where Russia and China are dangerous) because they want to be the next hegemons, according to Western media, but the multipolar world order we are all witnessing. We see traces of this multipolarity in Ukraine and Syria, in the China Development Bank, in the establishment of the BRICS states and the BRICS bank, in China's building of a new Silk Road Economic Belt, and in other initiatives still in the making.[12]

Dewesternization after the Cold War:
Changing the Content of the Conversation

Changing the content of the conversation is what dewesternization is doing. Dewesternizing states are as capitalist as Western imperial states, from where dewesternization borrow the idea. Their doing is similar, but the storytelling about their doing is different: the conflicts are manifested in interstate politics grounded on economic interest and national and civilizational pride and leadership: Western states want to continue being the leaders (rewesternization) and other states do not want to be led (dewesternization). It is in the storytelling that dewesternization opens up the process of changing the content of the conversations. One example: honest Western media admired many of Vladimir Putin's discourses countering Western media accusations (Western media are an instrument of rewesternization) after he seized Crimea and entered Syria in support of al-Assad to counter Western manipulation of terrorists and moderate terrorists. At the same time, dewesternization forces the updating of the rhetoric of modernity to justify the actions to contain dewesternization. Another notorious example was the much-commented-on three-and-a-half-hour speech by Xi Jinping to the 19th Party Congress.[13] The rhetoric of modernity has always been articulated to justify actions in the name of peace and civilizational or national interest. Currently, NATO's maneuvers to contain Russia are justified by a renewed rhetoric of danger and demonization: this is what I call rewesternization. Dewesternization and rewesternization are setting up the rules of the world order, a world order that is capitalist, but there are no longer universal principles justifying capitalism. Local histories are being enacted by large and small states in the name of dewesternization.

In response to the aggressive consolidation of Western civilization between 1500 and 2000, and continuing through the rewesternizing politics launched by President Barack Obama in Cairo in 2008 and by Secretary of State, Hillary Clinton in Honolulu in 2011 and continuing through the rhetoric of "Make America Great Again" enarbolated by Donald Trump, the project of delinking from Western domination has gained momentum, manifesting itself in the discrete efforts of dewesternization and decoloniality. Conversely, since it is difficult to let go of privileges, the United States and former Western Europe (and NATO) are emphasizing rewesternizing impetus, as a way to revamp—under new circumstances—the global designs that were successful for five hundred years. Undoubtedly, the obstacles that dewesternization and decoloniality present to the West and the West's counterefforts to maintain the privileges it has acquired are at the core of the global chaos we are steeped in.

This brings me to the guesswork required by the second set of questions. I would say that any possible alternative or solutions could not come from Western countries that are the builders and managers of the present chaos. Enough evidence suggests that Western designs (conversion, progress, democracy, disenchantment of the world, racism and sexism, patriarchy) do not work, and I argue that they have failed because they are implicitly geared toward maintaining the world order created in the past five hundred years. Western cooperation will be necessary, but its leadership is simply not conducive to achieving a more just and sustainable world order. The solutions that the world needs cannot come from former Western Europe and the United States.

It may be strange for the consumer of Western media to consider that China and Russia should take the lead in moving us toward a peaceful global order. Any suggestion to this effect may sound like yet another high-flown public statement issued by Chinese and Russian officials and their manipulated media, in contradistinction to the self-proclaimed free press and democratic media of the West. We should pay attention to these statements, however. During the Seventy-Year Common Victory conference in September 2015, held in Khabarovsk, Russia, to celebrate the defeat of fascism, Liu Qibao, a member of the Politburo of China, reminded the audience that China and Russia are both founding states of the United Nations. Qibao stressed "that this feature bestows upon both China and Russia the responsibility to play a leading role in ensuring global and regional peace, security and cooperation" and "spoke of China and Russia's 'common responsibility' towards guaranteeing stability in the post-war international order."[14] You may express your disbelief in such commitments. But, if you do, you should also suspect whether the United States and former Western Europe are seriously engaged in bringing peace to West Asia or whether the Mexican government and the CIA are seriously working to eliminate the drug cartels. The multipolar world order is irreversible and, of course, the multipolar world order couln't be a universal project of rewesternization!

Decoloniality after Decolonization:
Changing the Terms of the Conversation

Decoloniality Is Not a Nation-State–Oriented Project

Dewesternization and decoloniality emerged from the crisis of decolonization during the Cold War. Dewesternization embraced capitalism to affirm its political dissidence and confrontation with Westernization. Decoloniality rejected the idea of building (or taking already constituted) nation-states.

Decoloniality focused on the necessity of changing the terms (rules, principles, assumptions) of the conversation. Changing the terms of the conversation cannot be expected from the state (for the state is one of the key institutions of CMP for political Westernization), the corporations, the banks, or international organizations such as the UN or the IMF. And it cannot be expected from dewesternization either. Dewesternization disputes the control of CMP, not its very existence while decoloniality aims at delinking from its very existence not to dispute who manages it. Interstate conflicts amount to a multipolar world order that of course shall not be idealized, although one should be aware that multipolarity prevents the universalization of one global design—that of driving Western civilization to every corner of the round planet. Moving toward decolonial horizons of pluriversality requires changing the terms of the conversation. Decoloniality is one road toward pluriversality.

Changing the terms (assumptions, presupositions, praxis of living, cultural and biological) of the conversation is the task of the emerging political society in doing and thinking. Since Westernization mounted—since 1500—a device of management and control, the CMP, both dewesternization and decoloniality aim at delinking from it, but in different ways. Dewesternization is delinking by disputing the control of the CMP and, therefore, changing the content of the conversation, while decoloniality is delinking to relink with memories, praxis of living and thinking that were disavowed by CMP. The first leads to a multipolar world. The second leads to conceptualizing the decolonial pluriversal option in two directions: (1) showing the presuppositions and underpinning of dewesternization and rewesternization, but at the same time showing the opening that dewesternization enacts by redrawing the maps of local histories and pushing aside the pretended universality of Western local histories; and (2) conceptualizing pluriversality and enacting/promoting the pluriversal option by delinking from the previous option.

Now, none of the three options at this point could win over the others. The three options on their changing faces, fluidity and mobility (for none of them is a fixed blueprint to be and do and think and act), will coexist for decades to come. Only a magician could anticipate what would come of these confrontations in their fluidity and mobility in their politics, although anchored in solid aims and principles in their existence. However, it is undeniable that the turmoil the world is in today is due to the crash of Westernization, the emergence of dewesternization, the counterreformation of rewesternization, and the reorientation of decoloniality detached from decolonization (where the goal was to take control of the state apparatus) and embracing the horizon of pluriversality.

In order to change the terms of the conversation, we (the people) must start from the assumption that the West (the United States, former Western Europe, and their allies) can no longer offer solutions to the problems they themselves have created, through their establishment, management, and control of the CMP. However, they could and should play a crucial role in global peace, by relinquishing the need to lead the world under Western regional universalism. The world today no longer needs *one* leader, and it is precisely this situation that is generating a domino effect in small states that still want to join the leader and in large states that do not want or need to be led anymore. Management shall de uncoupled from the idea of one leader at the top and the rest at the base of the pyramid. That Western dream is over.

Alternative visions of and pathways toward a multipolar and pluriversal horizon in the global order are emerging out of the local histories and sensibilities that have endured the humiliation and subjugation of the CMP—that is, of modernity/coloniality. Dewesternization is taking place in the spheres of the state (military included) and finance (the current currency war, for example). Decoloniality is marching forward in the emerging sphere of political society.[15] Dewesternization is marching towards a multipolar state world order.

The World Public Forum (that mutated into the Dialogue of Civilization Research Institute)[16] has been and continues its contribution to dewesternizing narratives: not only scholarly and journalist reports on the emerging global political society, but by conceiving itself (the Institute) and themselves (the actors) as advancing dewesternization and promoting the multipolar world order.[17] The weapons to all three trajectories (rewesternization, dewesternization, and decoloniality) are knowledge (e.g., military, as all other knowledge, has a technical dimension (how to make weapons) and an epistemic and cultural dimension (when and how to use or sell them) that could and should be directed toward changing both the content and the terms of the conversation held hostaged for five hundred years by the North Atlantic universal fictions and the unipolar world order that it created and supported. What is needed and it is taking place is the confrontation and delinking from the enunciation that controls the CMP by positing itself as universal truth in sciences, technology and in all order of knowledge and democracy in politics.

This same enunciation holds that whoever disobeys the rules (be it in the interstate system or in people's political organization to take care of their/our interests) and rejects true knowledge and deserves to be jailed, sacrificed, marginalized, disavowed, and all those signifiers of punishment that the rhetoric of modernity constantly invents to depose epistemic opponents, justify the physical elimination of political enemies (i.e., Israel's constant bombing of Palestinians), or create economic disturbance for economic and financial competitors (the Reserve Fund's management and manipulation of interests rates, the IMF and the European Central Bank's poker game with emerging economies).

Conceiving of ourselves (scholars, intellectuals, journalists, artists, curators, etc.) as decolonial members of a growing global political society means that our goals should be to intensify our work (as scholars, journalist, politicians, artists, activists, and artivists) of creating and promoting pluriversality, which involves delinking from *ego conquiro* and *ego cogito*, so much entrenched in the formation of modern subjects and subjectivities: the winner, the most successful, the number one, the world leader, and all the other social roles that modernity and its aftermath—globalism—have created, endorsed, and consolidated. It shall be emphasized, although it is never enough, that what sustains the CMP is knowledge and not some imagined "reality" that has to be changed. There is no "reality" without the knowledge that creates images of "reality" without the institutions that create and maintain knowledge creating "realities" and actors that are driving the institutions and epistemic belief to refill the tank of the CMP. Delinking from ego conquiro, ego cogito, and their successors means also delinking from the game of life that the ego cogito and conquiro has fashioned (Schirmacher 2015).

I want to insist that the pluriversal horizon I'm envisioning—coexisting with rewesternization and dewesternizaiton—is a space where changing the terms of the conversation (and, by changing the terms and reorienting the content of the conversation) is an ethically engaged project. By ethically engaged I mean that it put institutions at the service of the people rather than people at the service of the institutions, which was the spirit of westernization that is not (yet) absent from dewesternization. I am not envisioning in this horizon blind antiwestern violence in the name of dewesternization or decoloniality. Anti-*x* violence (whatever *x* may be) changes neither the content nor the terms of the conversation for any project. Instead, it leaves untouched the principles and the rules of the game, only confronts its content: such acts do not delink from the CMP but rather play their own game. And I am not referring either to the potential use of dewesternization and decoloniality as a mask for remaining within the rules of the CMP for whatever personal or familial benefit. I am underscoring that (a) for five hundred years the world order has been mapped by CMP and (b) that from it's domination/exploitation conflicts emerged that are today channeled through dewesernization and decoloniality.

Allow me now to introduce a prickly example to clarify what I am saying; prickly because readers may expect detailed ethnographic description of social movements that are enacting the pluriverse. However, the pluriverse cannot be enacted if there is no conceptualization of the pluriverse. But conceptualizing the pluriverse doesn't mean to design it. Who would be the designer? Conceptualization of the pluriverse shall come from both nonacademic political society and academic political society (theories and/or communal projects of conceptualizing pluriversality in thinking and doing).

Pluriversality, the Communal, and Decolonial Love

Humberto Maturana is a Chilean neurobiologist, working in the field of second-order (or second-generation) cybernetics. Maturana is regarded by the scientific establishment—in spite of the impact of his theories—as someone who thinks outside the box. And, fortunately, he does. His reputation as an unconventional thinker is not unrelated to his being a Third World thinker and scientist. Being a scientist in the Third World is quite different from being a scientist in the First World. Science could be said to be universal but scientists are not; and if scientists are not, then sciences can be neither global nor universal. The universality of the sciences is a myth and a fiction created by the rhetoric of Western modernity that projected to the universal a regional conception of knowing. It is coloniality of knowledge at its best.

Maturana's theories were advanced in the 1970s, right after the fall of Salvador Allende and the advent of Augusto Pinochet. He is neither oblivious to nor detached from this historical context. Of course, analyzing the nervous system of a pigeon is not related to the clash between Marxism and neoliberalism taking place in Chile in the early 1970s. But the reflections on knowledge derived from a pigeon's cognitive system could be related—as it is in Maturana's (2004) case. I would suggest that the mainstream scientific community finds Maturana problematic because he has changed the terms of the conversation, not merely the content.[18] But what are the connections between his work on biology and cognition and how does this relate to decoloniality?

Maturana's thesis that is most relevant to my argument can be condensed in the expression "the origin of humanness and the biology of love," which is the title of one of his books (2009). The species of living organisms that in the Western vocabulary came to be named *human* (in Aymara, *runa*; in Mandarin, *he*; in Persian, *bashar/ensan*; and so on) is a species of animal that walks with two of its extremities and uses its upper extremities as instruments for improving its biological living conditions (via hunting, shelter, agriculture) and for regenerating the species. These extremities can also be used to control and dominate other members of the species, which is not common among other animal species. What distinguishes this particular subspecies of animal is not only the uses of the hands to build instruments, cultivate and cook their own food; it is the use of the hands to caress for the communal engagement and coordination by means of languaging. Languaging was already a practice among hunters for the human-animal was the only animal that could build instruments to hunt other animals. Languaging makes conversation possible and conversations lead to coordinating behavior. Love is the outcome of communal praxis and, therefore, noncompetitive relationality among all living organisms.

It is well known that most species of animals nurture their newborn with love. Hating the newborns are rare manifestations in competitive society like the one we are living where extreme individualism and competitiveness destroy the communal and create living conditions of despair for parenthood. Love and the communal are necessary conditions for the regeneration of the species, from our ancestors thousands of years ago to today. For how could the subspecies human of the species animal have survived and expanded demographically without love and communal praxis of living to nurture the newborns? All the subspecies of the species animal have regenerated and survived for thousands and some millions of years. However, not all subspecies of the species animal use their hands to relationally engage in languaging. Languaging allows us to engage in conversation, to create and share knowledge and to build, communally, improved living conditions. Conversation brings knowledge into the picture— communal and shared knowledge. The question, then, becomes, at what point in the evolution of humanness did its very foundation, love and the communal, become overpowered by competition, by rulers who did not obey but wanted everyone else to obey, and by languages and knowledges that became tools of control and domination instead of conversation and communality? At what point in the history of humanness did the advent of society overrule the communal? This is the question that underscores the intersection of the origin and regeneration of humanness with the origin of coloniality and its consequences: westernization, decolonization, dewesternization and decoloniality.

Based on the narrative of the origin of humanness and the biology of love Maturana asks us to consider whether we want to preserve love and life for the planet and the communal, or competition and destruction unto death. Rewesternization and dewesternization are geared by competition. Of the three trajectories, decoloniality is the one that together with cultural biology and the biology of love, are equipped to push the resurgence of the communal, to delink from competitiveness and to relink with the biology of love. The biology of love and decolonial love shall not be confused with Christian and liberal loves, as both versions are imbedded in CMP. The future of humanness and of the planet depends on which choice prevails. As a biologist and a scientist, Maturana changed the terms of the conversation upon which Western sciences and biology were founded. And Maturana does it in constant awareness that, although Chilean, he has been trained in Western sciences. Two of the most distinctive departures are the rejection of the concept of "representation," he replaces with the agency of the observers who not "represent reality" but who are relationally in languaging constantly engaged in world-making. The second departure is his delinking from the theory of evolution by focusing on the origin (instead of the evolution) of humanness and the biology of love. Maturana underscores what has been preserved through the centuries instead of what has evolved. Ants have preserved their way to build anthills for perhaps millions of years and so did bees building their behives. The subspecies human still use our hands to caress and to cook. The regeneration of the species involves, for Maturana, not only biological regeneration but also the preservation and conservation in cultural languaging of love and the communal. And third, Maturana also introduced new questions and changed conversations within the study and understanding of languages: language is not an entitity that humans have but a set of relational activities that animal-humans engage to coordinate behavior, in love or in conflict.[19]

I could have selected cases from the political society to make my argument instead of the theories of a Chilean biologist. In the sphere of politics and economics, an obvious example would be the Zapatistas or La Via Campesina.[20] I opted instead to bring the example of a scientist and philosopher, Maturana, into the conversation, with two purposes in mind. The first was to illustrate what I mean by delinking from the CMP (in this case, in the domain of science) and changing the terms of the conversation, which is achieved by changing the questions. Delinking doesn't mean that you abandon whatever domain of the CMP you delink from; rather, it means that you become epistemically and politically disobedient, departing from standard questions allowed by the discipline or in everyday life, exposing the vulnerability and fictionality of what passes for reality, and engaging, as many people on the planet already do, in rebuilding the communal.[21]

Second, referencing Maturana allows me to stress that changing the terms of the conversation is an epistemic struggle and that the decolonial work should be equivalent and parallel to political societies on the move and to scientists such as Maturana. In fact, the control of knowledge in the sphere of the social sciences and the place of the social sciences in CMP would require to delink, a treatment similar to Maturana's treatment of the field of the hard sciences: changing the terms of the conversation would lead to bypass the positivity of the social sciences and to ask for their role in the constitution and dissemination of the narratives profiling the idea and the imaginary of Western "modernity."

Although I have alerted you to the prickliness of the Maturana example, as well as to my motives for choosing it, you may still have a negative reaction, worrying that it sounds New Agey rather than scientific, apolitical, and out of touch with reality. (Indeed, some scientists would call Maturana a metaphysician.) In the sphere of the political society, considering the case of the Zapatistas and La Via Campesina, you may think these enterprises are hopeless in their attempts to delink from the Mexican state and from massive corporations such as Monsanto. If you have such a reaction, I would suspect that you are still caught in the spider's web of the rhetoric of modernity and in preserving the disenchantment of the world.

If you do feel discomfort, it may help to know that Maturana's biology of cognition and the biology of love (I will leave aside the Zapatistas and Via Campesina for now) emerged out of the unexpected situation of his experience in Santiago de Chile, during the years of Salvador Allende and the military coup that ended democracy with the dictatorship of Augusto Pinochet. This was the historical moment when Chile became the launching pad and testing ground for neoliberal doctrine, and it was in precisely this moment that Maturana understood the iron cage of the scientific and true version of things, with its self-regulating rules. Maturana's well-known dictum summarizes the point: we do not see what there is; we see what we see. This tautology at once shows how the coloniality of knowledge works and points to the necessity of delinking from the irrational beliefs that sustain scientific rational arguments.

Certainly, it is not love and the communal that we see in today's state institutions, banks, corporations, media, army, police, and all the other institutions involved in the current world (dis)order. It would be futile to expect that anyone in the United Nations, the G7, or the G20 would engage with this kind of discourse and take seriously the need to change the terms of the conversation. For that would mean putting institutions exclusively at the service of the people and their well-being, and this is simply not something that existing institutions, and their defenders, are willing to consider. The most that is being considered is light reform's of existing institutions, which does not even amount to changing the content of the conversation. Only dewesternization is taking that more drastic step, and it has given rise to all the well-known fears, demonizations, and strategies of contention on the part of the West.

Given all of this, there is not much that we—scholars, intellectuals, activists, journalists, and former state officers—can decolonially and immediately do to remedy the situation and to intervene in the growing conflicts between rewesternization and dewesternization. But there is much we can and should do to create long-term alternatives and pathways toward a life of communal horizons, where care would take precedence over personal success, where working to live would supersede living to work, where competition would be displaced by cooperation, and where institutions would be at the service of people instead of people being at the service of institutions.[22]

Closing and Opening

In an attempt to address questions about the causes of the prevailing global chaos and malaise, I have argued that the current situation should be explained, at least in part, by the history and development of the CMP, and by the growing dispute over it (rewesternization versus dewesternization). The effect of this increasing disputes underscoring the mutation from the unipolar to a multipolar world order is to mobilize and reorganize local conflicts around a global power struggle. The extreme complexities unfolded in Syria are in large measure tangled up with the dispute over the control and management of the CMP—which means, for some, maintaining long-lasting privileges and, for others, ending a situation that has created privileges for some and humiliation for others.

Addressing the second of the two initial questions that provoked this argument I have suggested that alternatives to the current chaos cannot come from the creators and managers of the CMP, for the simple reason that neither the content nor the terms of the conversation can be changed without first questioning the rules, institutions, and subjectivities that established the hegemonic terms and contents of the CMP in the first place.

I have also suggested that changes to the content of the conversation are to be found in the vision and projects of dewesternization, while changes to the terms of the conversation lie with decoloniality. I have further specified that dewesternization is a set of state-led projects, while decoloniality is in the hands of an emerging global political society that is delinking from the system of knowledge and assumptions embedded in the CMP. The CMP is not an autonomous entity, self-created and self-functioning. It was created by individuals who established institutions and implemented rules and principles for these institutions to follow, all within a set of languages that defined the bounds and principles of knowing and sensing, thereby creating knowledge and forming subjectivities.

Neither of the large axes at work (dewesternization or decoloniality) will achieve short-term tangible results. Dewesternization and decoloniality are moved by the energy of liberation, but rewesternization is moved by the reluctance to lose the privileges that Westernization has created. And losing privileges is a difficult reality to accept. Some of the causes and reasons behind the current malaise can be found in the West's moves and strategies to maintain managerial control over the CMP, which means maintaining a unipolar world order. The multipolar world order that dewesternization is creating and the pluriversal delinking from both rewesternization and dewesternization that decoloniality is aiming at are both struggles for liberation, and liberation always comes with violence and chaos.

Changing the terms of the conversations is undoubtedly a complex issue that shall be enacted in all the domains of the CMP managed and controlled by the level of the enunciation: from beliefs fueling the hard sciences and technologies, to the social sciences and the humanities, to art and museums, to everyday imaginary managed by the mass media and the consumption of technological gadgets and services. Changing the terms of the conversation is necessary for delinking not only from the hegemony of Western knowledge but also from the hegemony of the content of the conversation, which entangles dewesternization with rewesternization today.

NOTES

1. See the famous Matteo Ricci's map, http://centrici.hypotheses.org/70. I have ellaborated on this map in *The Darker Side of the Renaissance: Literacy, Territoriality and Colonization* (Ann Arbor: University of Michigan Press, 2nd ed., 2003), chapter 5.

2. Klaus Schwab, *The Fourth Industrial Revolution* (Switzerland: World Economic Forum, 2016).

3. "North Alantic Universals: Analytic Fictions, 1492–1945", *South Atlantic Quarterly* 101.4 (2002): 839–58.

4. See, for instance, Council of Bioethics, *Beyond Therapy. Biotechnology and the Pursuit of Happiness* (Washington, DC: Council of Bioethics, 2003); Kaushik Sunder Rajan, *Biocapital: The Constitution of the Postgenomic Life* (Durham, NC: Duke University Press, 2007); Nikolas Rose, *The Politics of Life Itself: Biomedicine, Power, and Subjectivity in the Twenty-First Century* (Princeton, NJ: Princeton University Press, 2007).

5. "Decolonial Aesthetics/Aesthesis Has Become a Connector across Continents: A Conversation with Walter Mignolo," *C& Magazine*, August 7, 2014, http://www .contemporaryand.com/magazines/decolonial-aestheticsaesthesis-has-become-a -connector-across-the-continent/.

6. Nina Pacari speech at that conference. From what I said could be inferred, "La incidencia de la participación política de los pueblos indígenas: un camino irreversible." In Heriberto Cairo Carau and Walter D. Mignolo, eds. *Las vertientes americanas del pensamiento y proyecto des-colonial* (Madrid: Trama Editorial, 2008): 47–60.

7. For the conceptual structures (theory) known as modernity/coloniality/decoloniality, see Mignolo (2011).

8. I am assuming here—without space, unfortunately, for a longer explanation—that the consolidation and expansion of Western civilization (from 1500 to 2000) was also the consolidation and expansion of the idea of modernity, which I also render as the "rhetoric of modernity"—rhetoric in the sense of persuasive discourses.

9. Latouche's story begins mid-seventeenth century, mine (ours, shall I say) in 1500. If you start in 1650, or around there, you will not see the similarities between two events five hundred years apart: the dismantling of the great civilization of the New World makes it easier to see the similarities with the invasion of Iraq in 2003. This is not a linear history, but a spiraling one within the same project: the homogenization of the planet according to Western designs.

10. "Nomos (Greek: 'law,' or 'custom'), plural Nomoi, in law, the concept of law in ancient Greek philosophy." *Encyclopaedia Britannica*, http://www.britannica.com/topic/nomos-Greek-philosophy.

11. Schmitt's (2006) superb argument and narrative is half of the story—the European half of the story. Without reference to Schmitt, Siba N' Zatioula Grovogui (1996) argued and narrated the other half: how does one see and feel international law from Africa instead of seeing and feeling it from Europe?

12. See Clover and Hornby (2015). On the other side of the equation, see Escobar (2015).

13. Pepe Escobar, "Xi's Road Map to the Chinese Dream," *Asia Times*, October 21, 2017, http://www.atimes.com/article/xis-road-map-chinese-dream/; Charlotte Gao, "Three Majors Takeaways from Xi Jinping's Speech at the 19th Party Congress," *The Diplomat*, October 18, 2017, https://thediplomat.com/2017/10/3-major-takeaways-from-xi-jinpings-speech-at-the-19th-party-congress/.

14. Quoted in *Value Walk*, October 3, 2015: http://www.valuewalk.com/2015/10/china-russia-to-promote-and-protect-world-peace/.

15. Some examples: La Via Campesina (http://viacampesina.org/en/), the Zapatistas (http://enlacezapatista.ezln.org.mx/), the Kurdish revolution in Syria (Graeber 2014).

16. Dialogue (DOC) of Civilization Research Institute, https://doc-research.org/en/.

17. See for instance the essay by Richard Sakwa, "One Europe or None," October 27, 2017, https://doc-research.org/en/one-europe-none/.

18. The reader not familiar with Maturana's thoughts can find a summary in this lecture: https://www.youtube.com/watch?v=twne4EqY15w.

19. For Humberto Maturana on language, see Maturana, Mpodozis, and Letelier (1995); on language and cognition, see Maturana (1978).

20. The Zapatistas, http://enlacezapatista.ezln.org.mx/; La Via Campesina, http://viacampesina.org/en/.

21. Maturana's changing the terms of the conversation could be appreciated in this classical essay: "Reality: The Search of Objectivity or the Search for Compelling Arguments," *The Irish Journal of Psychology*, 9.1 (1988): 25–82.

22. I do not have space here to explore in more detail case studies and the theoretical explorations under the heading of "rethinking organization." Of interest in this unfolding mainly within developed countries is the fact that more people are delinking in different ways and intensity from global designs and working toward autonomic organizations (see Laloux 2014). The book theorizes and illustrates the degree of discomfort within the corporate world that leads to organizations based on human relations rather than

profit. Thus *New Stage of Human Consciousness* in the subtitle. What the book illustrates is that within the sphere of rewesternization there is an emerging tendency to change the content of the conversations while maintaining the terms. Dewesternization and decoloniality are different aspects of the "new stage of human consciousness" that has been reinventing organizations based on nonwestern local histories.

REFERENCES

Angie, Antony. 2007. *Imperialism, Sovereignty and the Making of International Law.* Cambridge: Cambridge University Press.

Chatterjee, Partha. 2004. *The Politics of the Governed: Reflections on Popular Politics in Most of the World.* New York: Columbia University Press.

Clover, Charles, and Lucy Hornby. 2015. "China's Great Game: Road to a New Empire." *Financial Times*, October 12. http://www.ft.com/cms/s/2/6e098274-587a-11e5-a28b-50226830d644.html#axzz3y1jOKbSV.

Escobar, Pepe. 2015. "The New Great Game between China and the US." *TomDispatch*, November. http://www.tomdispatch.com/blog/176072/tomgram%3A_pepe_escobar,_the_new_great_game_between_china_and_the_u.s./.

Graeber, David. 2014. "Why Is the World Ignoring the Revolutionary Kurds in Syria?" *Guardian*, October 8. http://www.theguardian.com/commentisfree/2014/oct/08/why-world-ignoring-revolutionary-kurds-syria-isis.

Grovogui, Siba N' Zatioula. 1996. *Sovereign, Quasi Sovereign and Africans: Race and Self-Determination in International Law.* Minneapolis: University of Minnesota Press.

Grovogui, Siba N' Zatioula. 2006. *Beyond Eurocentrism and Anarchy.* New York: Palgrave Macmillan.

Laloux, Frederic. 2014. *Reinventing Organizations: A Guide to Creating Organizations Inspired by the New Stage of Human Consciousness.* Brussels: Nelson Parker.

Latouche, Serge. 1989. *L'Occidentalizaton du monde: Essai sur la signification, la portée et les limites de l'uniformisation planetaire.* Paris: La Découverte/Poche.

Maturana, Humberto. 1978. "Biology of Language: The Epistemology of Reality." In *Psychology and Biology of Language and Thought: Essays in Honor of Eric Lenneberg*, ed. George A. Miller and Elizabeth Lenneberg, 27–63. New York: Academic Press.

Maturana, Humberto. 2004. *From Being to Doing: The Origins of Biology of Cognition.* Heidelberg: Carl Auer International..

Maturana, Humberto, Jorge Mpodozis, and Juan Carlos Letelier. 1995. "Brain, Language and the Origin of Human Mental Functions." *Biological Research* 28:15–26 http://www.enolagaia.com/MatMpo&Let%281995%29.html.

Maturana, Humberto, and Gerda Verden-Zoller. 2009. *The Origin of Humaness and the Biology of Love.* Exeter: Imprint Academic.

Mignolo, Walter D. 2009. "The Communal and the Decolonial." *Turbulence.* http://www.turbulence.org.uk/turbulence-5/decolonial/.

Mignolo, Walter D. 2011. "Modernity and Decoloniality." *Oxford Bibliographies.* http://www.oxfordbibliographies.com/view/document/obo-9780199766581/obo-9780199766581-0017.xml.

Mignolo, Walter. 2016. "The Making and Closing of Eurocentric International Law: The Opening of a Multipolar World Order." *Comparative Studies of South Asia, Africa and the Middle East* 36 (1): 182–95.

Mignolo, Walter, and Arturo Escobar, eds. 2010. *Globalization and the Decolonial Option.* London: Routlege.

Schirmacher, Frank. 2015. *Ego: The Game of Life.* London: Polity.

Schmitt, Carl. 2006. *The Nomos of the Earth in the International Law of the Ius Publicum Europaeum.* Translated by G. L. Ullmen. Candor, NY: Telos.

Smith, Linda. 1999. *Decolonizing Methodologies: Research and Indigenous People.* London: Zed.

Trenin, Dmitri. 2016. "The Revival of the Russian Military: How Moscow Reloaded." *Foreign Affairs,* May–June. https://www.foreignaffairs.com/articles/russia-fsu/2016-04-18/revival-russian-military.

5 · Internationalism and Speaking for Others

What Struggling against Neoliberal Globalization
Taught Me about Epistemology

This chapter is written mainly from the perspective of the North, but not quite. Having been born and raised in Germany, I was regularly reminded that people with the surname Ziai Ardastaninejad are not accepted as real Germans, no matter what their skin color is or what their passport states. Yet this chapter is based on experiences I had in the North in the struggle against neoliberal globalization, and the new ways to think about knowledge and politics I have learned in this movement. Like so many others, I was brought to the movement by the appalling injustices in the global economy, by the structural adjustment programs of the International Monetary Fund (IMF) and World Bank, and the free trade enforcement of the World Trade Organization (WTO). In this movement I learned a lot, not only about political economy, but also about knowledge claims, epistemology, and political utopias.

Not Answering the Question "What Do You Want?"

I cannot even remember whether it was in Geneva 1998 or Prague 2000 or somewhere else, but the words still stick in my mind today. We were a bunch of demonstrators determined not to let the G7, the IMF, the World Bank, and the WTO decide on the fate of hundreds of millions of people and push through their neoliberal policies—at least not without our protest, not without the little that we dared and could do against it. We probably should have been thankful when the journalist from the renowned TV station came up to us, picked a handsome guy with dreadlocks from the crowd, held out the microphone, and asked him, "So we understand you are against free trade agreements and the current world order. But what do you actually want?," to which he replied, "I can't tell you what 'we' want, because I cannot speak for all of us. No one can." And the crowd cheered and hooted in support. The journalist frowned and turned away, not understanding why the guy could not simply state some political demands and be done with it, but those of us cheering in the crowd would have said exactly the same.

My first claim—which I cannot prove in any serious way—is that this scene was typical of the spirit of what became known as the antiglobalization movement in the late 1990s and probably took place in a similar manner a hundred times. The difference from earlier left-wing movements was not the lack of political demands. The guy with dreadlocks could easily have replied that the WTO has to be shut down, Third World debt canceled, and the IMF and World Bank democratized, just as his predecessors would have said that the Sandinistas should be left alone, the apartheid system put down, and nuclear power plants abolished. The difference does not belong to the content of politics, the policy, but the frames and procedures of political processes, the polity. My second claim—which I elaborate in this chapter—is that the episode manifests a new way of thinking about politics, knowledge, and power. A way that is influenced heavily by Foucault and postcolonial criticism, but at least as much by the Zapatistas and debates about internationalism. A way that, some critical voices might add with a view to the anarchist tradition, is not entirely new after all.

So why did he refuse to answer? Because he was aware that in that moment, he was put in a position of power by the journalist, who took him as a representative of the movement. Unless there had been a prior consensus about the answer, he would have subordinated all the others' views and agendas. He would have been allowed to articulate or even establish what the political objective of the movement was. Answering the question would thus have constituted relations of power between the one who speaks and those he spoke for. And the other demonstrators were very sensitive to such a move.

Speaking for Others and the Postcolonial Critique

It is difficult to precisely establish the roots of sensitivity to such relations of power, but very likely that Foucault and postcolonial critique were major influences. As Foucault has shown in his inaugural address, "to speak is to do something" (1972, 209), to discursively construct what we perceive as reality according to certain rules, and the right to speak is often linked to certain professions, institutional sites, and subject positions (50–54). The question of who speaks and in general the production of truth through language are always linked to questions of power (Foucault 1980). This is why Foucault and Deleuze (1972) criticize "the indignity of speaking for others" and "the people who claim to be a representative, who make a profession of speaking for others" while aiming at "conditions that permit the prisoners themselves to speak, . . . to speak and act on their own behalf." Now many different groups of people in history have been denied the right to speak and act on their own behalf: prisoners, those defined as insane, children, the lower classes, the uneducated, or women in general. In the face of a five-hundred-year history of European colonialism, the claim to speak for so-called backward and colonized peoples and act as trustees on their behalf has been among the most pertinent.

Therefore, the question of speaking for others has been a significant issue in postcolonial studies. In "Under Western Eyes: Feminist Scholarship and Colonial Discourses," Chandra Mohanty (1984) has written a classic text that criticizes the construction of "Third World women" as a category based on a cross-cultural experience of patriarchal oppression in feminist texts originating in the North. Highlighting the political effects of categories and methods, it reveals the colonialist move of knowing and articulating what the Third World women's problem is while neglecting different forms of oppression and implicitly denying their capacity to act as subjects of emancipation without the help of the West. Thus well-meaning Western feminists speaking for the oppressed from a position of privilege end up reproducing relations of power between the West and its Other.

Interestingly, another classic text of postcolonial studies arrives at different conclusions. Gayatri Spivak's "Can the Subaltern Speak?" not only criticizes the British colonialists' desire to establish the principle of white men saving brown women from brown men; it also takes issue with Foucault and Deleuze's statements (1972) that reject speaking for the oppressed, and the author asks, puzzled, "What has happened to the critique of the sovereign subject in these pronouncements?" (Spivak 1994, 69). What irritates her is that the very theorists who have shown the subject to be not autonomous but constituted by manifold discourses suddenly, in their political activism, reintroduce the idea of an authentic, knowing, and oppressed subject. She criticizes their "indifference to ideology (a theory of which is necessary for an understanding of interests)" (68) and their refusal to speak for others as failing their responsibility as intellectuals, because, and here she quotes Marx affirmatively, oppressed groups such as peasants "cannot represent themselves; they must be represented" (71). The idea of self-representation, as put forward by the activist refusing to answer the question, for Spivak amounts to an "essentialist, utopian politics" (71).

Of course, the analogy to the globalization movement may seem unconvincing at first, as the person invited to speak was not an intellectual speaking for the oppressed, but apart from the differences of class, education, and experience within the group it has to be taken into account as well that we perceived ourselves as part of a global movement, the larger part of which was situated in the South and had no comparable opportunity to articulate itself. But is Spivak then not right in pointing to the responsibility to speak for those who have no voice? There seems to be a dilemma: on the one hand we are assuming a position of authority if we claim to know what others want and articulate their interest. From an antiauthoritarian perspective, this claim is unwarranted unless there is prior discussion and consensus among those concerned. On the other hand, political agency is certainly confined by such a perspective. From a different perspective, this amounts to political paralysis and failing the responsibility of the intellectual to use her or his privileged position appropriately.

Interestingly, this dilemma has been recognized as such and tackled similarly not only by postcolonial critics, but also by some thinkers in development studies—refining Sylvester's statement that "development studies tends not to listen to the subaltern and postcolonial studies tends not to be concerned whether the subaltern is eating" (1999, 703). Apparently a few theorists of both camps have been concerned with discursive as well as material relations of power. In postcolonial studies, Laura Alcoff in her brilliant treatment of the issue refers to the refusal to speak for others as the retreat response to the dilemma: "This response is simply to retreat from all practices of speaking for and assert that one can only know one's own narrow individual experience and one's 'own truth' and can never make claims beyond this" (1992, 17; for a discussion see Marino [2005]). While she argues this may be the "proper response" in some situations, she also warns that this "may result merely in a retreat into a narcissistic yuppie lifestyle in which a privileged person takes no responsibility for her society whatsoever" (17).

In development studies, Stuart Corbridge (1994, 103) claims that "an unwillingness to speak for others is every bit as foundational a claim as is the suggestion that we can speak for others in an unproblematic manner." This is very close to Spivak's position, who of course realizes the relation of power involved in speaking for others but insists on the political necessity of doing so in some contexts. According to Corbridge, the central question is "how can we argue for a minimally universalist politics . . . without rejecting the essential insights of post-modernism (that so-called universal claims are often no more than white mythologies which occlude a more purposive politics of local resistance)?" (1994, 103). He concludes, "The point is that to change the world it is first necessary to offer an account of the world and then to put into circulation a blueprint for change. . . . A related point is that a commitment to change the world need not take the form of a presumption to act for others on the grounds that what we know is best" (112).

Although one does not have to agree with Corbridge's solution, the dilemma is clear: how can we formulate political utopias and agendas if we must not speak for others and thus prescribe how the world we want to live in has to look? Let us see how political movements struggling against neoliberal globalization in the 1990s and 2000s have dealt with this dilemma. First, I deal with the globalization movement and People's Global Action (PGA), and then with the internationalist groups in Germany assembled in the BUKO (Bundeskongress entwicklungspolitischer Aktionsgruppen/Bundeskongress Internationalismus).

Zapatista Politics and People's Global Action

When the scene depicted in the first section took place, I was only vaguely aware of the theoretical discussion outlined above, and I assume this holds true for a good part of my fellow activists. Yet we were extremely sensitive to these questions of power, and our solution to the dilemma was based on what I call Zapatista politics. These politics are inspired by the uprising of the Ejército Zapatista de Liberación Nacional (EZLN) in Chiapas, Mexico, in 1994 and the subsequent political practices in the occupied territories, but probably even more by the messages of Subcomandante Marcos and the slogans supposedly describing the Zapatista position, that is, by the discursive construction of Zapatismo (for the following see Muñoz Ramírez [2003]; Hayden [2002]; for a more recent discussion see Guillén [2016]). Examining some of these slogans provides some insight into Zapatista politics.

"Un mundo donde quepan muchos mundos"—a world in which many worlds fit. This slogan is markedly different from that of the World Social Forum (WSF; "Another world is possible") in that it refuses to reduce the alternatives to the existing system to one model that is universally applicable. Based on the experience of the WSF, Santos (2014, 192) points out the "unprecedented confrontation between radically different conceptions of alternatives society, so much so that they cannot be brought together under the umbrella of a single totalizing alternative." The claim to have found the one alternative would again subordinate the heterogeneity of alternatives—in the face of different alternative conceptions it would be the equivalent of answering the journalist's question and speaking for all the others. Instead, there is no claim to know how another world should look apart from the demand that it has to be one where different conceptions of alternatives fit in so that none is subordinated, and self-determination can be achieved for all.[1]

"Preguntando caminamos"—asking questions, we walk. Again, the slogan manifests a rejection of the claim to know. The certainty to know the way forward—toward progress, development, or communism—has been a characteristic feature of Western modernity and in particular of teleological philosophies of history after the fashion of Hegel, Marx, Comte, or Rostow, not least among the political left.[2] The Zapatistas explicitly do not claim to know the way and how society should look at its end. Yet they feel they know enough to start walking, without knowing where they will end—the loss of modern certainties does not lead them to political paralysis. Yet there is an awareness of the danger that certain knowledge entails: as Bauman (1992) has shown, foundational knowledge legitimates foundational politics, and the violent historical record of regimes based on scientific socialism is no mere coincidence. A related diagnosis can be found in Scott's (1998) critique of high modernism.

The awareness of the dangerous implications of certain leftist politics also seems to lie at the basis of the last quote: "No es necesario conquistar el mundo. Basta con que lo hagamos de nuevo. Nosotros hoy." (It is not necessary to conquer the world. It is enough that we remake it. Us, today.) Distancing themselves from earlier guerillas in Latin America, the Zapatistas reject the notion of taking power and conquering the state apparatus—either by force or by elections (see also Holloway 2002). The creative power of people is highlighted instead, in line with the post-structuralist idea that structures exist only as long as they are continuously reproduced by agents (see also Gibson-Graham 1996).

Some of these concerns can also be found in People's Global Action against "Free" Trade and the WTO (PGA), which was—inspired by the Zapatistas—created in 1998 as a platform for dialogue between social movements, not an organization. Arising from the intercontinental meetings called for by the Zapatistas in Mexico (1996) and Spain (1997), PGA was founded in Geneva 1998 shortly before the WTO ministerial meeting. Present were delegates from organizations and movements such as the Movimento dos Trabalhadores Rurais Sem Terra (MST) from Brazil, the Karnataka Rajya Ryota Singha (KRRS) from India, the Movement for the Survival of the Ogoni Peoples (MOSOP) from Nigeria, Mama 86 from the Ukraine, the Canadian Union of Postal Workers, and the student network Play Fair Europe! During the late 1990s and early 2000s PGA was very active, but it has seen relatively little activity (at least under the name PGA) during the past decade.

Concerning the question of speaking for others, one of PGA's five hallmarks stresses "an organisational philosophy based on decentralisation and autonomy. PGA is an instrument of coordination, not an organisation. It has no members and no legal representation. No organisation or person can represent PGA" (PGA 2001; Habermann 2014, 47; see also Banse and Habermann 2012).

There was thus no leadership. During PGA conferences only the convenors of the next conference were elected.

The PGA manifesto began with the following quote: "If you come only to help me, you can go back home. But if you consider my struggle as part of your struggle for survival, then maybe we can work together" (PGA 1998). The quote was ascribed to an "Aboriginal woman." Her name was Lilla Watson, from Brisbane, and the exact wording was slightly different: "If you come only to help me, you are wasting your time. But if you come because your liberation is bound up with mine, then let us work together!" (Habermann 2014, 46). This expresses a clear commitment to globalization in what is still sometimes mistakenly called the antiglobalization movement—concerning, however, a globalization of struggles for emancipation, not a neoliberal globalization of the economy. Yet it also expresses an understanding of international solidarity that is different from the idea that people in the North support the struggle of people in the South by donating money or joining brigades—an understanding that was common during the 1970s and 1980s in western Europe, but one that perceives solidarity as a one-way street and reproduces the Eurocentric division between those who help and those who need help, and thus establishes relations of power. By donating the five hundred dollars he was to receive for an interview of Italian factory workers who were on strike, Subcomandante Marcos subverted this pattern, establishing a two-way solidarity. "Your struggle is our struggle, too," was his comment (Sternfeld 2010). In rejecting the traditional pattern, PGA and Marcos already engaged in what has been called postmodern internationalism.

Postmodern Internationalism and Undeveloping the North

In this section, I do not focus on the whole debate on internationalism in Germany and Austria (see Fischer and Zimmermann 2008; Foitzik and Marvakis 1997; Gruppe Demontage 1998; Hanloser 1994; Hierlmeier 2002; Kößler 1988; Kössler and Melber 2002; Rössel 1994; for an overview of the international debate see Sluga, Clavin, and Amrith 2016), but focus on the debates within BUKO in the late 1990s (BUKO 2003; Redaktion Alaska 1998; Schwertfisch 1997; Spehr 1998; Wissen 1998). Formerly BUKO stood for Bundeskongress entwicklungspolitischer Aktionsgruppen, a federal congress of development policy action groups. In 2002, it was renamed Bundeskoordination Internationalismus, federal coordination of internationalism, which was by then a more adequate description. In particular, I would like to highlight how in some of these debates the critique of speaking for others and in general of a positivist epistemology led to the incorporation of new elements under the heading "postmodern internationalism."

While there was widespread agreement in these debates during the 1990s that the new world order after the demise of Soviet-style socialism required rethinking traditional assumptions of internationalism (as it had been understood since 1968), few went as far as the BUKO journal *Alaska* in their contribution (Redaktion Alaska 1998). While they maintain that the traditional focus of internationalism on posing questions about domination and liberation on a global scale and its perception of the current order as one based on the history of imperialism and resistance is still correct (Redaktion Alaska 1998, 8), they argue that in the (then) current historical situation, some revisions are necessary. The concept of new internationalism reflected these revisions:

- There is no revolutionary subject. Processes of emancipation are as diverse as the politicization of the subjects.
- The concept of an avant-garde is finished. All of us are constituted by relations of domination, albeit in different ways, and emancipation requires self-determination, not leadership.
- There is no central contradiction in the relation between labor and capital. Different relations of oppression and their historical dynamics are fundamental.
- Taking over the state and enforcing emancipatory social change from above does not work. Emancipation has to arise from society and can merely be supported by state policy.
- Progress and development do not automatically lead to democracy or socialism, but often take the form of violence and oppression.
- There is no objectivity that can determine other people's position and what they need.
- Socialization and economic planning are not necessarily the keys to a better world. (9)

Thus new internationalism prioritized resistance against domination in one's own country, recognizing the equal value of different struggles for emancipation, and abandoned the idea of universalizing the Northern model of development. Yet, the *Alaska* editors argue, it still clings to a typically modern concept of emancipation: There is a radical divide between emancipation and existing social relations; emancipation has to encompass all aspects of life (otherwise it is not radical); emancipation is the liberation of something that is already there (as if it was not shaped by the relations to be liberated from);

and because emancipation deals with the foundation or real cause of inequality and domination, it will do away with asymmetrical power (so there is no need to think about power afterward). The problems with this concept are the following: the radical divide privileges those who can best escape the necessities of reproduction under the existing social relations—typically men. The postmodern concept of emancipation promoted by them does not compete for the maximal distance from existing social structures nor search for the real cause of oppression. It sees emancipation as a process, not a one-time revolution, so that there will never be a point when emancipation becomes unnecessary (the classless society). It further rejects the division between leftists and the masses who have to be educated or at least convinced and is suspicious of ideas that can legitimize domination and violence, even in the name of emancipation (Redaktion Alaska 1998, 10ff.).

The debates about this kind of internationalism within BUKO were manifest in the concept of undeveloping the North (Abwicklung des Nordens[3]—see Bernhard et al. 1997; Hüttner 1997; Spehr 1996, 209–36; Spehr 1997), which consciously opposed the idea of developing the South as well as the discourse of sustainable development. The latter was seen as an ecological modernization of corporate capitalism that reproduced ideas of Western superiority, patriarchal faith in science and technology, and unjustified trust in planning and development (Hüttner 1997, 141). Instead, the concept suggested a political program that took into account the criticism of traditional internationalism yet refused the solutions proposed by ecofeminist subsistence approaches as too focused on agriculture and too little concerned with macropolitical alternatives and struggles— in the end as building a noncapitalist niche (Bernhard et al. 1997, 195ff.).

Undeveloping the North perceives the North not primarily as a geographical area, but as a model of society and a system of domination (Spehr 1997, 4), in which some groups are forced to provide their productive, reproductive, and emotional labor for a pittance while others (disproportionally often found in the North) enjoy unjust privileges. It is explicitly focused not on niches, but on general social structures that are to be tackled from the bottom up, and it aims at reducing the amount of work and nature to be exploited within these structures, thus on strengthening autonomy. Its five principles are:

1 Preventing the capacity of the North for military interventions to maintain its access to labor and nature ("No blood for oil" was the corresponding slogan against the wars in Iraq).
2 Pushing back the global sector, which forces local initiatives into global competition and thus eliminates economic alternatives.

3 Deprivileging of formal labor, which excludes major parts of the
   population from the benefits of the welfare state through the provision of basic social security for all.
4 Direct appropriation of spaces and relationships for the satisfaction
   of needs ("land and freedom").
5 Measures for securing survival, preventing the use of large areas for
   the global sector instead of for local food security in the South, and
   rebuilding structures to achieve this goal also in the North, where
   people have profited from a colonial division of labor until today.
   (Spehr 1996, 214–23)

In contrast to some ideas of sustainable development, undeveloping the
North insists that it is not legitimate, for example, for Northern actors to prevent deforestation of the Brazilian rain forest in the name of a global environmental consciousness ("saving the planet"). In contrast to some ecofeminist
approaches, it is not centered around an individual ethics of ecological production and consumption, nor does it accept a spiritual proximity of women
and nature. In contrast to some postdevelopment approaches, it does not want
to prevent Westernization, modernization, and industrialization. This is the
point where the concept is linked to debates about Zapatista politics and not
speaking for others: undeveloping the North explicitly avoids statements on
how societies should organize and produce, except for the principle that they
must not do so on the basis of exploiting other groups' work and resources.
However, this principle would severely limit attempts to modernize and indus-
trialize (Spehr 1996, 224). Undeveloping the North does not abolish capitalism,
patriarchy, and racism, but offers a way of dealing with social and ecological
crises that does not reproduce these structures. It merely aims at providing a
frame for the future arrangement of society (Spehr 1996, 226). Recently, the
concept has been taken up in the context of the degrowth debate in Germany
(Bendix 2016; Habermann 2012).

Free Cooperation

The most explicit political theory arising out of these discussions in BUKO was
articulated by Christoph Spehr. In his lighthearted, creative, and funny writings about very serious political and theoretical issues, he has attempted to deal
with the dilemma of formulating a political program of emancipation without
becoming guilty of formulating blueprints on the basis of privileged knowledge, which then merely need to be implemented, reproducing authoritarian

implications. This program elaborates the concept of undeveloping the North in the politics of free cooperation (Spehr 1996, 1999, 2003). The most elaborate of these attempts (Spehr 2003) has won the Rosa Luxemburg Foundation prize for answering the question, "Under which conditions can social equality and political freedom be united?" Spehr's answer was that there is no policy, no set of political institutions that can guarantee such a condition, and that of course political freedom in democratic capitalism is not freedom, just as social equality in socialist dictatorships is not equality. But, he argues, there is a politics that will best allow conditions of freedom and equality, and that is the politics of free cooperation (Spehr 2003, 27).

Inspired by Rousseau's image of people being free to leave the tree, that is, the social place where they live, the theory assumes that people are free and equal under the condition of free cooperation, which is based on three rules: (1) the existing rules and the existing distribution of property are not sacrosanct and can be changed at any time through negotiations; (2) all members of a free cooperation can limit their contribution and demand conditions for their cooperation in order to change the rules or leave it, and they have to be able to do so at costs that are affordable and comparable for everyone; and (3) free cooperation needs to ensure the condition of affordable and comparable costs (Spehr 2003, 28). Emancipation arises from leaving cooperations in which we are exploited, mistreated, or humiliated and/or from changing the rules of the cooperation on the basis of credible threats to leave it.

The point is that conditions must ensure that we can afford to leave a cooperation. That women can leave their abusive husbands. That workers can threaten to leave or take over the company. That those suffering racist or sexist or other kinds of discrimination can resist it and end it without having to fear the consequences. That colonized peoples can chase off the colonizers without being killed or starved. Conceptualizing domination as enforced cooperation, Spehr (2003, 36) distinguishes between different levels of domination, between different methods of forcing people to live and work in cooperations which are not free:

1 The exertion or threat of physical violence—the military level of domination, ranging from fists to nuclear bombs.
2 Structural subordination, the establishment and reproduction of rules and distributions in a social cooperation leading to a systematically biased accumulation of goods and power—the economic level of cooperation, ranging from the division of labor within the household to the terms of trade in world trade.

3 Discrimination, the excluding solidarity of one group against the rest—the social level of domination. This could be social ostracism for those exhibiting deviant sexual behavior or not renting flats to people of color in certain neighborhoods or any other form of exclusion.[4]

4 Control of the public, that is, influence on how people think and speak, and which interpretations and norms are dominant—the institutional level of domination. I think this one should be renamed the discursive or ideological level.

5 Dependency, that is, the elimination of alternatives for other partners in the cooperation, making it impossible to leave—the existential level of domination. This dependency can be technical— produced by terminator seeds, for example—but also psychological or emotional.[5]

To ensure domination, the instruments of domination of the different levels have to be translated: translating military superiority into economic subordination of others, or translating economic superiority into control of the public, or using a mixture of both to ensure the exclusion and isolation of deviant persons or countries (think of Cuba or Iran and other so-called rogue states). A German professor may never use violence to force a cleaning woman into a certain cooperation, but he or she may well profit because she was forced to flee from Bosnia or Russia by physical violence or economic necessity, as well as because her diplomas were not recognized by German authorities (social exclusion), and thus leaving her few alternatives apart from working as a cleaning woman. He or she may also profit from cleaning women not being organized in a union, their work being regarded as unqualified, and their having little influence on the public debate (Spehr 2003, 37). The point is to reflect on why people enter such cooperations instead of resorting to a simple liberalism that assumes everyone is free to choose the cooperations he or she wants. The political objective of the theory is to abolish or at least diminish these relations of domination to ensure a free and equal, or at least a more free and equal, cooperation.[6]

The theory of free cooperation thus formulates a political utopia, but at the same time takes into account the criticism that diverse actors (Foucault, the postcolonial critique, the Zapatistas, and the guy with dreadlocks who refused to answer the journalist's question) have formulated. It does not prescribe how the good life, the classless society, a decent relationship, or a state of emancipation looks; it merely seeks to strengthen the capacity of actors to negotiate and fight for their own version of it (56). Therefore it does not claim to have any privileged knowledge and rejects any form of condition for people's concerns to be legitimate (being at least eighteen years old, able to read, or having read Marx or Fanon or Beauvoir, for example) (57). Neither does it postulate privileged conflicts or relationships that are more important for emancipation than others—dealing with one kind of oppression while deferring to deal with the other kinds is rejected, recalling the experience of rapes in the "liberated" (i.e., cop-free) zones in the antipolice riots in Brixton in 1985 (57ff.). Consequently, radicalism in this concept means to include every aspect of our lives in the attempt to implement principles of free cooperation, not excluding those that are supposedly private and nonpolitical, such as questions of child rearing and toilet cleaning (58ff., see also 20ff. and 84). The basic principle of negotiation has been demonstrated by Zapatista women who, in preparation for the armed uprising of 1994, made their participation conditional on the men's consent to a revolutionary women's law and its implementation prior to any successful revolution (66).

Nevertheless, the theory of free cooperation does have a positive program. Corresponding to the different levels of domination, Spehr also outlines five strategies to attain the goal of free and equal cooperation. The first is the strategy of undeveloping the North already discussed above. The second is called "politics of relationships—alternative socialization." It strives to realize the condition that in relationships no other principle shall be relevant than the affordable and comparable costs for leaving it, not even constitutions or democratic majority decisions (84ff.). It also includes the exception of refugees: if people have no alternative because of war or persecution, we cannot legitimately refuse to enter into a cooperation with them by using Frontex (the EU's border management agency) to protect our borders (88). The third strategy is building social skills—which entails reflecting our histories and privileges as well as unlearning the skills of hierarchical cooperation (92). The fourth strategy, "practical critique of democracy/emancipatory democratization," entails perceiving democracy as merely one possible mode of dealing with conflicts of interest in a capitalist and patriarchal world. It also entails the decentralization of political power, affirmative action, and a basic income which guarantees that people cannot be forced into exploitative forms of cooperation (100–105). The fifth and last strategy is simply organization. It requires solidarity of individuals and groups and alliances that are not necessarily based on a unitary ideology but are recognizing the legitimacy of one another's struggle (108ff.).

"All theories," Robert Cox reminds us, "have a perspective. Perspectives derive from a position in time and space, specifically social and political time and space" (1996, 87). The political utopia of free cooperation—which has been sketched here only briefly—certainly bears the marks of its context and origin: a European political Left after the demise of the Soviet bloc. It recognizes how dangerous blueprints are in terms of dictating how people should live. It is entirely secular. And it is very much oriented toward communities made up of individuals consciously and voluntarily entering them. But it avoids the domination inherent in every argument that can be made against people's decisions to leave the tree and end some form of cooperation. According to this model, there can be no knowledge about other people's interests and about what is good for them, no speaking for others without their consent. Spehr's answer to Spivak's concerns discussed above would be: yes, there may be something like ideology, but to deny people's wish to leave some cooperation on the basis of knowledge about their being (supposedly) manipulated is to engage in the same type of ideological legitimation of force the (non-Stalinist) political Left wants to avoid.

Yet despite its discernible origin, the theory claims to be based on engagement with different types of struggles against domination and the corresponding theories. It argues that different theories in different social movements have usually focused on different aspects of domination, on different archetypes of oppression and struggle (Spehr 2003, 33ff.): Marxist theory has focused on the archetype of the worker who is exploited by the capitalist; feminist theory on the woman performing unremunerated reproductive labor and/or suffering sexual harassment and violence; theories of black emancipation on the slave being deported to a new world and treated as an object, not a human being; queer theory on the person constructed as a monster because of his or her sexuality in order to maintain conventional gender and family norms; and anticolonial theories on societies being invaded and destroyed, subordinated and controlled. Spehr argues that the more a theory focuses sharply on one of the archetypes and one type of oppression, the more the other types blur and fade away. This may lead to estrangement between different theories of emancipation (and even different generations: new ones may have a different experience of domination precisely because of the successes of the struggle of the old ones; 34). The crucial thing is to be aware of which perspective and which archetype we are focusing on.

CONCLUSION

This volume, after "having deconstructed Western-centric explanations of the Global South," argues that "we need to replace the old political philosophies and frameworks with new ones." The plural is important: there can be no question of us altogether converting to the Andean philosophy of buen vivir, as desirable as this might seem to some. Different contexts and struggles will produce different solutions. What I have done in this chapter is to present one possible new political philosophy that has its (superficial) origin in western Europe, yet has been very attentive to the postcolonial critique of speaking for others. The theory of free cooperation presents one attempt to deal with the dilemma of formulating a political alternative to the current imperial, patriarchal, and capitalist world order while avoiding the subject position of trusteeship (Cowen and Shenton 1996), of the expert who knows how a better world looks because he (less often she) possesses privileged knowledge about the subject matter. So the theory provides not a blueprint of a good society, but a blueprint for the struggle for a society in which those who are oppressed today have more agency in shaping it. It aims at strengthening the autonomy of individuals and groups by enhancing their capacity to influence relationships in which they live—or simply end them. In this way, it avoids the relation of power inherent in every attempt to formulate how other people's future should look, yet insists on emancipation as a political goal. In its refusal to accept such relations of power even in the struggle for emancipation, it can be seen as an interesting reformulation of anarchism in the twenty-first century—albeit one that has learned the lessons of postcolonialism, thus recognizing its specificity and renouncing any claim to provide a universal blueprint.

NOTES

1. One could argue that this is the ontological equivalent of Santos's negative general epistemological stance: "a general epistemology of the impossibility of a general epistemology" (2014, 192).

2. A curious counterpoint could be found in Fukuyama's claim that after 1989, we had reached the "end of history."

3. The German noun *Abwicklung* is translated here as "undeveloping," because of its opposition to *Entwicklung* (development) and its more active, process-oriented connotation. In the 1990s, the noun was often used in relation to the organized disposal of the GDR and its political, social, and economic structures. ("Disposal of the North" would thus be an alternative translation.)

4. Refusing to rent is an interesting case leading to more complex ramifications, because it involves refusing to enter into cooperation with someone rather than keeping someone in an unwanted cooperation.

5. Agricultural engineering has led to the invention of plants whose harvested seeds cannot be used to plant for the next growing season, making the farmer buy new seeds from Monsanto or similar companies every year.

6. The German title of the book, *Gleicher als andere*, alludes not only to Orwell's "some animals are more equal than others" but also to this perspective.

REFERENCES

Alcoff, Laura. 1992. "The Problem of Speaking for Others." *Cultural Critique*, no. 20: 5–32.

Banse, Frauke, and Friederike Habermann. 2012. "Vom Ende der Globalisierungsbewegung—und dem, was kommt. Ein Rück- und Ausblick." *Forschungsjournal Neue Soziale Bewegungen* 25 (1): 51–60.

Bauman, Zygmunt. 1992. *Intimations of Postmodernity*. London: Routledge.

Bendix, Daniel. 2016. "Post Development: Beim globalen Umgang mit dem kolonialen Erbe geht es um mehr als Wachstumskritik." *Degrowth in Bewegungen*, May 7. https://www.degrowth.info/wp-content/uploads/2016/06/DIB_Post -Development-1.pdf.

Bernhard, Claudia, Bernhard Fedler, Ulla Peters, Christoph Spehr, and Heinz-Jürgen Stolz. 1997. "Bausteine für Perspektiven." *Schwertfisch*, 1883–2000.

BUKO, ed. 2003. *Radikal global: Bausteine für eine internationalistische Linke*. Hamburg: Assoziation A.

Corbridge, Stuart. 1994. "Post-Marxism and Post-colonialism: The Needs and Rights of Distant Strangers." In *Rethinking Social Development: Theory, Research and Practice*, edited by David Booth, 90–125. Essex: Longman.

Cowen, Michael, and Robert Shenton. 1996. *Doctrines of Development*. London: Routledge.

Cox, Robert. 1996. "Social Forces, States and World Orders: Beyond International Relations Theory." In *Approaches to World Order*, 85–123. Cambridge: Cambridge University Press.

Fischer, Karin, and Susan Zimmermann, eds. 2008. *Internationalismen: Transformation weltweiter Ungleichheit im 19. und 20. Jahrhundert*. Vienna: Promedia und Südwind.

Foitzik, Andreas, and Athanasios Marvakis, eds. 1997. *Tarzan—was nun? Internationale Solidarität im Dschungel der Widersprüche*. Hamburg: Verlag Libertäre Assoziation.

Foucault, Michel. 1972. *The Archaeology of Knowledge and the Discourse on Language*. New York: Pantheon.

Foucault, Michel. 1980. *Power/Knowledge: Selected Interviews and Other Writings, 1972–1977*. New York: Random House.

Foucault, Michel, and Gilles Deleuze. 1972. "Intellectuals and Power: A Conversation between Michel Foucault and Gilles Deleuze." Libcom.org. https://libcom.org/library /intellectuals-power-a-conversation-between-michel-foucault-and-gilles-deleuze.

Gibson-Graham, J. K. 1996. *The End of Capitalism (as We Knew It): A Feminist Critique of Political Economy*. Minneapolis: University of Minnesota Press.

Gruppe Demontage. 1998. *Postfordistische Guerilla: Vom Mythos nationaler Befreiung.* Münster: Unrast.

Guillén, Diana. 2016. "Societies in Movement vs. Institutional Continuities? Insights from the Zapatista Experience." *Latin American Perspectives* 20 (30): 1–25.

Habermann, Friederike. 2012. "Von Post-Development, Postwachstum und Peer-Ecommony: Alternative Lebensweisen als 'Abwicklung des Nordens.'" *Journal für Entwicklungspolitik* 28 (4): 69–87.

Habermann, Friederike. 2014. *Geschichte wird gemacht! Etappen des globalen Widerstands*. Hamburg: Laika Verlag.

Hanloser, Gerhard. 1994. "Von 'Riots' und 'Modernisierern.' Eine kritische Würdigung des Neuen Anti-Imperialismus." *iz3w*, no. 200: 31–33.

Hayden, Tom, ed. 2002. *The Zapatista Reader*. New York: Thunder's Mouth/Nation.

Hierlmeier, Josef (Moe). 2002. *Internationalismus: Eine Einführung in die Ideengeschichte des Internationalismus—von Vietnam bis Genua*. Stuttgart: Schmetterling.

Holloway, John. 2002. *Change the World without Taking Power: The Meaning of Revolution Today*. London: Pluto.

Hüttner, Bernd. 1997. "Von Schlangen und Fröschen—Abwicklung des Nordens statt Öko-Korporatismus." *Schwertfisch*, 139–52.

Kößler, Reinhart. 1988. "Internationalismus, internationale Konkurrenz und Solidarität: Versuch einer Besinnung." *Peripherie*, no. 33/34: 40–48.

Kössler, Reinhart, and Henning Melber. 2002. *Globale Solidarität? Eine Streitschrift.* Frankfurt a.M.: Brandes und Apsel.

Marino, Lauren. 2005. "Speaking for Others." *Macalester Journal of Philosophy* 14 (1): article 4. http://digitalcommons.macalester.edu/philo/vol14/iss1/4.

Mohanty, Chandra Talpade. 1984. "Under Western Eyes: Feminist Scholarship and Colonial Discourses." *boundary 2* 12 (3): 333–58.

Muñoz Ramírez, Gloria. 2003. *EZLN: 20 + 10: El fuego y la palabra*. Mexico City: Revista Rebeldía.

PGA. 1998. "People's Global Action Manifesto." February–March. https://www.nadir.org/nadir/initiativ/agp/en/pgainfos/manifest.htm.

PGA. 2001. "Hallmarks of Peoples' Global Action." https://www.nadir.org/nadir/initiativ/agp/free/pga/hallm.htm.

Redaktion Alaska. 1998. "150° West 60° Nord: Eine Standortbestimmung jenseits vom neuen Internationalismus." *Alaska*, no. 223: 8–15.

Rössel, Karl. 1994. "Zwei Millionen Daumenabdrücke gegen den Imperialismus? Zum Stand der Internationalismusarbeit." *iz3w*, no. 200: 22–26.

Santos, Boaventura de Sousa. 2014. *Epistemologies of the South: Justice against Epistemicide*. Boulder, CO: Paradigm.

Schwertfisch, ed. 1997. *Zeitgeist mit Gräten: Politische Perspektiven zwischen Ökologie und Autonomie*. Bremen: Yeti.

Scott, James C. 1998. *Seeing Like a State: How Certain Schemes to Improve the Human Condition Have Failed*. New Haven, CT: Yale University Press.

Sluga, Gelnda, Patricia Clavin, and Sunil Amrith, eds. 2016. *Internationalismus: A Twentieth-Century History*. Cambridge: Cambridge University Press.

Spehr, Christoph. 1996. *Die Ökofalle: Nachhaltigkeit und Krise*. Vienna: Promedia.

Spehr, Christoph. 1997. "Hanna und die Abwickler." *Forum entwicklungspolitischer Aktionsgruppen*, no. 210: 4–7.

Spehr, Christoph. 1998. "Perspektiven der Internationalismusbewegung und Krise des BUKO." *Alaska*, no. 220: 39–42.

Spehr, Christoph. 1999. *Die Aliens sind unter uns! Herrschaft und Befreiung im demokratischen Zeitalter*. Munich: Goldmann.

Spehr, Christoph. 2003. "Gleicher als Andere: Eine Grundlegung der freien Kooperation." In *Gleicher als Andere: Eine Grundlegung der freien Kooperation*, edited by Christoph Spehr, 19–116. Berlin: Karl Dietz.

Spivak, Gayatri. 1994. "Can the Subaltern Speak?" In *Colonial Discourse and Postcolonial Theory: A Reader*, edited by Patrick Williams and Laura Chrisman, 66–111. New York: Columbia University Press.

Sternfeld, Nora. 2010. "Wem gehört der Universalismus?" *Jungle World*, December 2. http://jungle-world.com/artikel/2010/48/42190.html.

Sylvester, Christine. 1999. "Development Studies and Postcolonial Studies: Disparate Tales of the Third World." *Third World Quarterly* 20 (4): 703–21.

Wissen, Markus. 1998. "Der BUKO in der Neuen Unübersichtlichkeit." *Alaska*, no. 220: 36–39.

Part II. **Other Ontologies**

6 · Local Aquatic Epistemologies among Black Communities on Colombia's Pacific Coast and the Pluriverse

In 1991, Colombia passed a new constitution that was to significantly reshape the relations between the nation and its Afro-descendant population. Among other moves, it provided for legislation that would grant collective land titles to rural black communities living along the myriad of river basins in the Pacific Coast region. While much has been written about the subsequently passed law—known as Ley 70 of 1993 (e.g., Agudelo 2005; Oslender 2016; Paschel 2010; Wade 2002)—in this chapter I want to examine the universe of which this legislation talks. In particular, I want to show how what I call local aquatic epistemologies—the place-based and culturally specific ways of knowing a profoundly aquatic environment—are at the center of a rural Afro-Colombian worldview in the Pacific Coast region, which have underpinned the political organizing process. These local ways of knowing may be seen as constituting a relational ontology on the Pacific Coast that challenges Euro-Americanist frameworks of development thinking (Escobar 2008). They may thus be seen as a contribution to thinking toward and imagining the pluriverse, or a world of many worlds. I explore this relational ontology in this chapter through ethnographic vignettes that are the result of extended fieldwork and participant observation that I conducted in the Pacific Coast region in the late 1990s and early 2000s.

However, I should also say what this chapter is not going to do: it does not engage in great depth the emerging theoretical literature about pluriversality. And it does not do that for two principal reasons: first (and most obvious perhaps), the reader may find these conceptual developments exhaustively debated in the other chapters of this collection (see in particular chapters 3 and 4). I find it tiring when edited books become a mere collection of essays that cross-reference each other. Second, I find that debates on pluriversality (or is it pluriversity?—Mignolo seems to use both terms in the foreword here) often lack concrete ethnographic evidence to back up conceptual claims that some readers may find shrouded in unnecessarily convoluted language. I therefore want to do something quite different here; I want to let ethnography speak, to invite the reader to come with me and "dwell in the border," as Mignolo might say, if only for the duration of this chapter, to imagine, feel, dream, and smell what a pluriverse world might be like in particular places.

The basic idea of the pluriverse is (and maybe should be) simple: there are worlds out there (and have always been) that have historically been marginalized and suppressed by a Western cosmology and universalizing tendency that claimed a superior position for itself vis-à-vis those other worlds. Edward Said's (1978) *Orientalism* is one big excavation site of the power differential that enabled Western epistemology and hermeneutics to enact its superiority over a multiplicity of worlds that became categorized as the Orient and opened up for Western imperial exploitation. The notion of pluriversality, in contrast, is born out of a decolonial desire to break those bonds of dominance and a call for a coexistence of many worlds as an acknowledgment of the entanglement of diverse cosmologies, of which Western universalism is but one.

In this sense there have been important critical theories of the West's universalizing tendency that provide a conceptual bedrock for pluriversal thought, including genealogies of development (Escobar 1995), of Western cosmology and hermeneutics (Mignolo 2011), and of modernization theory and imperial globality (Slater 2004). Yet this theoretical critique of Western modernity's drive to disavow, silence, and delegitimize other cultures, peoples, and cosmologies should at the same time be accompanied by meaningful ethnographic engagements with those invisibilized worlds—those "territories of difference" as Escobar (2008) refers to them—in order to put flesh onto the pluriversality discourse and to enable a deeper, rooted decolonial engagement with the on-the-ground, lived experience of what it means to live in a pluriverse. It is the latter that I intend to foreground in this chapter, while the theory simmers on the back burner. My narrative here proposes an encounter with a particular territory of difference—Colombia's Pacific Coast region—an encounter that profoundly redirected my own way of seeing and sensing landscape and space. I want to invite the reader to join me (at least attempt) to dwell in the border and dive into the ontology of the aquatic space.

The Aquatic Space in Colombia's Pacific Lowlands

With a coastline of around 1,300 kilometers, stretching from Ecuador in the south to Panama in the north, the Pacific lowlands cover an area of almost ten million hectares of tropical rain forest.[1] Set apart from Colombia's interior by the western Andean mountain range, the lowlands have variously been described as the "hidden littoral" (Yacup 1934) or the "periphery of the periphery" (Granda 1977) due to their perceived physical and economic marginality in relation to the rest of the country. Initially of interest to Spanish colonizers for its rich alluvial gold deposits, the region has been characterized by boom-and-bust cycles, such as *tagua* (ivory nut) and rubber exploitation in the first half of the twentieth century, timber extraction since the 1960s, and more recently agro-industries such as oil palm plantations and shrimp farming. Throughout these changing economic paradigms, a resilient local population—made up overwhelmingly of people of African descent—has continued to practice a diversified subsistence economy in the rural areas based on fishing, hunting, agriculture, gathering, and small-scale artisanal gold panning for their everyday needs.

That was just about all I knew about this region back in February 1995, when I got off the small Satena plane at the airport in Tumaco, the Pacific Coast's most southern and third largest town. In Bogotá I had met Robin Hissong, who worked on the World Bank–funded biodiversity conservation program Proyecto Biopacífico. As a geographer in the making, I was generally interested in conservation, biodiversity, and sustainable development. The Pacific lowlands seemed an exciting place, where these notions overlapped in complex ways with an emerging identity politics of the region's Afro-descendant population. Therefore, I didn't hesitate when Robin extended an invitation to accompany her to Guapi, a small coastal town some 150 kilometers north of Tumaco, where she needed to deliver equipment to Proyecto Biopacífico's regional office.

This speedboat trip was a first taste of traveling through the maze of mangrove swamps that make up the southern coastline of the Pacific lowlands. Our captain suggested we should travel *por dentro*, slowly threading our way along the numerous meandering brooks and channels that cut through the mangrove landscape. He warned against navigating *por fuera*—on the open sea—as the Pacific Ocean was rough that day. Fine by me, I thought. That way I would get to see the area even better.

It was midday by the time we set off. The sky was overcast with dark clouds as we left the Bay of Tumaco. Humidity was near 90 percent. It was hot, and I didn't understand why we had waited so long. It was going to be a lengthy journey, eight hours plus. Robin had even mentioned that we might have to spend a night on the way.

"Who are we waiting for?" I asked the captain, who had said something about *esperando la marea*.

"When's Marea coming?"

Laughter all around. That was one of these silly gringo questions, of course. *Marea* means tide. And apparently there wasn't enough water in the mangrove's river channels. So we had to be patient, and wait for high tide to arrive. Later, I would realize how this seemingly mundane routine—the daily tidal changes—impacted everyday life patterns in a thousand and one ways. Traveling schedules are set according to the tides, calculating not only water availability in the coastal mangrove swamps but also further up the rivers. The alluvial plains have such a low gradient that the tidal impact can be felt up to twenty kilometers upstream. High tide also pushes salt water far up the rivers, a bad time for washing clothes or fetching drinking water from the river, for example.

Sitting at the landing steps in Guapi the day after we left Tumaco, I took in the majestic leisureliness with which the Guapi River descended to its meeting with the Pacific Ocean. A number of dugout canoes on the river, powered by the paddled strength of a single occupant, were making their way toward the landing steps from downstream, as the rising tide was giving them a helping hand. They would return later that day to their hamlets downstream, when the low tide facilitated a speedier journey.

It was there, at the landing steps in Guapi, where I spent innumerable hours in years to come, that the idea of the aquatic space began to take shape. Anthropologists and geographers have described the interactions of rural populations with the tropical rain forest in terms of human adaptation to an often unforgiving natural environment (Arocha 1999; Friedemann 1974; West 1957; Whitten [1974] 1986). Yet, sitting at the landing steps in Guapi overlooking the busy activities taking place—canoes arriving, women washing clothes on the river's edge, children playing in the water, travelers awaiting embarkations to upstream locations—I felt that these were more than merely adaptive responses. The discourse of adaptation maintains those boundaries of culture and nature that seemed to dissolve in practice in front of my eyes. The idea of the aquatic space that was taking root then owes more to a Deleuzian understanding of these complex and changing relations between humans and nonhumans in terms of assemblages. It wants to break with the notion of exteriority of an already existing nature that culture merely adapts to.[2] In particular I mean by *aquatic space* the particular assemblage of spatial relations that results from human entanglements with an aquatic environment dominated by intricate river networks, significant tidal ranges, labyrinthine mangrove swamps, and frequent inundations (Oslender 2004, 2016).

In 1999, I would spend many evening hours in the half-covered courtyard of the house I rented on Calle Segunda in Guapi, sitting with Doña Celia Lucumí Caicedo, a traditional healer and midwife, with whom I shared this living space. As the rains pummeled the rooftops, generating a thunderous noise that drowned out all possibility of conversation, we just stared ahead watching sheets of rainwater hammering the patio's tropical plants and quickly filling up the four barrels, one in each corner, which became a full week's household water supply in no time. These were moments when it seemed we all became one with the rain. No one in Guapi left their homes during these deluges. No conversation could be had for the deafening roar of Changó's fury unleashed on the rooftops of Guapi. Doña Celia was also lost in her thoughts then. Walking along the shores of her river in her imagination—as she would later tell me—she brought to life memories of her childhood growing up along the headwaters of the Guapi River. "A mi río, no lo olvido," Doña Celia would murmur. "I don't forget my river." She was one with her river, as she was sitting on our patio.

Sitting on this patio in Guapi, with the rains pummeling the iron roof, I began to wonder how the particularities of this place—its year-round humidity, its water-based cultures, its river thoroughfares, its listening-to-the-tides folks—figured in the making of the social movement of black communities that had begun to mobilize since the early 1990s around a newly formed constitutional discourse on blackness and black cultural and territorial rights. I have examined these questions in detail elsewhere (Oslender 2016). Here I want to explore the particularities of place that I found in Guapi through the notion of local aquatic epistemologies—the place-based and culturally specific ways of knowing a profoundly aquatic environment—as they were revealed to me by one of the region's *sabios*.

Embodying Local Aquatic Epistemologies: Doña Celia Lucumí Caicedo—in Memoriam

I was born in Balsitas, at the headwaters of the Guapi River, three streets below the village of Balsitas, in a place called La Corriente.[3] I was still a little girl when my mother already sent me to Balsitas to run errands. Even though I didn't know how to swim. When the current came, I took my little dugout canoe, and splash, splash, splash, on foot, I pushed it to the top of the current. Then I sat down in my canoe, and plap, plap, plap [making sound of paddle in the water], that's how I went up all three currents. The one near the house was street, street, street, until one got to another street. And then there was a little stream. That's how I got to Balsitas.

The notion of street (*calle*) requires an explanation here. In the rural areas of the Pacific lowlands there are very few streets. The humid, often inundated environment with its myriad rivers and smaller streams is highly inappropriate for the construction of roads. When Afro-Colombians talk about streets in this environment, they apply urban descriptive parameters to a rural landscape. What they measure with the denomination *street* is in fact the distance between two river bends. When Doña Celia talks about traveling three streets upstream, this means navigating three river bends before reaching her destination. The notion of street is therefore a flexible measurement, as the metric distance between river bends changes. It assumes that one knows the river section in question and thus forms central part of the local aquatic epistemologies in the Pacific lowlands.

> *In Balsitas I went to the now-deceased Joaquín Ledesma. He was a good friend of my parents. My mother put something into a handkerchief and sent it with me to the late Joaquín. Then he put something in my bag and said, "Take this, my child, take it to Ms. Lucha. And tell Ms. Lucha not to send you anymore, because you cannot swim. Sit down, child, you hear me!" There, comfortable and well sent as I was, I put my things in the prow of the canoe, and then I took my little paddle and proom, I sat down on the bottom of the canoe. And I arrived home faster than running the errand. When my mum thought that I was just arriving at Balsitas, I was already back home. And I told her, "Mum, the day you go to Balsitas, you should go and see Don Joaquín."*

It is said that children in the rural areas of the Pacific Coast move around in small dugout canoes well before they actually learn how to walk on their feet. The river is not just the place where they play. It is also the main road that connects them to neighbors, friends, and relatives who live along the same river. From an early age, children are incorporated into adult life. Girls help their mothers in the household, wash clothes, clean dishes, and look after their smaller brothers and sisters, while boys go fishing to supplement the family's meals. Doña Celia, like many other young girls, also worked alongside her mother and grandmother in the gold mines, panning sand and gravel in her *batea*, when she was only eight years old.[4] As Doña Celia tells us here, her mother used her as a kind of fluvial messenger to send information or goods to friends, neighbors, and relatives. The river in this context functions as the main road that little Celia had to navigate, an action in which she acquired considerable skill. Celia, the fluvial messenger on her aquatic road to the upper reaches of the Guapi River, remembers:

> *One day my mother sent me to my granddad Juan Gregorio on an errand. So I took my little canoe and left. When I arrived at my grandfather's I told him, "Granddad, here, my mum sends you this." He was a fisherman. . . . Many a time when I brought him his lunch, I found him sitting there on the beach. He caught mojarra, he caught sábalo, he caught sabaleta [common*

river fish]. . . . *He loved my mother, and she also came to love him, so my mother cooked the food at home and sent it to his house with us. We lived one street apart. Around the corner. One had to take the canoe. There was no path. . . . And I also went to my grandmother, taking food to her, too, to my grandmother Juana María. Well, my grandmother lived further away; she lived much higher up with her other sons. She came down to my mother only occasionally. Because my grandfathers, I knew them all divorced from their women.*

In Doña Celia's account, the river is the site not only providing dwelling, shelter, and living space, but also of performing family. Relations to family members are enacted in the daily movements around the riverscape. As such, the river is also a source of emotional attachment and of a particular sense of belonging; what I call an aquatic sense of place. U.S. American cultural geographer Robert West commented already in the 1950s on this close and intimate relationship between the individual and the river. As he observed, the river was a central point of reference in identity formation and everyday discursive practices: "People living on a given river consider themselves as a single community. . . . Negroes [*sic*] and mixed bloods speak of 'nuestro río,' or mention, for example, that 'somos del Río Guapi,' or 'somos Guapiseños' [*sic*], indicating their social attachment to a given river" (West 1957, 88).

Today, the river is still the most immediate geographical reference for the people of the Colombian Pacific Coast. Rather than referring to a settlement or village, when asked about their place of origin, Afro-Colombians name the particular river where they live. As Alfredo Vanín, a poet from Guapi and an authority on local history, told me, "If someone asks, 'Where are you from?,' then the answer would be, 'I am from the Chagüí River,' here in Nariño, or 'I am from the Saija River,' in the Cauca Department. Rather than talking of the village, first is the river."

The rivers are in fact considered the places out of which individuals emerge and in which they submerge again when the time has come for the final voyage, returning in body if possible, but always in spirit, to the river of origin the moment that death approaches. Such was Doña Celia's imaginative journey, when some years back she suffered from high fever and felt that the time had come for her body to leave this life. Reflecting "the dialogical nature of people's relationship to place" (Buttimer 1976, 284), she returned to her river in her imagination, to her origin, as her life was coming full circle:

There I went to all the places of my river where I grew up. I was walking them the very moment I was dying.

The Logic of the River

The river is central to all economic, domestic, and social activities in the Pacific lowlands. Houses are constructed on stilts along riverbanks, transport is river based, and fishing and collecting of shellfish are important contributors to the local diet. The river is also the space of social interaction per se, where people bathe, women wash clothes and fetch water, and children come to play. In these sociospatial constellations, the river emerges as a collective space of everyday social interactions that are based on cooperation and solidarity. As Silveria Rodriguez, a community leader in Guapi, told me in April 1996, "I remember, as a girl, I never went alone to wash clothes in the river. We were always at least four. Or to do the dishes. We always did things together."

In the local geographical imagination, various river sections are intrinsically connected, and *el río* refers not only to the principal river but also to tributaries and surrounding lands. Communities in the middle section or at the headwaters, for example, depend on the productive activities of communities living near the river delta, especially the provision of fish and mollusks. "Family territoriality" extends along the entire river basin in that people living upstream may own lands further downstream or vice versa (Romero 1998, 123). During one of my first interviews in the Pacific region in April 1996, the aforementioned Afro-Colombian historian and poet Alfredo Vanín explained, "The family spread out along the river in such a way that there was a piece of land, the forest backland, that belonged to a member of a family that dispersed along the river basins. The land in general belonged to the family and could be divided between the children as well. But it was in the name of the head of the family. That is to say, there was ownership of the land, although it was not titled." Thus the interconnectedness along a river basin is evident not only in terms of exchange of foodstuffs, but also in terms of land distribution and property relations. Activists from the *Proceso de Comunidades Negras* (PCN, (one of the leading groups in the larger social movement of black communities in Colombia) have referred to these spatialized social relationships along the river basins as "the logic of the river" (see also Oslender 2002):

> In the logic of the river, the characteristics of land use are determined
> by location: in the upper section of the river, emphasis is given to tra-
> ditional gold mining, and hunting and gathering activities are exercised
> in the forest hills; towards the middle section, emphasis is placed on
> agricultural production and small-scale logging, as well as hunting and
> gathering activities in the forest backlands; towards the lower section,

emphasis is given to fishing and the gathering of shells, mollusks and crabs, together with agricultural activities. Between all sections there exists a continuous relation between the upper and the lower parts and vice versa, and of the middle section with both, characterized by a mobility that follows the natural course of the river and of nature. Its dynamics strengthen and permit kinship relations and the exchange of products, with the productive unit in these dynamics being the dispersed family along the river. (PCN 1999, 1)

This river is very different from the river described in Gabriel García Márquez's ([1967] 2006) literary masterpiece *One Hundred Years of Solitude*. There, José Arcadio Buendía is desperate at the backwardness of his village and enthralled by the latest magnificent scientific instruments that Melquíades and his troupe of traveling gypsies periodically bring to the people of Macondo. From false teeth to flying carpets to the secrets of alchemy, all these marvelous advances come from somewhere beyond the river, a river that separates Arcadio Buendía and his people from modernity. One day he confesses to his wife Úrsula in desperation, "Incredible things are happening in the world.... Right there across the river there are all kinds of magical instruments while we keep on living like donkeys" (García Márquez [1967] 2006, 8). This river separates the local and backward world from another, scientifically advanced world. The river is a border, a hindrance, an obstacle; it holds people and their imagination back.

Not so in the Pacific lowlands. There, the river connects and displays a distinct spatial orientation. The river is seen not as necessary to cross (although that does of course happen as well), but to travel along, following its current. The river is regarded not as a separating but as a connecting line. One does not look beyond the river, but up and down, *arriba y abajo*. The entire orientation toward the river is different from the one portrayed in García Márquez's novel.

The landscape in the Colombian Pacific lowlands also has its own temporality. More than any other phenomenon maybe, it is the tidal rhythm that has given rise to time patterns that resist being molded into a 24/7 clockwork of modernity. Instead, the tides provide a temporal rhythm that bows to the lunar cycles, one that locals seize and run with. You go against this rhythm at your own peril. As Robert West related in his navigations around the southern Pacific Coast in the 1950s, "Travel *por adentro* along the inland channels, however, must be closely timed to correspond with periods of high tide. More than once the writer has been stranded for several hours in a canoe stuck on the muddy bottom of an *estero* at low tide, being pestered to distraction by black flies and mosquitoes until the water slowly rose with the incoming tide" (West 1957, 70).

Convivencia Acuática: Seizing the Tides

The town of Guapi lies some seventeen kilometers from the Guapi River mouth at an altitude of two meters above sea level. The newcomer to the region who arrives in the morning can be forgiven if she is surprised in the afternoon by the fact that the river flow seems to have changed direction. A tidal range of 4.5 meters and a low river gradient mean that twice a day at high tide brackish water reaches far beyond Guapi. During relatively dry periods, levels of saltwater intrusion can be significant. This also means that activities such as washing clothes in the river are performed at low tide in order to avoid contact between the laundry and salt water. Locals are very much aware of the rhythm of the tides and plan the day's activities according to the tidal clock rather than a tide-insensitive wristwatch.

Moreover, at low tide the receding waters expose the coastal mangrove swamps, an important zone of ecological productivity and economic activity (Arocha 1999, 73). Women shellfish pickers known as *concheras*, for example, travel into mangrove areas, oftentimes from afar, to collect shellfish that live buried in the mud. In order to extract them more easily, they do so at low tide, when the mudflats are exposed. The concheras meticulously plan their travels into the mangrove areas, calculating their departure at such time during low tide that the receding waters of the Guapi River speed up their journey and that on arrival the mudflats are exposed. They may spend up to five hours picking shellfish, after which they wait for the rising waters of the high tide to give them a helping hand when navigating upstream in their dugout canoes, known as *potrillos*. This system of transport makes it possible for the concheras to travel large distances to and from the mangrove swamps with relative ease. It is just one of many activities that draw on and coproduce the aquatic space as an assemblage of complex relations.

It is not just the concheras who set their traveling schedules according to the tidal rhythm. Lumberjacks are also listening-to-the-tides folks, whose workdays show changing temporalities. Colombian anthropologist Eduardo Restrepo has spent much time among tree cutters in the *guandal* forests, a back swamp of palm thickets of largely inundated lands found mainly in the southern part of the Department of Nariño. Analyzing their work patterns, he observes that the effect of the tides "not only determines the appropriate time to set off for work, but also for returning from work, so that the working days get either shorter or longer" (Restrepo 1996a, 366).

Logging activities are in fact dependent in many more ways on the rhythm of the tides, particularly when timber has to be transported over larger distances from felling site to sawmill. Once felled, a tree is pulled over the forest floor to a nearby water channel or river. According to Restrepo (1996b, 252–53), there are two distinct and complementary forms of transporting the logs. One way is over land and implies the temporary construction of *carreteras* (literally "roads") by placing thin logs some three meters apart and parallel to one another from the felling site to a watercourse. The felled tree (*tuco*) is then pulled over these logs, until it reaches the waterway on which it can be transported downstream. A longer-lasting road for the transport of logs is often constructed in the form of ditches of one meter width and two meters depth. These *cunetas* fill up with water after prolonged periods of precipitation or at high tide. When they fill with enough water, the logs are placed in them and floated to a larger and wider waterway. There, depending on the channel's width, various logs are tied together with natural fibers to form a raft, which then floats downstream until it reaches the sawmill. It may be argued that both the cunetas and carreteras constitute the fundamental infrastructure for timber extraction on the southern Pacific Coast, an infrastructure that embodies to me the workings of the aquatic space as an assemblage of relations in which the human and nonhuman interact in always complex ways.

Instead of Conclusions . . . Openings: Thinking the Pluriverse

I have foregrounded in this chapter an approach to the Pacific lowlands of Colombia not through legislative texts or political mobilization, but through a deep ethnography that reveals a rural Afro-Colombian lifeworld entangled in complex relations with the region's aquatic environment. The aquatic space as an assemblage of relations, I argue, is at the heart of a relational ontology in the Pacific region that sectors of the social movement of black communities—in particular the PCN—have mobilized in their demands for cultural and territorial rights (Grueso, Rosero, and Escobar 1998).

One may argue, of course, that the aquatic space these days is being transformed, with locals often deeply entangled as agents in technologies and processes of modernity. Some work on oil palm plantations, others use mercury or mechanical dredgers in gold mining, many are now involved in illegal coca cultivation, and much river travel today is by engine-driven speed boat. All of these things do happen. Rural black populations are modern, too. Yet, at the same time, traditional production practices and local subsistence economies are still central to resilient rural lifeworlds that form the backbone to visions of alternative life projects promoted by PCN based on difference. Theirs is a vision of pluriversality that demands a place for the aquatic relational ontology of the Pacific lowlands. They defend a world understood through and based on "local models of nature" (Escobar 2008), or what Restrepo (2004, 2013) calls a *gramática local del entorno*, a local environmental grammar. The politicization of this vision may be seen as constituting a political ontology (Blaser 2009; Escobar 2008, 15), a challenge to Western universalism implicit in the project of modernity. From this viewpoint, ontological conflicts point to a multiplicity of ways of being in the world. In other words, they are witness to a real existing pluriverse.

NOTES

1. The ethnographic narrative in the remainder of this chapter is adapted from my monograph *The Geographies of Social Movements* (Oslender 2016).

2. Most recent work on assemblage theory draws on Deleuze and Guattari ([1983] 2007). For an application to political ecology and environmental anthropology, see Escobar (2008) and Ogden (2011).

3. The quotes in italics in this section stem from over fifty hours of transcribed interviews with Doña Celia Lucumí Caicedo that I recorded in Guapi between March and July 1999 and subsequently translated. Doña Celia passed away on December 21, 2013.

4. A batea is a round, shallow bowl carved out of wood, which is used in traditional placer gold mining on the Colombian Pacific Coast, an activity usually performed by women and small girls, the *bateadoras*. For more on colonial placer mining, see the fascinating account in West (1952).

REFERENCES

Agudelo, Carlos. 2005. *Retos del multiculturalismo en Colombia: Política y poblaciones negras*. Medellín: La Carreta Editores.

Arocha, Jaime. 1999. *Ombligados de Ananse: Hilos ancestrales y modernos en el Pacífico colombiano*. Bogotá: CES.

Blaser, Mario. 2009. "Political Ontology: Cultural Studies without 'Cultures'?" *Cultural Studies* 23 (5–6): 873–96.

Buttimer, Anne. 1976. "Grasping the Dynamism of Lifeworld." *Annals of the Association of American Geographers* 66 (2): 277–92.

Deleuze, Gilles, and Félix Guattari. [1983] 2007. *A Thousand Plateaus: Capitalism and Schizophrenia*. Translated by Brian Massumi. Minneapolis: University of Minnesota Press.

Escobar, Arturo. 1995. *Encountering Development: The Making and Unmaking of the Third World*. Princeton, NJ: Princeton University Press.

Escobar, Arturo. 2008. *Territories of Difference: Place, Movements, Life, Redes*. Durham, NC: Duke University Press.

Friedemann, Nina S. de. 1974. "Minería del oro y descendencia: Güelmambí, Nariño." *Revista Colombiana de Antropología* 16:9–52.

García Márquez, Gabriel. [1967] 2006. *One Hundred Years of Solitude*. New York: HarperCollins.

Granda, Germán de. 1977. *Estudios sobre un área dialectal hispanoamericana de población negra*. Bogotá: Instituto Caro y Cuervo.

Grueso, Libia, Carlos Rosero, and Arturo Escobar. 1998. "The Process of Black Community Organizing in the Southern Pacific Coast Region of Colombia." In *Cultures of Politics, Politics of Cultures: Re-visioning Latin American Social Movements*, edited by S. Alvarez, E. Dagnino, and A. Escobar, 196–219. Oxford: Westview.

Mignolo, Walter. 2011. *The Darker Side of Western Modernity: Global Futures, Decolonial Options*. Durham, NC: Duke University Press.

Ogden, Laura. 2011. *Swamplife: People, Gators, and Mangroves Entangled in the Everglades*. Minneapolis: University of Minnesota Press.

Oslender, Ulrich. 2002. "The Logic of the River: A Spatial Approach to Ethnic-Territorial Mobilization in the Colombian Pacific Region." *Journal of Latin American Anthropology* 7(2): 86–117.

Oslender, Ulrich. 2004. "Fleshing Out the Geographies of Social Movements: Black Communities on the Colombian Pacific Coast and the Aquatic Space." *Political Geography* 23 (8): 957–85.

Oslender, Ulrich. 2016. *The Geographies of Social Movements: Afro-Colombian Mobilization and the Aquatic Space*. Durham, NC: Duke University Press.

Paschel, Tianna. 2010. "The Right to Difference: Explaining Colombia's Shift from Color Blindness to the Law of Black Communities." *American Journal of Sociology* 116 (3): 729–69.

PCN. 1999. "El concepto de territorio en las comunidades negras del Pacífico Centro y Sur." Proceso de Comunidades Negras.

Restrepo, Eduardo. 1996a. "El naidí entre los 'grupos negros' del Pacífico Sur colombiano." In *Renacientes del guandal: "Grupos negros" de los ríos Satinga y Sanquianga*, edited by J. I. Del Valle and E. Restrepo, 351–83. Bogotá: Biopacífico-Universidad Nacional de Colombia.

Restrepo, Eduardo. 1996b. "Los tuqueros negros del Pacífico Sur colombiano." In *Renacientes del guandal: "Grupos negros" de los ríos Satinga y Sanquianga*, edited by J. I. Del Valle and E. Restrepo, 243–348. Bogotá: Biopacífico-Universidad Nacional de Colombia.

Restrepo, Eduardo. 2004. "Ethnization of Blackness in Colombia: Toward De-racializing Theoretical and Political Imagination." *Cultural Studies* 18 (5): 698–715.

Restrepo, Eduardo. 2013. *Etnización de la negridad: La invención de las "comunidades negras" como grupo étnico en Colombia*. Popayán: Universidad del Cauca.

Romero, Mario Diego. 1998. "Familia afrocolombiana y construcción territorial en el Pacífico Sur, siglo XVIII." In *Geografía humana de Colombia: Los afrocolombianos*, vol. 6, 103–40. Bogotá: Instituto Colombiano de Cultura Hispánica.

Said, Edward. 1978. *Orientalism*. London: Routledge and Kegan Paul.

Slater, David. 2004. *Geopolitics and the Post-colonial: Rethinking North-South Relations*. Oxford: Blackwell.

Wade, Peter. 2002. "Introduction: The Colombian Pacific in Perspective." *Journal of Latin American Anthropology* 7 (2): 2–33.

West, Robert. 1952. *Colonial Placer Mining in Colombia*. Baton Rouge: Louisiana State University Press.

West, Robert. 1957. *The Pacific Lowlands of Colombia*. Baton Rouge: Lousiana State University Press.

Whitten, Norman. [1974] 1986. *Black Frontiersmen: Afro-Hispanic Culture of Ecuador and Colombia*. Prospect Heights, IL: Waveland.

Yacup, Sofonías. 1934. *Litoral recóndito*. Bogotá: Editorial Renacimiento.

7 · The Griots of West Africa

Oral Tradition and Ancestral Knowledge

Translated from the French by CHARITY FOX

The resurgence of the relevance of the griot in our modern society is not so much the result of a literary fad as of a repositioning of a sociocultural actor whose radiance has never ceased, showing traces of a living and enduring memory. The concept of the griot, in traditional African society, sends us back to two important dimensions which, while different in form, are very close in substance—those of history and education. Indeed, the knowledge and recognition of the existence, as well as the organization and the future, of the traditional society in Africa is the work of the griot, considered to be the repository of the tradition of the people he represents. Thenceforth, the griot's mission as historian causes us to pass through three temporalities, understanding the present as connected to the past; and past and present as conditioning the possibilities of the future. Through the art of the griot, through his manipulation of different forms of symbolic organization of the world, affiliations and relationships within a community or between different communities are reflected and expressed. In doing so, the griot is able to reunite the distant and near past with the immediate present with the imminent future.

It is in this regard that the role of the griot as an educator is decisive in the sense that his historical discourse necessarily conveys political, sociocultural, and economic values of an entire people. The (re)discovery of thoughts and actions of a people by itself or by other people falls within the scope of the necessary knowledge of various people around the world as to what they have in common or how they differ culturally.

Consequently, the multiple risks that underlie the spatial and temporal activity of the griot make of this relayer of cultures a man steeped in knowledge and endowed with a genuine understanding of the formation and transformation of the society of which he is a part. But beyond that, it is in reality by the work of historic and cultural (re)construction that the discourse of the griot proves to be the most revealing. Such a singular vision of the griot obviously generates multiple pertinent questions, such as: What is the place of the griot in traditional African society? What part do his knowledge of history and his storytelling ability play in the understanding and the (re)construction of African identities? What is the role of this determinant actor in the culture of universal citizenship?

By a diachronic and sociocritical analysis of the griot's rhetoric, this essay seeks to demonstrate first of all that the griot is the voice and the path of African history, and, second, that he rightfully embodies the survival of cultural identities, of which the partition of the construction of universal citizenship is an intrinsic reality.

The Griot: The Voice and Path of African History

The griot is a multifaceted character. He is compared to a needle and thread, which must work together to guarantee the resistance and the cohesion of social tissue. For the elders, usage of the word mobilizes three indispensable organs for the maintenance of social relationships: the foot, the hand, and the mouth. In order to maintain contact with others, it is the foot that provides the ability to take steps in their direction—walking in order to meet together, or, stated otherwise, to make mutual visits. The hand is used to give, to receive—to exchange gifts. As for the mouth, it helps to exteriorize one's intimate thoughts, to talk to one another, to understand one another, to communicate, and to dialogue. Here, the ear, which is the instrument of reception, is not specifically mentioned, undoubtedly because it is the counterpart of the mouth, which it represents. As soon as one or all of these three organs cease to function, that is, no longer bringing people together, there is necessarily a partial or total rupture of social ties.

The multifaceted character of the griot guarantees these social ties by means of diverse interactions between all the actors of the community. Generally this makes of him a public character and an intellectual among the intellectuals of society. For he knows more about the proper functioning of social structure and succeeds at resolving its problems.

Griots are craftsmen without equal since they engage in an activity that is more intelligible than sensible. Indeed, the subject matter that is at the heart of their work has a strong influence on the sensible world by means of the oratorical power that they wield over people. The word, of divine essence, constitutes the raw resource entrusted to the griot, who labors for the transformation of society and the maintenance of the social system. The word is life.

And griots ensure its survival. To them, their vocation, the *djéliya* (*djéli* = griot; *ya* = activity or practice), is a work of divine creation. They repeat whenever they wish, generally in their introductory words or a phrase, "I yo djéliya aaa, allah lè ka djéliyaya dan" (the djéliya emanates from divinity).

Griots believe, therefore, that they continue the work of creation and of social transformation initiated by the supreme creator. A craftsman, a created creator, the griot is an agent of transformation. And the order of griots exists to completely permeate the social fabric in order to control it, to correct its malfunctions, and to improve its performance—which explains the metaphorical role of this character. He is assimilated with the djéli (blood), which circulates throughout the organism. This translates all of the symbolism of the name attributed to the griot, who is to the social organism what the blood is to the biological organism. The griot symbolizes, therefore, vitality, social dynamic, and the source of life. Consequently, in the Manding region there is a saying "the griot is the liquor of the noble and of the people."[1] He sits at the heart of society and serves its leaders, whom he is able to mobilize around sociocultural, economic, and political actions and activities.

The blacksmith is also presented as an indispensable figure for the military glory of the ruler, as he guarantees his power, whereas the griot is presented as the figure who cares for his name, that is, his social and political image. This is taught through this saying about griots: "Noumou té e môgô mi bolo, i tè tôgô-tiguiya, djéli tè mogô mi bolo i tè saramaya" (He who has no blacksmith will have no fame; he who has no griot cannot be famous and loved by the people).

This formula shows the complementarity of oral and political art in the construction of society. The blacksmith represents metallurgical technology in the service of the army as the griot does in regard to the media.

The African griot is a member of the caste of the *nyamakala*, which also includes cobblers, blacksmiths, and potters, indefatigable workers of metal, leather, wood, and clay.[2] However, the significance of the word *griot* makes of this caste a social parasite, always dependent upon the generosity of his host, of his master, of society, simply put. This image is supported by the Malinke expression derived from *djiya* (to provide housing). It is not a question of the one who receives but of the one who is received and taken care of. The social condition that reveals the etymology of the word *griot* does not suffice to fully express his patrimonial dimension in society. Dominique Zahan gets the credit for shedding light upon the power of the word and the cultural riches that the voice of the griot provides: "The djéli works with language (verbe). He is a craftsman of the word as the other castes are with tangible materials."[3]

Language constitutes the tool of the griot's labor. It is by means of language that he presents the word to the public, as a deliverable product. He is therefore a man with a profession, as are the other members of his caste. In a word, the griot lives from the product of his art, which is nothing other than the spoken word, the word that reconstitutes the truth of history, the greatness of the ancestors, and the riches of African civilizations. Therefore, he is not a parasite, but a (re)builder of cultural identities in certain black African civilizations from which he draws all of his substance and authority, and he even has the force of law. Djélis are "men of the word," as in the evocative title of Sory Camara's (1992) *Gens de la parole*. They treat the word as a resource to bring to life history, traditions, and oral cultures. For the word of the griot is not only the identifying voice but also the path of authenticity.

In African society, the griot is historian, storyteller, chronicler, musician, and so on. He is above all else the keeper of the art of speaking well and of speaking truth. This observation, rather than being twofold, expresses in reality a single and unique entity: the language singularity of the griot in his function as master of the word. His mastery of the word makes him an adept of the times who seeks the affirmation of the identity consciousness of Africans, in order to accompany him toward a better understanding of the social system. Jansen observes, "The fasa (discourse) does not deal with the personal prestige of an individual but of his social prestige. This social prestige is determined by the patronymic, *jamu*, which implicitly refers to a heredity via a succession of glorious ancestors. The Griot, craftsman of the word, accomplishes his task therefore by transforming raw human material into socialized persons" (2000, 100).

The griot or djéli (referring to the blood in the Maninka[4] and Bambara languages) never praises an individual in an isolated manner as does his caste homologue, the blacksmith, who integrates different metals to make a homogeneous product.[5] He addresses the individual as belonging to a family, a collective identity blended in the *jamu*, since the latter derives its value from its lineage.[6] From this perspective, the discourse of the griot favors the representation of the people by large families, which constantly develop the *badeya*, literally "the child of the same mother" and by extension language, stemming from a common renowned ancestor. This is why the griot presents the prestige, the quality of the individual, as an ancestral legacy. We come to realize, through the philosophy of the griot, that traditional African morals are not individual morals but social morals which include the entire fabric of the community.

Emerging from the griot's position of genealogist is the role of an educator. In this capacity, he teaches that the African must never hold to morals that are his alone. His morals must be, first of all, the reflection of shared ethics.

It is with good reason that the griot, although belonging to a social group that is traditionally endogamous, the caste of the Nyamakala as opposed to that of the Woron (nobles), by the power of his fertile word reaches the awareness of the individual and, beyond, the general public. His strategy of communication can help provide pertinent answers to the current problems of society. Here, in fact, "the word is a benefit which is not the prerogative of the powerful but which, when expressed, liberates, discovers, cares for" (Hourantier 1990, 12).

The word, viewed as a possession, is able to satisfy the needs of an individual or of a community. But it is not the property of the strongest, of those in power, of the authorities. In other words, the power of the word is not destined to dominate. Instead, it should be therapeutic, to the extent that, in addition to the catharsis that it performs in the individual, it contributes to the (re)construction of cultural identities.

The word of the djéli is marked by a power of persuasion that surpasses the art of speaking. It awakens the consciousness of identity of the individual. Thenceforth, each time he speaks, the griot attends to the style of his phrases, works on their rhythm, their alliterations and playful tones, and their forceful imagery so that his eloquent rhetoric leads to action. His word is all the more effective in that it reaches back to the origin of populations, of the community, of the village, of the family. For this reason his word is viewed as being derived from a line of initiates.

The rhetoric of the griot is actually a word that is always reinvented, reincarnated, which edifies and leads one to self-consciousness of being. It appears that the "speaking well" and the "speaking truth" of the djéli are opposite sides of the same coin. Indeed, the word of the griot is not limited to a ceremonial imagination that praises the beauty of words, of language, but rather his word calls upon the concrete imagination that speaks to the depth of his words in their primitive state and above all renders them eternal.

This is why the African griot, in private or in public, is not stuck on a fixed text so much as a dovetailing of syntax. He always extends his word beyond its material form by surpassing his own point of view. Hence, what the word of the djéli seeks, essentially, is to always pass on a spirit, that of the ancestors. Jacques Chevrier thinks that the word "remains ... both the priority and majority cultural support par excellence to the extent that it weaves between past and present generations a link of continuity and solidarity without which neither history nor civilization exists" (1983, 13).

The metaphorical use of "cultural support" presents the griot as an undeniable means for upholding or always keeping alive the culture and certain civilizations of black Africa. Not only is he the solid element who serves as a support for the survival of the history of populations, of their cultural identity; he also appears in a classic diagram of communication as the means to guarantee their diffusion and to render them more distinct, perceptible, comprehensible, and even emotional. In other words, he is the path that can readily connect the man of today and tomorrow with his past, with his history, with his ancestral wisdom. He incarnates this popular African teaching: "Never forget our origins; the future is full of unknowns" (Traoré 1970, 25).

This advice, borrowed from the wisdom of the elders, is a warning to Africans against the risk of straying culturally, that is, of alienation. What is certain for black people, since it is already known, lived, and experienced, is indeed their past, their history, their traditions. They define, through the analysis of this popular thought, the path of survival of black people. The path laid out by the griot should not be understood here as simply connecting different cultural periods, namely the past, the present, and the future. But this path roots blacks in their values before directing them toward others. This path becomes in the end that of otherness and of diversity for the survival of black cultural identities.

On the Survival of a Consciousness of Being and Cultural Identity

The goal of research on oral literature is to question current events or modern creations by referring to the substance of African culture. Obviously, the main mission of this literature is to pass on, from generation to generation, the values of oral traditions. This cultural survival is allotted to the griot who, traditionally, is a chronicler, a genealogist, and a historian. Djibril Tamsir Niane speaks to this, where he is fully cited despite the length:

> I am a griot. It is I, Djéli Mamadou Kouyaté, son of Bintou Kouyaté and Djéli Kedian Kouyaté, master in the art of speaking. Since ancestral times the Kouyatésare in service to the princes Kéita of Manding: We are carriers of words, we are the bags that contain secrets that are secular several times over. The Art of speaking holds no secrets for us; without us the names of kings would fall into oblivion, we are the memory of men;

with the word we give life to the actions of kings in front of young generations. I have received my sciences from my father Djéli Median who also has received it from his father. History is no mystery to us; we teach the vulgar that which we are willing to teach him, we are the ones who hold the keys to twelve doors in Manding.

I know the list of all the sovereigns who succeeded to the throne of Manding. I know how black men divided themselves into tribes, because my father bequeathed to me all his knowledge. I know so and so is called Kamara, another Keita, another Sidibé or Traoré; every name has a meaning, a secret significance.

I have taught kings the history of their ancestors so that those lives can serve as examples, for the world is old, but the future comes out of the past.

My word is pure and stripped of all lies; it is the word of my father; it is the word of my father's father; I will tell you the word of my father in the way that I received it; the royal griots ignore lies. When a quarrel breaks out between tribes, we settle the dispute for we are the custodians of the oaths that the Ancestors have lent us. Listen to my word, you who want to know. (1960, 9–10)

To decrypt without discord and fathom the heuristic quintessence and especially the hermeneutics of the Griot Kouyaté, a diagram of this descriptive system becomes necessary. "A descriptive system is a constellation of words associated with a concept, a core word, or a nucleus" (Prud'homme and Guilbert 2006).

In other words, the descriptive system is a graphical representation technique that consists of highlighting a key word around which other satellite words revolve and whose semantic range is unclear. It must be emphasized that the said satellite words operate as a metonym of the core or nucleus word. Madame Kouyate attests to the descriptive system example shown in figure 7.1, which has been developed from the word of the griot. In this diagram, each field is linked to the core or nucleus word *griot* by an underlying semantic relationship. Born into a caste in a society without writing, the griot "can intervene to comment on his own narrative in order to didactically emphasize the aspect that he would like to draw the public's attention to" (Ndiaye 2004, 67). In this case, what he says commits entirely to a single matrix that consists of exalting the mission or role that is assigned to the griot for black Africans.

So that the mission is underlined with a double line and attracts public attention, the poet-griot appeals didactically, educationally, and instructively with an oratory technique that is essentially dominated by the incantatory

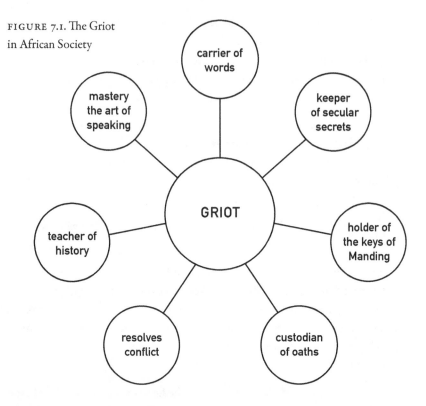

FIGURE 7.1. The Griot in African Society

- carrier of words
- mastery the art of speaking
- keeper of secular secrets
- GRIOT
- teacher of history
- holder of the keys of Manding
- resolves conflict
- custodian of oaths

power of an anaphora. Indeed, the accentuating process through using the personal deictic *I* that punctuates the beginning of each stanza in

> I am griot . . .
> I hold onto my science . . .
> I have taught . . .
> I know the list . . .

to which must be added the repetition of the personal deictic *we* and its synonymous variants, the possessive deictics such as *my*, which can be found in

> We are the carriers . . .
> we are the memory . . .
> We teach; I possess the sciences of my father . . .
> (. . .)
> for my father has bequeathed to me . . .
> (. . .)
> the word of my father's father . . .
> Listen to my words

In short, by creating meaning, all these semantic obliquities (to use Michael Riffaterre term [1983, 12]) reflect the efficient power of the speaking subject in the topics that he allows himself to narrate.

We know that the griot is an object of scorn, admiration, and even fear in society. He enjoys the license of expression and limitless immunity before any assembly. Who could present it to the public better than himself? The griot Djéli Mamadou Kouyaté, as stated, engages in this activity with immeasurable ease: "To signify ... is to exclude and conversely, difference, opposition, any mark is plagiarism and conversely, all figures are presence and absence, all that is posed is first presupposed" (Hamon 1984, 11).

The griot Djéli Mamadou Kouyaté does not say otherwise when he tries to signify, to explain, to lay out the mission that is his within society. By proclaiming himself "master in the art of speaking," he joins a large social group and unconsciously and paradoxically affirms his exclusion of that group since he belongs to the caste of the Nyamakala. The griot is no ordinary man because he exercises a power that is vested wholly and solely in him thanks to his mastery of the language and his instrument of perfection. He limits access, due to the particularity of his social status, but he also unlimits insofar as his words are predestined to take on very important functions. The griot jealously holds to his vast knowledge, a pluridimensional knowledge that he distributes and teaches to others. It follows from this statement that he assumes, in most occasions, a position of superiority, since he always believes himself to be in front of a more or less uncultivated assembly that is fully committed to his cause.

The griot enjoys identifying himself as "a carrier of words / a bag that encloses secular secrets"; in other words, he equates himself with an object of great value whose ability to contain timeless secrets overflows with exuberance. The griot, by his unrivaled power to reveal the "matters that are hidden from kingdom, family, princes and dignitaries" is a privileged or perhaps predestined individual who is fortunate since birth to be part of a small number of people able to retain that which can never be publicly spoken.

The griot preserves deeply inside himself the speech that he knows how to dissect and interpret with ingenuity. He defines himself as the memory of men, the knower and the known, the repository of knowledge, the ability to promote and especially to keep with discretion, wisdom, and determination the cultural heritage of the people; the sum of the past and present that characterizes this people and that keeps them alive despite the upheavals of the time. It goes without saying that the absence of this memory makes the construction of cultural identity within a society impossible.

The role of the griot is to create the meaning of these memories to keep them awake to avoid the amalgams that often lead to hatred and misunderstanding. Therefore, the griot plays the role of history teacher perfectly and remains the ideal person to decipher the past of the people and allow it to efficiently build the present and face the future with much more serenity. Christiane Ndiaye summarizes all these ideas in the following words: "The most intense and formal training is that of the so-called 'traditional' Griots, part of West African castes who are initiates, whose science is secret and who are attached to a royal family whose origins, the genealogy and all the highlights of the history of the people of this kingdom they do not forget" (2004, 66).

Very influential in the decision making of his society, the griot "resolves discord," prevents and alleviates conflict, cultivates love for one's neighbor by a solid training with the elders of his caste, easily deciphering the secret science and its mystical impacts related to the survival of a royal family of whom he remembers the origins. He is therefore, as stated earlier, a historian, a genealogist, a mediator, and a grand custodian of oaths, of sacred and solemn promises, the basis for all social, spiritual, economic, and political development. The griot Djéli Mamadou Kouyaté is therefore right in saying that he is the "keeper of the keys of Manding," the one-man band by which everything passes, the emeritus curator of secret methods, capable of destroying or protecting the kingdom and far beyond that precise framework. He is the archivist par excellence: "The Griot finds himself to be, among the Malinké, the individual most able to perform such a function. And he performs it competently. We know his presence in all critical moments of every member of society's life (male and female circumcision, marriage, as well as on the battlefield). Note that this is a function of arbitration and publication that explains the diversification of the types of Griots and their specialization. Indeed, one can say that each State or profession has its Griots" (Camara 1992, 22).

The *djéli*, as indicated by the blood metaphor, impacts all members of the social organism. He acts according to the nature and need and the "critical moment of every member of society's life: male and female circumcision, marriage, and even on battlefields." In this context, more than his ability to say it well, it is his saying it as it is that grants him the status of savant, bringing out what is right.

Accordingly, the African griot does not belong to only one place. The principles of truth, proceeding from his specialization in serving people, are qualities that reflect his role in fostering universal citizenship.

On Citizenship

The griot, we know, is the knower of the history of the peoples, of tradition. His presence alongside social actors and historical players in the community is justified by the fight against institutionalized fear, forgetfulness, laziness, and idleness—and it serves to promote understanding, mutual respect, cohesion, and peace. By his function and his genre, the griot is not only master of the word, he is primarily a specialist in social sciences, psychology, pedagogy, communication, history, rhetoric, music, law, and development, to mention only those classic skills of universal scope.

When it comes to circumcision, for example, the company uses kênê-djeli, or the griot of circumcision. His role is to psychologically prepare the candidates for the test of iron. Thus, before the test, this griot will have the candidates publicly swear to their ability to withstand the test; otherwise they will not be given a wife when they have reached adulthood. The child comes to the griot. He reveals his identity, family, or clan. The griot reminds him of his ancestors' deeds through the motto of his clan. The child greets his fathers and his mothers and many other people who are dear to him. Then he gives his oath swearing in their name and his own name.[7]

This ritual of preparation for pain, the most important in the village or community, serves to highlight and showcase the youth who will move from one age to another. The kênê-djéli contributes to the psychological and moral training of the candidate, who, the following day, must meet the blacksmith and his iron circumcision. The dissipation of fear and the overcoming of the test ensures the future man of pride and honor for both himself and his family, including his mother, who finds herself enhanced by the bravery of her son. The tears of perjury dishonor the mother whose son accompanies the nephew to the site of circumcision. The mother could be asked concerning the purity of her son's blood if the latter dishonors his father's family by betraying his oath of the day before.

The kênê-djéli, who communicates to the youths the laws, rules, and values that govern the age group they are going to integrate, plays an educational role that values bravery and stoicism. For a man should never cry. He faces the trials of life by preserving his honor and his human dignity. In other words, the future head of the family could be called to higher social responsibilities, including the possibility of being the first of the city's defenders: the *kèlè-massa*.

The griot's role in upholding citizenship can be justified by his dexterity in the politics of economic and social development. The *donzo-djéli*, *serewa* (griot of the hunters), through his art, inscribes the names of the valiant fighters in the texts devoted to hunting adventures. The story of these hunting adventures gives way to the name *dozo-mana* or hunting narrative. Such literary compositions are the work of *dozo-ngoni fola* (player of the harp for the hunters) and incite dance and reflection. He knows how to drive the hunters into the virtual field of bravery and magic even before the completion of any meritorious action. These griot-musicians animate the *konsi* (hunting vigil) and the *simbo-si* (funeral vigil of the masters of the order).

Indeed, he sings to the dead in the presence of the living; he invites others to perform renowned actions that will echo in the collective memory posthumously. For they are surely subject to the *somayèlèma* (city change), a euphemism that refers to the history of the deceased. The use of this term indicates that the model never dies. It just passes from the concrete world to the abstract world of later fame. It is by performing acts of extreme bravery, such as an encounter with a buffalo or other mystical and ferocious animals, that the hunter is crowned with the very rewarding title of *simbo* by the donzo-djéli.

The citizen acts of the griot fall within the educational field by the transmission of historical, cultural, and political memory of the hunters. These skills also extend themselves to the ideological field insofar as they tell of the great deeds of the hunters by the revelation of a model to be followed. To this must be added the domain of magic-religion as it organizes rituals, purification vigils during the konsi, simbo-si, and *bade* (funeral).[8] At the aesthetic or artistic level, verbal competence magnifies the identity of the brotherhood. This is achieved through praise, songs, and humorous and philosophical discourses that encourage the hunters to follow through on their exploits. Apart from hunting, agriculture produced griots as well: the *sènè-djéli* (griot of the fields).

Land reforms imposed on the Mandingue by the emperor Sosso clearly put agriculture at the center of the main concerns for the city. These reforms were reinforced by Soundjata, who believed the city should meet his needs and prevent annual food crises. From that point, agriculture was expected to determine the new personality of the Maninka in addition to hunting. It needed to be encouraged and promoted. It was necessary for the griots, committed to raising awareness and promoting social equity, to also become interested in this vital area. Farmers were able to acquire an extensive knowledge of nature and time. This allowed them to control the planting calendar. The extension process supported by the sènè-djéli has, in turn, given rise to ideal farmers of this type.

The sènè-djéli also compose texts to the glory of the heroes. They design models to imitate and convey knowledge about the land, crops, animals, astronomy, seasons, and so on. These texts are imbued with literary creativity, which produces a new sensation every time one listens. Like the other kinds of griot, the sènè-djéli celebrates the memory of the great deceased in order to motivate the living, as expressed by Kabinè Cônô, a well-known sènè-djéli of the Guinean farmers.[9] The chorus sings of the pangs of hunger and the effort to fight the famine of the city. He reminds the living that the brave deceased peasants cannot come back to work for the living. Here we see the psychological and economic functions, interwoven with the literary art of the *sènè-djéli*. The griot who struggles for a just and peaceful society also knows how to encourage the troops in case of war and to get them to exercise respect for the rights of the captured or prisoners of war, or for human rights in general, similar to the Red Cross and other humanitarian organizations of the world today.

This kèlè-massa-djéli is a griot who accompanies warlords on the battlefield. His mission is to galvanize the troops. In this capacity, he drives the *tchèkan tèguè* (man-word-cutter), which is a debating contest motivating the warriors on the eve of an announced attack. The tchèkan tèguè consists of giving challenges without the presence of the enemy. On this occasion, the griot sets the stage. He plays great epic tunes such as the *djandjon*, the *djouga*, the *safinata-woulou*, the *siba*, the *bangoron*, and so on. This awakens the military sensitivities of the warriors who aspire to glory and fame.

The griot makes postwar narratives while evoking the promises they held. He sets the stage for the war that is still to be waged. Then he invites each warrior to make an oath for what he will do to the enemy on the set day of their meeting. Besides the griots who accompany the warlords, there are those who attach themselves to certain families for whom they will be the main griot. Their elected representatives are a part of the royal courts. They are called massa-djéli (griot of the court).

They should rightfully be called both griot of the warlord and griot of the court, because Mandingue society is an aristocratic society. Many men are able to become masters in their field. These kinds of people are statutorily appointed based on their performance, including kèlè-massa (warlords), *djao-massa* (trade lords), sènè-massa (lords of agriculture), and so on.

Each activity has its lord, his massa (king). Each would retain the services of a griot for his social standing, *djamou*, and his legacy. The griot is concerned with strengthening the personality, the reputation, and the prestige of his client. Every citizen of the city that seeks the services of the griot becomes the *djatigui* (soul-owner), that is, a master. The griot is entirely at his service. He protects the client's social interests, advises him, builds up his confidence in everything that he should or should not do, and makes known to the city everything that the master has done that is worthy of recognition. The type of bond that is formed between the djatigui and the djéli is based on an oath or contract. The bond covers the present and the future. Thus, djéli clans are forever joined to djatigui clans.

The griot solves all of the master and his family members' social problems. He represents them wherever he finds the need. He plays the role of lawyer, or ambassador, for the family. He is considered a member of the family, since he is the confidant. He is a social worker, and a full-time social worker at that. His interventions as a social worker are truly remarkable for energizing family life as well as in the daily management of conflicts. He guards and transmits the history of the allied clans, the deeds, failures, friendships, enmities, and especially the family trees, which determine the social relationships with other families, for the prosperity of the family. This work of memorization requires the griot to be a composer of genius with an identity matrix of being a master in order to become known by his original essence and actions.

Another type of griot, hardly the least, is the master in the art of scribing texts addressed to the clans, the *djéli-n'gara*. For services rendered, this griot receives, above all, respect and consideration. However, the beneficiaries of his social intervention also pay according to their means in order to meet the material needs of the griot. The massa-djéli and the hostess djatigui are reflections of this griot's power. A saying is, "The world belongs to the favorite and to the griot."[10] The highest-ranked and most feared griot is undoubtedly the djéli-n'gara (imperial griot).

The djéli-n'gara is a craftsman of public speaking. He embodies rhetoric and eloquence. He surpasses the ordinary kèlè-massa-djéli. As one who inspires heroes, the character of the djéli-n'gara is an emblematic intellectual figure. He is an anthropologist, gifted with the qualities of a historian-geographer, and has literary talents. In the city, he is a knowledgeable man since he travels extensively, rubbing shoulders with other kings and their people. He is steeped in knowledge that he owes to the learning and mastery of his craft. Curiosity is his best quality, and research is his method. He is recognized by the whole city as one to be imitated for his mastery of culture and conduct concerning social, legal, and political affairs. This type no longer belongs to a group or private clan like the *doundougouma-djéli* (private griot), but to the very universe itself. He represents what is called *froba-djéli* (griot of the people). The djéli-n'gara is sought out in the royal courts for his wisdom and experience of the word. He is at once the adviser, the diplomat, and the lawyer who reconciles the people and their king while ensuring proper conduct of public affairs. He is the king's king.

In the public sphere, where the *bélén* (pulpit) is set up, he is the great master of ceremonies, because he has the perfect knowledge of protocol and precedence that is required for good practice. This traditional communicator, great master of the hasp, is thus called *béléntigui* (master of the public pulpit). The peculiarity of the djéli-n'gara is that he specializes in the transmission of the historical, cultural, and political heritage of the city at a higher level than the other kinds of griots. He is a communicator of culture writ large, and he has great fame. He conveys the ideological values of the social model that was collectively built, and he observes its application in the city. He is the confidant of the emperor, the massa of massas. As such, he can receive or command to see every personality according to his rank, his qualities, and his honorable attributes that he claims in his creed. What is most interesting about the djéli-n'gara and all the other types mentioned above is the literary character of the texts they produce. They reveal the prodigious memory and the creative genius of this individual who represents the collective and historical memory of the city—and hence the intellectual qualities that bind him to the whole world.

CONCLUSION

This study aims to reveal that Africa has kept alive to this day the practice of a verbal art through the voice of the griot. Indeed, in oral tradition, nothing is free. There is no art for art's sake, because the word of the griot is a lesson, a truth that restores the past while simultaneously committing society to its future. His voice is not a way to express selfish and individual feelings. Instead, he is the spokesperson for collective values.

Thenceforth, the griot, despite being a member of society, retains through principles of truth a position of authority and of law. In short, the griot is a savant. He teaches the world what is right for the survival of their consciousness of being, for the identity of black people and for the historical truth. He promotes the establishment of knowledge, etiquette, and expertise. His word is the mirror of virtues and ideologies. Ultimately, the African griot restores the past, guarantees the present, and predicts the future of the African.

NOTES

1. Djéli yé djatigui ya dolo lé yé" (the blood is the liquor of the *djatigui*).

2. The collective name *nyamakala* indicates a social and occupational group whose members possess forces of opposition (*kala*) of the evil power (*gnama*) in any subject matter. Bokar N'Diagne says (1976, 13), on one hand the term derives from Bambara, where *nyama* means "fertilized, garbage," and *kala* means "a bit of," that is, "a bit of garbage." On the other hand, he attributes the origin of the word to spoken Toukouleur, where *nyama* means "you will eat," and *kala* means "all." In other words, the term *nyamakala*

might come from a Maninka language and mean "one who does not hesitate." This is not convincing, since many of the nyamakala guarantee sociocultural codes. They are invested in the defense of public morality. Therefore, they reject bad values. On the other hand, it seems the Bambara etymology can be understood as far as fertilizer and garbage are recoverable and reusable resources for the craftsman. This power of recycling the resource is a means of formal demand, which not only translates the meaning of *stalk*, by which the craftsman would hold the resource, but evokes the creative genius of the man whose hand reflects the power. So the power of the craftsman over the resource appears as a force of opposition to natural decomposition (cf. Kouyate 2013).

3. Dominique Zahan, quoted in Camara (1992, 108).

4. Manding people are Maninka but often referred to as Malinke.

5. Maninkas or Malinkes are West African groups present in Mali and Guinea, culturally related to the Bambaras. The Malinkes share the same origins as the Bambaras; their societies are identical. There is a strong lineage between the two ethnicities in spite of occasional conflicts between the two. The language they speak is Maninka or Malinke of the Mandé family. The Bambara are West African people of the large Mandingue group, mostly present in Mali. They are originally from Mandé. They allegedly left that region to escape Malinke domination, at the time of the empire of Mali. Thus their name came to signify "those who refused to submit" (*toban* or "refuse" and *mana* or "master"). Others understand this etymology as meaning those who refused to submit to Islam. But the quality of this people justifies itself through its cultural rigor.

6. The jamu is the patronymic. African tradition confers upon him gods in reference to the might of the wildcat and to the cunning that is generally attributed to certain animals such as the hare or the partridge (an attribute of the Ouattara, for example). It is evident that in traditional society, "Every name has a meaning, a secret significance," as stated by the griot Mamadou Kouyaté (Niane 1960, 10). Listen to the griot of Kourouma concerning the mottos of Fama: "Fama Doumbouya! True Doumbouya, father Doumbouya, mother Doumbouya, last and legitimate descendant of the princes Doumbouya of the Horodougou, panther totem" (Kourouma 1970, 11).

7. It is through the child's parents, uncles and aunts, and any member of the community that is from their generation.

8. This term is similar to an anagram, by reversing the two syllables. *Ba* (large) and *de* (assembly) become *dê/djéba* (the last assembly) held around the remains.

9. "Fôlô-fôlô dabala ni sè, sou tè monnè bô" (glory to the deceased farmers; one who is deceased can hardly avenge one who is living).

10. In polygamy, it is the favorite wife who has the most privilege, who is the most favored, because she is the confidant of the husband. Among the several wives, one is considered the confidante and hence the favorite.

REFERENCES

Camara, Sory. 1992. *Gens de la parole*. Paris: ACCT, Karthala, SAEC.

Chevrier, Jacques. 1983. *L'Arbre à palabre*. Paris: Hatier.

Courtes, Jean. 1976. *Introduction à la Sémiotique Narrative et Discursive*. Paris: Hachette.

Fayolle, Roger. 1987. *La Critique*. Paris: Armand Colin.

Fouet, Francis. 1984. *Direction, Littérature Africaine D'Engagement*. Abidjan, Côte d'Ivoire: NEI.

Hamon, Philippe. 1984. *Texte et Idéologie*. Paris: PUF.

Hanault, Anne. 1983. *Narratologie, Sémiotique Générale, Les Enjeux de la Sémiotique*. Paris: PUF.

Hourantier, Marie-José. 1990. "L'introduction de la technique du conteur dans le théâtre-rituel négro-africain." In *Séminaire de Méthodologie Derecherche et D'Enseignement du Conte Africain*, AUPELF, Abidjan, Côte d'Ivoire, April 3–6, 1989.

Jansen, Jan. 2000. *The Griots: An Essay on Oral Tradition Diplomacy*. Münster: LIT Verlag.

Kourouma, Ahmadou. 1970. *Les soleils des indépendances*. Paris: Edition Seuil.

Kouyate, Brahima. 2013. "L'Onomastique en Pays Mandingue: Le Cas de la Région du Denguélé." PhD diss., Université Alassane Ouattara.

N'Diagne, Bokar. 1976. *Les Castes au Mali*. Bamako: Editions populaires.

Ndiaye, Christiane. 2004. *Introduction aux littératures francophones*. Montreal: PUM.

Niane, Djibil Tamsir. 1960. *Soundjata ou L'Épopée Mandingue*. Paris: Présence Africaine.

Prud'homme, Johanne, and Nelson Guilbert. 2006. "Le Langage en Ligne." In *signe*, edited by Louis Hébert. Rimouski, Quebec. http://www.signosemio.com.

Riffaterre, Michael. 1983. *Sémiotique de la poésie*. Paris: Seuil.

Traoré, Issa Falaba. 1970. *Duel dans les falaises*. Abidjan, Côte d'Ivoire: NEA.

8 · Experimenting with Freedom
Gandhi's Political Epistemology

Mohandas Karamchand Gandhi (1869–1948) was the political leader of the Indian independence movement against British rule. In this capacity, Gandhi was undoubtedly the moral and political nerve center of the successful anticolonial struggle. His moral example inspired many other global political movements, and he is widely considered a beacon and the most compelling spokesperson for nonviolent (*ahimsa*) resistance (Hardiman 2011). This essay demonstrates the interconnectedness of his practices of *satyagraha* (civil disobedience), *ahimsa* (nonviolence), and *swaraj* (self-rule). I show that since moral experimentation was a key ingredient in how Gandhi conceptualized the application of these core principles, it offers an important window into his political epistemology.

Gandhi held fast to the belief that empirical and spiritual truths together give access to the Truth. His approach is thus at a theoretical remove from most European accounts of epistemology. Gandhi's spiritual epistemology is also a political program designed to bridge divides across racial, ethnic, religious, and linguistic lines. Accessing the truth requires dialogic engagement with others and taking active steps to improve the possibility of dialogue. This provides the political actor with empirical awareness of differing perspectives on the same issue. Even when such dialogic engagement falters, belief in the oneness of humanity ensures that accounts of irreconcilable differences are balanced against possibilities of cooperation and understanding.

Engaging others is an obviously crucial dimension of any political program. Gandhi insisted on a second dimension that was equally important to political emancipation. Without a corresponding commitment to crafting a better self, one cannot engage with others without devolving into violence. As the seat of desires, all of which have been greatly heightened because of modern civilization, the self seeks more than it should. As a result, the modern self ignores both empirical reality and spiritual insights for crass materialism. Disciplining this self is crucial for an honest engagement with difference, for a thorough accounting of the ills of modern civilization, and, of course, for battling colonialism. Gandhi's political epistemology is at once broad in its sway—nothing less than modern civilization demands the activist's constant attention—and focused enough to notice the nuances within the self. This epistemology is, in other words, simultaneously other- and self-directed.

The political expression of this epistemology is woven into nearly every feature of satyagraha, ahimsa, and swaraj. However, because this empirical-spiritual epistemology is sensitive to the reality the political actor shares with others, and guarded about the ways in which the self can become deluded, the implementation of this epistemology is necessarily tied to a practice of ethical experimentation. This experimentation takes the form of both practical policies designed to alleviate suffering and ascetic practices designed to liberate consciousness from the thrall of modern civilization. The results of an experiment are, in keeping with the scientific method, always provisional. At all times, however, the experiment in satyagraha, ahimsa, and swaraj deepens spiritual insight about the oneness and diversity of humankind.

Satyagraha, Ahimsa, and Swaraj

Given its appeal to a number of global political movements, it is important to understand what exactly satyagraha means within the framework of Gandhi's political thought. To that end, it is useful to begin with the concept of Truth, an area that, given the wide use of the concept of civil disobedience, is not usually associated with it. According to Gandhi (2007, 235), if "the quest for Truth is the *summum bonum* of life," then satyagraha is the engine of that quest. The term *satyagraha* itself was invented to give a new name to the struggle for rights that Gandhi had initiated during his years as a lawyer in South Africa. Gandhi's opponents and observers likened his movement to other historical instances of passive resistance or conscientious objection. Wary of these associations, and opposed to any merely passive resistance, Gandhi sought to emphasize the active dimension of civil disobedience. The broader question for Gandhi was, what principle did a civil disobedient seek to become active for? Gandhi's answer was *satya*.

Satyagraha is an amalgam of two words: *satya* and *agraha*, which together mean Truth and force. According to Bhikhu Parekh, a noted interpreter of Gandhi's thought, "When the two terms are combined there is a beautiful duality of meaning, implying both insistence *on* and *for* truth" (1989b, 143). There is a still deeper meaning to be gleaned from the term. For Joan Bondurant

(1988, 17), *satya* itself is derived from *sat*, which means being. Understood in this way, Truth is the essence of what exists, and *satyagraha* is an insistence on existence itself.

To complicate this picture, let us examine the principle of Truth in Gandhi's thought. Gandhi (1979b, 172) always insisted that he was a "votary of Truth," which meant for him that he was always seeking it. However, he always had an epistemological humility about the kinds of truths human beings could conceivably come to possess. Given the variations in human perspectives that are endemic to the diversity of forms of human organization, there cannot but be a profusion of multiple truths. To say, as Gandhi does, that he is a "votary of Truth" is not to claim access to an overarching Truth. It is, instead, to seek access to diverse truths that together constitute Truth. In the process, one comes face to face with what is, namely, the truths of plural human perspectives. Each perspective sheds a partial light on Truth, and without this partial access, Truth cannot even be said to exist.

The perspectivalism of Gandhi's approach does not imply that these multiple truths speak in a uniform voice. Gandhi argued that "every case can be seen from no less than seven points of view, all of which are probably correct by themselves, but not correct at the same time and in the same circumstances" (2009, 250). Let us unpack Gandhi's words. Reality is itself multifaceted. Everyone sees things from their own perspective. Gandhi allows that individual perspectives do indeed shed light on reality. There is, in other words, considerable value to be attached to how people view a situation and their own interests. However, the narrow perspective of one political actor cannot encapsulate the entirety of the Truth of a situation. The Truth is itself composed of "seven points of view." Gandhi's numerical choice of "seven points of view" might well be arbitrary. Nevertheless, it conveys the multifaceted nature of the Truth of reality.

Prima facie, there is nothing unfamiliar in what Gandhi is saying here, and indeed, to some extent, his views on this matter run parallel to those of empiricists such as John Stuart Mill. For Mill, "the steady habit of correcting and completing [a wise person's] own opinion by collating it with those of others . . . is the only stable foundation for a just reliance on [wisdom]" (1989, 24). Where Gandhi differs from Mill, as we shall see shortly, is on Mill's premise that a firm uneducated belief in the existence of Truth and its ultimate victory over attempts to suppress it are nothing more than "superstition" or "sentimentality" (Mill 1989, 31, 37). Despite the similarity in their thought, it is important to remember that Gandhi radically departs from Mill's position. Gandhi's faith that human beings can arrive dialogically at the Truth is utterly alien to Mill.

For Gandhi, the fact that the Truth exists is a sentiment, but for precisely that reason it is to be valued much more than brute empiricism.

Gandhi's differences from empiricists like Mill draw upon the writings of the nineteenth-century author John Ruskin. In *Unto This Last*, which had a profound effect on Gandhi, Ruskin argued that the brute rationalism of the economic theories of David Ricardo, Jeremy Bentham, and Mill belied the ultimately affective nature of mankind. Absent an acknowledgment of this aspect of human existence, the elegant theories produced by political economists depend upon faulty premises (Ruskin 1985). As such, they are not at all applicable to the motive forces that drive human actions. An individual's actions are predicated on affective attachments just as much as they are on rational calculation. To see the world only from the point of view of rationalism produces gross injustices. In contrast, forms of political and social organization that operate on the basis of affective attachments respect the dignity and humanity of all.

In Gandhi's hand—who, incidentally, translated *Unto This Last* into Gujarati and published it under the title *Sarvodaya* (Progress for all)—satyagraha becomes the strategy that seeks Truth by bringing into dialogue multiple and, at times, antagonistic truths. At its base, however, is a firm belief that Truth exists because humans have an affective attachment to Truth, even if they cannot themselves arrive at it singly. Politically, this faith is reflected in the very first step of any satyagraha struggle, which is to discover the conditions one seeks to address, from the perspective of both the aggrieved and those accused. Gandhi's initial attempts to *initiate* satyagraha in India began with a fact-finding mission in which he turned to both the oppressed masses and the colonial administration in order to understand the reality of the situation. Many years later, and in an altogether different context, Martin Luther King Jr. would also devote the first step of his mission in Birmingham, Alabama, to learning the truth of the conditions from the perspective of both the oppressed and the oppressors.

Devotion to accessing Truth in its multiple guises assumes the presence of goodwill. Political actors are more likely to reach compromise if they believe that their opponent is similarly motivated by a sincere search for Truth. While it might be tempting to assume that the very call for dialogic engagement between multiple truths would lead to compromise, the reality is not as simple. What is to prevent one actor from believing that his truth is the Truth that all parties should agree with? How does the sincerity of a votary of Truth link up with another equally sincere votary of Truth in dialogue? This is not an easy task. As we saw above, the term *agraha* in satyagraha stands for force. To deepen the etymology of the term, we can turn again to Bondurant, who notes that at its root, *agraha* means a "firm grasping" (1988, 11–12). While the compound term *satyagraha* would thus mean "Truth force" or "firmly grasping Truth," human psychology introduces an undeniable element of possessiveness into the term. How can we maintain the goodwill that should animate dialogic interactions between multiple truths?

The goodwill of satyagraha finds its theoretical and practical elaboration in the concept of ahimsa. This is because ahimsa prevents the willful assertion of one truth over another. It thereby acts as a necessary circuit breaker between a powerful attraction to Truth on the one hand and its forcible articulation on the other. As Gandhi notes, civility (or goodwill) "does not here mean the mere outward gentleness of speech cultivated for the occasion, but an inborn gentleness and desire to do the opponent good" (2009, 394). In order to get at this key Gandhian concept, it is helpful to again begin with its etymology. For Parekh, "Etymologically and in its standard usage, the term *himsa* means a *wish* to kill or harm and implies ill-will" (1989a, 110). Similarly, for Bondurant ahimsa is a negative of himsa, which means to injure, kill, slay. To practice ahimsa is therefore to avoid injuring, killing, or slaying (Bondurant 1988, 23–24). Understood along these lines, the cultivation of ahimsa as a political practice should be obvious. Faced with another truth, we are required to practice ahimsa in order to avoid political disagreements from devolving into violence. There is, however, a still deeper meaning to the practice of ahimsa. If human psychology is usually unequipped to deal with alternative perspectives on Truth, then it becomes very difficult to sustain the epistemological humility that goes along with the goodwill necessary for dialogue. Satyagraha can degrade into a firm grasp of the truth one already holds. Ahimsa, therefore, is also a moral position an actor takes toward oneself, and it prevents an attraction to the Truth from becoming an adamant assertion about possession of that Truth. To do otherwise would be to kill, injure, or slay (physically or metaphysically) the multiple perspectives that constitute Truth.

Ahimsa is therefore both the supreme political expression of the goodwill that animates dialogic engagement and the axiomatic core of Gandhi's political theory (Veeravalli 2014). More than just a negative injunction against killing or harm, ahimsa also calls for a broader engagement with others through love and compassion. We can see Gandhi's syncretic tendencies in how we developed the compassionate face of ahimsa. In ahimsa Gandhi combines the Hindu, Jain, and Buddhist practices of nonviolence with a Christian emphasis on love. In this guise, the goodwill underwriting ahimsa finds expression in an active desire for the well-being of others. Gandhi's emphasis on love is an attempt to bridge the divide between competing visions of the truth without diminishing the other's truth. This is achieved by showing the other that one shares the other's pain and, in the process, seeks to understand the other's position as she herself understands it. This desire for the well-being of the other explains Gandhi's sincere efforts during satyagraha movements to learn about both sides of a political dispute. It also stands behind Gandhi's ascetic self-cultivation (Howard 2013). His well-documented attempts at controlling his diet, his vow of celibacy, and, above all, his fasts undertaken to atone for the sins of others and his own attest to the cultivation of goodwill toward his political opponents. By disciplining the actor's basest impulses, these ascetic practices enable the open reception and transmission of goodwill. The political opponent sees that there is no base motive hiding behind public avowals of sincerity; by cleansing his very being of acquisitiveness in all its forms, the political actor shows that nothing but love and compassion animates his search for a dialogic encounter.

Ahimsa in its positive guise, therefore, also allows for constructive actions that help reduce areas of disagreement. Here Bondurant identifies the true brilliance of ahimsa and satyagraha: "The claim for *satyagraha* is that through the operation of non-violent action the truth as judged by the fulfillment of human needs will emerge in the form of a mutually satisfactory and agreed-upon solution" (1988, 195). The shared reality between political opponents, and what can be changed about it to make it better, becomes the true goal of satyagraha, and ahimsa enables that underlying unity of interests (the Truth) to emerge.

Gandhi's perspective on the indelibility of shared interests stands in direct opposition to the revolutionary rhetoric that animated many Indian political thinkers at the turn of the twentieth century. For these revolutionaries, violence was, if not the first, then certainly an acceptable route to political independence. Drawn to "European revolutionary movements and ideas—terrorism, Russian nihilism, Marxism, the ideologies of the Irish home rule movement and the Italian *Risorgimento*," these thinkers stood in the starkest contrast to Gandhi's views on the acceptable route to independence (Gandhi 2009, xxxvii). Given the importance they attached to the principle of swaraj (self-rule or independence), Gandhi's rhetorical appropriation of the term was designed to flip the usual sense in which the concept had been hitherto deployed.

For Gandhi, swaraj did not mean a simple expulsion of the British from India. Instead, *swaraj* implied a total critique of modern civilization and the correct diagnosis of its attendant diseases. In *Hind Swaraj*, Gandhi—in the guise of an Editor—engages a Reader whose rhetoric is clearly meant to mimic the revolutionary thinkers who held sway among the colonized intelligentsia. To the claim that India must follow the model of Japanese nationalism at the turn of the twentieth century, and thereby use violence and industrialization to expel the British, Gandhi's Editor makes a truly novel argument. To the Reader's proposal, the Editor says, "In effect [your proposal] means this: that we want English rule without the Englishman. You want the tiger's nature, but not the tiger; that is to say, you would make India English, and, when it becomes English, it will be called not Hindustan but Englistan. This is not the Swaraj that I want" (Gandhi 2009, 27).

Drawing out the premises of revolutionary rhetoric to their inevitable consequences, the Editor identifies that in effect, the use of violent methods fails on two grounds. First, it shows an imagination hostage to a vision of the future dictated by the colonizer. The Reader desires independent India to be an industrialized powerhouse, regardless of how dangerous this mode of social and economic organization would be to ordinary Indians. Second, and relatedly, the theoretical premises misdiagnose the problems that beset colonized India. The Reader assumes that it is a matter of who controls India, when in fact the real disease is the tiger itself, that is, modern civilization.

Gandhi's critique of modern civilization draws upon what he saw as the predatory impulses evident in modern capitalism. According to Gandhi, the earliest agents of colonialism were themselves amoral. Motivated solely by the desire "to increase [their] commerce and to make money," the agents of the British East India Company were uninterested in promoting civilizational ends (Gandhi 2009, 39). Internecine conflicts between Indian kingdoms made it possible for the company to increase its holdings in India by playing off one ruler against another. The company preyed on the petty ambitions and fears of Indian rulers. For this reason, "it is truer to say that [Indians] gave India to the English than that India was lost" (Gandhi 2009, 39). The security that the company guaranteed came at a terrible cost. The highest cost borne by India was the loss of its civilization. For Gandhi, properly understood, "civilization is that mode of conduct which points out to man the path of duty. Performance of duty and observance of morality are convertible terms. To observe morality is to attain mastery over our mind and our passions. So doing, we know ourselves" (Gandhi 2009, 65).

On this view, colonialism is much more than the acquisition of territory and an extraction of its resources for the benefit of the colonizers. It is, rather, a diminution in the mastery over mind and passions that enable civilization itself. By offering cheaper cloth, faster travel, better medical care, and so on, British colonialism increased desires manifold. In so doing, it drew India deeper into the tiger's domain, from which it could not even imagine escape. Like the Reader, all Indians could hope for was the substitution of one ruler for another. Against this tragic trajectory, Gandhi asks Indians to remember that true swaraj comes when "we learn to rule ourselves. It is, therefore, in the palm of our hands" (Gandhi 2009, 71). Commitment to duty and morality, both of which, on Gandhi's view, point us toward limiting the ambit of our desires, delivers swaraj. Just as importantly, swaraj is not a distant dream to be achieved when other conditions are met. It is, instead, available this very instant.

The most startling conclusion that Gandhi alerts us to is that the British Empire is itself lacking in civilizational merit. Given the ideological sway of Britain over the hearts and minds of many Indians, this was a remarkable claim. Indeed, much of British educational policy was designed precisely to show the poverty of Indian civilization in comparison to the supposed grandeur of Europe. In a famous minute on educational policy, the nineteenth-century British administrator Lord Macaulay deemed the entire history of Indian civilization less important in the lessons it had to offer than a "single shelf of a good European library." Most Indians had accepted this premise and therefore sought to imitate Europe. In contrast to these Indians, Gandhi argued that acquiring swaraj would not just be an Indian endeavor, but would also draw the British out from the tiger's domain. It would make the British realize how far they themselves had traveled from the path of civilization.

Surprising as Gandhi's diagnoses are, they are not without merit. Inspired by nineteenth-century accounts of factory life in industrialized England, Gandhi recognized the horrible conditions under which British laborers worked. Virtually enslaved by the factory owners, these workers lived in a condition "worse than that of beasts." Even if such conditions could be bettered, Gandhi argued that the English still remained enslaved. Only this time, "they are enslaved by temptation of money and of luxuries that money can buy" (Gandhi 2009, 35). Ruskin's influence is again in evidence here. Like Ruskin, Gandhi was clear that the search for greater wealth without regard for "social affections" was bound to lead a civilization astray. This was because it was these social affections that enabled the right distribution of rights and duties within a political system. This is why, and despite their civilizational boasts, Gandhi thought that the British had forgotten the example of Greece and Rome, from whom they claimed to draw their own civilizational impulses. As Gandhi once put it, the difference between Western and Eastern civilizations can be grasped in a series of oppositions. Western civilization is "destructive," "centrifugal," "disruptive," and "without a goal." In contrast, Eastern civilization for Gandhi is "constructive" and "centripetal"; it "combines" and "always has a goal before it" (Gandhi 1979a, 244). It is no surprise therefore that Gandhi thought that the British also lacked swaraj.

The purpose of satyagraha is to draw political opponents into a dialogue oriented around a desire for attaining Truth. The suffering of the political actor is meant to awaken a moral transformation in the opponent. It is meant to make the opponent realize how far he too has traveled from the Truth. Gandhi's long-standing belief in the essential wisdom of the British polity led him to believe that even the British could be morally swayed back to a search for Truth. Satyagraha would enliven in them their sense of swaraj and let them acknowledge how modern civilization had fundamentally confused their sense of moral duty. They too could then become civilized.

Experimenting with Truth

Satyagraha, ahimsa, and swaraj are central tenets of Gandhi's political thought. The harmony underwriting the three tenets is that each depends on the other for its proper functioning. Satyagraha would be impossible if the political actor were not driven by a desire for ahimsa. In turn, true ahimsa—in both its negative and positive dimensions—would be unattainable were it not for the self-control that *swaraj* asks the political actor to cultivate. Finally, to round the circle, swaraj itself would remain a distant dream were it not channeled into active political struggle on behalf of Truth, that is, satyagraha. There is an internal harmony between the three tenets.

It is important to note at this point that the harmony of the three principles is itself predicated upon an altogether different intellectual edifice. On its own, it is not clear why we should believe that civil disobedience allied with self-rule and nonviolence would yield positive results. Could we not say with Gandhi's critics that he made mistakes, and that the trajectory of historical events belies the harmonization of interests that he envisioned? How might Gandhi respond to these criticisms? What is the edifice that supports his faith in the harmonization of satyagraha, ahimsa, and swaraj?

This is where we enter the peculiarity of Gandhi's thought. A few words of caution are merited here, especially since aspects of Gandhi's underlying epistemology are so utterly foreign to European standards. According to Parekh, "For Gandhi the scientific spirit meant the spirit of rational inquiry, 'the spirit of search for the truth in place of being satisfied with tradition without question,' and implied intellectual curiosity, rigorous pursuit of truth and critical examination of established beliefs. Gandhi's admiration of the scientific *spirit*, however, did not extend to the scientific culture" (1989b, 31). This is because, as Anthony Parel notes, modern European epistemology is firmly grounded in "dogmatic empiricism" that "discounts any spiritual insights humans may have" (2000, 9). To the question that animates epistemology, How do we know that we know the Truth?, a European empiricist would answer, "By empirical evidence." In contrast, "Gandhi assumes that humans live by truths established by empiricism, reason, and spiritual insights" (Parel 2000, 9). Gandhi renounces neither empiricism nor reason. Instead, spirituality supplements these other methods. Turning to Gandhi without an acknowledgment of his spiritual beliefs would stymie our ability to understand his thought.

Still, exploring in depth the structure of Gandhi's thought on matters he deemed spiritual might take us too far afield from his epistemology. It certainly would require a deeper exploration of Hindu metaphysics. For our purposes, therefore, I focus on one basic Hindu concept from which Gandhi drew his spiritual beliefs. This concept is the interconnectedness of all life, also known as *Atman*. *Atman*, as Parel tells us, means "immortal spirit" (2000, 9). Although the concept has resonances in Christian theology, and while Gandhi almost certainly drew on biblical resources in articulating his conception of it, according to the indologist Wendy Doniger (2009), *Atman* implies the individual manifestation of the world soul *Brahman*. All beings are endowed with *Atman*, and this *Atman* is itself a reflection of *Brahman*. As Gandhi writes, "I believe in absolute oneness of God and, therefore, also of humanity. What though we have many bodies? We have but one soul" (quoted in Veeravalli 2014, 1). The interconnectedness of beings is one basis for the Hindu belief in the sacredness of all life and, by extension, the principle of ahimsa.

Ahimsa was earlier identified as an axiomatic principle underwriting Gandhi's thought. In a manner resonant with the tradition of thought associated with Parmenides and Plato, Gandhi believed that without the principle of nonviolence, because it maintains beings and reality (*sat*), the universe itself would have ended. While Hindu thought usually advocates ahimsa in its negative sense—that is, it asks its adherents to refrain from harming others—Gandhi, as we saw earlier, was also interested in exploring the positive dimensions of ahimsa. This he achieved through the practice of compassion or love. However, as we also saw, this compassion is not just a theoretical endeavor. It demands practical application in social, economic, and political life. It is only in its practical guise that the theoretical role occupied by ahimsa can make its fullest contribution to reducing political disagreement. This gives us something of an answer to the epistemological puzzle underwriting Gandhi's thought. Gandhi's epistemology was rooted in the belief that we are all interconnected, but the proof of this assertion needed constant validation. In turn, verifying the claim that we are all interconnected is possible through the practice of satyagraha. But the Truth (satya) toward which the political actor bends his resolve is not available without dialogue. In turn, dialogue is impossible without swaraj. But true swaraj needs constant vigilance against the enticements of the expediency modern civilization offers. The political actor learns to channel his resolve and acquires swaraj by constantly experimenting with forms of living that enable the highest attainment of self-control and humility.

It is not surprising, therefore, that Gandhi termed his autobiography *The Story of My Experiments with Truth*. Why did he make this choice? We saw earlier that ahimsa demands epistemological humility from the political actor. To assume that the actor already possesses the Truth is both a violation of the principle of ahimsa and a perversion of satyagraha. Gandhi touches upon this issue by addressing the literary medium of autobiographies. It is instructive to listen to him in his own words: "Supposing you reject tomorrow the things you hold as principles today, or supposing you revise in the future your plans of today, is it not likely that the men who shape their conduct on the authority of your word, spoken or written, may be misled? Don't you think it would be better not to write anything like an autobiography, at any rate just yet?" (Gandhi 2009, 13). In response, Gandhi admits that the issue bothered him as a writer. His doubts were resolved when he realized that he did not mean to write an autobiography at all. Instead, "I simply want to tell the story of my numerous experiments with truth, and as my life consists of nothing but those experiments, it is true that the story will take the shape of an autobiography. But I shall not mind, if every page of it speaks only of my experiments" (Gandhi 2009, 14).

We can appreciate Gandhi's theoretical maneuver. He is saying that because his whole life has been a series of experiments, he has learned that he cannot fully trust the results of any one experiment. Every experiment needs further validation when circumstances change; with each successive experiment, personal truth comes closer to Truth. While we can appreciate Gandhi's recognition of the role contingency plays in his epistemology, that still leaves the question, what exactly is experimentation? Unfortunately, Gandhi never tells us, and it is an area where many of his sympathetic and critical interpreters have not much to say.

Despite his relative silence on the issue, experimentation is the key to understanding Gandhi's epistemology. According to Anuradha Veeravalli, "The experiment establishes the reality of Truth and the truth of reality in illustrating/ being an expression of the laws that govern the relation between man and the world" (2014, 36). In other words, through experimentation, political actors disclose the underlying reality that they share not only with each other, but with the world itself. A useful illustration of how experimentation "establishes the reality of Truth and the truth of reality" would be Gandhi's experiments with his own attitude toward his diet and, in turn, how these experiments informed his broader understanding of the relation between satyagraha, ahimsa, and swaraj.

A subject of almost obsessive attention, the body and its care occupy a recurring role in Gandhi's writings. His experiments in medicine, together with a controlled diet, were an attempt to regain swaraj—understood here as bodily self-control—from the dangerous allurements of modern civilization. From his earliest days in London as a law student, Gandhi tried to find vegetarian alternatives for a meat-based diet. He learned early on "that the real seat of taste was not the tongue but the mind" (Gandhi 2009, 67). This meant that curtailing the violence the human body commits against other nonhuman bodies depends on disciplining the mind. But the cravings of the mind are themselves subtle. The patient actor uses experiments to discover which cravings cannot be removed, which can be limited, and others that can be done away with entirely.

The lessons that would be gleaned from these experiments would help advance human understanding of what swaraj truly requires. Gandhi often experimented on himself before recommending the results to others. For instance, during a recruitment drive for satyagraha, Gandhi subsisted entirely on a diet of fruits and lemon juice. He was convinced that this was all that the body needed to survive, and any more would only strengthen the mind's cravings. The strain of recruiting workers, however, proved to be more taxing than his diet could sustain. After Gandhi fell seriously ill, his doctors offered him beef broth and milk as supplements to his meager diet. He refused to take beef broth because it went against his very Hindu understanding of ahimsa. Milk, however, proved to be a more difficult substance to refuse. Gandhi was faced with the difficult choice between consuming milk and returning to his work, or maintaining the conditions of the experiment, but at the expense of ending his political activities. He chose to consume milk. Although he himself held onto the conviction that adult humans do not need milk, he learned an important lesson. He urged those who had sought to follow his example by eschewing milk "not to persist in the experiment, unless they find it beneficial in every way, or unless they are advised by experienced physicians" (Gandhi 2009, 252). Experiments therefore helped him understand the truth of reality; some cravings exist for a reason and must be fed.

Given the theoretical sophistication underwriting satyagraha, ahimsa, and swaraj, the example of milk in Gandhi's diet might appear to be a trivial choice. For Gandhi this was clearly not the case. He believed that the kind of substances someone consumed would inevitably shape the character of the person. In this, he was following the Indian proverb "that as a man eats, so shall he become" (Gandhi 2009, 251). As noted earlier, if swaraj is already in the palm of our hands, self-rule demands attentiveness to personal habits as much as the grand politics of the state. Self-control aimed at nonviolence in thought and deed would be essential for orienting oneself to the Truth. But whether the truth one held conformed to reality could be verified only through experimentation. The results of these experiments themselves could rarely be taken as final—Gandhi, after all, continued experimenting with a milk-free diet—and could never be imposed on others. Experimentation needed to be applied broadly for the Truth of a doctrine to emerge. Swaraj and ahimsa would together deliver satya (Truth) and sat (reality/existence).

CONCLUSION

Gandhi's successes and failures are still the subject of considerable debate (Chenoweth and Stephan 2011; Roberts and Ash 2009). It is not always the case that the practice of satyagraha, ahimsa, and swaraj necessarily yields beneficial political outcomes. Seen from an alternative historical lens, Gandhi failed to bring about Hindu-Muslim unity and a thorough reevaluation of the social values underwriting Hinduism. Further, although India did achieve freedom from British rule, Gandhi's fears that Indian leaders wanted not swaraj but an "Englistan" came true. The developmental path taken by postindependence Indian leaders was at some remove from Gandhi's own expectations of what swaraj would mean. In addition, the universality of Gandhi's strategy is not entirely obvious. For example, although Gandhi himself thought that satyagraha could be practiced by Jews against the Nazis, most of Gandhi's contemporary commentators and his more recent interpreters agree that satyagraha, precisely because it draws the oppressor into dialogue through goodwill, needs a legal framework to protect the oppressed. In the words of the letter the Jewish philosopher Martin Buber wrote to Gandhi, "*Satyagraha* is testimony. Testimony without acknowledgment is martyrdom" (Parekh 1989b, 169).

Whatever the limitations of Gandhi's political philosophy, its broad appeal and applicability attest to its importance. The very mobility of Gandhi's writings also speaks to their, at times maddening, inconsistencies. Indeed, in some respects, as foremost a political actor, Gandhi was not interested in theoretical consistency. The very principle of experimentation requires that almost all political axioms and received wisdom be deferred until empirical confirmation. A principle articulated one day might need to be reevaluated on another day based on new information. Regulating this commitment is Gandhi's altogether spiritual belief in the oneness of humanity and the primacy of ahimsa. Spiritual beliefs might have little effect on a determined opponent impervious to Gandhi's critique of modernity. The amalgam of the scientific spirit of empiricism and reason on the one hand, and spirituality on the other, does not make for a consistent political philosophy. Indeed, as Gandhi himself noted, his "experiments continue[d] at the expense of trusting friends" who turned to Gandhi for a stable framework within which to view their actions and the trajectory of the independence movement. Despite being faced with the expectations for consistency, Gandhi himself adhered only to "a little voice within us [that] tells us, 'You are on the right track, move neither to your left nor right, but keep to the straight and narrow way'" (Gandhi 2009, 154).

This is not in itself a failure. The principles of satyagraha and swaraj are flexible enough to accommodate a variety of political experiences. They work, however, only so long as we do not lose sight of an axiomatic commitment to ahimsa. To the degree that ahimsa guides the actor's forays into political life, Gandhi would argue that the method of satyagraha and the self-discipline needed for swaraj will automatically follow. What path political actors take (e.g., which laws they choose to break and which to keep), and how they conceptualize their critique of modern civilization (e.g., is modern medicine in all its forms bad? Do railroads and electricity diminish our capacity for self-rule?) will obviously change according to the circumstances a political actor finds himself in. Nevertheless, spiritual faith in the oneness of humankind will naturally delimit the kinds of choices and options political actors should consider.

From a political standpoint, and in Gandhi's own mind, these choices and options fall in favor of small grassroots-oriented democratic models, rather than sweeping state-level technocratic decision making. For instance, in his constructive program, Gandhi advocated employment by making *khadi* (homespun cloth) to combat the effects of imported British cloth, village sanitation in order to improve the health of the mass of Indians living in villages, basic education, and so on. Later in life, Gandhi came to recognize the need for factory-built equipment in agriculture. He also recognized that education, the provision of sanitation, the uplift of untouchables (in Gandhi's lexicon called Harijan, meaning children of God), and other key components of postcolonial reconstruction required state involvement. As Ronald Terchek notes, "[Gandhi's] formulation of politics is not meant to settle political questions but to keep them alive, and his experiments are not meant to discover perfectionist solutions but to be resilient to diversity and openness" (1998, 168). Keeping with his experimental epistemology, Gandhi was willing to modulate his vision of modernity by reality. As such, his critique of Western civilization was not total; Gandhi was willing to borrow elements of it in order to supplement core commitments in his own vision.

Still, Gandhi recognized that there have to be limits to how far India adopted the tools of modern civilization. As his dialogue with the Indian nationalists reveals, Gandhi was conscious of the fact that political actors should never efface the key distinction between means and ends. Where, for the nationalists, violence was merely a conducive means to independence, Gandhi warned that the use of violence would itself contort the soul of the political actor. As such, even the acquisition of the proposed end (independence) would ultimately be nullified through civilizational loss. Similarly, the policies of the constructive program can easily fall within the province of state policy, which often can act on a scale that individuals and village communities can scarcely dream of. For Gandhi, however, to accede to the efficiency and scope of state action is to implicitly sanction the kinds of violence that the state depends on. This violence is levied daily not only in the form of taxation, but in its investment in the tools of modern civilization that are the very source, in Gandhi's mind, of the ills that beset societies. In contrast, to draw upon the resources of village communities is not only to preserve the framework of moral duties and responsibilities that are the hallmark of civilization. It is also to delimit the ambit of violence at a broad scale.

To Gandhi, the tools of modernity and the goal of civilizational recovery pointed at contradictory ends. This contradiction, however, could not be resolved by returning to a rustic past. Much as Gandhi admired the rustic vision of authors such as Tolstoy, Ruskin, and so on, he was conscious of the fact that although modernity is unavoidable, it is also something that can be created anew by political actors. He points us, in other words, toward an alternative modernity. This alternative modernity cannot do without the tools of modern civilization, but their employment cannot be dictated by state policy. These instruments must be woven into the fabric of village life, where the civilizational edifice of rights and duties can remain palpable. In other words, by giving individuals and communities power over their own destinies, Gandhi's model of a grassroots democratic model provides a surer path to swaraj and, as we saw, the possibility for both ahimsa and Truth.

REFERENCES

Amin, Shahid. 1995. *Event, Metaphor, Memory: Chauri Chaura, 1922–1992*. Berkeley: University of California Press.

Bondurant, Jane. 1988. *Conquest of Violence*, rev. ed. Princeton, NJ: Princeton University Press.

Chenoweth, Erica, and Maria J. Stephan. 2011. *Why Civil Resistance Works: The Strategic Logic of Nonviolent Conflict*. New York: Columbia University Press.

Doniger, Wendy. 2009. *The Hindus: An Alternative History*. New York: Penguin.

Gandhi, Mohandas Karamchand. 1928. *Satyagraha in South Africa*. Madras: S. Ganesan.

Gandhi, Mohandas Karamchand. 1979a. *The Collected Works of Mahatma Gandhi, Vol. VIII (January–August 1908)*. New Delhi: Publications Division, Ministry of Information and Broadcasting, Government of India.

Gandhi, Mohandas Karamchand. 1979b. *The Collected Works of Mahatma Gandhi, Vol. LXXVII (December 17, 1942–July 31, 1944)*. New Delhi: Publications Division, Ministry of Information and Broadcasting, Government of India.

Gandhi, Mohandas Karamchand. 2007. *An Autobiography: The Story of My Experiments with Truth*. Translated by Mahadev Desai. London: Penguin.

Gandhi, Mohandas Karamchand. 2009. *Gandhi: "Hind Swaraj" and Other Writings*. Edited by Anthony J. Parel. Cambridge: Cambridge University Press.

Guha, Ramchandra. 2013. *Gandhi before India*. New York: Penguin.

Hardiman, David. 2011. "Gandhi's Global Legacy." In *The Cambridge Companion to Gandhi*, edited by J. M. Brown and A. Parel. Cambridge: Cambridge University Press.

Howard, Veena R. 2013. *Gandhi's Ascetic Activism: Renunciation and Social Action*. Albany: State University of New York Press.

Mill, John Stuart. 1989. *"On Liberty" and Other Writings*. Edited by Stefan Collini. Cambridge: Cambridge University Press.

Parekh, Bhikhu Chotalal. 1989a. *Colonialism, Tradition, and Reform: An Analysis of Gandhi's Political Discourse*. Thousand Oaks, CA: SAGE.

Parekh, Bhikhu Chotalal. 1989b. *Gandhi's Political Philosophy: A Critical Examination*. Notre Dame, IN: University of Notre Dame Press.

Parel, Anthony J. 2000. *Gandhi, Freedom, and Self-Rule*. Lanham, MD: Lexington.

Prasad, Rajendra. 1928. *Satyagraha in Champaran*. Madras: S. Ganesan.

Roberts, Adam, and Timothy Garton Ash, eds. 2009. *Civil Resistance and Power Politics: The Experience of Non-violent Action from Gandhi to the Present*. Oxford: Oxford University Press.

Ruskin, John. 1985. *"Unto This Last" and Other Writings*. Edited by Clive Wilmer. New York: Penguin.

Terchek, Ronald J. 1998. *Gandhi: Struggling for Autonomy*. Lanham, MD: Rowman and Littlefield.

Veeravalli, Anuradha. 2014. *Gandhi in Political Theory: Truth, Law and Experiment*. Farnham, UK: Ashgate.

9 · Development as Buen Vivir

Institutional Arrangements and (De)Colonial Entanglements

In a world long organized around the Western capitalist principle of living better and its correlate, having more, *development* is a term and concept with a historically weighted significance. For many, it is, in essence, the "paradogmatic" (not just paradigmatic) frame against which the Global South in general and Latin America in particular have both measured themselves and been measured. It is the developed West against and, at the same time, the model for the rest.

Such a framework has served not only to envelop humanity and the human condition in the lineal ideas of civilization and progress, but also to entangle modernity further with its underside: coloniality—that is, with a matrix of global power that has hierarchically classified populations, their knowledge, and cosmological life systems according to a Eurocentric standard. This matrix of power has legitimized relations of domination and superiority/inferiority, and has established a historical structural dependence related to capital and the world market (Quijano 2000). In this sense, development has always signaled more than just material progress and economic growth; it has marked a Western model of judgment and control over life itself.

The central question I would like to pose is whether and to what extent this model and its institutional arrangements are in a process of transformation. Does the shift toward new social and sustainable forms of development break with and shrug off the past? How can we understand the emergence in the Andes region and Ecuador in particular of buen vivir, living well or collective well-being, as the guiding principle for a new regimen of development? In the 2008 Constitution of Ecuador, this new regimen is defined as the organized, sustainable, and dynamic ensemble of economic, political, sociocultural, and environmental systems that guarantee the realization of buen vivir. What does such a regimen suggest and afford for development's (de)envelment? These are the guiding questions for what follows.

Integral and Sustainable Human Development

The twenty-first century in Latin America has seen a shift in the notion of development from economic progress toward a more humanistic view focused on the individual and the quality of life. This new framework, most often referred to as "integral and sustainable human development," finds ground in the perspectives of Manfred Max-Neef and Amartya Sen. It focuses on the interconnectedness of economics with the political, sociocultural, and environmental spheres, as well as in the necessities, capacities, and potentialities of human beings. Human development—on both the individual and social scale—is seen as necessarily oriented toward satisfying these necessities, improving these capacities, and enhancing these potentialities in the present. Human development permits the increase in capacities and continuance or sustainability in the future. In contrast to previous lineal models, the focus here is systemic, subject rather than object based. It is concerned with recuperating the molecular dimension of the social and deepening democracy and citizenship from below. Equity, democracy, participation, protection of biodiversity and natural resources, and respect for ethnic-cultural diversity serve as key elements of the framework.

At first glance, such a shift in focus, frame, and perspective appears innovative and positive. It offers perhaps the possibility to challenge the development paradogmas of the past and their colonial, imperial, and dependence-based designs and aspirations. However, a closer look at the criteria and suppositions of this framework, and its ambitions and usage on the national and transnational scale, suggests further scrutiny.[1]

Let us take, for example, the notion of quality of life. Quality of life is understood in the sense of the possibility of satisfying basic needs. It refers to the well-being of the individual according to ontological (being, having, doing) and axiological categories (subsistence, protection, affect, understanding, participation, creation, and leisure). Reaching this well-being is the responsibility of the individual. The possibility of development, therefore, does not rest on society per se, nor is it reliant on or related to the transformation of social institutions and structures; it depends on individuals. Social development depends on the manner in which people—particularly the poor—assume their life. When individuals take control of their lives, acting on their life conditions, then social development and progress occur.

These two principles—the individual and the quality of life—are sustained by four key criteria: liberty, autonomy, coexistence, and social inclusion. The first two encourage individual agency, willpower, and determination. The capacity of the individual to exercise control over her or his own life is central to both human development and the expansion of human liberties. As Sverdlick (2002) notes, these human liberties—understood as politics; the existence of opportunities for all to participate in the production, distribution, and consumption of goods; and access to quality education and health care, among others—are central to the liberty or freedom of the market. They are the goals of development as well as the means that make development possible.

The strategic value of liberty and autonomy can be most clearly observed in Latin America in the present reforming of education, from primary school to the university. Here education is being transformed into an individual and personal project, a consumer good in which competition—between students and among teachers—is the motor in the search for quality and excellence. Objective and quantifiable indicators of quality and control, including exams, standards, and accreditation benchmarks, are converting educational institutions into enterprises where public space and social responsibility operate under a privatized logic. Social gaps, social injustices, and educational failure are seen as personal and family problems that can be individually overcome. In a world that once valued solidarity, fraternity, reciprocity, and collective community-based relations, individual stamina and initiative are quickly becoming the guiding principle and force.

Social inclusion and coexistence are complementary criteria that permit the linking of individual autonomy and liberty to the social. These criteria, present in national educational policies and reforms as well as in the humanistic perspectives, proposals, and policies of international organisms such as UNESCO, the Inter-american Development Bank (IDB), and the United Nations Development Programme (UNDP), purport to anchor individual welfare and ensure conformity within a social system that increasingly works to control cultural diversity and make it functional to the system. For the UNDP, for example, "it is the sensation of social cohesion based in culture and in the values and beliefs shared that molds individual human development. If the people live together, cooperate in a way that enables them to reciprocally prosper, they amplify their individual options" (Guinazu 2008).

Of course, in a region characterized by social movement resistance, insurgence, and demands, social inclusion and coexistence are considered useful tools in preventing ethnic balkanization and controlling and managing ethnic opposition, the latter considered an increasing threat to (trans)national security. The application of these tools can be clearly witnessed in the emergent policies and programs of public social institutions that recognize and include Indigenous and Afro-descendant peoples, their cultural practices, and even their knowledges without changing the dominant nature or structure of these institutions, what can be understood as functional interculturality.[2]

But they can also be observed in the projects and initiatives of multilateral and transnational institutions, which endeavor to keep diversity in check in order not to threaten political and economic interests and stability. This was evident in the UNDP initiatives in 2007–8 in Bolivia. Through published texts, a documentary film, and a television series that involved leftist white-mestizo academics and interviews with Indigenous intellectuals and leaders, the UNDP promoted the urgency of a new *sentido comun* (common sentiment) grounded in social inclusion and cohesion. It was presented as the common sentiment of a nation that could surpass Indigenous nationalisms and the apparent aims of the Constituent Assembly, with the goal of keeping Bolivia under the dominion of the world market (Walsh 2009).

As such, the new paradigm—paradogma?—of human development seems only to envelop further the human condition. On the one hand, it suggests the continued operation in Latin America of the multicultural logic of neoliberal capitalism and its ability to condition modes of thought and conform to a common sense that legitimates the machines of power, making it increasingly difficult to search for alternatives (Torres, cited in Sverdlick 2002). In this sense and despite its holistic and integral language, it is bound to the continuance of Western modern-colonial imposition. The very idea of development itself is a concept and word that does not exist in the cosmovisions, conceptual categories, and languages of indigenous communities.

But while human development continues to reflect and reproduce a multicultural logic, this logic is not quite the same as that of the early 1990s. Then it was the (neo)liberal multiculturalism of the United States, with its guarantee of the freedom to be different, its emphasis on tolerance, and its marketing of diversity, that dominated the scene. In the twenty-first century, neoliberalization and globalization are experiencing a process of European humanization in which the European model of functional interculturalism and development is on the way to replacing the multicultural hegemony of U.S. neoliberal development policy. The manifestation of this shift is clearly evidenced in EUROsociAL, an alliance between the European Union, IDP, UNDP, and the Economic Commission of Latin America (CEPAL), with the support of the World Bank and the International Monetary Fund. In its first phase (2005–10), EUROsociAL described itself on its webpage as

> a plan of development for the European Union that seeks to make this region the most competitive and dynamic economy in the World, capable

of generating a growing sustainable economy, respectful of the environment, with more employment and greater social cohesion. . . . [It is] the [European] ideal of what should be a dignified society. A possible horizon for the politics of development in Latin America. . . . The incorporation of social cohesion in the agenda of Latin America is a product of the dialogue with Europe, using the academy, international organisms, and national governments to adapt the concept to the Latin American reality.[3]

In this description, the envelopment of human development and its entanglement is clear. Indeed some warn that the real agenda of such policies is a recolonization of lands and their natural resources by means of new programs of education, research, and development (Delgado 2006). Yet there is another side to the problem, which is the positing of integral sustainable human development as a regional, national, and even revolutionary alternative. This is the problem to which I now turn.

Human Social Development as (and versus) Buen Vivir

Buen vivir, roughly translated as living well or collective well-being, is the orienting concept of the Ecuadorian Constitution passed by popular referendum in September 2008.[4] As the Preamble states, "we decided to construct a new form of citizen coexistence, in diversity and harmony with nature, to reach el buen vivir, el *sumak kawsay.*"

In its most general sense, buen vivir denotes, organizes, and constructs a system of knowledge and living based on the communion of humans and nature and on the spatial-temporal-harmonious totality of existence—that is, on the necessary interrelation of beings, knowledges, logics, and rationalities of thought, action, existence, and living. This notion is part and parcel of the cosmovision, cosmology, or philosophy of the Indigenous peoples of Abya Yala but also, and in a somewhat different way, of the descendants of the African diaspora.

In a country that has long exalted its mestizo character, favored whitening and whiteness, and looked to the North for its model of development, the incorporation of buen vivir as the guiding principle of the Constitution is historically significant. Its new conceptualization as public policy is largely a result of the social, political, and epistemic agency of the Indigenous movement since the decade of the 1990s. It responds to the urgency of a radically different social contract that presents alternatives to capitalism and the culture of death of its neoliberal and development project. But more than a constitutional declaration, buen vivir affords, as Alberto Acosta (2008) makes clear, an opportunity to collectively construct a new model of development. It is based, according to Eduardo Gudynas (2009), in the generation of new equilibriums including quality of life, democratization of the state, and attention to biocentric concerns.

The grounds for this new model are evidenced in the triangular relationship that the Constitution constructs between the rights of nature, buen vivir, and what is referred to as the regimen of development. As the Political Charter states, "Nature or *Pacha Mama*, where life is reproduced and realized, has the right to the integral respect of its existence and the maintenance and regeneration of its life cycles, structure, functions, and evolutionary processes" (article 71). It also has the right to reparation or restoration (article 72).

Buen vivir, in addition to being the transversal axis of the Constitution (and the triangle), has its own regimen, with more than seventy-five articles, including water and food, nature, education, health, labor and social security, housing, culture, social communication, science, technology, ancestral knowledge, biodiversity, ecological systems, alternative energy, and individual and collective rights of historically unprotected groups, among other areas. What particularly stands out here is the social, economic, and epistemic significance given to buen vivir and the integral relations it constructs among beings, knowledge, and nature. Nature is broadly understood as the constitutive conditions and practices—sociocultural, territorial, spiritual, ancestral, ethical, epistemic, and aesthetic—of life itself.

The third element of the triangle is the regimen of development, described in the Constitution as "the organized, sustainable and dynamic ensemble of economic, political, socio-cultural, and environmental systems that guarantee the realization of buen vivir, or sumak kawsay. . . . Buen vivir requires that persons, [Indigenous] nationalities and peoples, effectively enjoy their rights and exercise responsibilities in the frame of interculturality, respect for diversities, and harmonic co-existence with nature" (article 275).

Seven objectives organize this regimen: improvement in the quality of life; a just, democratic, productive, and solidarity-based economic system with equal distribution of development benefits and dignified and stable work; the promotion of participation and social control, including equitable representation of diverse identities in all areas of public power; the recuperation and conservation of nature and the maintenance of a sane and sustainable environment; the guarantee of national sovereignty and Latin American integration; the promotion of an equitable, balanced, and articulated territorial order; and the protection and promotion of cultural diversity, social memory, and cultural patrimony.

With regard to development, this charter envisions a new society based in equality, fraternity, solidarity, complementarity, equal access, participation, social control, and responsibility. Its project is toward a new social, political, economic, and nature-based mode of development that creates distance from capitalism and requires a major reorienting from within.

The design for the realization and application of this project is detailed in the National Plan of Development, also referred to as the National Plan for el Buen Vivir 2009–2013, developed by the National Secretariat of Planning and Development (SENPLADES) and approved in November 2009 by president Rafael Correa.

For SENPLADES, this plan is considered to be "the first step in constructing a National Decentralized System of Participatory Planning that has as its goal the decentralization and deconcentration of power and the construction of the Plurinational and Intercultural State."[5] Here buen vivir is described as

> a wager for change from the demands for equality and social justice; from the recognition, validation, and dialogue of peoples and their cultures, knowledges, and modes of life. *Buen vivir* seeks to achieve the satisfaction of necessities, the attainment of the quality of life and a dignified death, to love and be loved, the healthy flourishing of all, in peace and harmony with nature and the indefinite prolongation of human cultures. . . . It recognizes the need for free time for contemplation and emancipation, and that real liberties, opportunities, capacities, and potentialities of individuals grow and flourish in the manner that they permit a simultaneous achievement of that which society, territories, diverse collective identities and each one—seen as both an individual and UNIVERSAL HUMAN BEING—value as the objective of a desirable life. It obliges us to reconstruct the public in order to recognize, understand, and value one another—as diverse but equals—with the goal of making possible reciprocity and mutual recognition, and with this, the self-realization and construction of a social and shared future.[6]

In the plan and its twelve strategies for change and twelve national specific objectives, buen vivir and development are understood as interchangeable. Development is the realization of buen vivir, and the construction and realization of buen vivir is what enables this new vision of human and social development. It is precisely this signification that raises a number of critical questions and concerns. For reasons of space, I take into account only two here.

The first question and concern has to do with the very origins of buen vivir. Its inspiration, as mentioned, finds ground in ancestral philosophies and cosmologies of life and living where development as a term and concept is nonexistent (Viteri Gualinga 2002). By making buen vivir central in the reconstituting of the Ecuadorian state and nation, both the Constitution and plan provoke an interculturalizing unprecedented in the country as well as in the Latin American region. It requires the general populace to think and act with ancestral principles, knowledges, and communities, assuming these principles and knowledges are valid for all. Yet this inspiration, it seems, is not the only one in operation. A closer analysis of the new plan and its predecessor (2007–9) makes evident that living well also—and possibly to an even greater degree—takes meaning from the alternative visions of development emerging in the Western world. More specifically, they come from the notions of integral sustainable human development discussed above. In this adaptation and hybridization of the concept and term, the conceptual rupture and intercultural potential appear to lose at least some of its radical force. The crucial question is whether buen vivir is becoming another discursive tool and co-opted term, functional to the state and its structures and with little significance for real intercultural, interepistemic, and plurinational transformation. Certainly such a question and concern are warranted when we take into account government actions in the months and years after the passage of the Constitution, including the approval of a mining law in December 2008 and a water law in August 2014, and the establishment of an extractive-based economy which continues until today, all of which clearly contradict the tenets of buen vivir.

The second question and concern has to do with the meaning and orientation of development. In both the previous plan and the 2009–13 one, development is conceived in the context of the state; that is to say, development is the strategy by which state reform will occur, permitting the state to recuperate its capacities of management, planning, regulation, and redistribution (SENPLADES 2009).[7] In this sense buen vivir as development is the state. And it is the state that signifies in technocratic, economistic, and humanistic terms what is development and buen vivir. Two of the strategies for change make particularly clear the technocratic and economistic orientation: "Transform the model of specialization of the economy through the selective substitution of importations for *el buen vivir*" and "inversion for *el buen vivir*, through the connecting of savings and inversion in a sustainable macroeconomy."[8]

In the humanistic sense, the plan takes much of its language and focus from the model of integral sustainable human development. Liberty, autonomy, inclusion, and social cohesion are key elements. Bettering the capacities and potentialities of the citizenry—understood as individuals and universal beings—improving their quality of life, strengthening democracy and participation, promoting the conservation and sustainability of biodiversity and natural resources, and the affirmation and respect for diversity appear as criteria thought and signified from a Western modernist framework. The possibility of thinking with other philosophies, cosmovisions, and collective relational modes of life not centered in the individual and in capacities and potentialities is noticeably absent.[9] Missing as well is an understanding and positioning of the problem that goes beyond individual responsibility and a strong state, a problem that rests in the legacies, reproductions, and reconstructions of coloniality and of the modern-colonial-world system with particular manifestations in Latin America, the Andes, and Ecuador.

As such, we might critically ask, to what extent does this new binary buen vivir–development enable a de-envelopment of the developmentisms present and past? And to what measure does the new paradigm (paradogma?) in Ecuador suggest a disentanglement of the colonial matrix of power? Or does all this rather suggest a new, more complicated envelopment and entanglement?

In Closing

What I have endeavored to show here is that the new institutional arrangements of human-centered development in the Americas of the South, and particularly in Ecuador, are not without problems, inconsistencies, and contradictions. While the rest of the world may consider this case hopefully, as the dismantling of neoliberal policies and the construction of endogenous development under a radically different life philosophy, the policies and practice emerging from day to day indicate that the so-called citizen revolution—if we can really call it that—has not eliminated but rather strengthened Western-conceived frames of modernization.

But what I want to bring to the fore are even deeper concerns with regard to the new paradigm—or paradogma—of integral sustainable human development. The universalizing of this model, enabling it to travel without question—or visa—to the Souths of the world, recalls the geopolitics of development in the past. Such recollection, however, is easily shrouded by this new humanistic face and agenda.

It seems that the European push to humanize capitalism and its neoliberal project is having an effect. In this new scenario, we must be ever-more vigilant of the institutional arrangements and colonial entanglements.

NOTES

This chapter was first published as an article with the same title in *Development* 53, no. 1 (2010): 15–21. It is reprinted here with permission of the author.

1. My interest as such is not in a critique of the authors associated with this new paradigm or their work, but rather with the paradigm's interpretation and application.

2. Functional interculturality can be understood as part of an institutional strategy that seeks to promote dialogue, tolerance, coexistence, and inclusion without necessarily addressing the causes of inequality; it makes diversity functional to the system (Tubino 2005). This contrasts with what I have referred to as critical interculturality, which begins with a profound questioning of this system and seeks its major transformation in social, political, epistemic, and existential terms—that is, a new ordering of structures, institutions, and relations (Walsh 2002, 2009).

3. The quotation cited here came from EUROsociAL's program description available in 2009 on its web page (http://www.programaeurosocial.eu), now no longer available.

4. It is also a central component of the Bolivian Constitution, passed by popular referendum in January 2009.

5. "Ecuador cuenta con un Ecuador cuenta con un nuevo Plan Nacional de Desarrollo para el período 2009–2013," Ecuador inmediato.com, November 5, 2009. http://www .ecuadorinmediato.com/index.php?module=Noticias&func=news_user_view&id =116173, last consulted October 31, 2017.

6. "Ecuador cuenta con un Ecuador cuenta con un nuevo Plan Nacional de Desarrollo para el período 2009–2013," Ecuador inmediato.com, November 5, 2009.

7. In 2013, the government launched its third National Plan of Buen Vivir, 2013–17. Since the present chapter was initially written in 2010, this latter plan is not included in the analysis. Suffice it to say that the same critique made here of the previous plans still holds.

8. SENPLADES 2009b.

9. See Escobar (2009) for a similar critique.

REFERENCES

Acosta, Alberto. 2008. "El Buen Vivir, una oportunidad por construir." *Ecuador Debate* 75:33–48.

Delgado, Freddy. 2006. "Presentacion." In *Educacion intra e intercultural: Alternativas a la reforma educativa neocolonizadora*, edited by Freddy Delgado and Juan Carlos Mariscal, 9–16. La Paz: Plural.

Escobar, Arturo. 2009. "Una minga para el desarrollo." *America Latina en movimiento*, no. 445:26–30.

Gudynas, Eduardo. 2009. *El mandato ecologico: Derechos de la naturaleza y politicas ambientales en la nueva Constitucion.* Quito: Abya Yala.

Guinazu, Maria Cecilia. 2008. "Ciudadania y desarrollo humano en America Latina." *Revista Latinoamericana de Desarrollo Humano*, no. 46, July.

Quijano, Anibal. 2000. "Coloniality of Power, Eurocentrism, and Latin America." *Nepantla: Views from South* 1 (3): 533–80.

SENPLADES. 2009a. *Recuperacion del Estado nacional para alcanzar el buen vivir: Memoria Bienal 2007–2009*. Quito: SENPLADES.

SENPLADES. 2009b. *República del Ecuador. Plan Nacional para el Buen Vivir, 2009–2013. Versión resumida*. Quito: SENPLADES.

Sverdlick, Ingrid. 2002. "Resena de Educacion en tiempos de neoliberalismo de Jurjo Torres (Madrid, Morata, 2001)." *Education Review*, no. 18.

Tubino, Fidel. 2005. "La interculturalidad crítica como proyecto ético-político." Encuentro continental de educadores agustinos, Lima, January 24–28. http://oala.villanova.edu/congresos/educacion/lima-ponen-02.html.

Viteri Gualinga, Carlos. 2002. "Vision indigena del desarrollo en la Amazonia." *Polis: Revista Latinoamericana* 3. https://polis.revues.org/7678?lang=en.

Walsh, Catherine. 2002. "(De)Construir la interculturalidad: Consideraciones criticas desde la politica, la colonialidad y los movimientos indigenas y negros en el Ecuador. In *Interculturalidad y Politica*, edited by Norma Fuller. Lima: Red de Apoyo de las Ciencias Sociales.

Walsh, Catherine. 2009. *Interculturalidad, Estado, Sociedad: Luchas (de)coloniales de nuestra epoca*. Quito: Universidad Andina Simon Bolivar/Abya Yala.

Part III. Other Sciences and Epistemologies

10 · Caribbean Europe

Out of Sight, Out of Mind?

From sociology's canonized classics up to present-day sociological approaches, an entity called Europe has clearly dominated sociological production about the modern world. In most accounts, the Europe hailed as a standard of civilization, modernity, development, capitalism, or human rights, was poorly or not at all defined and rarely broken down into any subdivisions, except when synecdochically reduced to its hegemonic variant, Western Europe. At the same time, this unspecified entity was overwhelmingly presented as an autonomous, institutionally self-sustaining, and, at least since the age of industry, economically and politically self-contained region. As such, Europe was supposed to be always a step ahead of the regions to which it was being compared, but unrelated to, and essentially unlike them.

This Europe—whose self-image and epistemic self-positioning I have elsewhere called "heroic" (Boatcă 2010, 2013, 2015)—features prominently both in the self-referential historiography of Western European colonial powers as well as in the social theory that emerged during European colonialism and it was subsequently seen as applicable to the entire world. Core sociological categories such as class, reflecting the specific historical and socioeconomic context of Western European industrial society, channeled attention to processes peculiar to that context rather than to those transcending it, and to Western Europe to the detriment of other regions. As a result, class conflict, pauperization, and social mobility within self-proclaimed industrial nations became more visible than colonialism, the trade in enslaved Africans, and European emigration to the Americas, and were disproportionately represented in mainstream sociological theory both within and outside the West. It is only in the past twenty years that sociology's systematic neglect of the dynamics of colonialism and imperialism and of the resulting structural entanglements of power between world regions has been denounced as Eurocentrism or Occidentalism (Chakrabarty 2000; Hall 2006) and calls for the decolonization of the discipline have ensued

(Connell 2007; Gutiérrez Rodríguez et al. 2010; Walsh, Schiwy, and Castro-Gómez 2002).

The present chapter advances instead a more encompassing notion of Europe as a creolized space: it takes into account the regional entanglements to which European colonialism and imperialism have given rise since the sixteenth century and rethinks Europe from its unacknowledged borders in the Atlantic and the Caribbean Sea. It thus builds on works that make the Atlantic world central to an understanding of modernity from coloniality, that is, from the very history of colonial conquest, dispossession, and enslavement (Gilroy 1993; Quijano and Wallerstein 1992; Stam and Shohat 2012). It also builds on notions of creolization developed from and about the Caribbean that emphasize the mutually constituting character of colonial and imperial entanglement, that is, the transformative effect of the Rest on the West as much as the other way around (Hall 2006; Mintz 1998).

In order to show how creolization as a term originally coined to describe processes specific to the Caribbean speaks to a different understanding of Europe up to this day, the history and the concept of Caribbean Europe are used to shed light on a previously developed notion of multiple and unequal Europes (Boatcă 2010, 2013, 2015). The chapter ultimately argues that a rethinking of Europe from its Atlantic and Caribbean borders successfully challenges Occidentalist notions of Europeanness and the modern nation-state, as well as related notions of citizenship, sovereignty, and modernity.

Europe as the Anomalous Norm

When a deduced "norm" turns out not to be the statistical norm, that is, when the situation abounds with exceptions (anomalies, residues), then we ought to wonder whether the definition of the norm serves any useful function. —IMMANUEL WALLERSTEIN, *The Essential Wallerstein*

Any attempt at defining Europe has to confront the controversial question of its external and internal borders, implicitly tied to its status as a continent. Although widely criticized as obsolete, inadequate, and irrelevant for both physical and human geography, the division of the world into seven continents is standard cartographic practice (Lewis and Wigen 1997)—and one with momentous political, economic, and cultural consequences. Among the continental landmasses commonly defined, the distinction between Europe and Asia is by far the least warranted on geographical terms. It sometimes leads professionals to group the two together as a single continent of Eurasia—in which tiny

Europe, however, is only one of six subcontinents (Lewis and Wigen 1997, 35ff.). For more than one reason, therefore, Europe is a cartographic anomaly. Yet not only is it still treated by geographers and nongeographers alike as a full-fledged continent—as Lewis and Wigen have noted—it is repeatedly presented as the norm, or the "archetypal continent": "Viewing Europe and Asia as parts of a single continent would have been far more geographically accurate, but it would also have failed to grant Europe the priority that Europeans and their descendants overseas believed it deserved. By positing a continental division between Europe and Asia, Western scholars were able to reinforce the notion of a cultural dichotomy between these two areas—a dichotomy that was essential to modern Europe's identity as a civilization" (1997, 36).

The metageographical East-West division has also served as the most common as well as the most long-standing internal differentiation within Europe, periodically transferring geopolitical, economic, and cultural divides into an ahistorical distinction between Eastern and Western Europe. The European East thereby sanctions Western Europe's position as the norm, while partly acquiring attributes of a larger East in being portrayed as Oriental or "somehow Asian" (Bakić-Hayden 1995; Lewis and Wigen 1997, 7). Various attempts at scientific orderliness have included pinpointing a third zone between East and West as well as further subdividing the shifty Eastern Europe into North, Central (nineteenth-century Mitteleuropa), and Southeastern Europe (the Balkans). Here, too, what Stuart Hall has termed "the Rest and its internal others" again appear as instrumental for the West "to recognize and represent itself as the summit of human history" (1992, 313ff.).

Thus, the concept of Europe has never had a mere geographic referent, but has instead always reflected the geopolitics as well as the epistemology of the various historical moments and the global power relations characterizing them. However, political maps that represent distinct continents not only naturalize them as commonsensical entities, but also suggest that they are made up of nation-states that fit continental borders. Transcontinental states such as Turkey, Egypt, or Russia are thus posited as anomalies in need of explanation (Lewis and Wigen 1997, 9). In the case of Europe in particular, such naturalization has the absurd effect of generating anomalies from the definition of a continent that is itself anomalous. Thus, many European states have territories outside continental Europe: Cyprus is, strictly speaking, located in West Asia, on the Anatolian Plate, while Malta and Sicily are on the African continental plate. If, however, geographical incongruities result in a few exceptions to the rule, it is colonial history that reveals exceptions as systematic and the rule itself as a function of the political economy of global capitalism. Today, the European Union (EU) includes thirty-four overseas entities resulting from the colonial involvement of six European member states: Denmark, France, the Netherlands, Portugal, Spain, and the United Kingdom. Of these, nine are part of France, Portugal, and Spain and thus full-fledged EU members; they are considered outermost regions of the European Union and are subject to EU legislation (the *acquis communautaire*) (European Parliament 2016). The remaining twenty-five, awkwardly described in official language as "countries that have a special relationship to one of the Member States of the European Community" (EEAS 2016), are colonies of Denmark, France, the Netherlands, and the United Kingdom; they are not part of the single market, yet their nationals are EU citizens. These Overseas Countries and Territories (OCTs) as a whole feature among the regions in the European Commission's list of partners in "international cooperation and development," which also includes both Africa and sub-Saharan Africa, both Asia and Central Asia, the Americas, the Caribbean, the Pacific, and "the Gulf" (meaning, but not specifying, the Persian Gulf) (European Commission 2016b). Thus, while the entire list bespeaks blurry borders and inconsistent criteria, including the OCTs as a "region," it is telling not only for the anomalous status they hold within the EU and ironic in the face of their being geographically spread across three of the world's oceans. It reveals the extent to which geographical and political categories— from "countries" and "territories" to "regions"—are used as placeholders for the appropriate term, "colonies," while their historical genealogies are disguised under euphemisms such as "special relations."

In spite of such formal acknowledgment, official EU discourse foregrounds continental Europe to the detriment of all other territories—most of which are former colonies—that are part of European countries, but are geographically located on other continents. In the process, it links Europeanness to a narrowly defined physical location that excludes both the memory and the present of Europe's colonial ties to other regions. With the discourse of the European Union, we thus witness the reemergence of a "moral geography" of the continent, with profound implications for the identity politics, citizenship rights, and military and monetary policy of the excluded countries (Muller 2001). The pervasive civilizing discourse situates the EU at the top of a value hierarchy derived from the historical legacy and the current political role of its member states, viewed as exemplary in both cases. This "moral geopolitics" (Böröcz 2006) of the EU results in a racialized identity politics and a related moral geography underlying it that continually shape political discourse and public perception of Europe and the European Union.

Introducing Multiple Europes

The discourse surrounding the emergence, establishment, and, later, expansion of the European Union has been gradually monopolizing the label of "Europe" such that only its twenty-eight member states or at most those about to become members are considered European and consequently included in the term. As a result, processes of accession to the EU have consistently been defined as "Europeanization," irrespective of the already geographically European location of the candidate states, from the 2004 enlargement round to the 2007 inclusion of Romania and Bulgaria.

At the same time, Europe's remaining colonies overseas are graphically represented as part of the EU in official maps, yet play no part in the definition of either the normative European ideal or the corresponding common identity. The fact that they are situated outside a continental European location was never mobilized in a discourse of exclusion from Europe directed at these territories on account of any supposed cultural, political, or economic difference. As shown above, administratively, most either are a part of the European states that colonized them and, by extension, of the EU, or have associated status within it; they are included in official EU maps, and their citizens have EU citizenships; Portugal's "autonomous regions" the Azores and Madeira, Spain's "autonomous community" of the Canary Islands, and the French overseas departments all use the euro as their official currency and are represented on euro banknotes, which the European Central Bank (2017) claims "show a geographical representation of Europe." The presence (and absence) of overseas territories on the banknotes is explained away with reference to their size, while their connection with Europe appears to be nothing but accidental: "The tiny boxes near the bottom of the banknote show the Canary Islands and *some overseas territories of France where the euro is also used*."[1]

In fact, as Karis Muller pointed out early on, when superimposed on the official EU map, the areas covered by the euro provide "a time lagged photograph of colonization" (2000, 328). Against this background, the discursive construction of a singular notion of Europe crucially depends on the silencing of the historical role of its member states and their predecessors in creating the main structures of global political and economic inequality during European colonial rule. As Böröcz and Sarkar have argued, the member states of the EU before the 2004 Eastern enlargement were "the same states that had exercised imperial rule over nearly half of the inhabitable surface of the globe outside Europe" (2005, 162) and whose colonial possessions covered almost half of the inhabited surface of the non-European world. The thirty-four colonial possessions still under the direct control of EU member states today represent more than half of the fifty-eight remaining colonies worldwide (The United Nations and Decolonization 2017). This is not a coincidence. The overseas empires of today's EU states such as Britain, the Netherlands, France, and Belgium had been many times larger than the current size of their territories. The loss of colonial empires after World War II therefore significantly fueled the political impetus behind the creation of the European Economic Community (EEC), the EU's predecessor, to which the contribution of remaining colonies was seen as decisive (Hansen and Jonsson 2014; Muller 2001). Upon its founding in 1957, the EEC included not just Belgium, France, Italy, Luxembourg, the Netherlands, and West Germany, but also their colonial possessions, officially referred to as "overseas countries and territories," the same label used today for the remaining colonial possessions: "They included, most importantly, Belgian Congo and French West and Equatorial Africa, whereas Algeria, which in this time was an integral part of metropolitan France, was formally integrated into the EEC yet excluded from certain provisions of the Treaty" (Hansen and Jonsson 2014, 7).

In turn, the moral geography at work today denotes the symbolic representation of the European continent reflecting the civilizing discourse advanced by its main colonial powers. Most telling in this regard were the official maps of the EU made shortly before the 2004 enlargement round, in which the European continent was color-coded to reflect the different speeds of accession and, by extension, the candidate countries' closeness to the European ideal. Yellow represented the member states until 2004. Blue represented the ten new members that joined that year. Romania and Bulgaria, which were denied access in the 2004 enlargement round, were represented in purple, as was Turkey, which has been a candidate for accession since 1986. At the same time, Europe's overseas colonial territories, while graphically represented as part of the EU, played no part in the definition of either the European ideal or the corresponding common identity.[2] Their location outside continental Europe never triggered a discourse of exclusion. At most, their existence is instrumentalized in triumphalist and celebratory discourses of the metropole, as in the case of France's Année de l'Outre Mer in 2011—which, among other things, claimed the biodiversity of the French overseas departments for Europe as a whole (Éduscol 2011; Vergès 2015). The very opposite is the case for Turkey, whose "semi-Asian" location—across the anomalous continental divide between Europe and Asia—has repeatedly been part of the arguments of denying it EU membership since decades before the start of the Erdogan regime.

The implicit geopolitical imaginary at work here presupposes an equally implicit ontological and moral scale. Such a scale ranges from a geographically western Europe, whose modern, democratic, and pacific character (and therefore superiority) remain unquestioned, up to a backward, violent, and inferior part (thus of questionable Europeanness) frequently located in the eastern part of the continent. However, Eastern Europe and the Balkans represent only the other extreme on the ontological scale of Europeanness, which seems to encompass various intermediate degrees. The criteria for one's location in any one position on the scale are nevertheless far from clear. I have previously argued that such graphic representations rely primarily on a discursive practice within a power structure, or imperial maps (Boatcă 2013; Coronil 1996). They combine the typical claim to objective truth with a territorial project of a colonial or imperial nature that lends legitimacy to the particular representation of the world and with the definition power necessary for imposing that representation as valid both internally and externally. The discourse of European unity and singularity thus paradoxically reinforces a historically consistent politics of difference within Europe that can best be described as a hierarchy of multiple and unequal Europes emerging in the sixteenth century.[3]

At that time, the changing geopolitical context of Europe prompted the rearticulation of existing religious differences. On the one hand, "imperial differences" (Mignolo 2006) within Europe became more pronounced—non-Christian and non-European peoples such as the Turks and the Moors were relegated to an inferior status vis-à-vis the European Christians of the emerging Spanish Empire; on the other hand, "colonial differences" between Europe and the overseas colonies started taking shape—the indigenous people of the New World territories were increasingly constructed as faithless barbarians to be Christianized by the colonizers (Mignolo 2000, 2006). Beginning in the eighteenth century, hierarchies that structured Europe according to principles similar to those applied to the colonial world gradually started taking shape. After the change in hegemony from the old Spanish-Portuguese imperial power to the Low Countries, France, and England, the logic underlying the spread of Eurocentrism in the non-European world also accounted for the propagation of Occidentalism in Europe. Within Europe, evolutionary thinking served to justify the temporal division of the continent: while the East was still considered feudal, the South had marked the end of the Middle Ages, and the Northwest represented modernity. On the other hand, the dualism behind constructed categories such as primitive/civilized, irrational/rational, or traditional/modern allowed both a spatial and an ontological division within Europe. The geographically European, (predominantly) Christian and white Southeast of the continent, and especially the Balkans, could not be constructed as an "incomplete Other" of Western Europe, as the Far East had been. The region emerged instead as Europe's "incomplete Self" (Todorova 1997). Its proximity to Asia and its Ottoman cultural legacy located it halfway between East and West, thus giving it a condition of semi-Oriental, semi-civilized, semi-developed, in the process of catching up with the West. In the same vein, the European South, epitomized by the declining Spanish Empire and its Moorish legacy, was gradually defined out of the Western core both for its proximity to Islamic North Africa and for its reputation as a brutal colonizer of the New World, constructed as the opposite of England's own benevolent colonialism.

The construction of the colonial difference overseas thus went hand in hand with the emergence of the double imperial difference in Europe (stretching into Asia): on the one hand, an external difference between the new capitalist core and the existing traditional empires of Islamic and Eastern Christian faith—the Ottoman and the tsarist ones; on the other hand, an internal difference between the new and the old capitalist core, mainly England versus Spain (Mignolo 2006). From this moment on, we have at least two types of European subalterns to the hegemonic model of power, as well as the first imperial map of multiple Europes.

I therefore propose to distinguish between four types of Europes with different and unequal roles in shaping the hegemonic definition of modernity and in ensuring its propagation: decadent Europe (which had lost both hegemony and, accordingly, the epistemic power of defining a hegemonic self and its subaltern Others), paradigmatically represented by the early colonial powers Spain and Portugal; heroic Europe (self-defined as the producer of modernity's main achievements), primarily represented by the successive colonial powers, France and England, which were at the same time the self-proclaimed leaders of modernity's main revolutions, the French Revolution and industrialization (also conceived in terms of a revolution rather than a result of colonial extraction); epigonic Europe (defined via its alleged lack of these achievements and hence as a mere reproducer of the stages covered by heroic Europe), best epitomized by Southeastern Europe and the Balkans; and, last, forgotten Europe, the colonial possessions never included in the definitions of Europe, modernity, or the Western nation-state, although they were economically indispensable for these achievements and administratively integral parts of Western European states until well into the twentieth century and some even today (table 10.1). While decadent Europe and epigonic Europe were both characterized by a semiperipheral position, their different trajectories in having achieved this position acted toward disuniting rather than uniting them in their interests: in Spain and Portugal, the memory of lost power and the dominion of imperial languages induced the awareness of a decline from the core, that is, an imperial

TABLE 10.1. Multiple and Unequal Europes

EUROPE	PROTOTYPE	ROLE IN THE HISTORY OF MODERNITY	WORLD-SYSTEM POSITION	ATTITUDE	ROLE IN COLONIALITY
Decadent	Spain, Portugal	Participant	Semi-periphery	Nostalgia	Founding
Heroic	France, England	Producer	Core	Hegemony	Central
Epigonic	Balkans	Reproducer	Semi-periphery	Aspiration	Accomplice
Forgotten	British Virgin Islands	Reproducer	Periphery	Ambivalent	Instrumental

nostalgia.[4] Instead, in that part of the continent that had emerged as Europe only due to the increasing demise of the Ottoman Empire—that is, Eastern Europe and the Balkans—the rise to the position of semiperiphery within the world economy alongside the enduring position of periphery within Europe itself made the aspiration to Europeanness, defined as Western modernity, the dominant attitude. In the case of forgotten Europe, attitudes have ranged between the strong desire for decolonization, leading to the independence of most territories under European domination in the wake of World War II, to the voluntary relinquishing of sovereignty in exchange for EU citizenship and economic integration in the monetary union that to this day characterizes parts of the Dutch Antilles, the British Virgin Islands, and the French overseas departments—which, since 2011, also include the Indian Ocean island of Mayotte.

Thus, the subdivisions underlying the imperial map of multiple Europes had served to positively sanction the hegemony of "heroic Europe." France, England, and Germany, as epitomes of what Hegel had called "the heart of Europe," became the only authority capable of imposing a universal definition of modernity and at the same time of deploying its imperial projects in the remaining Europes or through them. On the one hand, Northwestern Europe's rise to economic prosperity, during which hegemony was disputed among Holland, France, and England, would use the territorial gains of the first, Spanish-Lusitanian colonial expansion in order to derive the human, economic, and cultural resources that substantiated the most characteristically modern achievements—of which the "Industrial Revolution" is a paradigmatic example (Moraña, Dussel, and Jáuregui 2008). However, this would occur without integrating the contribution either of the declining European South or of the colonized Americas in the narrative of modernity, which was conceived as being both of (North)Western and of inner European origin.

On the other hand, and especially as of the mid-nineteenth century, the Western European core of the capitalist world economy benefited from the end of Ottoman rule in the east of the continent by establishing neocolonies in the rural and agricultural societies of the region and thus gradually gaining control of the strategic trade routes of the Black Sea and the Danube. The subsequent "modernization" of the Balkans and the European Southeast, through the introduction of liberal institutions and legislation, aimed at making the region institutionally recognizable to the West and financially dependent on it. At the same time, it involved the shaping of political and cultural identities of countries in the region in relation to the Western discourse of power. Consequently, from Austria and Poland to Romania and Croatia, states periodically described their contribution to European history as "bulwarks of Christianity" against the Muslim threat. Every country in "Eastern" Europe designated itself as a "frontier between civilization and barbarism" or as a "bridge between West and East," thus legitimizing Western superiority and fostering the same Orientalism that affected themselves as Balkan, not Christian enough, or not white enough. Remapping Eastern Europe and the Balkans in the context of a hierarchical model of multiple and unequal Europes reveals that the blindness to the (neo)colonial logic prevalent in these areas' political and identity discourses rather makes them accomplices of the colonial project of power underlying the emergence of modernity. Taken together, the Europeanness as affirmed by heroic Europe, mourned by decadent Europe, or pursued by epigonic Europe resulted in an understanding of a single valid, untainted, white Western Christian Europe with which brown, black, Muslim, and Eastern identities and legacies were incompatible and which to this day excludes and discounts on this very basis (Essed 2009).

Such a model is nevertheless inevitably incomplete and meant to serve heuristic purposes, not to exhaustively or even partially explain the trajectory of any European region in the *longue durée*. This has been systematically done a number of times and has yielded widely differing taxonomies, depending on whether the focus of the categorization was economic or political or a mixture of the two (see, e.g., Rokkan 1999; Therborn 1995). On the basis of its most prototypical examples, however, the model of multiple Europes as sketched above does help illuminate the impact that the direct or indirect involvement in the extra-European colonial endeavor has had on the definition power associated with a region's structural position within the modern/colonial world system in general and within Europe in particular. In other words, the further away from the historical experience of heroic Europe a part of Europe is or has been, the less definition power it has tended to have with respect to discourses of modernity, European identity, or both.

Creolizing Europe through the Caribbean

Thus, in a hierarchy of multiple and unequal Europes that ranges from heroic to decadent to epigonic in terms of the role attributed to each in the achievement of modernity, the EU's overseas territories appear as "forgotten Europe"—they are literally off the chart in terms of Europe's self-representation and modernity's checklist, yet on the map in terms of the claims laid to them by continental European states. While there is a—however imprecise—geographical referent for heroic Europe in the (North)Western part of the continent, decadent Europe in the South(west), and epigonic Europe in the (South)East, there is none for forgotten Europe. This is not only due to the fact that Europe's overseas countries, territories, and outermost regions are spread out across the Atlantic Ocean, the Caribbean Sea, and the Pacific and Indian oceans and thus not easily pinpointed to any one location. Rather, the lack of a referent for what ultimately are colonial outposts is a result of the coloniality of memory—the systematic omission of enduring colonial ties from public discourse on Europe alongside the systematic avoidance of any overarching classification of current colonial territories as regions of Europe: when made at all, references to parts of forgotten Europe in official discourse tend to be linked to the imperial history of individual states, as in the case of labels such as the Dutch Caribbean, the British West Indies, or Françafrique. Yet they never point to the integral part that colonial possessions have played in the consolidation of European economic and geopolitical power as a whole or to the present-day continuities in Western Europe's entanglement with and policies toward them.

As an overarching category, "forgotten Europe" therefore helps stress the fact that some of the multiple Europes are more unthinkable than others: epigonic Eastern Europe is white but not quite, Christian but not Western Christian, while parts of it are not Christian at all. Its geographical location in Europe is unquestioned, although its EU accession was piecemeal and remains incomplete. The modernity of individual Eastern European states has repeatedly been tied to their EU membership status and seen as a gradual process of Europeanization. In turn, in the case of the Caribbean territories of current EU members, it is the African and Asian heritage of their populations and their predominantly syncretic religions that, together with their remote geographical location, decisively unsettle Europe's prevailing self-definition as continental, white, and Christian. The Caribbean's history of slavery, linked to backward, inefficient, unfree, and nonwhite labor, served for a long time as a stark contrast to the presumed freedom, modernity, and high productivity of the wage labor of white Europeans. The more attributes were added to each side of the Europe and the non-Europe thus constructed, the more unrelated their history and present seemed to be. In the end, "if it is perceived to be relevant at all, the history of slavery is somehow assigned to blacks. It becomes our special property rather than a part of the ethical and intellectual heritage of the West as a whole" (Gilroy 1993, 49).

Within forgotten Europe, the Caribbean colonies thus offer both a prime vantage point for upending the dominant understanding and representation of Europe and a concrete basis for a coherent geographic referent of this hitherto unthinkable category. The fact that more than a third of the EU's colonial possessions are located in the Caribbean today warrants an engagement with what I would like to call Caribbean Europe—the integral but invisibilized part of an otherwise highly visible Europe. I view it as encompassing all Caribbean territories previously colonized by a European power and presently administered as dependencies of an EU member. The formal colonial relation to EU members still figures in the euphemism of the Caribbean territories' current official denomination—from "territory" to "municipality," "community," or "department" *of* a European state. This is not to discount the coloniality of power underlying the many nonadministrative ties of dependence still tying the formally independent Caribbean to Europe. Instead, my goal is to highlight the enduring colonial (rather than neocolonial) nature of administrative ties still in force today. According to this definition, Caribbean Europe currently includes the French overseas departments of Martinique, Guadeloupe, and French Guiana and the French overseas community of St. Martin from among the EU's outermost regions; and the French St. Barthélemy, the British Virgin Islands, Anguilla, Bermuda, the Cayman Islands, Montserrat, and Turks and Caicos as well as Dutch Aruba, Curaçao, Sint Maarten, Bonaire, Saba, and Sint Eustatius from among the EU's OCTs.[5]

As such, Caribbean Europe represents only one instance of the multiple Europes actively forgotten through the coloniality of memory at work in the dominant EU discourse (yet very much present in the everyday reality of those living in the occupied territories). A similar case could be made for an African Europe on account of the French outermost regions of Réunion and Mayotte and Spain's enclaves Ceuta and Melilla, or for a Pacific Europe on account of

French Polynesia and Wallis and Futuna as well as the British Pitcairn Islands. However, as the first region in the Americas to be claimed by European powers as early as 1492 and one that received more than a third of the 12.5 million Africans trafficked in the European slave trade from the sixteenth to the nineteenth centuries, the Caribbean has had the longest and the most complex history of entanglement with Europe (Hall 2015; Mintz 2010).[6] It also has been the site of several strategic EU projects and activities throughout the twentieth century and until today: as the coloniality of memory actively and consistently produces these territories as absent from and unthinkable within the European discourse, it repeatedly taps into their potential to act as Europe's military and naval bases, sites of medical experiments, spaceports, and tax havens, as well as laboratories of neoliberal economics or warfare, to name but a few of their functions (for more, see Bonilla 2015, 184ff.; Hansen and Jonsson 2014, 2).

The notion of Caribbean Europe advanced here is not intended to claim the Caribbean or parts of it for Europe in a renewed, theoretically and epistemically colonial gesture. Rather, it is meant to creolize the very notion of Europe by drawing attention to the decisive shifts that colonial possessions operate in both its historical legacies and its present borders when colonial possessions are consistently taken into account. The project of creolizing Europe is therefore contingent upon creolizing social theory so as to reinscribe the transnational experiences of non-European, non-Western, and nonwhite regions such as the Caribbean as well as the multiple entanglements between Europe and its colonies in sociological thought. In this sense, the notion of Caribbean Europe can be seen as an instance of what Lionnet and Shih have called "the becoming theory of the minor"—thinking through and with invisibilized, peripheral, or subaltern formations, or thinking from coloniality: "If minor formations become method and theory, then new analytics will be brought to the foreground to creolize the universalisms we live with today, doing so from the bottom up and from the inside out. It is this process of becoming theory of the minor that we are also calling creolization" (2011, 21).

What does the creolization of Europe through the lens of its Caribbean colonies look like concretely? In other words, what does Europe look like when its Caribbean component is remembered? In the following, I discuss two different but related aspects impacted by this shift of perspective and point at other areas where this impact can be felt.

One of the most immediate effects of rethinking Europe through the Caribbean is a drastic redrawing of European and EU borders. Tellingly, there are no available maps depicting these borders, yet the map of the EU's OCTs and outermost regions comes closest to offering an accurate image.[7]

The first shift that occurs when considering Caribbean Europe an integral part of the European Union concerns the latter's external western borders. The EU's western boundary has never been questioned in official discourse and has never constituted the object of accession negotiations (there was no western enlargement of the EU). Very much unlike both the eastern and the southern boundaries, it is mostly considered unproblematic. Often conflated with the western border of the European landmass, it is seen as beginning with the Atlantic Ocean on the western coast of Portugal—although, in the case of the EU, this already leaves both the Spanish Canary Islands and Portuguese Azores and Madeira unaccounted for. When both these Atlantic colonies and Caribbean Europe are taken into account, however, the western borders of the EU are suddenly relocated to the Americas—more precisely, to French Guiana in South America and Guadeloupe in the Caribbean, which, as overseas regions of France, are integral parts of the French Republic and consequently of the European Union. The shift also affects the external borders of the EU more generally: through French Guiana, France borders Brazil and Suriname, while the Netherlands shares a maritime border with Venezuela and the United States through the Lesser Antilles, which include the U.S. Virgin Islands.[8]

Accounting for Caribbean Europe impacts not only the EU's external but also its internal borders. Since the territories of European member states in the Caribbean are differently positioned than on the European landmass, France borders the Netherlands only on the island of St. Martin/Sint Maarten; in turn, the Netherlands comes to share maritime borders with France and the United Kingdom in the Caribbean Sea.

If claiming that the westernmost point of the EU lies in the Caribbean or that France borders Brazil seems spectacular or extreme, this only goes to show the extent to which the coloniality of memory is ingrained in the public perception of Europe. From an official EU position, the above are uncontested formal borders. The statements therefore rather resonate with the official claim that the EU's overseas territories range "from the poles to the tropics" (European Commission 2016b)—a phrase highly reminiscent of both the Spanish and the British Empire's self-descriptions as the empire on which the sun never sets.

Apart from the drastic formal corrections operated on the borders of the European Union described above, this shift of perspective also impacts the conventional geographic understanding of Europe as a coherent continent and the modern political norm of a united state territory. If French, Spanish, and Portuguese national territory spans Europe, the Atlantic Ocean, the Caribbean, and South America, then transcontinental states such as Turkey are no longer the exception to European geography, but the rule. When the Treaty on the European Union states that "any European country may apply for membership if it respects the democratic values of the EU and is committed to promoting them" (European Commission 2016a), it however conflates both geographic and political criteria in the phrase "European country." Yet not even geographic Europeanness makes sense as a criterion for EU accession. Most of the EU's founding members did not meet it in 1957, when the EEC was created and their overseas colonies were included, and some would still not meet it today. Here, too, the history and present-day reality of Caribbean Europe help shed light on the type of polity to which official or scholarly references to European countries implicitly or explicitly point.

Creolizing European Statehood

The notion of European country invoked in the language of the European Commission is based on the notion of the sovereign nation-state that emerged with the Peace of Westphalia in the seventeenth century and was consolidated in the aftermath of the French Revolution at the end of the eighteenth.

For a long time, mainstream historiography and social science viewed the rise of nation-states as the gradual overcoming of multinational political organizations and multiethnic empires throughout the world. The resulting conceptualization of empires and nation-states as mutually exclusive and chronologically discrete political formations and of the nation-state as the modern norm generated its own anomalies. The existence of the Habsburg, the Ottoman, and the tsarist empires well into the twentieth century had to be explained away accordingly as survivals of the old order, "anachronistic holdovers from an age of aristocracy, clinging to their imperial identifications in the face of the inevitable national challenges that mounted over the course of the nineteenth century" (Cooper 2005, 156).

State formations that are still colonized in the twenty-first century, such as the European and U.S. Caribbean territories, continue to be viewed as exceptions to the above trajectory from empire to nation and as anomalies in a modern world of sovereign nation-states. A growing literature tries to capture the paradoxical logic behind the functioning of state structures in the nonindependent Caribbean using concepts such as "extended statehood" (De Jong and Kruijt 2005), "postcolonial sovereignty games" (Adler-Nissen and Gad 2013), or "non-sovereign futures" (Bonilla 2015). The same ambiguous status with regard to these territories' populations is echoed in Françoise Vergès's notion that, for the inhabitants of France's overseas possessions, French republican principles of citizenship, equality, and fraternity are "inflected: citizens but colonized, equal but not completely, brothers—but junior brothers" (2005, 75, my translation).

While scholars of global history and postcolonial scholars have provided ample evidence for the coexistence of imperial and national state structures in the nineteenth century and most of the twentieth, the dominant view is that they no longer coexist in the twenty-first. Thus, in his detailed analysis of the transformations undergone by the French state in the aftermath of the French Revolution and the Napoleonic era, Frederick Cooper convincingly argues that France remained an empire-state for most of its modern history. Despite viewing the French overseas departments in the Caribbean as decisive for this argument, and a rethinking of France from its colonial borders as necessary, Cooper chooses Algeria's independence as the moment that marked France's transition from empire to nation-state: "If one wants to rethink France from its colonies, one might argue that France only became a nation-state in 1962, when it gave up its attempt to keep Algeria French and tried for a time to define itself as a singular citizenry in a single territory" (2005, 22).

Thus, even a radically critical view of empire in the European context manages to once again forget (or disregard) Caribbean Europe in the endeavor of characterizing present-day state structures and to conclude that "the most important fact about empires is that they are gone" (Cooper 2005, 203). When taking the French outermost regions into account, however, the very definition of *empire* Cooper provides becomes a more apt characterization of post-1962 France than any available definition of a unitary nation-state, for which France has been seen as paradigmatic. Cooper defines empire as "a political unit that is large, expansionist (or with memories of an expansionist past), and which reproduces differentiation and inequality among people it incorporates" (2005, 27). Whether it is empire, extended statehood, or sovereignty games that best describes the state structures in twenty-first-century Caribbean Europe, is however of little consequence in this context. What is important is that its history and present as integral parts of European states and suprastate organizations such as the EU or the British Commonwealth of Nations effectively creolize the norm of the sovereign nation-state. It is in this sense that the notion of Caribbean Europe ties into conceptualizations of the Black and the Red Atlantic that not only transcend the nation-state but provide ways to rethink Western statehood from the political and cultural history and the present-day reality of black and indigenous populations in the Americas (Gilroy 1993; Stam and Shohat 2012).[9]

As Yarimar Bonilla has shown, the nonindependent Caribbean encompasses multiple political forms and overlapping zones of affiliation that fall outside the legal definition of either independent states or formal colonies (categorized here as Caribbean Europe), but also "a large number of nonsovereign enclaves: military bases, privately owned islands, semiautonomous tourist resorts, free-trade zones, tax havens, wildlife preserves, satellite launching stations, detention centers, penal colonies, floating data centers, and other spaces of suspended, subcontracted, usurped, or imposed foreign jurisdiction that challenge the principles of bounded territorial authority associated with the Westphalian order" (2015, 10). Thus, when the norm itself becomes questionable—in this case, the sovereign nation-state—it is not the nonsovereign, nonemancipated, or non-decolonized state structure that is in need of explanation, but the universality of the nation-state norm as well as the continuities of distinct formations to which it gave rise under colonial and imperial rule.

Mapping Caribbean Europe

In his discussion of national identity and consciousness in "Ethnicities and Global Multiculture," Jan Nederveen Pieterse (2007) noted, "Nations typically unravel at the borders; they come loose at the seams." Rethinking Europe from its Caribbean periphery, as the present chapter has aimed to do through the category of Caribbean Europe, arguably has a similar effect on received knowledge of Europe's physical and moral geography as well as its political topography.

The questions of European borders and European statehood dealt with in this chapter represent two instances of a wider array of theoretical, methodological, and political issues that a consistent consideration of Caribbean Europe could help rethink. Among them is the question of modernity linked to debunking the necessity of transition from empire to nation-state as a myth as well as to the different claims to statehood in several parts of the nonindependent Caribbean (Bonilla 2015, xiii; Cooper 2005, 343). Closely related to the notion and the narrative of modernity are questions of migration, whiteness, and citizenship linking Europe and the Caribbean since the former's colonization of the latter in the sixteenth century, or what Paul Gilroy referred to as "the difficult journey from slave ship to citizenship" (1993, 31). To this day, the gap between rich and poor is smaller in those Caribbean countries where no large indigenous population survived the European invasion and no slave plantation economy was set up, such as Costa Rica. Due to the very existence of overseas colonies to which many poor Europeans emigrated as indentured servants and to the region's inadequacy for large-scale export economies, white Europeans in Western Europe constituted a racially less stratified basis for the emergence of free-labor economies to which Caribbean slave plantations are still contrasted (Boatcă 2014). As has been documented for the postcolonial migration flows between several Western European countries and their former colonies, as well as for the United States and its protectorates, the possession of the citizenship of the former metropole remains today a crucial factor deciding the timing and the destination of ex-colonial subjects' emigration as well as the struggle for independence in the remaining colonial possessions: people in today's occupied territories are more likely to migrate to the metropole whose citizenship rights they hold as long as the colonial relationship allows it. Instead, relinquishing such rights by claiming statehood lowers the occupied territories' incentives for achieving independence. Thus, fear of losing Dutch citizenship and the privileges it bestowed led to a dramatic increase in Surinamese emigration to the Netherlands in the years preceding Surinam's independence from the motherland in 1974–75 and remains the main reason behind the lack of political pressure for independence in the Dutch Antilles and Aruba (van Amersfoort and van Niekerk 2006).

Focusing on Europe's remaining colonial possessions in the Caribbean and their corresponding geographical referent, the notion and the reality of Caribbean Europe thus challenge, that is, effectively creolize, established understandings of Europe, a white European identity, and the European Union. Incorporating Caribbean Europe as a legitimate part of Europe makes the concept and the reality of black Europe more than an exception or a new addition to an otherwise homogeneous and white European space (Hine, Keaton, and Small 2009; Sharpley-Whiting and Patterson 2009). Instead, it connects the peoples of the Caribbean diaspora living in continental Europe with Caribbean Europe and fits both into a more encompassing notion of a black, brown, white, Muslim, Christian, and syncretic Europe. Mapping the theoretical and political implications of Caribbean Europe therefore offers a way out of systematically producing exceptions, anomalies, and residues to a singular European norm by researching rules through a historical and global perspective from multiple and unequal Europes instead.

In more general terms, the perspective delineated here goes to show that the systematic incorporation of the transregional, transcontinental, and other transborder entanglements linking colonies and metropoles since the sixteenth century decisively transforms the theoretical, conceptual, and methodological apparatus of social theory developed in the West on the one hand and our understanding of the functioning of key global institutions such as citizenship or regional ones such as the European Union on the other.

NOTES

1. See the map of Europe on EU banknotes, accessed June 27, 2017, https://www.ecb .europa.eu/euro/banknotes/design/html/index.en.html.

2. See the map of EU enlargement 2004 (blue) and pending (purple). Accessed June 27, 2017, http://www.eu-cu.com/europe.gif.

3. The remainder of this section summarizes arguments initially elaborated in Boatcă (2013; 2015, ch. 7).

4. That the loss of empire generates imperial nostalgia whether or not it is linked to loss of hegemony or of military, political, and epistemic dominance in the world-economy is demonstrated by Gilroy's (2004) analysis of the phenomenon in the case of Britain. In turn, the argument advanced here focuses on the role imperial nostalgia plays in shaping the self-definition of a declining hegemon and the consequences for the geopolitical rearrangements in Europe following the shift of hegemony from the Spanish to the British core.

5. See map at EU Overseas Countries and Territories and Outermost Regions 2015, accessed June 27, 2017. https://upload.wikimedia.org/wikipedia/commons/7/72/EU _OCT_and_OMR_map_en.png. Also see overview in Bonilla (2015, 7ff.).

6. Hall dwells on Glissant's notion of entanglement in order to elaborate on his own understanding of creolization as a process always premised on unequal power relations rather than on mixing of equal elements: "Writers like Édouard Glissant use the term 'creole' in a broader sense, to describe the entanglement—or what he calls the 'relation' between—different cultures forced into cohabitation in the colonial context. Creolization in this context refers to the processes of 'cultural and linguistic mixing' which arise from the entanglement of different cultures in the same indigenous space or location, primarily in the context of slavery, colonization, and the plantation societies characteristic of the Caribbean and parts of Spanish America and Southeast Asia. . . . This does not mean that in creole societies cultural elements combine on the basis of equality. Creolization *always* entails inequality, hierarchization, issues of domination and subalterneity, mastery and servitude, control and resistance. Questions of *power*, as well as issues of *entanglement*, are always at stake. It is important to keep these contradictory tendencies together, rather than singling out their celebratory aspects" (Hall 2015, 15ff.).

7. See map at EU Overseas Countries and Territories and Outermost Regions 2015, accessed June 27, 2017. https://upload.wikimedia.org/wikipedia/commons/7/72/EU _OCT_and_OMR_map_en.png.

8. See map of the Caribbean with its European and U.S.-American colonial possessions, accessed June 27, 2017. http://reservationsbvi.com/maps/Caribbean%20Map.gif.

9. Robert Stam and Ella Shohat point out that, "while the 'Black Atlantic' evokes the
Middle Passage and the African Diaspora, the notion of a 'Red Atlantic' registers not
only the dispossession of indigenous peoples by Europeans but also the impact of indigenous ideas on European thinking" (2012, 3). Alongside the ways in which indigenous
communities in the Americas have historically represented challenges to the Western
notion of the nation-state, the fact that the present-day boundaries of many indigenous
communities straddle the borders of nation-states in the Americas today is of particular
importance in this context (see Stam and Shohat 2012, 6ff.).

REFERENCES

Adler-Nissen, Rebecca, and Ulrik P. Gad. 2013. *European Integration and Postcolonial
Sovereignty Games: The EU Overseas Countries and Territories*. London: Routledge.

Bakić-Hayden, Milica. 1995. "Nesting Orientalisms: The Case of Former Yugoslavia."
Slavic Review 54:917–31.

Boatcă, Manuela. 2010. "Multiple Europes and the Politics of Difference Within."
In *The Study of Europe*, edited by Hauke Brunkhorst and Gerd Grözinger, 51–66.
Baden-Baden: Nomos.

Boatcă, Manuela. 2013. "Multiple Europes and the Politics of Difference Within." *Worlds
and Knowledges Otherwise* 3 (3). https://globalstudies.trinity.duke.edu/volume-3
-dossier-3-uneasy-postcolonialisms.

Boatcă, Manuela. 2014. "Inequalities Unbound: Transregional Entanglements
and the Creolization of Europe." In *Postcoloniality-Decoloniality-Black Critique:
Joints and Fissures*, edited by Sabine Broeck and Carsten Junker, 211–30. Frankfurt:
Campus.

Boatcă, Manuela. 2015. *Global Inequalities beyond Occidentalism*. Farnham, UK: Ashgate.

Bonilla, Yarimar. 2015. *Non-sovereign Futures: French Caribbean Politics in the Wake of
Disenchantment*. Chicago: University of Chicago Press.

Böröcz, József. 2006. "Goodness Is Elsewhere: The Rule of European Difference."
Comparative Studies in Society and History 48:110–38.

Böröcz, József, and Mahua Sarkar. 2005. "What Is the EU?" *International Sociology*
20:153–73.

Cassano, Franco. 1996. *Il pensiero meridiano*. Bari, Italy: Laterza.

Chakrabarty, Dipesh. 2000. *Provincializing Europe: Postcolonial Thought and Historical
Difference*. Princeton, NJ: Princeton University Press.

Connell, Raewyn. 2007. *Southern Theory: The Global Dynamics of Knowledge in Social
Science*. Cambridge: Polity.

Cooper, F. 2005. *Colonialism in Question: Theory, Knowledge, History*. Berkeley: University of California Press.

Coronil, Frederick. 1996. "Beyond Occidentalism: Toward Nonimperial Geohistorical
Categories." *Cultural Anthropology* 11:51–87.

Dainotto, Roberto. 2006. *Europe (in Theory)*. Durham, NC: Duke University Press.

De Jong, Lambert, and Dirk Kruijt. 2005. *Extended Statehood in the Caribbean: Paradoxes of Quasi Colonialism, Local Autonomy, and Extended Statehood in the USA, French, Dutch, and British Caribbean*. Amsterdam: Rozenberg.

EEAS. 2016. "European Union External Action: Overseas Countries and Territories." European External Action Service. https://eeas.europa.eu/headquarters/headquarters -homepage/343/overseas-countries-and-territories_en.

Éduscol. 2011. "Année des Outre-Mers Français: Enseigner l'Outre-Mer, enseigner en Outre-Mer." http://eduscol.education.fr/cid57163/2011-annee-des-outre-mer-francais .html.

Essed, Philomena. 2009. Preface to *Black Europe and the African Diaspora*, edited by Darlene Clark Hine, Trica Danielle Keaton, and Stephen Small. Urbana: University of Illinois Press.

European Central Bank. 2017. "Design Elements." Accessed June 6. https://www.ecb .europa.eu/euro/banknotes/design/html/index.en.html.

European Commission. 2016a. "European Neighbourhood Policy and Enlargement Negotiations: Conditions for Membership." https://ec.europa.eu/neighbourhood -enlargement/policy/conditions-membership_en.

European Commission. 2016b. "International Cooperation and Development: Overseas Countries and Territories (OCTs)." http://ec.europa.eu/europeaid/regions/octs_en.

European Parliament. 2016. "Fact Sheets on the European Union: Outermost Regions (ORs)." http://www.europarl.europa.eu/atyourservice/en/displayFtu.html?ftuId =FTU_5.1.7.html.

Gilroy, Paul. 1993. *The Black Atlantic: Modernity and Double Consciousness*. Cambridge, MA: Harvard University Press.

Gilroy, Paul. 2004. *After Empire: Multiculture or Postcolonial Melancholia*. London: Routledge.

Gutiérrez Rodríguez, Encarnación, Manuela Boatcă, and Sérgio Costa. 2010. *Decolonizing European Sociology: Transdisciplinary Approaches*. London: Routledge.

Hall, Stuart. 2006. "The West and the Rest: Discourse and Power." In *The Indigenous Experience: Global Perspectives*, edited by Roger C. A. Maaka and Cris Andersen, 165–73. Toronto: Canadian Scholars.

Hall, Stuart. 2015. "Créolité and the Process of Creolization." In *Creolizing Europe: Legacies and Transformations*, edited by Encarnación Gutiérrez-Rodríguez and Shirley A. Tate, 12–25. Liverpool: Liverpool University Press.

Hansen, Peo, and Stefan Jonsson. 2014. *Eurafrica: The Untold History of European Integration and Colonialism*. London: Bloomsbury.

Hine, Darlene C., Trica D. Keaton, and Stephen Small. 2009. *Black Europe and the African Diaspora*. Urbana: University of Illinois Press.

Lewis, Martin W., and Kären Wigen. 1997. *The Myth of Continents: A Critique of Metageography*. Oakland: University of California Press.

Lionnet, Françoise, and Shu-mei Shih. 2011. *The Creolization of Theory*. Durham, NC: Duke University Press.

Mignolo, Walter D. 2000. *Local Histories/Global Designs: Coloniality, Subaltern Knowledges, and Border Thinking*. Princeton, NJ: Princeton University Press.

Mignolo, W. D. 2006. "Islamophobia/Hispanophobia: The (Re)Configuration of the Racial Imperial/Colonial Matrix." *Human Architecture* 5 (1): 13.

Mintz, Sidney W. 1998. "The Localization of Anthropological Practice: From Area Studies to Transnationalism." *Critique of Anthropology* 18:117–33.

Mintz, Sidney W. 2010. *Three Ancient Colonies: Caribbean Themes and Variations.* Cambridge, MA: Harvard University Press.

Moraña, Mabel, Enrique D. Dussel, and Carlos A. Jáuregui. 2008. *Coloniality at Large: Latin America and the Postcolonial Debate.* Durham, NC: Duke University Press.

Muller, Karis. 2001. "Shadows of Empire in the European Union." *European Legacy* 6:439–51.

Pieterse, Jan N. 2007. *Ethnicities and Global Multiculture: Pants for an Octopus.* Lanham, MD: Rowman and Littlefield.

Quijano, Aníbal, and Immanuel Wallerstein. 1992. "Americanity as a Concept: Or, the Americas in the Modern World." *International Social Science Journal* 44:549–57.

Rokkan, Stein. 1999. "A Model and Conceptual Map of Europe." In *State Formation, Nation-Building, and Mass Politics in Europe,* edited by P. Flora, S. Kuhnle, and D. Urwin, 135–49. Oxford: Oxford University Press.

Sharpley-Whiting, Tracy, and Tiffany R. Patterson. 2009. "The Conundrum of Geography, Europe d'outre mer, and Transcontinental Diasporic Identity." *Black Europe and the African Diaspora* 89:84.

Stam, Robert, and Ella Shohat. 2012. *Race in Translation: Culture Wars around the Postcolonial Atlantic.* New York: New York University Press.

Therborn, G. 1995. *European Modernity and Beyond: The Trajectory of European Societies, 1945–2000.* London: SAGE.

Todorova, Maria. 1997. *Imagining the Balkans.* New York: Oxford University Press.

United Nations. 2017. "The United Nations and Decolonization." https://www.un.org/en/decolonization/nonselfgovterritories.shtml.

van Amersfoort, Hans, and Mies van Niekerk. 2006. "Immigration as a Colonial Inheritance: Post-colonial Immigrants in the Netherlands, 1945–2002." *Journal of Ethnic and Migration Studies* 32:323–46.

Vergès, Françoise. 2005. "L'Outre-Mer, une survivance de l'utopie coloniale républicaine?" In *La fracture coloniale,* edited by Nicolas Bancel, Pascal Blanchard, and Sandrine Lemaire, 67–74. Paris: La Découverte.

Vergès, Françoise. 2015. "Creolization and Resistance." In *Creolizing Europe: Legacies and Transformations,* edited by Encarnación G. Rodríguez and Shirley A. Tate, 38. Liverpool: Liverpool University Press.

Wallerstein, Immanuel M. 2000. *The Essential Wallerstein.* New York: New Press.

Walsh, Catherine, Freya Schiwy, and Santiago Castro-Gómez, eds. 2002. *Indisciplinar las ciencias sociales: Geopolíticas del conocimiento y colonialidad del poder. Perspectivas desde lo andino.* Quito: Abya Yala.

11 · How Spinoza and Elias Help
to Decenter Our Understanding of Development

A Methodical Research Proposal on the Pluriverse

The master stories of modernity are under pressure. Economic crises, declining social and political participation, ecological limits, and a pluriversal—more complex—world order generate growing insecurity even in the Western centers. The "end of history" appears to have come to an end and is being superseded by the question of whether the successes of our growth regimes and democratic state forms are not merely historical exceptions (Crouch 2004; Piketty 2014). In many regions of the world, development has ceased to follow Western values and patterns. There is a need to redefine what social development may mean in the future and what logics it may follow outside the Western centers. This requires, first and foremost, putting the two central dimensions of the Western understanding of development to the test.

Since its beginnings, engagement with the development of the Global South has mostly been characterized by one constant: a persistently strong and unabated Eurocentrism that shapes the methodical and theoretical-normative assumptions of most analyses while positing Western development as a reference. Western development, first in its centers and subsequently through North American colonization, is stylized as something universal, essentially as a totality that precludes alternatives. This Eurocentrism, however, comprises two dimensions: the first level is an understanding of development as an evolutionary process oriented toward the achievement of an abstract telos, projected onto the future and judged by European and North American experiences and standards, and imagined in strictly sequential terms rather than also as simultaneous coexistence. The second dimension is an androcentric, individualistically theorized subject concept, mostly informed by liberal theory and conceiving social development as shaped by rationally acting, self-interested maximizers of freedom.

Based on these premises, the countries of the Global South are still today commonly interpreted and analyzed as mostly expressions of deficient Western development logics.[1] To be sure, the cultural turn managed to make this

Eurocentric tunnel vision wider. Universal evolutionism, in particular, has in recent decades become profoundly deconstructed. Postcolonial studies have been of particular importance in this regard: in four decades, they have attempted to identify the intellectual and ideological origins of the historical, ethnic, gender-specific, and other restrictive conceptions of development and statehood. Great importance is attached to local and ethnic contexts, as well as gendering, in an effort to trace development in its different facets (Amin 1989; Chakrabarty 2000; Cooper 2005; Coronil 1997; Escobar 2005; Said 1978; Spivak 1990).

However, postcolonialism has been criticized for often going too far in trying to deconstruct the Western understanding of development, neglecting or completely ignoring the economic and political conditions of development (classical: Dirlik 1994).[2] Furthermore, these approaches have as yet not managed to develop a coherent methodical framework open enough to capture relevant particularities while demonstrating sufficient consistency as a basis for decentered development research that would permit generalization and systematic comparison beyond the Western world.[3] In my view, this endeavor cannot succeed without taking into account the second dimension of Eurocentrism, that is, the subject level. In this regard, postcolonial approaches distinguish themselves most notably through contributions on (political) nonrepresentability or the absence of the possibility of the analytical portrayal of subaltern subjects in the countries of the Global South (Spivak 1988). More far-reaching contributions, which would devise a methodical framework for development analyses that draws from a non-individualistic theoretical understanding of subject constitution, however, are (as yet) not readily available.

This chapter, therefore, engages with this dimension. To do so, a theoretical introduction of Baruch Spinoza is first followed by a portrayal of subject constitution by reason and affect. Second, by recourse to Norbert Elias, the interdependences of the individual and the social collective are systematically explored. Finally, it is discussed what methodical potentials (and limitations) Elias's toolbox of figuration offers for decentered development research and how with him structures can be made to rejoice.

Searching the Subject in Developmental
Theory: A Plea for Passion

A debate on the subject level in development analyses has to consider at the outset that the concept of the individual is a cultural concept of the secularized West, which, however, is always counterposed by personal and collective forms of identity. This means that the individual does not act on the grounds of a rationally guided individualism—an ideal typically assumed in the West following Max Weber and to some extent empirically demonstrable—but that individuals simultaneously tend to identify themselves through collectives (often the family, tribe, sex, class, nation, and state), organize themselves in these, orient their action in accordance with them, and are in this regard also guided by affections.

To avoid misunderstandings: the following considerations do not pursue a fundamental critique of individualism. Rather, they should merely be understood as an effort to integrate subjective collective relations and affections more strongly in social analysis. After all, within actions, emotions cannot be fully separated from cognitive understanding, nor are ritual acts, such as state ceremonies, performed completely unreflectingly or unwittingly. Furthermore, I do not suggest that the actions of the subjects of the countries of the Global South are in principle more strongly shaped by the group or by affect. Rather, it is assumed that different developmental trajectories—such as that of the West—have led to a different balancing between rationality and affect and between the individual and the collective.[4] An examination of the particular relations and intertwinings of affective collective action then would facilitate a decentered and context-specific analysis without having to define all subjects by the specific Western rationality–affect balance. At the center of the observation would then be the respective relations and intertwinings, rather than the individual or the affect per se.

Therefore, this chapter essentially advocates for a changed subject perspective within which a complementary focus can be taken on the rationally and affect-guided interrelations between humans and their social environment, that is, the ongoing and visible reciprocal forms of articulation of development. From such a perspective, development is studied not only in its political-institutional and economic dimensions, but as a dynamic form of interwovenness in which humans order their social relations within specific historical contexts; that is, a multiplicity of individual and collective actors who define, (re)produce, or change everyday social practices, forms, functions, and mechanisms.

To search for such a complex subject conception that adequately considers the dimension of affect, it is recommended to consult the classics. For approaching the ratio–affect relation it is helpful to draw from (development) economist Albert O. Hirschman, who strongly influenced development studies and who is still today remembered for his nonconformist thinking.[5] Of particular relevance to the outlined problematic is his *The Passions and the Interests*, which according to Hirschman himself is the only book he wrote out of pure passion for scholarship—and here, the motivation became the program. Based on the European philosophy of the state, this treatise is a trenchant exposition of the history of ideas that traces how the category of passions—such as greed (for power), covetousness, acquisitiveness, and sexual and other cupidities—was gradually pushed into the background as action-determining moments in social development and state formation (Hirschman 1977). While since Plato human action had been considered to move between (volatile and often exorbitant) passions and (frequently ineffective) rationality, from the sixteenth century onward two tendencies can be observed: the reappraisal of rational control as a virtue to be internalized, first comprehensively outlined by René Descartes; and the development of the category of interest, in which the positive attributes of the former dichotomy appeared to merge. While rationality was to suppress the destructive forces of passion, the latter would lend the former direction and vigor.

According to Hirschman, the growing influence of this understanding in Europe had quite pragmatic advantages for that epoch: it promised calculability and reliability of the actually irrational, the human being. In politics, it turned the power- and glory-obsessed despot into a calculating and calculable ruler; and making money was no longer the reprehensible expression of greed and avarice, but a sober—that is, rational—desire. As unrestrained passions transmuted into cherished interests, acting increasingly became strategic pondering and, at the same time, calculable. Hirschman views this change of heart as the historical genesis of capitalism and of the bourgeois state.

For Hirschman, it was Adam Smith's postulate in the *Wealth of Nations* that all passions can be satisfied through the individual pursuit of economic interests that established the theoretical tradition of the rational-utilitarian individual.[6] This led to the overwhelming neglect of the affect dimension and to the narrowness of the field of study that still prevails today. After all, as measurability and calculability are central to science, the practicable liberal conception of the subject as a rational, self-interest-maximizing individual asserted itself in the social sciences as well as in development research, and remains powerful today. Its triumph since Adam Smith has resulted in an economization of social science methods and definitions, which soon would interpret societal institutions principally as an incentive structure and aggregation of rational actions (North, Wallis, and Weingast 2009), despite the very diverse, partially counterproductive consequences for social development (Acemoglu and Robinson 2012). Through the idea of freedom and self-responsibility, the human being became systematically and simultaneously historically, socially, gender-specifically, culturally, and locally decontextualized—a basis upon which also Locke constructed his political theory. Later (neo)structuralist, functionalist, and regulation-centric social analyses equally fail to question this liberal conception of subjects, as do most of the theoretical approaches to development. Often they at least implicitly presume individual action to be interest determined and rational.

A reintegration of affect in development analysis, however, is confronted with an obvious problem: how can the irrational be made calculable? Certainly, passions can be felt, enjoyed, or suffered; however, can they also be measured and weighed without restricting the inquiry to the individual or small group, as we know it from sociopsychological and ethnological methods? How can we imagine rationality and passion not as antipodes, where one side offsets the other, but as forming a complementary relationship in which the consideration of both dimensions generates an understanding of social action and social development?

Hirschman responds to this question by proposing to return, in ideal historical terms, to pre-Smithian thinking and engage more strongly with the Dutch philosopher Baruch Spinoza. With his rigid method borrowed from geometry and his insistence on the individual, which, however, he understands as aggregate individuals always interrelated with society, together with his monism that understands spirit and matter as a unity and in conjunction with his skepticism toward rational judgment, Spinoza attempts to methodically analyze and empirically study passions (Nadler 2015; Soyarslan 2016). In his *Ethica, Ordine Geometrico Demonstrata*, posthumously published in 1677, Spinoza (2015) defines passions as affects that enlarge or reduce the human capacity to act, while identifying over fifty affections with differing degrees of efficacy (Lord 2010, 83ff.).

It is beyond the scope of this chapter to attempt to present in detail Spinoza's cataloguing of affections, which starts with the basic affects of pleasure (lust) and grief (unpleasure) and their realization as craving, which then leads to secondary affects, of which hate and love are fundamental. What deserves highlighting, however, is that for Spinoza affections in principle are constitutive—that is, humans are always rational and passionate at the same time. Put differently: rationality, in order to be effective, has to be rooted in affections. Or, in even more radical terms: passions create or destroy society and make it humane. Therefore, in Spinoza's ontology, affections have an effect not only on the individual but also on other relational categories, such as identity, power, and politics, while in turn being influenced by them (Kisner and Youpa 2014).

More profound engagement with Spinoza thus appears to offer an interesting approach to how the neglected dimension of affect can more strongly inform an analysis of contemporary developments of the Global South. Nonetheless, even though Spinoza's systematizations are an important reference for the elaboration of categories for an affect analysis, this does not warrant measurement of the irrational. Yet, if subject action is conceived as always related to collectives, as Spinoza did, and (rational as well as affective) behavioral variables are understood as a constitutive part of social fabrics, which in turn require a certain degree of constitutedness in order to shape subject actions, then descriptions of the configurations of societies permit us to draw conclusions regarding the references of individual action and—provided the research focus is designed accordingly—the influence of affections. Therefore, just as Max Weber's ([1922] 2013) sociology of authority (*Herrschaftssoziologie*) viewed institutions as sedimented forms of subject action (*Akteurshandeln*), in which actors' interpretive patterns and moral concepts are important determinants of orientations that shape the structures and objectives of institutions as much as they are shaped by them, it may then equally be possible to research subjects and (societal or state) institutions by means of an affect analysis. This requires viewing the actors as social beings while both the social structure that underlies concrete action and the action itself have to be methodically analyzed as integral to the processes that take place within the very structures that they may transform.

With this approach Spinoza permits an analysis of power structures that cannot be adequately depicted or explained through a geographical (the nation) or philosophical understanding of sovereignty (the state). This predestines his theory for a decentered analysis of, for instance, forms of political organization beyond the Western state. For while the modern state is unanimously understood as an autonomous apparatus separated from society and economy, ensuring rule in the form of an "impersonal power" (Gerstenberger 2007), many states of the Global South are generally characterized by an overlapping coexistence and reciprocal interpenetration of heterogeneous, formal, and informal systems of power and regulation, which reduce the homogeneity and integrity of the state and may even constitute regulatory systems inconsistent and antagonistic to it (Schlichte 2005). Furthermore, often the power of subjects and/or collectives predominates over impersonal power. To date, however, these are not conceptualized as distinct, influential social and institutional practices, but simply as deficits that have to be overcome. Therefore, they are mostly not at all understood.

Debates on the contemporary failing states approaches illustrate this. Here, Western analyses principally diagnose a weakness or absence of the sovereign and/or of insufficiently developed degrees of institutionalization and formalization, while attempting to approximate the Western ideal through institution or state building. Notoriously, these efforts fail and may even be counterproductive.[7] In Spinoza's sense, however, a so-called failing state territory has to be understood not as a deficient institutional framework but as a field of power whose specific form is the outcome of the social practices and (partially competing) efforts of actors to achieve superior regulatory competence. In addition to institutional and formal framings, other contextual and legitimation factors, such as the environment, history, culture, ethnicity, religion, and so forth, have their corresponding efficacies.[8] In summary, it becomes clear that Western development analysis not only debilitates knowledge production; in the guise of political consulting it may even become costly and dangerous.

Bring Passion into Structure: Elias's Figuration Approach

The efficacy of affections in social development can thus be examined by determining the efficacy of structure and agency. This insight, however, means having to deal with another challenging issue, which numerous scholars have already engaged with (such as Bourdieu, Elias, Fraser, Foucault, Giddens, Habermas, and others). Since space constraints do not permit the necessary critical appraisal of the state of knowledge in this regard, especially if one includes non-Occidental perspectives, the following restricts itself to the one classic that in my view has most notably shaped the respective debates while prominently dealing with the affect dimension: Norbert Elias's ([1939] 1994) figuration model, which he develops and applies in his work *The Civilising Process*.

In the following, these positions are presented and examined with respect to their usefulness for further developing the subject concept for decentered development research. This follows the categories derived from the previous critique of Eurocentrism by (1) determining the basic conceptualization of central modes of action and socialization; (2) the distinct research focus; (3) the question of whether and how the relation between structure and agency within development processes is empirically measured; (4) the significance of affections in this, and to what extent a contextualization of the individual in social institutions occurs; whereby (5) particular attention is paid to the critique of androcentrism. This is complemented by (6) the question of how this connects to the critique of the first dimension of Eurocentrism, that is, the postulated contextualization through an extended space-time dimension; and (7) how this approach relates methodically to the countries of the Global South. Since an exhaustive introduction to Elias's works is not possible here, the outline limits itself to the findings of a first systematic review.

Within the smallest social constellation, Elias identifies (1) archaic fear as the ultimate motive for social action, and he largely assumes an anthropological lens rooted in social coercion to compete for power—processes that are influenced by affections as much as they produce structure. He then attempts, methodically and theoretically, to uncode the relations between subjective and collective action and to contextualize this through the affect dimension. In this his contemplations concentrate on social practice (2), as to him it is within social processes in particular that the individual and the collective become identifiable and describable in their totality. He rigorously opposes static analyses and criticizes the method of generating isolated factors or variables, instead proposing to approach the object of investigation via its relationship dynamics.[9] Thus he considers and explicitly balances both sides (structure and agency) (3), thereby gaining a clear understanding of the fact that theory has to be empirically sustained and informed (4) (for an overview, see Dépelteau and Landini 2013; Elias [1970] 2012). Elias also makes theoretical reference to the problematization of androcentrism and to the countries of the Global South respectively. Although his main work largely ignores gender relations (5), essentially, however, the thesis of "situated knowledge" (Haraway 1991) is immanent to it. Moreover, in other works, Elias explicitly engages with this issue and, by applying his figuration approach, formulates key ideas that today are intensely discussed within gender research generally, and the intersectional approaches in particular.[10] As regards social development, Elias imagines this strictly as models in space and time (6) and emphasizes that not only intra- but also intersocietal influences have to be integrated in the analysis, understanding the latter as an extension of chains of interdependence. Subsequently, Elias's elaborations make concrete reference to countries of the Global South (7), and he is convinced of the openness of his methodical framework of figuration, which in principle makes it applicable to different forms of social development (e.g., Elias [1970] 2012, 162ff.).

With this approach, Elias radically breaks with the two narratives of Eurocentrism and provides a number of productive impulses for decentered development research: he underscores that structure and agency have principally to be analyzed in social practice and in processes. After all, the human being is not simply in processes, it is the process; the only immutable thing about humans is their mutability emanating from evolutionary change (Elias [1970] 2012, 108ff.). Thus Elias encourages prospective development research to bank less on quantitative analyses and to adopt a more relational perspective, rather than a strictly static and/or (field) isolated one. New empirical research foci could be distinct development fields and institutions, such as gender, social, and labor policies. They are not merely characterized by functions and their equivalents, but are state-generated and -regulated spaces in which struggles over domination and distribution take place. Again, the research focus then should not be static analyses but (reform) processes, as for instance pursued by institutional change research and transformation studies.

Furthermore, Elias explicitly rejects an understanding of rationality and affect as antipodes, simultaneously attempting to illustrate the interrelation of structure and action by means of empirical examples. The integration of the affect dimension in addition creates a contextual connection between development research and history, culture, and the local, beyond a micro perspective. Thus he is convinced that the *homo clausus*—the essentialist individual isolated from society—does not exist.[11] Rather, humans can only be thought of in the plural, as they are integrated in intergenerational interdependences that shape them as much as they are shaped by their affections, thoughts, and actions. Thus Elias disaggregates social development as figurations in which a multitude of persons—who by no means are individuals—are bound together in different ways through numerous interrelations and various labile power balances.

Elias describes this conception metaphorically as a group dance, such as a tango, in which the music, pairing, and dance steps are in principle prescribed. The figuration of the dance thus is relatively independent of the individual; however, without a plurality of the reciprocally related persons there would be no dance. While the individual is not determinative, the dance cannot be performed without the group. The actions of all dancers are interdependent and move within a power-imbued tension structure, whose change can also change the figuration.

This means that the figuration approach is based on a theory of power relations that, while viewing power as control of resources, understands the exercise of power not as a unipolar mechanism but as fluctuating transformations of power. The social force field of power rests not in individual human beings (and not only in the political), but in what happens between people and in what is changing. Power is the dynamic essence of interpersonal relationships, which means that integral to power is also always its recognition, legitimation, counterpower, and the possibility of the empowerment of those over whom power is exercised. For Elias, power is the central relationship attribute between humans, and the engine of social development.

This relational understanding of power bears a double advantage for development research: on the one hand, it per se avoids power-blind reductionism, still today often practiced with a control-oriented and technical bias, as well as the economistic or functionalist narrowness of power-sensitive approaches. On the other hand, it does not limit the definition of power to the Weber-influenced, still widespread notion of power as a unilateral assertion of one person's will in a social relation, that is, the exertion of influence (power over)—an interpretation of power that improperly simplifies the contextual analysis of complex power relations.[12]

In accordance with Elias's conception of power, the volitional acts, plans, and passions (as articulations of power) of many actors together generate social and political structures. However, social processes are due to the existing interdependences and fluctuations and are, in their totality, uncontrolled: development is always contingent.

Elias's Toolbox: An Instrument
for Systematizing Postcolonial Analyses

Transferring such figuration onto social developments appears difficult. However, the Eliasian focus on social interdependencies permits us to develop some suggestions regarding how the characteristics shared between the individual and society may be systematically explored, categorized, and thus made accessible for empirical measurement. On the one hand, Elias here makes recourse to the category of affective valences, that is, an affectually shaped web of relationships between people, whereby for Elias human satisfaction is always primarily oriented toward other humans. With regard to larger units, such as the state, such affective attachments are not restricted to humans but also involve unifying symbols such as coats of arms, flags, and emotive concepts or emotionalized big events such as football.[13] Here, affect articulation is already becoming directly related to social collective articulation.

This example in particular shows how Elias, with his focus on affect, avoids cultural relativism. While culture and the state usually have the nation or some other myth of origin as their reference points, affects for Elias always also refer to social positionings: traditions, for example, are not only locally or ethnically rooted, but directly tied to social and political change (also see Hobsbawm and Ranger 1983). Change itself shifts into the focus of observation, rather than the state exclusively as the origin and place of its respective shaping power. In addition, Elias's ([1970] 2012, 133ff.) categories of integration and differentiation facilitate measurement of the quality and quantity of social interdependences: integration, above all, is a physical violence–reducing group survival function that produces social structures, societal organization, and, finally, state monopolies; and differentiation, and the division of labor in particular (which in capitalism reached a new quality), deepens and broadens the interdependencies. Both processes are inextricably intertwined: this means, for example, that the becoming of bourgeois society cannot be separated from the emergence of capitalism. Therefore, Elias places at the center of analysis not economic structural constraints or political regime configurations but the power differentials and balances that hold these chains of interdependence together.

Elias ([1970] 2012: 147ff.) systematizes these three categories into a basic regulatory triad, in which differentiation represents the control dimension of extrahuman contexts of events; integration represents the control of interhuman relationships; and his proposed affect reduction represents self-control. Therefore, with this approach, which combines psycho- and sociogenetic studies, Elias developed definable and empirically deployable categories that permit the analysis of social and personal structures within a specific social process. They thus appear to offer an open, sensitive, while consistent methodical framework for inquiry into development patterns, which is particularly useful for tracing the particularities of societies of the Global South.

This is so for the following reasons: first, Elias's figuration model focuses on affections and explicitly examines these also with regard to their collective expressions, for example, in the form of state symbols. Second, it is nonessentialist with respect to its understanding both of the subject and of structures, as it seeks to relate social and political with economic and other determinants, whose interdependencies, which have to be empirically determined, can lead to varying developmental modes and patterns of society and socialization. This means that the figuration model is neither state- nor market-centric, and it is free from normative presuppositions. This comes very close to an unreserved approximation to the countries of the Global South. Third, the model's category of integration also allows it to scrutinize perpetuated and naturalized social and political exclusion as simultaneities of endogenous and exogenous dynamics (also see Elias and Scotson 2008). This is an important component in countries of the South, which is scarcely taken into account by, for instance, Weber and Bourdieu, and still receives insufficient attention in contemporary inequality research. Via the notion of fluctuating power balances, however, Elias takes account of the dynamics of spaces of social order as well as their forms of legitimation. In this, fourth, he places power and social positioning at the center of observation.[14] Therefore, without neglecting affect and context, Elias conceives a form of analysis that avoids slipping into cultural relativism and ethnologization. And, fifth, with its notion of space-time, the concept offers not only the possibility of a strong contextualization of social development but also a methodical-analytical perspective of how social processes in societies can be traced and explained as interdependent—including transnational—multilevel trajectories.

This methodical understanding is best illustrated by a concrete example. For this purpose, we select a major country of the Global South, which at the beginning of the twentieth century had the same per capita income as Germany, and that in 1940 was considered by agricultural economist Colin Clark (1940) to become one of the four nations with the highest per capita income worldwide within the next thirty years: Argentina. Soon after this prognosis, Argentina became characterized by severe social and political dislocations and economic decline, and instability, poverty, and deep inequalities have since become key features of its society. Most commonly, this is attributed to structural (e.g., deferral of agricultural reform) and institutional (e.g., hyperpresidentialism, dictatorial tendencies, and weak rule of law) distortions. However, the Eliasian figuration approach could expand such stunted explanations by introducing the following considerations: on the one hand, the emergence of the Argentine nation was based on massive external resource influx. Referred to as the Belle Époque, which lasted until World War I, this nourished an almost forty-year economic boom during which the nation experienced cultural blossoming. The leading agricultural elites quickly learned to optimize the use of their fertile soils while banking on a poorly diversified export basket of everyday necessities (wool, grain, meat), which ensured a relatively steady demand also during international sales crises. On the other hand, liberal migration laws that demanded few concessions to be made to the new homeland led to a remarkably high immigration rate: at the turn of the century, a third of the population consisted of migrants. The economic boom facilitated high collective upward mobility, leading relatively early within the region to the formation of a broad middle class while easing integration in a general sense. At the same time, however, this complicated the emergence of identity-establishing collectives and intensified the strong self-referential acting of the subjects, motivated by gains in freedom. Ideal (family) relations shaped by the European countries of origin remained important reference points of the elites and later migrants; Argentina viewed itself more as a European outpost than as a nation of its own. Such collective experiences in state formation generally favored outward-oriented solution, which truncated efforts for national identity politics, the development of political institutions, and the consolidation of conflict resolution mechanisms. Therefore, due to the massive resource influx and the immigration background of broad sectors of society, no profound integration and differentiation occurred in Argentina. The elites never had to struggle for a central monopoly as the cash inflows initially ensured sufficient resources (and power) for all relevant groups. It did not appear necessary to build up a strong central state: institutions, such as a currency, laws, state bureaucracies, and even a capital city were in their majority only created after state formation, and the pronounced noncompliance of (not only) the elites to pay taxes down to the present day demonstrates the limited legitimation and powers of self-assertion that the state (has) had. Self-interests were best realized through the development of social conflict potentials (and violence) rather than through active participation in the state; progressive affect control was neither necessary nor conducive to this. The economic concentration on exports—which due to a redistribution of export revenues was never abandoned in its final logic even during periods of inward orientation—further reduced the need for social differentiation. Therefore, growing interdependence, to which Elias by reference to Europe attributes first consolidation followed by gradual horizontalization and depersonification of state power, never occurred. This explains why populism and violence are still important political means today in Argentina. The latter, in particular, is remembered in the form of the most recent military dictatorship, which even in the regional comparison was extremely brutal and perfidious. For Elias, social interdependence is inextricably intertwined with affect control: if the first is coarse grained, the probability of the use of political violence increases.

This cursory illustration alone gives us some ideas of the kinds of questions that may be posed and engaged with through the methodical toolbox of figuration. For example, the figuration model permits us to understand the state fiscal monopoly, which in contrast to democracy and the monopoly on the legitimate use of force has barely been enforced in Latin America, not as a premodern system deficiency or technocratic implementation failure but as an expression of a specific, historically grown, and to date—in essence political regime neutral—legitimating power asymmetry between empirically delimitable groups. A research program based on a figuration analysis could help to determine whether such nonexistent resource monopolization, for instance, is an expression of inadequate interdependence chains or restricted integration conditions, and what culture of rule contributes to legitimating or naturalizing the exclusion entailed. Therefore, this could permit us to concretely identify the extent to which functional considerations (power and resource maintenance) and/or affective guiding patterns (such as traditional external orientation of elites) play a central role, in order to explain why, for example, more recent reforms for increasing tax revenue in the region have often remained ineffective.

Transcending Elias with Elias

Despite these inspirations provided by Elias, development theoretical debates, including the contemporary ones, and with them the analysis of countries of the Global South, have a strained relationship with his approach. After all, the title of his *The Civilising Process* already evokes a normative and teleological understanding of development and, on top of this, it explicitly refers to European social trajectories. Thus it has provoked numerous disputes and accusations of a marked Eurocentrism, and even of racism. However, these kinds of reactions, alongside the persistent ignorance of making the Eliasian approach fruitful for decentered (and especially postcolonial) research practice, are probably due to the tragic fact that Elias's text is not only among the most frequently cited classics in the social sciences, but also one of the most misinterpreted ones.

Elias's civilization theory has frequently been criticized not only for its historical representations and interpretations, but also for its theoretical premises. For example, Elias stylizes competition as the principal source of social dynamics while, just like Weber and Bourdieu, insufficiently engaging with cooperation. Elias assumes as the driving force of such competitive constellations the individual's archaic fear of the Other (nature, humans), which can be transformed into security principally through domination—an interpretation that in principle follows Hobbesian natural law and Sigmund Freud's conception of the human being (Wickham and Evers 2012). And even though Elias vehemently rejects the accusation of evolutionism, in fact a consistent application of his categories in principle only permits a unilineal course of social and political development—not in a teleological sense, however, but as a progressive, stagnating, or regressive tendency. Also, the idea that the development process of the Western states is best described as a process of increasing affect control can undoubtedly be questioned. After all, the destructive tendencies and extreme acts of violence of modern European states in the twentieth century can hardly be simply understood as temporary regressions—perhaps they even were only made possible by civilization (Bauman 2000). Furthermore, neither are the two Eliasian categories for measuring social processes (integration/differentiation) completely alien to theoretical beliefs in modernization, nor are his stated arguments for social differentiation far off from structural functionalism, which he himself had critiqued.

These multifarious and indeed justified criticisms, however, have largely overlooked that the model of figuration represents a model that excellently accomplishes the complementary integration of affections in social analysis and development research, while its rational understanding of the individual and the collective simultaneously facilitates new methods and approaches. This in fact would be in Elias's spirit: as he once stated, the notion of figuration seeks to provide a conceptual tool through which the false duality of society and the individual can be dissolved (Elias [1970] 2012, 123ff.). In order to make the figuration model work for research, however, it would be necessary to address its existing deficits and the criticisms voiced, and update it to the current state of knowledge.

This task should be guided by the three categories of the Eliasian triad. With respect to the category of affective valences, it should first be positively noted that this implies historical retrospective, which in principle promises a post-colonial analysis, as here Elias works with a three-generation view. Nonetheless it has to be asked whether this approach could not be optimized in research economic terms in order to keep the data collection effort feasible. Of further advantage is that both a historical perspective and the integration of affections provide key criteria that permit a systematic contextualization of social processes without having to restrict oneself to local particularities.

However, it would be necessary to clarify whether Elias's interest in progressive affect control and, therefore, self-control would not have to be significantly extended toward motives of action other than fear and hope, in order to capture more relevant aspects of social change. After all, social cohesion requires not only internal renunciation of violence, but also empathy and solidarity. Here, a synthesis with Spinoza's affect categorization is useful as it also recognizes such affects as lust, cupidity, and love, thus permitting a more broadly conceived research focus (Bodei 1995). The hitherto unattempted experiment of calibrating, and potentially synthesizing, Elias and Spinoza warrants the possibility of elaborating a framework of methods that not only perceives development with passion, but also makes it operational. It thus facilitates a new access to the social dynamics of today's Global South.

As regards the issue of integration, the assumption that the diffusion of affections primarily occurs as an elitist top-down tendency has to be corrected—this assumption has already been largely made relative by more recent historical analyses. And although Elias explicitly differentiates his category of differentiation from structural functionalist assumptions, he nonetheless implicitly draws from them in his own analysis. In this respect it would have to be examined, inter alia, whether a less passionate engagement with theoretical approaches opposed by Elias could not facilitate new syntheses that would permit the development and operationalization of indicators without having to neglect the research focus on the social praxis of development patterns. In addition, the degree of integration and the thickness of differentiation that state interdependence chains would have to dispose of in order to maintain their efficacy and not to rupture would further have to be specified. This is above all significant if the analytically relevant transnational dimensions of social interweavings, as also considered by Elias, are to be analyzed with respect to their degrees of efficacy (Mann 1986).

In addition, two other tasks are of cardinal importance. On the one hand, further development of the figuration model would have to make an effort to take seriously in all respects the criticism of androcentrism (Walby 2009), and build this into the figuration model. For example, within the category of affective valences it would be possible to collect data in a gender-sensitive way; in the category of integration, to pay particular analytical attention to women's social positions and rights; and, in the category of differentiation, for instance, to research changes in male and female professions in order to capture their social ascription as a specific mode of gender construction. On the other hand, the Eliasian model's understanding of social change and the subject–structure relationship would have to be vigorously calibrated with the positions and knowledge of non-European doctrines and worldviews, as well as with the state of knowledge of postcolonialism, in order to clarify whether and what analogies exist and where syntheses are possible for an even more adjusted application of the figuration model to the states of the Global South. Not least, it would also have to be examined how Elias is perceived and received in the countries of the Global South, and whether this provides further starting points for a research program based on the figuration approach.

These are, undoubtedly, only some first explorations of the direction into which the figuration model may further be developed as a toolbox of decentered development research methods. The central objective would be to sharpen its categories and to update it to the latest state of knowledge and the corresponding conditions of the countries of the Global South, in order to elaborate new indicators for empirical inquiries. The debates on postcolonialism and post-development, in particular, could thus gain constructive stimulation, as the figuration model provides both methodical and analytical responses to the central critiques of these approaches: first, the categories of integration and differentiation sufficiently consider the material conditions of development without relapsing into a Western economism, while the category of affective valences simultaneously ensures subject sensitivity, which rightfully is a key tenet of postcolonialism. Second, the figuration model proposes a method and design that permit us to context-specifically relate structure and subject in the analysis without having to forgo systematization and comparison. If a research program of such orientation could in practice contribute to an improved, empirically grounded understanding of the countries of the Global South, this would be of particular benefit to developmental theories—and to science as a whole.

1. This dictum, which is already contained in the grand development theories, modernization theory, and—influential from the 1960s onward—dependency theory, has perpetually returned in different variants: the first strand of thought transfigures non-Western development as premodern, temporary mal- or underdevelopment, which has to be countered by European-style economic development and state and administrative reforms. By contrast, the second strand views observed developmental anomalies often as an expression of a peripheral, distorted, and dependent capitalism, implying that capitalism is also the dominant mode of social organization in the countries of the Global South. Following September 11, 2001, development studies regained impetus, however, with a shift in perspective, from a developmentalist to a security policy focus via the new deficit concept of the failing state, which has often quite blatantly become aligned to Western principles through state building (Fukuyama 2004; for the current Western and, above all, North American dominance in international politics research, also see Tickner [2013]).

2. As Sylvester (1999, 703) has succinctly stated: "Development studies does not tend to listen to subalterns and postcolonial studies does not tend to concern itself with whether the subaltern is eating."

3. Different studies either employ differing (though to some extent disciplinarily justifiable) parameters and categories, or lack profound empirical substantiation, which renders them methodically imprecise while undermining comparability. They are then often characterized by a high level of abstraction that lacks empirical grounding, rather than by precise concepts, or they operate with absolute explanations (such as colonialism), which do not do justice to the complexity of social change in the countries of the Global South (Santos 2014). From the same perspective, certain popular postdevelopment approaches that attempt to transfer the state of knowledge from postcolonial studies to development theory, discourse, and practice can be accused of a mirrorlike inversion of the orthodox development discourse: when grassroots movements, local initiatives, and subsistence communities are promoted as an alternative to modern industrial society, they appear to simply invert the normative parameters of the modernization discourse. Analytically, therefore, they run the risk of promoting in a reductive or culturally deterministic way the conceptual framework of the development discourse as the central inequality-generating mechanism, while bracketing out other central aspects of social change, such as the (global) economy and politics.

4. This is, essentially, what Weber ([1922] 2013) also says: in contrast to what is frequently claimed today, for him, the development from the Protestant ethic to capitalism was not a causal or linear process. Rather, the intentional behavior of numerous individuals (religious salvation) led to a nonintentional overall change (rational modernity). This "paradox of rationalisation" (Schluchter 1979) in which, as a form of demystification, religious meaning, and identity-giving norms and practices mutated in the West into a rational-efficient but meaningless dominion, is for Weber quite unique. His theory of the development of worldviews (*Weltbilder*) thus makes a universal historical claim but is not, in contrast to the positions of many of his apologists, universalistic.

5. To be sure, rigorous methodical scrutiny leaves little substance from Hirschman's postulates in favor of a self-subversion of thinking or a possibilism in the social sciences.

However, the real interest of his interventions arguably consisted in an effectively staged catalysis, with which he attempted to break up the monodisciplinary orthodoxies and conventional research traditions.

6. Certainly, by reference to Smith's earlier writing *The Theory of Moral Sentiments*, it has been pointed out that this ascription would do the Scottish moral philosopher wrong (Máiz 2010; Silver 1990). However, what can be stated with certainty is that *The Wealth of Nations* became a key foundation of rational interest–focused social studies and research.

7. Generally, failing states are understood as partially erupted, locally limited, but on the whole controllable security problems. On this basis, recommendations for political action are made, and their implementability supported by an alleged scientific base. Ironically, however, the scientific justification of such recommendations—Weber's conception of the state—is precisely the reference through which the frequent failure of efforts of state or institution building can be explained. These policies understand the building of administrative capacities as a lever of Western modernization, seeking to increase individual rationality by increasing state rationality. However, in accordance with Weber, this represents an inversion of cause and effect: in the West it was individual rationality that, once internalized, provided the basis for rational rule. However, when, as in the West, the transferred instrumentally rational-functional principles have a destructive effect on the existing structures of meaning, they generate counterreactions, such as extreme traditionalism and fundamentalism.

8. While, for instance, a Western development approach often understands the epidemic existence of corruption as simply bad governance, a decentered understanding of social and cultural tolerating and sanctioning of corruption (which actually may be grounded in rationality) would open up a fundamentally different (policy) perspective (Blundo and de Sardan 2006). Moreover, in those places where politics and administration are strongly personality driven, the promotion of administrative capacities increases not efficiency, but the influence of particular groups. For example, the privatization programs in Africa led not to greater market efficiency but to an extension of traditional elite power (Tangri 1999).

9. Pierre Bourdieu, Michel Foucault, and Anthony Giddens, among others, whose influential social theories are also based on studies of social practice, were strongly influenced by this approach. Also see Gabriel and Mennell (2011b) for Elias's international impact on social science research.

10. For Elias, gender relations too are dynamic power balances that unfold between the sexes at the macro level of the states and the gendered division of labor, as well as in the subjective and affective relations at the micro level. Today's gender research analyzes the latter as "doing gender" (West and Zimmermann 1987). Elias showed in his studies that power balances between men and women always operate simultaneously in the public space, in the economy and politics, the family, matrimony, and sexuality (Klein and Liebsch 2001). Conversely, changes in political framework conditions, such as through reforms, obviously also shape gender relations.

11. Elias thus by far transcends Weber's analysis. Both classics share the claim of analytically relating structure with agency. Weber's self-conception by no means corresponds with today's popularly propagated universalist idea of development as an evolutionary process guided by Western modernity, but actually takes into account local contextualization.

However, with his simplified subject notion centered on reasonableness or instrumental rationality, Weber undoubtedly is one of the origins of the second dimension of Eurocentrism. This key idea, which culminates in the coupling of the concept of the incorporated public law institution (*staatlichen Anstaltsbegriffs*) with rational rule (*rationale Herrschaft*), itself based on the rational behavior of the individual, renders Weber largely unsuitable for decentered research. In my assessment, this also applies to the more recent efforts to rehash Weber's categories for analyses of contemporary global changes of state and society.

12. If such a one-dimensional approach (often also by reference to Weber) is coupled with a formalistic and institutionalistic angle, this can barely be expected to produce valid knowledge about, in particular, the countries of the Global South. However, there is more to Elias's relational understanding than just transcending Weber's. His view that dominant power figurations are also, and in particular, articulated outside the political, and that they become inscribed or reflected in the individual, has also influenced Bourdieu's and Foucault's definitions of power. In fact, his engagement with the issue of the genesis of power may even have been more profound than theirs. Furthermore, the figuration approach may provide inspiring contributions to more recent debates of power, which address both the repressive and productive character of power through the concepts of power over and power to, aspiring to an integral concept of power (for an overview, see Clegg and Haugaard 2009). It is therefore quite striking that Elias's positions continue to receive little attention in contemporary sociological and political science debates in the United States. Gabriel and Mennell (2011a, 18) explain this ignorance, quoting an email from Alan Sica: "The reason Americans don't take to Elias is that he writes about European historical and cultural change and American sociologists don't feel comfortable with that sort of thing, except for [Jack] Goldstone and that small lot; and because he is theoretically very adventurous and synthetic, and they don't go for that; and because he trashed Parsons, who many of them liked back in the day; and because he could be mistaken for a closet Freudian, which they don't like; and because he brings up really obnoxious qualities of humankind, which they particularly don't like; and because he wrote a helluva lot of stuff, which takes a long time to read, they don't have time; and because 'figuration' is a word that has a distinctly effete connotations in this country, and sounds like art history."

13. For the second, on sport and social development, also see Elias and Dunning (2008).

14. This is exactly what Gayatri Spivak (2003) would argue later, pointing out that all struggle of cultural discrimination equally is a struggle of social advancement.

REFERENCES

Acemoglu, Daron, and James Robinson. 2012. *Why Nations Fail: The Origins of Power, Prosperity, and Poverty*. New York: Crown Business.

Amin, Samir. 1989. *Eurocentrism*. New York: Monthly Review Press.

Bauman, Zygmunt. 2000. *Dialectic of Modernity*. London: SAGE.

Blundo, Giorgio, and Jean-Pierre Olivier de Sardan. 2006. *Everyday Corruption and the State: Citizens and Public Officials in Africa*. London: Zed.

Bodei, Remo. 1995. *Una geometría de las pasiones*. Barcelona: Aleph.

Chakrabarty, Dipesh. 2000. *Provincializing Europe: Postcolonial Thought and Historical Difference*. Princeton, NJ: Princeton University Press.

Clark, Colin. 1940. *The Conditions of Economic Progress*. London: Macmillan.

Clegg, Stewart R., and Mark Haugaard. 2009. *The Sage Handbook of Power*. London: SAGE.

Cooper, Frederick. 2005. *Colonialism in Question: Theory, Knowledge, History*. Berkeley: University of California Press.

Coronil, Fernando. 1997. *The Magical State: Nature, Money, and Modernity in Venezuela*. Chicago: University of Chicago Press.

Crouch, Colin. 2004. *Post-Democracy*. Cambridge: Polity Press.

Dépelteau, François, and Tatiana Landini. 2013. *Norbert Elias and Social Theory*. London: Palgrave Macmillan.

Dirlik, Arif. 1994. "The Postcolonial Aura: Third World Criticism in the Age of Global Capitalism." *Critical Inquiry* 20 (2): 328–56.

Elias, Norbert. [1939] 1994. *The Civilising Process: Sociogenetic and Psychogenetic Investigations*. Oxford: Blackwell.

Elias, Norbert. [1970] 2012. *What Is Sociology?* Dublin: University College Dublin Press.

Elias, Norbert, and Eric Dunning. 2008. *Sport and Leisure in the Civilizing Process*. Dublin: University College Dublin Press.

Elias, Norbert, and John L. Scotson. 2008. *Established and Outsiders*. Dublin: University College Dublin Press.

Escobar, Arturo. 1995. *Encountering Development: The Making and Unmaking of the Third World*. Princeton, NJ: Princeton University Press.

Fukuyama, Francis. 2004. *State Building: Governance and World Order in the 21st Century*. Ithaca, NY: Cornell University Press.

Gabriel, Norman, and Stephen Mennell. 2011a. "Handing Over the Torch: Intergenerational Processes in Figurational Sociology." *Sociological Review* 59 (s1): 5–23.

Gabriel, Norman, and Stephen Mennell, eds. 2011b. *Norbert Elias and Figurational Research: Processual Thinking in Sociology*. Hoboken, NJ: Wiley-Blackwell.

Gerstenberger, Heide. 2007. *Impersonal Power: History and Theory of the Bourgeois State*. Leiden: Brill.

Haraway, Donna. 1991. *Simians, Cyborgs and Women: The Reinvention of Nature*. New York: Routledge.

Hirschman, Albert Otto. 1977. *The Passions and the Interests: Political Arguments for Capitalism before Its Triumph*. Princeton, NJ: Princeton University Press.

Hobsbawm, Eric, and Terence Ranger. 1983. *The Invention of Tradition*. Cambridge: Cambridge University Press.

Kisner, Matthew J., and Andrew Youpa, eds. 2014. *Essays on Spinoza's Ethical Theory*. Oxford: Oxford University Press.

Klein, Gabriele, and Katharina Liebsch. 2001. *Egalisierung und Individualisierung: Zur Dynamik der Geschlechterbalancen bei Norbert Elias*. In *Soziale Verortung der Geschlechter: Gesellschaftstheorie und feministische Kritik*, edited by Gudrun-Axeli Knapp and Angelika Wetterer, 225–55. Münster: Westfälisches Dampfboot.

Lord, Beth. 2010. *Spinoza's Ethics*. Edinburgh: Edinburgh University Press.

Máiz, Rámon. 2010. "La hazaña de la Razón: La exclusión fundacional de las emociones en la teoría política moderna." *Revista de Estudios Políticos* 149:11–45.

Mann, Michael. 1986. *The Sources of Social Power:* vol. 1, *A History of Power from the Beginning to AD 1760.* Cambridge: Cambridge University Press.

Nadler, Steven. 2015. "On Spinoza's 'Free Man.'" *Journal of the American Philosophical Association* 1 (1): 103–20.

North, Douglas, John Wallis, and Barry Weingast. 2009. *Violence and Social Orders: A Conceptual Framework for Interpreting Recorded Human History.* Cambridge: Cambridge University Press.

Piketty, Thomas. 2014. *Capital in the Twenty-First Century.* Cambridge, MA: Harvard University Press.

Said, Edward W. 1978. *Orientalism.* London: Vintage.

Santos, Boaventura de Sousa. 2014. *Epistemologies of the South: Justice against Epistemicide.* Boulder, CO: Paradigm.

Schlichte, Klaus, ed. 2005. *The Dynamics of States: The Formation and Crisis of State Domination.* Aldershot, UK: Ashgate.

Schluchter, Wolfgang. 1979. "The Paradox of Rationalisation: On the Relation of Ethics and World." In *Max Weber's Vision of History: Ethics and Methods,* edited by G. Roth and W. Schulchter. Berkeley: University of California Press.

Silver, Allan. 1990. "Friendship in Commercial Society: Eighteenth-Century Social Theory and Modern Sociology." *American Journal of Sociology* 95 (6): 1474–505.

Soyarslan, Sanem. 2016. "The Distinction between Reason and Intuitive Knowledge in Spinoza's Ethics." *European Journal of Philosophy* 24 (1): 27–54.

Spinoza, Baruch de. 2015. *The Ethics: Ethica Ordine Geometrico Demonstrata.* Translated by R. H. M. Elwes. Wokingham, UK: Dodo Press.

Spivak, Gayatri Chakravorty. 1988. "Can the Subaltern Speak?" In *Marxism and the Interpretation of Culture,* edited by Cary Nelson and Lawrence Grossberg, 271–313. Chicago: University of Illinois Press.

Spivak, Gayatri Chakravorty. 1990. *The Post-colonial Critic: Interviews, Strategies, Dialogues.* Edited by Sarah Harasym. New York: Routledge.

Spivak, Gayatri Chakravorty. 2003. *Death of a Discipline.* New York: Columbia University Press.

Sylvester, Christine. 1999. "Development Studies and Postcolonial Studies: Disparate Tales of the 'Third World.'" *Third World Quarterly* 20 (4): 703–21.

Tangri, Roger. 1999. *The Politics of Patronage in Africa—Parastatals, Privatization and Private Enterprise.* Oxford: James Currey.

Tickner, Arlene B. 2013. "Core, Periphery and (Neo)Imperialist International Relations." *European Journal of International Relations* 19 (3): 627–46.

Walby, Sylvia. 2009. *Globalization and Inequalities: Complexity and Contested Modernities.* Los Angeles: Sage.

Weber, Max. (1922) 2013. *Economy and Society.* Berkeley: University of California Press.

West, Candace, and Jon H. Zimmermann. 1987. "Doing Gender." *Gender and Society* 1 (2): 125–51.

Wickham, Gary, and Barbara Evers. 2012. "Elias in the Footsteps of Hobbes?" *Human Figurations: Long-Term Perspectives on the Human Condition* 1 (1): 2–11.

12 · In Quest of Indigenous Epistemology

Some Notes on a Fourteenth-Century Muslim Scholar,
Ibn Khaldun (1332–1406)

Background

Discourse on the decolonization and indigenization of knowledge, particularly in the non–Organisation for Economic Co-operation and Development (OECD) countries has been going on for at least the past three decades or so. However, in general, the debate is still peripheral and has yet to take center stage in the academic circle of native scholars. Until recently, not many have made serious efforts or directly engaged in this initiative.

Nevertheless, a sign of contestation over what is now termed colonial knowledge has already surfaced in many former colonized nations. A new wave of academic movement among native scholars has emerged. The mission is to end the syndrome of intellectual dependency and to detach from the colonial mentality. No doubt the colonials established an educational system and institutions; however, one must also be aware of the fact that the education system was chiefly meant to serve the interests of the colonial masters. When they left, the educational system and institutions remained. Even though these institutions were taken over and operated by the natives, the philosophy and the curriculum used were still what was inherited from the colonial system; hence the question of indigeneity was raised.[1]

For a newly independent nation, a nation-building curriculum would certainly be the top priority in their education policy. Knowledge and values in the education system should be imperative in carrying out this mission. Nation building involves many aspects of human life, including identity, integrity, patriotism, national pride, culture, tradition, and belief systems, among others. All these elements, plus the traditional or native values, should be the underpinning philosophy of the indigenous education system.

At the tertiary level, the issue of knowledge orientation has gradually become a matter of concern. In fact, some universities have even gone a step further in their nation-building curriculum—to the extent of offering courses on indigenous epistemology.[2] We believe that knowledge is epistemologically value laden. And, logically, colonial knowledge would carry the spirit, identity, and values that conform to the traditions of the colonial masters. We cannot expect the colonial education system to produce indigenous knowledge; hence the need for reform and reorientation.[3] There is a necessity to reconstruct and derive the epistemological framework that is rooted in native values and at the same time to wash away the remnants of the colonial marks in the native education system (see, among others, Alatas 1977; Shamsul 1999, 2008).

Since the colonial influence is already deeply entrenched in the minds of native intellectuals, this task is not going to be an easy one. It requires widespread awareness. A prominent Malaysian sociologist, the late S. H. Alatas, in the early 1970s developed a concept that he called the captive mind to describe this mentality. By captive mind, he meant an uncritical and imitative mind dominated by an external source, whose thinking is deflected from an independent perspective (Alatas 1974). This endeavor is continued by his son, another eminent academic, Syed Farid Alatas (see, e.g., Alatas 2005, 228–41). Certainly, this move requires a serious and systematic deconstruction project as well as a strong commitment on the part of these native scholars.[4] It goes beyond the mere mass struggles for political independence. In this respect, intellectual independency is even more crucial. It entails a substantial deconstruction and reform of the basic epistemological principles that lay the foundation of colonial knowledge.

The call for decolonization is meant to deviate from the domain of colonial mentality and cultural imperialism. For the native, colonial knowledge had proven to be inept at providing solutions to local problems. They believe that human society is heterogeneous, unique, and distinctive. This subsequently makes a society different from the other. It is this uniqueness that determines the character of that society and its problems. A society needs to be perceived and understood from a perspective peculiar to that society, as Battiste describes: "Today, indigenous peoples around the world continue to feel the tensions created by a Eurocentric educational system that has taught them not to trust indigenous knowledge, but to rely on science and technology as tools for their future, although those same sciences and technologies have increasingly created the fragile environmental base that requires us to rethink how we interact with the earth and with each other" (2010, 16).

The notion that the West is the sole champion of knowledge advancement and modernity is not always agreeable. Among native scholars, the jinx of the dependency theory is no longer bearable. Knowledge developed in the West might not be applicable in non-Western societies.[5] This would leave a significant knowledge gap in the way one analyzes and understands one's own society. The different nature, culture, and value systems of an indigenous society require an understanding from the very root of a native perspective. The knowledge frameworks developed in Western traditions might only be best applied in the Western social and cultural milieu, where they originated.

Knowledge and sciences are acquired and developed to fulfill human needs and solve human problems. The right epistemology would guide us to the correct understanding of particular human needs and problems. Assumptions constructed based on a specific culture or tradition might be different from the other. The gap between indigenous and colonial knowledge needs to be practically addressed. The colonial education system would not be expected to produce a native-oriented knowledge. In my view, native scholars need to carry out two things, namely, decolonization and indigenization, simultaneously. An education system that is based on colonial values requires a systematic process of decolonization. At the same time, the process of indigenization has to take place.

In the Muslim world, this awareness has already existed since the 1970s and early 1980s. There was a movement propagating the idea of Islamization of knowledge, that is, the reorientation of knowledge to suit the principles of Islam. The term was first used by S. M. N. Al-Attas (1993) in his *Islam and Secularism*, first published in 1978. This was followed by Ismail R. al-Faruqi (1982) in response to what he believed to be the incompatibility of the principles, categories, concepts, and tools originating in the secular West. Al-Attas's approach is to desecularize and de-Westernize knowledge as he believes that secular elements have corrupted knowledge and diverted it from its original functions.

It is important for native scholars to develop knowledge and sciences that will serve the purpose—to solve society's problems and to fulfill its needs. Similarly, knowledge or assumptions used to diagnose society's problems and to propose solutions need to be strongly rooted in a specific social environment. This can be done in many ways, including, among others, the revisiting of the rich indigenous traditions and values that have long been unattended. This is where our present study of Ibn Khaldun is relevant.

This chapter dwells on a fourteenth-century Muslim thinker, Abdul Rahman Ibn Khaldun, better known as Ibn Khaldun (1332–1406). I introduce Ibn Khaldun here for the following reasons: (1) he was a native thinker and can be recognized as representing the indigenous perspective, and (2) he pioneered a new science of society and civilization known as *'umran*. In this science, he detailed the methodologies, the principles, and the systematic analysis of the formation of human society and the rise and decline of a civilization. This is consistent with the main purpose of this study, that is, to look for an indigenous epistemology.

Ibn Khaldun was a versatile scholar who spent most of his life roaming around North Africa and some parts of Europe.[6] As a scholar, he produced an important masterpiece known as *Muqaddima* (The Prolegomena) in which he outlined his notion of civilization. More importantly, he believed that a civilization is developed and constructed in a specific sociocultural context and value system that eventually forms the identity particular to that civilization.

Why Indigenous Epistemology?

The present volume has a noble mission, that is, to construct a pluriverse. The major aim is to look for native indigenous epistemologies, for a couple of reasons: first, we believe that the main purpose of knowledge and science is to serve human purposes, fill human needs, and solve human problems; hence it is value laden. Knowledge has to be rooted and ingrained from within the value system and tradition of a society. Second, the current orientation of the development of knowledge and science are very much Western-centric (read: colonial-centric) and often incompatible with native values and traditions.

Since our main concern is the study of society and to understand epistemology through an indigenous mirror, it is crucial that we look for the correct authentic and representative references. We expect that these references would give us an indigenous or native perspective and a proper understanding distinctive to our society. Most literature and textbooks available today do not really serve this purpose. Such books were produced by and mostly belong to the Western tradition, crafted by Western academics, and carry Western-centric models that reflect the experience, empirical studies, experiments, traditions, and value systems of Western society. In view of this, we now look for literatures and thinkers whose ideas and conceptual framework reflect the native understanding of our own society.

The process of indigenization requires a return to the roots, where we could learn and formulate our own native epistemology. We have to look for native scholars and native literatures that can represent the native worldview. These figures must be acquainted with the tradition and represent the value of the native society. More importantly, their epistemology is firmly rooted in the native values and traditions. We are in dire need of authentic sources that are profoundly ingrained and developed within the indigenous value system. We seek native scholars who can provide us with an indigenous perspective or an epistemological framework for matters pertaining to knowledge and values. It is for this reason we look at Ibn Khaldun as one of these personalities, an Eastern intellectual icon, who could represent an indigenous non-Western epistemology.

Contextualizing Ibn Khaldun: An Indigenous Thinker with a Universal Outlook

Ibn Khaldun was a classic native thinker who left us with an invaluable treatise on the study of human civilization, a magnum opus known as the *Muqaddima*. In the *Muqaddima*, he crafted a science of society that he named *'ilm al-umran*. In it, he drew our attention to the importance of understanding the progress of human civilization, how and why it develops, and, more importantly, the philosophical underpinning of the development, rise, decline, and fall of a civilization. He employed two terms, namely *'umran badawi* (primitive culture) and *'umran hadhari* (civilized culture), to differentiate between uncivilized and civilized society. He articulately theorized the process and stages of development from 'umran badawi toward umran hadhari. Mahmoud Dhaouadi (1990, 320), a Tunisian scholar, for example, noted that Ibn Khaldun's social thought may be considered the only authentic indigenous intellectual, sociohistorical knowledge about human society that the Third World possesses.

In terms of period, Ibn Khaldun preceded other prominent Western social scientists such as Machiavelli (1469–1527) and Vico (1668–1744). Marx (1818–83), Weber (1864–1920), and Freud (1856–1939) were much later. The credit and recognition Ibn Khaldun received from some Western scholars also indicate that they had access to his works. Scholars such as Yves Lacoste (1984) recognized Ibn Khaldun as an eloquent academic who formulated a systematic approach to the study of history and human civilization. His status has no parallel in the history of social thought of other societies and civilizations prior to his time (Lacoste 1984). Arnold Toynbee, a prominent British historian, ostensibly claimed that Ibn Khaldun "has conceived and formulated a philosophy of history, which is undoubtedly the greatest work of its kind that has ever yet been created by any mind in any time and place" (Toynbee 1961, 372). A British-Czech social anthropologist, Ernest Gellner (2000), considered Ibn Khaldun to be the best interpreter of Islamic society and a sociologist whose theoretical insights are comparable to those of Durkheim and Weber. From remarks of those commentators, it certainly appears that Ibn Khaldun was recognized as an original philosopher, who had developed and produced his own conceptual and theoretical scheme for understanding society.

The concept of 'umran is the center of the Khaldunian scheme. For modern readers, it is understood and translated in various ways. Nonetheless, 'umran is mostly defined as civilization, while others understand it as culture (see, e.g., Chabane 2008, 333–34). Muhsin Mahdi (2006), for instance, translated *umran badawi* as primitive culture, *umran hadari* as civilized culture, and *hadara* as civilization. *'Umran* is also translated as sociology or a science of society as understood in modern terms. In short, 'umran can be considered as the progression of a society from a primitive state toward a civilized state. Hadara is the last stage of the progress of 'umran and subject to change, in line with the changes in human society (see Chabane 2008, 321–32). Ibn Khaldun's thought continues to be a field for research and reflection. Although the concept was developed more than six hundred years ago, the principles and the theoretical foundations are still germane. A lot can be learned from this wisdom and brilliance of the past. It is in this context that Ibn Khaldun's thought remains relevant and should become a subject of interest to those who look for an original and native sociophilosophical discourse.

The Epistemology of Ibn Khaldun

A series of discourses have taken place on various aspects of Ibn Khaldun's epistemology. However, no one disputes the presumption that his epistemology is indigenous in nature. We take a look at his magnum opus, the *Muqaddima*, which was written as an introduction to a bigger historical treatise, named *Kitab al-'ibar wa-diwan al-mubtada' wa-al-khabar fi ayyam al-'Arab wa-al-'Ajam wa-al-Barbar wa-man asara-hum min zawi al-sultan al-akbar* (Book of lessons, record of beginnings and events in the history of the Arabs and the Berbers and their powerful contemporaries). Intentionally, he wrote this book out of his own personal dissatisfaction. He was not happy with the way history was written prior to his time. He believed that knowledge of history is essential in understanding human society and civilization; therefore it must be accurately recorded. He was meticulous about the authenticity and reliability of his information. Any report was carefully examined and supported by evidence that went through strict verification procedures. He criticized his predecessors, including al Mas'udi (896–956/7) for not being careful enough in recording historical events. Ibn Khaldun developed his method and applied the principles of rationality and logic. He insisted that historians must acquire necessary methodological and analytical skills in documenting historical events. Historians must have a clear knowledge and understanding of the nature of people, including way of life, culture and value systems, occupations, doctrines, and so forth. Apart from that, a good knowledge of the social, political, and geographical environment where the events took place is also equally important.

The *Muqaddima* consists of six chapters. The first deals with human civilization in general, followed by the second chapter on Bedouin civilization, including the living conditions of tribes and "savage" nations. The third chapter dwells on the rise of dynasties, the caliphate, and royal authority, including discussion on government ranks. The fourth chapter discusses sedentary civilization and the formation of countries and cities. The various aspects of making a living, such as profit and the crafts, are elaborated in the fifth chapter. Chapter 6, which occupies almost one-third of the book, deliberates on the various kinds of sciences, including educational tradition, instruction methods, the process of knowledge acquisition, and the classifications of sciences. Taking history as his point of departure, Ibn Khaldun drew his theoretical conception of the formation of human civilization. He pointed out conditions and factors that determine the sustainability and life span of a civilization. This information can be gathered from knowledge of history. He wrote, "It should be known that history, in matter of fact, is information about human social organization, which itself is identical with world civilization. It deals with such conditions affecting the nature of civilization as, for instance, savagery and sociability, group feelings [*asabiyya*], and the different ways by which one group of human beings achieves superiority over another" (Ibn Khaldun 1990, 1:57).

It is in chapter 6, that Ibn Khaldun systematically presented his views on knowledge and science—his epistemology. He wrote about the basic notion of human beings as they differ from the world of animals. The human ability to think is the key to the process of establishment of human society and the emergence of civilization, as it enables human beings to deal and interact with other living beings. "It should be known that God distinguished man from all the other animals by an ability to think which He made the beginning of human perfection and the end of man's noble superiority over existing things" (Ibn Khaldun 1990, 3:545).

The ability to think provides the capacity to reason out and to find ways and means to overcome problems and to fulfill human needs. More importantly, it empowers human beings to acquire knowledge and to arrange social and political life. Mastery of knowledge and sciences through inquiries and education would lead to the establishment of sedentary life and the emergence of civilization.

To better understand the essence of the Khaldunian epistemology, it is important to look at the background of Ibn Khaldun's conception of the nature and form of various aspects of knowledge, classification of science, how knowledge is acquired, and what would be the limit of human knowledge. This notion is built on the basis of the ontological position of human existence. This leads to an understanding that Ibn Khaldun's epistemology, which he brilliantly developed, corresponds very closely to his ontological conception. He wrote further, "The ability to think is the quality of man by which human beings are distinguished from other living beings. The degree to which a human being is able to establish an orderly causal chain determines his degree of humanity. Some people are able to establish a causal nexus for two or three levels. Some are not able to go beyond that. Others may reach five or six. Their humanity, consequently, is higher" (Ibn Khaldun 1990, 3:548).

For Ibn Khaldun, the human mind has the ability to grasp three different spheres, that is, the world of senses, the world of humans, and the world of angels. The first and lowest sphere is the world of the senses ('alam al-hiss). This sphere consists of minerals, plants, animals, and human beings. We become aware of this sphere by means of sense perception (see, e.g., Ahmad 2003, 15). The next level is the sphere of intellect ('alam al-'aql), which uniquely belongs to humanity. At this level, a human being can understand matters through the power of the intellect. The world of intellect deals with concepts and ideas, or scientific perceptions that are above the world of the senses. Above the world of intellect is another sphere, the angelic world ('alam al-mala'ika; see Ahmad 2003, 15). This is a spiritual realm that consists of pure understanding beyond ordinary reasoning and/or intellection. At this level, a human being can only grasp knowledge in general and not the particulars. Since the position of human beings is in the middle of this hierarchy, human spirituality has the ability to ascend to a higher spiritual sphere and return to the physical world. However, this ability to attain a higher spiritual sphere is only for selected individuals, that is, those who were chosen by God among the prophets and the sages (see further in Ardic 2008, 16).

On human intellect, Ibn Khaldun gives a detailed account of its nature and how the process of thinking takes place. Thinking comes from perception (idrak). Perception is the consciousness of the perceiver outside his or her essence. Perception is peculiar to the living being. Things outside their essence can be perceived through the external senses, such as hearing, vision, smell, taste, and touch. However, human beings have the advantage of being able to perceive things outside their essence not only through the external senses but also through the power of intellect in their brains. With this power, human beings can obtain pictures of the sensibilia and apply intellectual power to them. Thinking is the occupation of forming pictures beyond sense perception and mental wandering for the purpose of analysis and synthesis. This is the meaning of the heart (af'ida).

Explaining the process of intellection, Ibn Khaldun divided human intellect into three stages, namely, (1) the discerning intellect, (2) the experimental intellect, and (3) the speculative intellect. The discerning intellect consists mostly of perception. It enables humans to obtain things that are useful to them and their livelihood and repel things that are harmful. The experimental intellect provides humans with the ideas and behavior needed in dealing with one's fellow humans and leading them. The speculative intellect provides knowledge or hypothetical knowledge of an object beyond sense perception. The end of the process is the perception of existence together with its various kinds, differences, reasons, and causes. And, because he is a Muslim scholar, the last part of Ibn Khaldun's theory of knowledge reflects very much the doctrine of Islamic metaphysics (Ahmad 2003, 12; Ibn Khaldun 1990, 2:444). In the Khaldunian epistemological scheme, the connection between the physical and metaphysical worlds is clearly demonstrated. At the same time, he brilliantly elucidates the division between the world of humanity and the world of other creatures. It is the whole scheme that forms the basis of Khaldunian conceptions of the formation of human society and the development of human civilization.

Having said this, the crucial question is still how to reappropriate the ancient Khaldunian scheme and modern thought in social sciences and humanities. How can we read conceptions proposed in the fifteenth century and contextualize them with a modern globalized digital age? It is apparent that Khaldunian epistemology is deeply rooted in the native values and belief system of the society in which he lived; in this case, the Muslim Arabs and Berbers of North Africa. His epistemology reflects the value systems practiced in the society that shaped his outlook toward social progress and the establishment of civilization.

What we can learn here is that the notion developed by Ibn Khaldun reflects the nature, culture, belief system, and values of his own society—the society he belonged to, and where he was brought up. More importantly, his works were written in his native language using native terminologies. On this basis, Ibn Khaldun's work has fulfilled the criteria of a native literature produced by a native scholar. Hence, his view can be considered as representing an indigenous view. Next I revisit and study part of Ibn Khaldun's thought and the notions he formulated to see how they can be applied as guiding principles in the current situation.

Urbanism: What Khaldunian Epistemology Has to Offer

Since the central theme of our discussion here is the idea of human progress, it would be proper to highlight certain issues that fall within the scope of development and growth. For this purpose, we pick up one of the major issues as a case in point, that is, the issue of urbanism. We believe that urbanism is one of the current topics of interest that attracts the attention of many—leaders, scholars, educators, and the public at large. This is due to the rapid migration from rural areas to urban areas. In many countries, the urban population is now much bigger than the rural. It is noteworthy to see how Ibn Khaldun formulated his theory of urbanism, in what way he implemented his epistemology, and in what manner urbanization should take place.

In the Khaldunian scheme, 'umran is about progress from a simple or primitive society ('umran badawi) to a civilized society ('umran hadhari). The achievement of the level of a civilized society is characterized by, among other things, sedentary life, advancement of knowledge and skills, and other sophistications including technology and science. In modern terms, sedentary life is equivalent to urbanism.

We are aware of the fact that life in cities is complex. Cities offer a vibrant life with all kinds of attractions, cultures, entertainments, employment opportunities, and other urban stimulation. Despite that, cities are also filled with problems—abject poverty, filth, high crime rates, pollution, traffic gridlock, and the list continues. Generally, there are many positive and negative aspects of cities.

In the Khaldunian order, urbanism is the final stage of 'umran. Chabane relates Ibn Khaldun's concept of 'umran to urban studies. The expansion of industrial society in the Western world resulted in the development of an academic discipline called urbanism. Chabane believes that the theories of urbanism can be applied to understand Khaldun's thought. Therefore, it is quite logical to translate 'umran as "urbanization" (see Chabane 2008, 332–33).

It is worth noting here that Ibn Khaldun proposed some important principles regarding planning of cities. We find that his conception of urbanism carries a very modern flavor and, more importantly, the principles he outlined are still relevant in the context of contemporary urban issues. He believed that city and urban development undergo a cyclical process. Based on his observations, he described the pattern of cultures, lifestyles, forms, structures, and problems of towns and cities in his time. He touched upon almost every component of city life, including well-being and physical and spiritual development as well as environment, ecosystems, and sustainability.

Civilization theories substantiate that human beings are the planners and architects responsible for creating the ecological environment, physical and cultural. This concept is certainly in agreement with the notion of humans as the agents of change par excellence. As a devoted Muslim, Ibn Khaldun took the basic Islamic doctrine of God's vice-regent (*khilafa*) as his point of departure (Ali 1992; see also Ahmad 2000). This notion positions humans as the responsible beings who create their living space and environment. In other words, civilization is no other than the manifestation and realization of human dreams, ideas, and planning of the ideal living environment. The human living environment is not something that exists as merely the outcome of the law of nature. It is human beings who plan and carry out the process and progress of civilization, anchored in physical and technological ability (Bennabi 2001, 25; see also Hassan 1969).

Civilization is the product of human thought, ideas, creativities, and intellectual abilities. However, civilization too is not value free. Human civilization is underpinned by various assumptions and ideological doctrines as well as the culture, tradition, and values of the society. It is vital at this juncture to appreciate the epistemological foundation that forms the basis of its paradigm and ideology. Equally important is to identify the actual form and pattern of paradigm that lays the foundation of that idea. In this way, it is hoped that we will be able to see the pattern of ideology adopted by its proponents. Furthermore, we will be able to assume its impacts on the nature of thought adopted in urban studies.

Today, as we notice, urbanism cannot escape the clutches of contemporary ideologies. This is manifested by the striking phenomenon of intellectual domination of the advanced nations over the rest. As a result, it becomes a kind of doctrine that whatever comes from the advanced countries (read: Western) should be regarded as modern and trendy, and to be adopted without question. It is even worse when this situation exists not only in the realm of physical development but extends over areas of education, values, and culture.

In his discourse, Ibn Khaldun dwelled on all facets of development—both physical and nonphysical. For him, development is the manifestation of the dynamic transformation human society has undergone, that is, from nomadic to sedentary, from simple to complex, from rural to urban and from badawi to hadhari (see Ahmad 2003, 2005). This transformation eventually results in the emergence of new settlements, with the formation of new towns and cities together with the creation of urban life and culture. This is exactly what we understand as urbanization in current terminology. In the context of civilization, towns and cities can be considered as the visible indicators of the level of achievement a particular society has reached. Ibn Khaldun was fully aware of the importance of towns and cities as they represented the faces and façades of a particular civilization. This is explained in his civilization discourse in section 5 of chapter 4 of the *Muqaddima*, which deals particularly with the process of town and city planning and development (Ibn Khaldun 1990, ii).

Back to our primary questions. What does Khaldunian epistemology have to offer in terms of urban development? What lessons and principles can we learn from the *Muqaddimah*? Can these principles be of benefit in dealing with the questions of the quality of life, well-being, and sustainability of our cities? As societies become more developed, cities play an important role as centers of settlement as well as centers of political, social, and cultural activities. Currently, about half of the world's population lives in cities. Cities are becoming larger. No doubt, the metropolis and megalopolis will characterize future human settlements.

In the *Muqaddima*, written over six centuries ago, one of the sections also deals with similar questions, outlining the principles to be employed in addressing current urban crises. Ibn Khaldun particularly stressed the importance of governance or political organization. Governance or khilafa, as he called it, is the prerequisite for the establishment of cities. Cities emerge as the result of policy and planning imposed by the authority. In this case, the dynasty is the authority that will determine the form, image, and characteristics of a particular city. Generally speaking, the concept of governance is not new. It has been known, developed, and understood since the formation of human social organization. In political science, the more commonly used term is government or political system. However, the term governance becomes more important now as we discuss the complexity of urban society and its problems. Simply put, governance means management of the people's affairs, the process of decision making, and the process by which decisions are implemented. The term governance can be used in several contexts such as corporate governance, international governance, national governance, and local governance.

Ibn Khaldun also emphasized a major principle in city planning, namely geographical location. The reason for finding and choosing the right location is to ensure the safety of the city and the presence of basic necessities (such as shelter, fresh air, and water). Social institutions are needed to support and sustain human activities (such as religious, administrative, security, and health institutions), to guarantee a better quality of life. Ibn Khaldun wrote, "Towns are dwelling places that nations use when they have reached the desired goal of luxury and of the things that go with it. Then, they prefer tranquility and quiet and turn to using houses to dwell in. The purpose of building towns is to have places for dwelling and shelter. Therefore, it is necessary in this connection to see to it that harmful things are kept away from the towns by protecting them against inroads by them, and that useful features are introduced and all the conveniences are made available in them" (1990, ii).

It is apparent that Ibn Khaldun viewed shelter as the important require-
ment of city development. Certainly this is about humanizing the cities, where
shelter is one of the fundamental, basic rights of the people. Ibn Khaldun also
stressed safety, for example, by situating the city inside protective walls. While
this may not be feasible in the current context of city development, the issue of
safety has always been a universal concern. As cities become larger, they are also
becoming more and more unsafe. As human society becomes more advanced,
the concept of safety and security becomes wider. It could no longer be confined
within the limited definition of facing the crimes and enemies, but also includes
environment and health as well as mental well-being (see Mohamad 1998).

The United Nations Conference on the State of Safety in World Cities in
2007 recognized that one of the most significant causes of fear and insecurity
in many cities today is the increasing rates of crime and violence. Between 1990
and 2000, incidents of violent crime per 100,000 persons increased from 6 to
8.8. Studies show that 60 percent of all urban residents in the world have been
victims of crime (see UN Habitat 2007). Crime, whether it includes violence
or not, is a growing and serious threat to urban safety all over the world. Another study on urban environment and mental well-being by Guite and Ackrill (2006) shows that factors such as noise, overcrowding, dissatisfaction, and
feeling unsafe significantly detract from the well-being of urban populations.

A study by Savard, Clergeau, and Mennechez (2000) suggests applying the
concept of biodiversity to urban ecosystems. Again, we find it in Khaldunian
principles of how a city should be developed. Expanding cities have such far-
reaching and intractable effects both on social structures and on the natural
environment. Hence, a forward-looking approach should be adopted. The
principle of responsible urban development and respecting the rights of future
generations should be introduced.

The impact of economic inequality is another issue. While more economically affluent groups will get the benefit of the city's wealth, there is also the
emerging group of the urban poor. This social class gap leads toward the deterioration of human attitude, lifestyles, and values.

In making cities habitable, a just and balanced development approach is
important to ensure that all will benefit from city development. This is in line
with the concept of sustainable city development, where it becomes the center
of democracy, culture, and innovation (Alam 1960; Zen 2007). The poor have
the right to voice their grievances and predicaments just like the rich, and this
is where governance is required to ensure justice is done for all.

One of the major points that Ibn Khaldun emphasized, to which current
urban planners and city authorities should pay attention, is the deterioration

of cities caused by the sedentary or urban lifestyle associated with consumerism among the urban population. He gave the example that, just as man has his life span, a city also has its physical limit. As he put it, a city will be destroyed by rampant corruption among members of the society. The culture of consumerism, luxury, leisure and pleasure (or hedonism), opulence and indulgence among city dwellers will be the reason for the city's downfall. The attitude of the residents will be the main cause of the city's destruction. Ibn Khaldun (1990) explained, "All this is caused by excessive sedentary culture and luxury. They corrupt the city, generally in respect to business and civilization. Corruption of the individual inhabitants is the result of their painful effort to satisfy the needs caused by their luxury customs; the result of the bad qualities they have acquired in the process of obtaining those needs; and of the damage the soul suffers after it has obtained them, through acquiring another quality."

As we witness conditions in many cities, this is not far from the truth. Cities are filled with people who earn their living through immoral activities such as selling drugs and human trafficking, money laundering, and white-collar crimes. The physical limits of a city are very much affected by various factors including the physical (such as the quality of building materials and technology used), the social (such as the size of the population and its level of education), and the environmental (such as the availability of natural resources) as well as economic factors and the income gaps between the various segments and classes of city dwellers.

A study conducted by Matheson et al. (2006) shows that stressed neighborhoods have higher levels of depression. In this study, he argues that daily stress, where residential lack of mobility and material deprivation prevail, is connected with depression. Women were found to be more reactive to chronic stress that resulted in a higher risk of depression. Faris and Dunham conducted a study in 1939 (quoted in Matheson et al. 2006) on the issue of environment and mental health, and found that psychiatric admissions in Chicago were varied, with higher rates for those living in the inner-city center than in outlying areas. Social disorganization such as poverty was found to be one of the contributors to depression among inner-city populations (Latkin and Curry 2003). In the fifteenth century, Ibn Khaldun already cautioned, all these symptoms are no other than the manifestation of corruption of the individual inhabitants. Ibn Khaldun particularly emphasized that human misbehavior became the major source of disaster in cities. All these can be seen in contemporary cities if the planners lose sight of controlling urban sprawl as well as providing alternative strategies for future development of the city. In the current context of urbanization, this can be interpreted as the issue of urban agglomeration that has a detrimental effect on the overall quality of life of the population and eventually may lead to the destruction of the city if any parts of the system stop functioning. The ecological footprint proposed by William Rees in 1992, which measures human needs in earth's ecosystem, is about the size, capacity, and sustainability of a city, and is also consistent with Ibn Khaldun's concept of an optimum city size, economically, socially, physically, and environmentally balanced (see Ibn Khaldun 1990).

A just city is a city that upholds the principles of justice and provides forums for the voice of the marginalized, socially excluded, and minorities. This can be achieved through the establishment of good governance and fair representation of the people, enhanced by a strong civil society and public participation. Good governance will also ensure an equitable distribution of wealth and efficient management of resources. These are primary issues in the new millennium when resources are becoming scarce and yet the population keeps increasing and cities become more urbanized.

Based on Ibn Khaldun's cyclical theory, a city will also experience the process of rise and fall. A city is the manifestation of human desires to progress. The sustainability of a city very much depends on how it is organized and managed. If a city is not properly managed in accordance with the prescribed principles of justice and balance, it will eventually fall into ruin. The rise and fall of a city in most cases is the consequence of the acts of humankind. Greed and corrupt practices are among the biggest factors that destroy cities. This can be learned from Ibn Khaldun's notion of city development and sustainability. Also, the sedentary nature of urban dwellers can weaken their sense of social cohesion, which leads to social, political, and economic instability as suffered by many cities throughout human history.

Concluding Remarks

To conclude, several key points can be highlighted here. First, the reappropriation of classical knowledge is essential, as we believe that history repeats itself, but in different forms and conditions. This means that, epistemologically, knowledge of the past is needed for the projection of the future. This is consistent with the major theme of the present volume, that is, toward construction of the pluriverse. We view current economic, social, ecological, and other drawbacks as the manifestation of the failure of current knowledge to provide solutions to human problems. The current economic catastrophes hitting various so-called advanced high-income countries, for example, is evidence that knowledge alone, without the right sense of purpose and identity, will not provide effective solutions to these problems. This particularly supports our earlier argument of why understanding indigenous epistemology is so vital in making sense of human knowledge and sciences.

Second, the need for indigenization of knowledge is also crucial as a majority of the former colonized nations are in the midst of planning, developing, and, more importantly, filling needs and solving society's problems. It is for this reason that indigenous epistemology needs to be established as the underpinning of the development of knowledge and sciences, especially among the non-OECD nations.

Third, widespread awareness is needed among native scholars as this indigenization initiative will have to be carried out seriously and systematically. The process of indigenization and decolonization of knowledge should be in the mainstream agenda, particularly in developing countries and former colonized societies, if they are to develop and progress with a sense of character and identity.

Fourth, this study of Ibn Khaldun's epistemology is just to pave the way toward more studies of this kind. Ibn Khaldun formulated a science of society founded on native understanding; based on native experiences; deeply rooted in native culture, values, and belief systems; and written in a native language using native terminologies. In fact, besides Ibn Khaldun, many more native intellectuals and scholars from many other traditions can be grouped in this category, as they have significantly contributed to the world of knowledge and disciplines of all sorts. What is more important is the indigenous root that forms the foundation of knowledge and sciences they produce.

Finally, I have to note here that despite all the enthusiasm and eagerness to decolonize and to indigenize the epistemological foundation of knowledge and sciences, it does not mean we should resort to a totally anti-Western attitude in a literal sense. Indigenization does not mean a total rejection of the West or any other tradition. One must not run away from the fact that the West and the colonizers have contributed tremendously to modernity, development, and the triumph of human civilization. A lot more can be learned from the West and the former colonists or even from the OECD nations. Thus, decolonization in this context is meant to be understood as the development of knowledge and the establishment of its epistemology based on the native tradition, language, and belief and value systems of indigenous society.

NOTES

1. A good review of current debates on indigenous knowledge can be found in Hart (2010). A prominent Malaysian scholar, A. B. Shamsul, is also working on this topic. In his article "Colonial Knowledge and the Construction of Malay and Malayness," he speaks about how colonial perspectives influenced the way Malay society is viewed and the impact on the construction of Malay identity (Shamsul 1999).

2. For example, UC San Diego has offered a course on indigenous epistemology in the Department of Ethnic Studies (see "Graduate Courses," UC San Diego, accessed 2015, http://www.ethnicstudies.ucsd.edu/graduate-studies/courses.html).

3. For further discussion on indigenous knowledge, see, e.g., Maurial (1999, 62) and De La Torre (2004, 174–90).

4. In similar discussions, other terminologies are also employed such as desecularization, dewesternization, and indigenization, and in the Muslim world, the term Islamization of knowledge is widely used.

5. In fact, heavy criticisms have been initiated by a number of scholars, which can be found in some outstanding books of this nature, among them Edward Said's (1978) masterpiece *Orientalism*. Said concludes that it was Western literature that has depicted negative characteristics of Eastern societies. Another scholar, Arturo Escobar (1995) in his *Encountering Development*, for example, has proposed an alternative discourse on development in the Third World.

6. Apart from his own autobiography, many biographies of Ibn Khaldun have been written. For a glance at Ibn Khaldun's life and works, see, for example, Fromherz (2010) and Enan (2007).

REFERENCES

Ahmad, Khurshid. 2000. "Islamic Approach to Development." In *Political Development: An Islamic Perspective*, edited by Zeenath Kausar. Petaling Jaya, Malasia: IIUM Press.

Ahmad, Z. 2003. *The Epistemology of Ibn Khaldun*. London: RoutledgeCurzon.

Ahmad, Z. 2005. "Ibn Khaldun's Approach in Civilization Studies." In *Studies in Ibn Khaldun*, edited by M. Campanini. Milan: Polimetrica Scientific.

Alam, Shah Manzoor. 1960. "Ibn Khaldun's Concept of the Origin, Growth and Decay of Cities." *Islamic Culture* 34 (2): 90–106.

Alatas, S. F. 2005. "Indigenization: Features and Problems." In *Asian Anthropology*, edited by Jan von Bremen, Eyal Ben-Ari, and Syed Farid Alatas. London: Routledge.

Alatas, S. F. 2008. "Islam and Civilization in the Writings of Abd Al-Rahman Ibn Khaldun." *IAIS Journal of Civilization Studies* 1 (1).

Alatas, S. F. 2012. *Makers of Civilization: Ibn Khaldun*. Oxford: Oxford University Press.

Alatas, S. H. 1974. "The Captive Mind and Creative Development." *International Social Science Journal* (UNESCO) 26 (4).

Alatas, S. H. 1977. *The Myth of the Lazy Native: A Study of the Image of the Malays, Filipinos and Javanese from the 16th to the 20th Century and Its Function in the Ideology of Colonial Capitalism*. London: Frank Cass.

Al-Attas, S. M. N. [1978] 1993. *Islam and Secularism*. Kuala Lumpur: ISTAC.

Ali, Muhammad Mumtaz. 1992. *The Concepts of Islamic Ummah and Shariah*. Petaling Jaya, Malasia: Pelanduk.

Ardic, Nurullah. 2008. "Beyond 'Science as a Vocation': Civilisational Epistemology in Weber and Ibn Khaldun." *Asian Journal of Social Science* 36:434–64.

Battiste, M. 2010. "Nourishing the Learning Spirit: Living Our Way to New Thinking." *Education Canada* 50 (1).

Bennabi, Malik. 2001. *The Problem of Ideas in the Muslim World*. Translated by Mohamed Tahir el-Mesawi. Kuala Lumpur: Islamic Book Thrust.

Chabane, Djamel. 2008. "The Structure of 'umran al-'alam of Ibn Khaldun." *Journal of North African Studies* 13 (3).

Clark, D. 2003. *Urban World Global City*. New York: Routledge.

De La Torre, J. 2004. "In the Trenches: A Critical Look at the Isolation of American Indian Political Practices in the Non-empirical Social Science of Political Science." In *Indigenizing the Academy: Transforming Scholarship and Transforming Communities*, edited by D. A. Mihesuah and A. C. Wilson. Lincoln: University of Nebraska Press.

Dhaouadi, M. 1990. "Ibn Khaldun: The Founding Father of Eastern Sociology." *International Sociology* 5 (3).

Enan, M. A. 2007. *Ibn Khaldun: His Life and Works*. Kuala Lumpur: Other Press.

Escobar, A. 1995. *Encountering Development: The Making and Unmaking of the Third World*. Princeton, NJ: Princeton University Press.

Faruqi, I. R. al-. 1982. *Islamization of Knowledge: The Problem, Principle, and Work Plan*. Herndon, VA: IIIT.

Fromherz, A. J. 2010. *Ibn Khaldun: Life and Times*. Edinburgh: Edinburgh University Press.

Gellner, E. 2000. *Muslim Society*. Cambridge: Cambridge University Press.

Guite, H. F., and G. Ackrill. 2006. "Impact of the Physical and Urban Environment on Mental Well-Being." *Journal of the Royal Institute of Public Health* 120:1117–26.

Hart, M. A. 2010. "Indigenous Worldviews, Knowledge and Research: The Development of an Indigenous Research Paradigm." *Journal of Indigenous Voices in Social Works* 1 (1): 1–16.

Hassan, Riaz. 1969. "The Nature of Islamic Urbanization: An Historical Perspective." *Islamic Culture* 63 (3).

Ibn Khaldun, Abdul Rahman. 1990. *The Muqaddimah*. Translated by F. Rosenthal. Princeton, NJ: Princeton University Press.

Lacoste, Yves. 1984. *Ibn Khaldun: The Birth of History and the Past of the Third World*. London: Verso.

Latkin, C. A., and A. D. Curry. 2003. "Stressful Neighborhoods and Depression: A Prospective Study of the Impact of Neighborhood Disorder." *Journal of Health and Social Behavior* 44 (1): 34–44.

Mahdi, Muhsin. 2006. *Ibn Khaldun's Philosophy of History*. Kuala Lumpur: Other Press.

Matheson, F. I., R. Moineddin, J. R. Dunn, M. I. Creatore, P. Gozdyra, and R. H. Glazier. 2006. "Urban Neighborhood, Chronic Stress, Gender and Depression." *Journal of Social Science and Medicine* 63:2604–16.

Maurial, M. 1999. "Indigenous Knowledge and Schooling: A Continuum between Conflict and Dialogue." In *What Is Indigenous Knowledge? Voices from the Academy*, edited by L. M. Semali and J. L. Kincheloe. New York: Falmer.

Mohamad, Jamilah. 1998. "Building Heaven on Earth: Islamic Values in Urban Development." *Journal of Usuluddin* 8:121–34.

Rees, W. 1992. "Ecological Footprints and Appropriated Carrying Capacity: What Urban Economics Leaves Out." *Environment and Urbanization* 4 (2): 121–30.

Sabir, Imran. 2002. "Indigenous Culture and the Western Concept of Development." *Fountain: On Life Knowledge and Belief*, no. 40, October–December.

Safi, Louay. 2000. "Development Trends in Contemporary Muslim Experience." In *Political Development: An Islamic Perspective*, edited by Zeenath Kausar. Petaling Jaya, Malaysia: A. S. Nordeen.

Said, Edward. 1978. *Orientalism*. New York: Vintage.

Sardar, Ziauddin. 1978. *Science, Technology and Development in the Muslim World*. London: Croom Helm.

Sardar, Ziauddin. 1986. *Islamic Futures: The Shape of Ideas to Come*. London: Mansel.

Savard, J. P. L., P. Clergeau, and G. Mennechez. 2000. "Biodiversity Concepts and Urban Ecosystems." *Landscape and Urban Planning* 48:131–42.

Shamsul, A. B. 1999. "Colonial Knowledge and the Construction of Malay and Malayness: Exploring the Literary Component." *SARI Journal of Malay World and Civilization*, no. 17:3–17.

Shamsul, A. B. 2008. "Colonial Knowledge and the Deepening of Orientalism: The Asian Experience." In *Occidentalism and Orientalism: Reflections of the East Asia and the Perception of the West*, edited by B. Azizan and N. M. N. Faridah. Kuala Lumpur: Centre for Civilization Dialogue, University of Malaya.

Toynbee, Arnold. 1961. *A Study of History*. Oxford: Oxford University Press.

UN Habitat. 2007. *International Conference on the State of Safety in World Cities*. Monterey, Mexico, October 1–5.

United Nations Conference on Human Settlement. 1996. "Humanizing the City." *Habitat 2 City Summit*. Istanbul.

Zen, Ismawi. 2007. "Vision of an Islamic City." In *Islam and Urban Planning*, edited by Azila Ahmad Sarkawi and Alias Abdullah. Selangor, Malaysia: Scholars' Press.

13 · Anekāntavāda

The Jaina Epistemology

Jainism, a religion rooted in India, belongs to the *śramaṇa* tradition and is known for its cardinal principles of *ahiṁsā* (nonviolence), *aparigraha* (nonpossession), and *anekāntavāda* (nonabsolutism). Jainism dates its beginning to the seventh to fifth centuries BCE. It developed into a religious system that has significantly contributed to Indian philosophy and logic. The word *Jainism* derives from *jina*, which literally means "a conqueror," one who has by determined effort conquered the worldly passions such as desire, anger, hatred, pride, greed, and so on, and has been liberated from the bonds of *saṃsāra*, the cycle of birth and death. Jainism was founded by human spiritual teachers known as the *tirthankaras*. In all, there were twenty-four tirthankaras. Mahāvīra is considered the last of the tirthankaras who preached and extended the philosophy and ethical teaching of Jainism. Jainism regards *mokṣa* as the major and final aim of human life and coordinates with the doctrine of karma and ethical codes and practices. The principle of anekāntavāda, its epistemological theory, is the most significant contribution of Jainism to the world.

Epistemology for Pluriverse and Anekāntavāda

Epistemology, the ways of knowing and processes of cognition, has acquired a central position in the reflections of different scholars for centuries. Epistemic cognition occurs at various levels ranging from our daily life activities to definite scientific or academic tasks. At every occasion, the capability of epistemology impacts how we make meaning of facts and information. Epistemological models or theories are focused on determining an individual's perception of the world, what sense one makes of it, and how knowledge is constructed. When reflecting on which models of epistemology have dominated the world so far, one may begin to discuss the deep-rooted impact of Eurocentrism and the Western way of knowing as prominent models. Eurocentrism, at its crux, denies identity to any non-Western culture or epistemology. Western-Eurocentric views present themselves as the center of the world and attempt to establish a historical linearity that indeed lacks plurality in the process of cognition. Moving toward pluralism and plurality requires considering seriously other epistemological theories and models that provide alternative options to Eurocentrism and established Western ideologies. By doing so, we can contribute to the urgent task of constructing the pluriverse (Mignolo 2002). Walter Mignolo's concerns join this discussion as he challenges us to examine the reasons for social and political chaos. In his words, "I would argue that the underlying causes of the prevailing chaos are, on the one hand, the persistence of global coloniality and, on the other, the fact that since approximately the year 2000 we have been witnessing the economic and political reemergence of cultures and civilizations that have historically been undermined by global coloniality" (Mignolo 2017, 40). His arguments include discussions of epistemology as an important element of understanding diverse issues and events in the world. He points out that epistemological coloniality has become a powerful phenomenon, severely reducing the possibilities of knowing and explaining the world and forcing the world to follow the cognitive models of colonizers.

Mignolo presents the concept of pluriversality as a key to ending the cycle of Western hegemony and to opening a window to an epistemology that is free from the shackles of supremacy or centricity. Mignolo's description of pluriversality asserts that the universal can only be pluriversal, which, according to him, also matches the Zapatistas' idea of a world in which many worlds can coexist. In Mignolo's words, "The theoretical revolution grounded in double translation makes it possible to imagine epistemic diversity (or pluriversality) and to understand the limits of the abstract-universals that have dominated the imaginary of the modern/colonial world from Christianity to liberalism and Marxism" (Mignolo 2002, 250). According to him, pluriversality is about border thinking, border epistemology, border gnosis; and it emphasizes acceptance of a pluriverse and thinking pluritopically, which allows for an opening toward other, non-Eurocentric epistemologies.

Feminist standpoint theorist Donna Haraway (1988) expands discourses on epistemological theories and proposes a case for reflecting on the notion of Eurocentrism. She argues for the embrace of partial knowledge and situated knowledge production that includes one's standpoint in the analysis. She opens the discourse of feminist objectivity to introduce and discuss the need to rethink knowledge construction and production. Haraway proposes an argument for a doctrine and practice of objectivity as one "that privileges contestation, deconstruction, passionate construction, webbed connections, and hope for transformation of systems of knowledge and ways of seeing" (1988, 585). She critiques traditional notions of objectivity that claim an absolute point of view on a given issue. For Haraway, situated knowledge is a solution for the uncomfortable concept of objectivity. She argues that situated knowledge methodology helps to construct a more profound understanding of a given issue, because situated points of view allow taking into account the content and context in a richer way. She explains her proposal thus: "'Subjugated' standpoints are preferred because they seem to promise more adequate, sustained, objective, transforming accounts of the world" (Haraway 1988, 584). Haraway thus replaces the orthodox concept of objectivity and replaces it with a fresh method of situated knowledge that integrates cognitive processes into standpoint theory. She points out that we can grasp and explain the world better if we consider facts in context, from a situated standpoint.

The works of Donna Haraway and Walter Mignolo function as stimulus and prepare the ground for introducing the Jaina philosophy of anekāntavāda, an ancient Indian epistemology. This Jaina philosophy is very similar to the concepts presented by Haraway and Mignolo. Anekāntavāda, as an epistemology, corresponds to Mignolo's notion of pluriversality. Moreover, anekāntavāda, with its two related theories of *syādvāda* and *nayavāda*, complements and expands the usage of objectivity and partial knowledge.

Epistemological Theory of Anekāntavāda

The origin of anekāntavāda is difficult to trace in the Jaina literature. Subjects such as ontology and metaphysics can apparently be considered roots for the development of anekāntavāda. Knowledge, logic, and epistemology are innate parts of Jaina literature and are widely noticeable. Mahāvīra, in the Jain Āgam (Jaina canonical text) *Bhagavatī-Sūtra*, referred to four means of valid knowledge, such as perception (*pratyakṣa*), inference (*anumūna*), analogy (*upamāna*), and authority (*āgama*). Umāsvāti in the *Tattvārtha Sūtra* describes five varieties of knowledge as empirical (*mati*), articulate (*śruta*), clairvoyant (*avadhi*), mind-reading (*manaḥparyāya*), and omniscient (*kevala*). These five varieties of knowledge are further divided into two classes: acquired and innate. Discussion on knowledge in Jaina literature gradually advanced and focused on pure logic and epistemology. It can also be proposed that anekāntavāda played a vital role in comprehending concepts such as liberation and karma. In Jaina understanding, karma is seen as an instrument for an individual to attain liberation. The soul (self) needs to be released from the negative influence of karma, and it becomes important for an individual to begin right conduct. Jainism in this regard asserts that comprehending right conduct is essential to determine and regulate the karmic inflow; and right conduct is acquired only by developing an enlightened worldview and enlightened knowledge. The epistemological theory of anekāntavāda thus was marked as a rudimentary method to comprehend the right worldview and the right knowledge. Necessary conditions such as the right conduct, the right worldview, and the right knowledge made anekāntavāda an operative epistemology, as Jainism does not isolate ethical practices from cognition. For Jaina philosophy, ethical practices and cognition are affiliated and facilitate each other.

It is important to discuss the nature of reality in Jaina understating in order to recognize the relevance of anekāntavāda. Reality, according to Jain metaphysics, consists of six eternal substances, and each substance is associated with certain qualities. The six substances are space, the principles of motion and rest, physical order, existence, and time. The quality of each substance has a mode of existence, which is subject to change. Zaveri points out the significance of anekāntavāda as a method for grasping the nature of reality and explains that "*anekāntavāda*'s originality lies in that it seeks to reorientate our logical attitude and asks us to accept the exposure of contradictions as the true measure of the nature of reality. The law of *anekānta* affirms that there is no opposition between the unity of being and plurality of attributes. A thing is one and many at the same time—a singularity and a plurality rolled into one" (2009, 6–7). This attribution of anekāntavāda agrees with Mignolo's notion of pluriversality as both propose a comprehensive view for perceiving an object or reality. In this regard, anekāntavāda and pluriversality emphasize plurality and discourage an absolute state of reality. Anekāntavāda and its methods of nayavāda and syādvāda also correspond with Haraway's concept of situated knowledges, for both impart concepts of a standpoint-oriented cognitive process. Both anekāntavāda and situated standpoints substantiate the use of individual standpoints to develop more sustained and objective understanding.

Anekāntavāda's development can also be discussed with reference to Jainism's rich traditions of nonviolence and tolerance. The Jaina principle of respect for the life of others gave rise to the principle of respect for the views of others. Mahāvīra carried the concept of nonviolence and tolerance from the domain of practical behavior to that of intellectual and philosophical discussion. Jaina canonical literature provides details. Anekāntavāda was not overtly discussed in Jaina literature before its establishment as the central philosophy of Jainism but was found in discourses on the nature of ahiṁsā. For example, the Jain Āgam *Acharang Bhasyam* elaborates on practices that stabilize the vow of nonviolence such as controlling speech, controlling the mind, moving carefully, and so on. *Acharang Bhasyam* stresses an enlightened worldview and asserts that confusion and doubt can undermine the observance of the vow of nonviolence and all worldly violent activities, which are to be comprehended and given up. It is explained in *Acharang Bhasyam* that a person with unbiased perception under the consideration of transcendental and empirical standpoints can distinguish between right and wrong and can adopt the attitude of equanimity. In this regard, anekāntavāda was considered as the conceptual tool to determine nonabsolute and plural standpoints, allowing an individual to know the right way.

Anekāntavāda can be tracked in Mahāvīra's answers to the questions of his disciples regarding the nature of soul, the nature of matter, and the permanent and impermanent nature of the universe. The following dialogues between Mahāvīra and Gautama can be taken as an example:

> Are the souls, O Lord, eternal or non-eternal?
>
> Gautama! The souls are eternal in some respect and non-eternal in some respect.
>
> For what reason, O Lord! has it been said that the souls are eternal in some respect and non-eternal in some respect?
>
> Guatama, the souls quâ substance (noumenal entities) are eternal; the souls quâ states (phenomenal modes) are non-eternal. It is for this reason, O Gautama! that it has been said that the souls are eternal and in some respect and non-eternal in some respect. (Mahāprajña and Tulsi 2005, 542)

It can be observed from the dialogues that Jaina philosophy believes in both eternalism and noneternalism. The dialogue is the mark of rejecting absolute being and absolute nonbeing and suggesting acceptance of the synthesis as the concrete feature of any entity. Mahāvīra accepted both the ends and alternatives and came closer to anekāntavāda.

Anekāntavāda is also discussed extensively in noncanonical Jain literature. For example, *Anekāntajayapatā* is one of them. *Anekāntajayapatā* means "a treaty which is a banner of victory of many-sided (doctrine)" and was written around the seventh or eighth century AD by Haribhadra Sūri, a Jaina scholar. Kapadia has critically studied *Anekāntajayapatā* and noted, "When this *ahiṁsā* is allowed to play its role on the intellectual plane it teaches us to examine and respect the opinion of others. This implies that *ahiṁsā*—the Jaina attitude of 'intellectual *ahiṁsā*' is the origin of *anekāntavāda*. In other words the Jaina principle of 'respect for life' (*ahiṁsā*) is the origin of 'respect for the opinion of others' (*anekāntavāda*)" (1947, cxiv). He adds, "This doctrine of *anekānta-vāda* helps us in cultivating the attitude of toleration towards the views of our adversaries. It does not stop there but takes us a step forward by making us investigate how and why there are different views and how the seeming contradictories can be reconciled to evolve harmony. It is thus an attempt towards syncretism" (cxix).

According to Matilal (2012), all-around development of *anekānta* philosophy took place when the Sanskrit language came to be used by Jaina writers. Etymologically, the meaning of *anekāntavāda* can be described in two ways: (1) *un + eka + anta + vada*, that is, not one side of theory, viewpoint, or object; or (2) *un + ekanta + vada*, that is, not-one-sided theory. Thus, anekāntavāda lays emphasis on two points: first, characteristics of a reality or the object signify plurality; and second, many mutually contradicting characteristics of reality or of an object coexists; all are valid from its point of view. *Anekāntā* literally means non-one-sided and *vāda* is translated as theory, discourse, doctrine, or thesis. Anekāntavāda has been described with various expressions. Long describes it as "the Jain doctrine of relativity" (2009, 141); and Padmarajiah defines it as "theory of manifoldness" (1986, 7). It is also described as the doctrine of nonabsolutism.

The central theme of anekāntavāda is manifested through its noteworthy use in harmonization of conflicting views and upholding the validity of multiple viewpoints as true. The epistemological use of anekāntavāda is to understand that each object is made up of many forms, attributes, relations, and modes; and thus self-contradictory traits may coexist simultaneously in the same object at the same time or even at different times. According to the norms of anekāntavāda, reality can have antagonistic dimensions; it can be one or many; and also it can be universal or particular at the same time. Anekāntavāda does not adopt extreme positions in regard to the theory of being, either emphasizing identity or describing difference as pointing to the essential nature of reality.

Anekāntavāda began to appear in Jaina literatures through discussion and reference of syādvāda and nayavāda, which are discussed briefly here and in detail later. *Tattvārtha Sūtra*, an ancient Jaina text written by Acārya Umāsvāti sometime between the second and fifth centuries AD, eloquently explains the nature of anekāntavāda. Umāsvāti, in the text, talks about the nature of substance and existence as the character of substance, and discusses that existence is a combination of origination, cessation, and persistence (Umāsvāti 1994, 135). The discussion of Jaina ontology suggests that Jainism denies absolute existence and permanence or absolute nonexistence and impermanence but defends the concept of nonabsolutism. The method of understanding the concept of nonabsolutism is further explained by Umāsvāti. He states that the ungrasped (unnoticed) aspect of an object is attested by the grasped (noticed) one (Umāsvāti 1994, 135). Here he explains that an object or reality has two fundamental aspects, eternal and noneternal; and a particular attribute or mode of an object is brought to light by the observer for a specific purpose, relegating the other attribute and modes to the background. Hence, one mode may be grasped at the expense of others. Thus, while explaining the nature of substance, Umāsvāti asserts anekāntavāda in the form of nonabsolutism and brings forth the method of syādvāda (synthesis). Further, *Tattvārtha Sūtra* defines that the goal of human life is liberation and asserts that the path to liberation is through enlightened worldview, enlightened knowledge, and enlightened conduct (Umāsvāti 1994, 5). Enlightened worldview is the source of enlightened knowledge and conduct. Umāsvāti asserts that the path of liberation is determined by this integrated trinity and discusses it in the commentary: "The world-view which sees the many and the whole is enlightened. It is true understanding, informing an individual's thought and action in solving the ethical and spiritual problems of worldly bondage and of release from that bondage" (1994, 23).

Discussion of liberation in *Tattvārtha Sūtra* provides the preferred method of gateways and standpoints as the means of undertaking one's own exploration of truth. Umāsvāti (1994, 24) extensively discusses how the method of standpoints allows different estimates of reality using various frames of reference. The philosophical *nayas* (standpoints) mentioned in the text by Umāsvāti (1994, 23) are the common person's view, generic view, practical view, linear view, and literal view. Here, he introduces nayavāda as the analytical method. Another major discussion of anekāntavāda is found in the Jain scholar Siddhasena Divākara's *Sanmati Tarka*, written in the fifth century AD. He explicitly describes the functions of naya and the significance of anekāntavāda. Siddhasena Divākara's proposition on anekāntavāda and nayavāda is highly relevant to knowledge and perception and their means and method through naya. He suggests the method of naya as a means to reach anekāntavāda. He proposes two fundamental nayas—*dravyārthika* (noumenal) and *paryayārthika* (phenomenal)—as the analytical methods of inquiry and two fundamental methods that cover the general and the particular viewpoints of things. All other analytical methods of inquiry fall under these two headings only (Sanghavi and Doshi 1939, 3). Divākara describes the nature of the naya as follows: "Just as emerald and other jewels of rare quality and of excellent kind do not acquire the designation of a necklace of jewels even though all of them be priceless jewels on account of their lying unconnected with or disunited with each other, similarly every *naya* in its own sphere is right, but if all of them arrogate to themselves the whole truth and disregard the views of rival *naya* then they do not attain the status of a right view" (Sanghavi and Doshi 1939, 26).

Similarly, if all the nayas arrange themselves in a proper way and supplement each other, then alone they are worthy of being termed the whole truth or the right view in its entirety. But in this case, they merge their individuality in the collective whole (Saṅghavi and Doshi 1939, 27). Divākara then focuses on the function of the naya with reference to developing perception and knowledge, asserting that "perception is the cognition of the general; and knowledge means the cognition of the particular. This is the import of the two *nayas* respectively."[10] This explains that a thing is cognized by the soul (an individual) either in its general form or with its particulars, using both the nayas. The concept of naya, with its method of perception, reveals a multidimensional method for reaching reality or that reality seen from any standpoint is correct within its own position. The discussion on anekāntavāda here signifies that it is a method for developing perception and knowledge that supports the concept of nonabsolutism.

The introduction of Siddhasena Divākara's *Sanmati Tarka* states, "to examine a thing from every possible point of view, to have a frame of mind favorable for such examination and to try to examine in this manner, is what is called the *Anekāntavāda*." The description goes on and describes the person with a nonabsolutist viewpoint: "a man who holds the view of the cumulative character of truth, *anekāntajña* never says that particular view is right or that a particular view is wrong" (Saṅghavi and Doshi 1939, 63). Epistemologically, the theory of anekāntavāda, in order to function, is supported by the two methods of nayavāda and syādvāda. Nayavāda is understood as the doctrine of standpoints; and syādvāda is known as the doctrine of conditional predictions.

According to Ācārya Mahāprajña (2010), naya, anekāntā, and syādvāda are essentially the forms of knowledge and are the means to know it. Sometimes we have a propensity to know it wholly, sometimes part by part. The theory of anekāntavāda finds its implications through nayavāda and syādvāda. Padmarajiah states, "*Anekāntavāda* as the theory of reality, according to which reality is infinitely manifold, or relativistic in its determinations have been observed to be inherent in the co-ordinate conception of identity-in-difference" (1986, 303).

Nayavāda and Syādvāda

Anekāntavāda as a larger system combines nayavāda and syādvāda for its complete application. Nayavāda is a partial process that delineates viewing an object one single aspect at a time. Syādvāda, the principle of conditional predictions, is a method of inspecting inferences of an object by examining it from seven different standpoints. According to Mardia and Rankin, "Jaina theory of knowledge has three major components. Naya (standpoint); [and] anekāntavāda (holistic principle of many-sidedness), of which syādvāda (conditional precondition) forms an essential part" (2013, 48–49). As a holistic system, anekāntavāda forms a method of looking at subparts of an object through the principle of standpoint and conditional predictions. Logically, nayavāda and syādvāda are two complementary processes that form a natural development toward the epistemology of anekāntavāda. Nayavāda is an analytical method that investigates a particular standpoint among a multitude of different viewpoints in their totality. Syādvāda is essentially a synthetic method designed to harmonize the different viewpoints arrived at by nayavāda. Padmrajiah quotes Upadhyaye's assertion that "nayavāda is primarily conceptual while syādvāda is mainly verbal" (1986, 304). Thus, nayavāda is epistemological in character while syādvāda is a mode of verbal hypothesis.

A naya is a particular viewpoint or opinion. Since reality can be viewed from infinite numbers of qualities and modes, an object or matter can be analyzed with several nayas. A naya takes into account the validity of each viewpoint and does not eliminate other diverse viewpoints. Gopalan describes the use of naya or nayavāda: "Jainism does not merely maintain that there are many reals but also accepts that each of the reals, in its turn is complex reals and the numbers of relations into which they enter point to the fact that Reality many be comprehend[ed] from different angles. The attempt at comprehending from [a] particular standpoint is known as *naya*—a view arrived at from one angle" (1973, 145). Jain philosophers explicitly articulate seven nayas and term the process of such sevenfold analysis nayavāda. Padmarajiah explains the concept of nayavāda as an important component of the Jaina epistemological system: "Theoretically the viewpoints from which an object or an event could be perceived are not merely numerous but infinite in number because even the humblest fact of existence is infinitely manifold and therefore can be an object of various modes of analysis" (1986, 312).

Siddhasena Divākara describes two main nayas as the principle nayas, and other nayas fall under the two categories of the noumenal (dravyārthika) and the phenomenal (paryayārthika). That is, the analytical methods of inquiry are the two fundamental methods (the two nayas) that cover the general and the particular view-points of things as stated by tirthankaras (Saṅghavi and Doshi 1939). All other analytical methods of inquiry fall under these two headings only. The nayas are categorized as *naigama*, the common point of view or universal-particular point of view; *saṃgraha*, the general point of view or class point of view; *vyavahāra*, the specific or practical point of view; *ṛjusūtra*, the momentariness point of view; *śabda*, the verbal or synonymous point of view; *samabhirūdha*, the subtle or etymological point of view; and *evaṃbhūta*, the "such like" point of view. The various standpoints or viewpoints offer an analysis of manifold reality from their respective angle or point of vision. Such an analytical method adds understanding to the partial truth.

The first standpoint is naigama-naya, which denotes the common or universal-particular point of view. This naya is described in two senses. First, it emphasizes the teleological character of an object, which refers to the purpose elaborated in the object. Second, it denotes a method with reference to an entity. Padmarajiah describes this naya with examples: "For instance, a person is carrying fuel, water, and rice, when asked 'what are you doing?' says 'I am cooking' instead of saying 'I am carrying fuel' and so forth. This means that the general purpose of cooking controls the entire series of actions which are represented by one or more of them" (1986, 314). The second sense described in naigama-naya is the standpoint of the nondistinguished. This sense refers to the absence of division between the generic or the universal and the specific or the particular. Padmarajiah gives an example for this viewpoint: "One of the instances given in illustration of this non-distinction is that of the term 'bamboo.' When we use this term in a statement such as 'Bamboo grows here in plenty,' from the non-distinguished point of view, the distinction between the generic and the specific features of the bamboo is not within the focus of our attention, although it is undoubtedly at the back of our minds" (1986, 314–15).

The second standpoint is saṃgraha-naya, which represents the class or general point of view and emphasizes the universal features of an object. Saṃgraha-naya is a step further than naigama-naya and concerns the class or general character of a factual situation. In the saṃgraha-naya viewpoint, general qualities of an object are taken into consideration, without overlooking the specific qualities of the object. The third viewpoint is vyavahāra-naya, which stands for the particular viewpoint and contrasts with the naigama-naya and saṃgraha-naya. This viewpoint is based on empirical knowledge and represents a conventional viewpoint. A particular characteristic of an object or reality is emphasized in this viewpoint. The fourth naya is ṛjusūtra-naya. Matilal defines it as the "straight-thread" viewpoint: "Siddhasena has called it the prototype (*mūla*) of the 'modification exists' standpoint. It emphasizes the here-and-now aspect of a thing" (2012, 50). This viewpoint represents the extraction of the present from the empirical. Gopalan explains ṛjusūtra-naya thus: "This standpoint considers only the present from the object to be significant. It merely does not consider the past and the future but considers that even the whole of the present is of no consequence. It extracts the mathematical present, the momentary state of existence of the object" (1973, 148). The fifth standpoint is śabda-naya, which refers to the verbal point of view of an object. This also relates to the synonyms, verbal and grammatical variations of the word, and its meaning. Matilal (2012) explains this standpoint by giving an example of variation of grammatical inflections. He quotes two sentences: (1) The king sees the boy (*rājā paśyati māṇavakam*). (2) The boy sees the king (*nāṇavakaḥ paśyati rājānam*). With this example he explains, "The Sanskrit grammarians argue that although the same nominal stem 'rājān' ('king') is used in both cases, it is proper to distinguish between the different function of the word in both the sentences indicated by their grammatical inflections" (Matilal 2012, 51).

The sixth standpoint is samabhirūdha-naya, which represents the subtle or etymological point of view. In a sense, it is the reverse of the last naya. This standpoint focuses on the dissimilarities between words, and synonyms are no exception. It is about making subtle distinctions in the meaning of words that are supposed to denote the same object; and such distinctions can be based upon the etymological roots of the words concerned. Words such as *rājan*, *nṛpa*, and *bhūpa* refer to the same person, the king, but each has a different etymological meaning. This naya states that all words derive from some root or other; however, it can be admitted that there can be very few, if any, true synonyms in a natural language. Padmarajiah explains, "The truth of this viewpoint is based on the two principles in the Jaina philosophy of language. The first principle is that whatever is knowable is also expressible. That is, knowledge or the meaning of anything in reality is not possible except through the means of words. The second principle is that, strictly speaking, there can only [be] one word for one meaning and vice versa. Accordingly, several words which are conventionally supposed to convey one and the same meaning, have in actual fact as many meanings as the number of words found there" (1986, 323). The seventh viewpoint is evaṃbhūta-naya, which represents actuality or the "such like" standpoint and restricts the meaning of words to their concrete and immediate usage. Gopalan states, "the term *evaṃbhūta* is true in its entirety in the word and the sense" (1973, 150). This standpoint is an extension and specialized form of the application of the verbal method. It restricts the meaning of a specific word to its particular use; and thus, according to this standpoint, each word is supposed to have one unique and single meaning.

The method of nayavāda supports viewing things with various perspectives from different standpoints and becomes an important epistemological element of anekāntavāda and facilitates cognitive characteristics such as reflective thinking, critical thinking, and interpretation. Nayavāda allows an individual to know about a thing beyond a single standpoint. It can be discussed that nayavāda, like the concept of situated knowledge, fosters the comprehension of any subject at hand through viewing and knowing it from different viewpoints. According to both these models, naya and situated standpoint, every object or reality is understood more thoroughly as it is examined carefully with its specific range and nature.

The second important method of epistemology of anekāntavāda is syādvāda or *saptabhaṅgī*, which presents the number of possible or alternative truths under the conditional method of sevenfold prediction. It is the most distinguishing feature of Jaina metaphysics and is considered complementary to nayavāda. The term *syādvāda* means conditional or relativistic dialectic and is synonymous with saptabhaṅgī. Some of the English equivalent words for *syat* are *probably, perhaps, indefinitely, in some way,* and *in a certain sense.* The term *syat* also brings out the meanings of "from a certain point of view." Three fundamental concepts that make up the seven predicates within the method of syādvāda, in the seven modes, all together are "is," *asti,* "is not," *nāsti,* and "inexpressible," *avaktavya.* Thomas describes Malliṣeṇa's explanation of syādvāda as given *Syād-Vāda-Mañjarī*: "'*syād*' is a particle signifying 'not unequivocally': and so '*syād*-doctrine' is the doctrine of 'non-unequivocality.' And that is the acceptance of a single entity variegated by a plurality of attributes" (1960, 22).

Emphasis on syādvāda is the synthetic approach to reality, prominently stressing that the different viewpoints together help in comprehending the real. Syādvāda indicates that the nature of an object itself is understood synthetically from the modes of proposition. Padmarajiah quotes Malliṣeṇa's definition of *syādvāda*: "*syādvāda* or *saptabhaṅgī* is that conditional method in which the modes, or predictions (*bhaṅgaḥ*) affirm (*vidhi*), negate (*niṣedha*) or both affirm and negate, severally (*pṛthag-bhūta*) or jointly (*samudhita*), in seven different ways, a certain attribute (*dharma*) of a thing (*avirodhena*) without incompatibility (*praśnavaśāt*) in a certain context" (1986, 336).

The seven modes, propositions, or predictions are described as follows: (1) *syād-asti* (in some ways it is); (2) *syād-nasti* (in some ways it is not); (3) *syād-asti-nasti ca* (in some ways it is and it is not); (4) *syād-asti-avaktavyo* (in some ways it is inexpressible); (5) *syād-astyacaktavyaśca* (in some ways it is and is inexpressible); (6) *syatnasti ca avaktavyaśca* (in some ways it is not and is inexpressible); and (7) *syadasti nasti ca avaktav-yaśca* (in some ways it is, is not and is inexpressible). It can be observed that the partial truth expressed by syādvāda does not represent half-truth, but truths presented by the sevenfold prediction are alternative truths that individually touch every aspect of the thing or reality and suggest a synthetic system of knowledge. These seven modes are made up of three fundamental concepts: They are "is," "is not," and "inexpressible."

A predicate with any one of three describes simple judgment and a predicate with two or all three describes a complex judgment. The term *syat* qualifies the indeterminate reality of an object, made against the background in all these seven judgments, either simple or complex.

All seven predictions can be understood through the example of an object, 'a pot.' First proposition: "In a certain sense, the pot is" signifies the obvious existence of the pot. The prefix *syat*, may imply or in a certain sense implies that this proposition is not an absolute truth, because the prediction excludes the truth of all the other propositions. It suggests that this one proposition is valid from only one point of view. To elaborate further, it can be explained that if the pot is looked at from the point of view of substance, clay, then, if the pot is made of clay, and only if it is made of clay, can we state the existence of the pot. Second prediction: "In a certain sense, the pot is not" is not the contradiction of the first one. It signifies that the pot does not exist as something else.

The third and fourth predictions: "In a certain sense, the pot is and is not" and "in a certain sense, the pot is inexpressible," respectively, can be treated conjointly to understand their differences more clearly. These two predictions present being and nonbeing together, out of which the third mode presents successive presentation, and the fourth prediction presents simultaneous presentation. These two predictions are referred to as "copresentation" and "differenced togetherness" of the attributes. The fifth prediction: "In a certain sense, the pot is and is inexpressible" means that from the point of view of existence the pot is describable, but if both its existent and nonexistent forms are reflected concurrently, it becomes inexpressible. The sixth prediction: "In a certain way, the pot is not and is inexpressible" describes denial and joint and simultaneous affirmation and denial. The seventh prediction: "In a certain way, the pot is, the pot is not, and not and is inexpressible" describes successive presentation of two aspects, positive and negative, and they jointly show an inability to express any description of the pot (Gopalan 1973; Padmarajiah 1986).

Syādvāda, the sevenfold prediction system, provides the language of anekāntavāda for a precise synthesis obtained from multiple viewpoints. The concept of seven predictions expresses partial truth, which does not firmly and logically go together necessarily, but the truth of each prediction is independently true in its partial point of view. This method of syādvāda provides a process of cognition to understand the manifoldness of an object. Vaidya (1928) points out that each of the *nayas* comprehends things from only one particular standpoint; knowledge derived from a *naya*, therefore, is partial and incomplete. To comprehend things in all their aspects, therefore, a special mode or form must be found. *Syādvāda* provides that mode or method. The method of

Syādvāda, being synthetical in nature, supports epistemology of constructivism in which previous knowledge allows to synthesis with new and different knowledge. Naylor and Keogh assert, "The central principles of this approach are that learners can only make sense of new situations in terms of their existing understanding. Learning involves an active process in which learners construct meaning by linking new ideas with their existing knowledge" (1999, 93). Syādvāda facilitates cognitive conditions for deep dialogue, discovery, and inquiry-based learning.

Significantly, nayavāda and syādvāda as epistemological tools can be compared with the twentieth-century concept of Bloom's taxonomy, a conceptual tool for theorizing levels of cognition, used to develop learning systems dedicated to constructive and critical thinking, logic, and reasoning. Nayavāda, with its method of analysis, and syādvāda, with its method of synthesis, complement Bloom's taxonomy. Nayavāda and syādvāda, similarly to his taxonomy levels, facilitate a step-by-step process. Methods of nayavāda can be applied, knowing, comprehending, and examining an object of study from different viewpoints; while syādvāda allows integrating the ideas with predictions from various standpoints. Nayavāda, in this regard, offers an opportunity to experience analytical activities that help take into consideration diverse viewpoints and avoid absolutism. It allows acknowledging multiplicity, exploring the dimensions of difference, taking multiplicity into full account in constructing nonabsolutistic and multiperspectival knowledge of an object and reality. Nayavāda facilitates conducting experiments with various approaches and allows assessing multiple possibilities. Syādvāda supports a process of exploration with various steps and allows checking the result with multiple hypotheses. Thus, nayavāda and syādvāda can be proposed as a method of precise unity-in-multiplicity, meaning pluriversality. Moreover, viewing a particular aspect of an object or subject under study is equally important and valid to knowing its entirety and aptness. Both situated standpoints and syādvāda and nayavāda as cognitive processes make a strong case for a validity that denotes examining and knowing a thing from its objective point of view.

The holistic logic of anekāntavāda increases the potential of comprehension through critical examination, trial and error, and the evolution of ideas. This very nature of anekāntavāda with its companion theories of nayavāda and syādvāda fosters the attitude of constructing the pluriverse. Therefore, all opinions, even those that appear to be manifestly wrong, should be respected and at the same time engaged with and challenged positively with the sense of the pluriverse. Moreover, anekāntavāda, similarly to Mignolo's pluriversality, allows border thinking, border epistemology, and border gnosis, and it emphasizes acceptance of a pluriverse and thinking pluritopically. It is a call for an opening toward others, a non-Eurocentric epistemology that proposes a cognitive system of pluriversality that emphasizes diverse viewpoints and aspects.

Anekāntavāda is distinct from Eurocentric thought and rejects the attitude of absolutism and embodies a philosophy that each class has its own viewpoint that deserves to be understood and considered seriously. Anekāntavāda dovetails neatly with current trends in scientific and philosophical thoughts and goes against the inharmonious Eurocentric epistemological fundamentalism and sense of superiority. It remarkably features nonabsolutism and a doctrine of manifoldness. Anekāntavāda and its two methods of nayavāda and syādvāda also foster the attitude of intellectual ahiṃsā as well. Intellectual ahiṃsā is characterized with an attitude that there should be no discrimination between us (our thoughts) and others (their thoughts). Anekāntavāda as the doctrine of manifold viewpoints can help in developing the attitude of intellectual ahiṃsā in the form of tolerance toward diverse viewpoints, which prevents absolutism or extremism. Tähtinen (1976) refers to the *Puruṣārtha Siddhyupaya* and *Sūtrakṛtaṅga Sūtra* and argues that the root of violence is ignorance. He adds that Jaina philosophy also recognizes that ignorance cannot lead to right conduct, which is based on knowledge. One has first to strive for right belief, then knowledge, and conduct becomes right. Arriving at the right understanding of the four passions (ignorance, greed, pride, and anger) one can practice self-control, compassion, and tolerance that make intellectual ahiṃsā applicable in reality. Tähtinen further argues in support of anekāntavāda as a tool for intellectual ahiṃsā and states that "when we extend non-violence from reverence for life to reverence for thought, we are led to non-absolutism. Therefore, non-absolutism is held as important as non-violence by Jain philosophers" (1976, 85). Anekāntavāda is a thesis not of disbelief or uncertainty, but of an unlimited number of characteristics, reconciling opposite viewpoints. This marks the relevance of anekāntavāda in today's world for adopting an attitude of intellectual ahiṃsā for peaceful and progressive interactions. The anekāntic method, which has its origin in exploring the nature of truth and reality with nonabsolute characteristics, found its application in developing perception to understand diversity, precisely to understand multiple standpoints, and evaluate and synthesize them as and when required. Its representation in today's world should be put into application to explore a wider outlook, to avoid mental conflicts and confrontations, and to establish tolerance between ideologies.

CONCLUSION

Anekāntavāda is not only about the diversity of reality but provides opportunity to construct knowledge through diversity and allows a situated standpoint with more adequate and objectively unique understanding of the world. It also accelerates the concept of constructing the pluriverse in order to develop complex forms of thought including developing the ability to engage with plurality. Anekāntavāda, nayavāda, and syādvāda analytically and synthetically feature a comprehensive arrangement of epistemology, designed to aid an apprehension of the complex construction of reality. Anekāntavāda is an epistemology of synergy and pluriversality that emphasizes acceptance of a pluriverse and thinking pluritopically. Methods of nayavāda and syādvāda enhance cognitive experience, which makes use of critical and inquiry-based comprehension and creates a case for a methodology of situated knowledge. Anekāntic vision has a robust potential to explore the truth with different shapes yet hold every shape substantially valid in its own perspective and reference. Anekāntavāda was developed during the period of classical antiquity but, certainly, it can embolden epistemology, which has promising implications for the present time.

REFERENCES

Gopalan, S. 1973. *Outlines of Jainism*. New York: Halsted.

Haraway, Donna. 1988. "Situated Knowledges: The Science Question in Feminism and the Privilege of Partial Perspective." *Feminist Studies* 14:575–99.

Haraway, Donna. 1991. *Simians, Cyborgs, and Women*. London: Free Association.

Harding, Sandra. 1986. *The Science Question in Feminism*. New York: Open University Press.

Harding, Sandra. 1991. *Whose Science? Whose Knowledge?* New York: Open University Press.

Harding, Sandra. 1993. "Rethinking Standpoint Epistemology: What Is 'Strong Objectivity'?" In *Feminist Epistemologies*, edited by Linda Alcoff and Elizabeth Potter, 49–82. London: Routledge.

Harding, S., and U. Narayan, eds. 2000. *Decentering the Center: Philosophy for a Multicultural, Postcolonial, and Feminist World*. Bloomington: Indiana University Press.

Hofer, Barbara K. 2002. "Introduction." In *Personal Epistemology: The Psychology of Beliefs about Knowledge and Knowing*, edited by Barbara K. Hofer and Paul R. Pintrich. Mahwah, NJ: Erlbaum.

Holmwood, J. 1995. "Feminism and Epistemology: What Kind of Successor Science?" *Sociology* 29 (3): 411–28. http://journals.sagepub.com/doi/abs/10.1177/0038038595029003003.

Kapadia, H. R. 1947. "Introduction." In *Anekāntajayapatā by Haribhadra Sūri with His Own Commentary and Municandra Sūri's Supercommentary*, vol. 2, ix–cxxviii. Gaekwad's Oriental Series 105. Baroda, India: Oriental Institute.

Long, Jeffery D. 2009. *Jainism: An Introduction*. London: I. B. Tauris.

Mahāprajña, Ācārya. 2010. *Anekānta: Philosophy of Co-existence*. Ladnun, India: Jain Vishva Bharti.

Mahāprajña, Ācārya, with Vāchanā Pramukh Gandhipati Tulsi, eds. 2001. *Acharang-Bhasyam*. Translated by Nathmal Tatia, Muni Dulaharj, and Muni Mahendra Kumar. Ladnun, India: Jain Vishva Bharti.

Mahāprajña, Ācārya, with Vāchanā Pramukh Gandhipati Tulsi, eds. 2005. *Bhagvaī Viāhapaṇṇattī*. Translated by Muni Mahendra Kumar. Ladnun, India: Jain Vishva Bharti.

Mardia, K. V., and A. D. Rankin. 2013. *Living Jainism: An Ethical Science*. Hants, UK: Mantra.

Matilal, B. K. 2012. *The Central Philosophy of Jainism (Anekātavāda)*. Ahmedabad: L. D. Institute of Indology.

Mignolo, Walter. 2002. "The Zapatistas's Theoretical Revolution: Its Historical, Ethical, and Political Consequences." *Review (Fernand Braudel Center)* 25 (3): 245–75. http://www.jstor.org/stable/40241550.

Mignolo, Walter. 2013. "On Pluriversality." October 20. http://waltermignolo.com/on-pluriversality/.

Mignolo, Walter. 2017. "Decoloniality after Decolonization and Dewesternization after the Cold War". In *A World Beyond Global Disorder: The Courage to Hope*, edited by F. Dallmayr and E. Demenchonok, 39–60. Newcastle upon Tyne, UK: Cambridge Scholars Publishing.

Naylor, S., and B. Keogh. 1999. "Constructivism in Classroom: Theory into Practice." *Journal of Science Teacher Education* 10:93–106.

Padmarajiah, Y. J. 1986. *A Comparative Study of the Jaina Theories of Reality and Knowledge*. Delhi: Motilal Banarasidas.

Sanghavi, Pandit Sukhlālji, and Pandit Bechardāsji Doshi. 1939. *Siddhasena Divākara's Sanmati tarka with a Critical Introduction and an Original Commentary*. Edited by Pandit Dalsukh Malvania. Bombay: Shri Jain Shwetambar Education Board.

Tähtinen, Unto. 1976. *Ahiṃsā: Non-violence in Indian Tradition*. London: Rider.

Thomas, F. W. 1960. *Śri Malliṣeṇasuri's Syād-Vāda-Mañjarī*. Delhi: Motilal Banarsidass.

Umāsvāti, Ācārya. 1994. *Tattvārtha Sūtra—"That Which Is": With the Combined Commentaries of Umāsvāti, Pūjayapāda and Siddhasenagaṇi*. Translated by Nathmal Tatia. New York: HarperCollins.

Vaidya, P. L., ed. 1928. *The Nyayavatara of Siddhsena Divākara*. Pindavada, India: Seth Kalyanji Pedhi.

Zaveri, J. S. 2009. *Samaysāra by Ācārya Kundakunda*. Ladnun, India: Jain Vishva Bharati University.

Part IV. Rethinking Politics,
Democracy, and Markets

14 · First People of the Americas

Lessons on Democracy, Citizenship, and Politics

The eastern hemisphere produced wisdom, western Europe produced knowledge.
—VINE DELORIA, *Custer Died for Your Sins*

In this chapter, I offer a reflection on the nature of politics in what I call a true democracy. True democracy is a phenomenon rarely observed today. I find it most present among some indigenous, native, or First People of the Americas and this chapter thus focuses on them to a great extent. Native Americans, probably because of their devastating experience with white, European civilization, have formulated the most radical and convincing critique of this society, which some of them call a cannibal disease—*wétiko* (Forbes 2008). Based on my reading of Native American literature—both academic and novelistic—as well as empirical field research conducted with the Wintukuas of Colombia in 2014, I seek to first develop what aspects of reality and practice the concept "politics" can and should cover in a democracy. From politics, I move into democracy—its emergence, its meaning, and its connection to community and culture. Work in game theory helps to support my argument that democracy must rely on a strong sense of community and culture—and that relative equality is its core condition. I support these conclusions, again, from my reading of Native American writing and analysis, offered by such authors as Vine Deloria (1969, 2007; Deloria and Lytle 1984), Jack Forbes (2008), and John Snow (1977).

I then expand my scope to take a closer look at Latin American indigenous groups, such as the Zapatistas (Stahler-Sholk 2008, 2014), but most centrally the Wintukua, whose political organization I have witnessed in person when conducting research in Colombia. I conclude this chapter with a reflection on the true meaning and potential of democracy and its connection to culture. I find the lessons we can all learn from Native American or First People to be clear. They show us the path toward true democracy, that is, rule by the people and self-rule. This is not to say that all of them actually practice true democracy. It merely means that among them, many institutions and solutions to collective problems of democratic community life can be observed—even if sometimes partially or in rudimentary form. Vine Deloria (2007) thus titled one of his books *We Talk, You Listen.* He has a lot to say—and so have others from the thousands of tribes of the Americas. The question is: are we listening?

Politics

Politics, properly understood, is the realm of collectively and publicly debating and deciding how to live. Politics is the task of everyone living in a democracy. It is not an option, or a choice, as a democracy without a citizenry making its own decisions and crafting its own laws ceases to be a democracy proper (Rousseau [1762] 2003).

Many of the debates about liberalism, communism, participation, civil society, and the state miss this point. For if the term *democracy* means anything at all, rule must be an active exercise of all citizens. It must be self-rule. The core of self-rule is for citizens to decide the rules under which they want to live—in open, public debate (Rousseau [1762] 2003).

This is how democracy started—not in ancient Athens, but everywhere in the world. According to Elman Service (1975), pre-Neolithic societies were all egalitarian and humankind moved into the construction of social hierarchies only slowly and reluctantly—the rule of some over others never being accepted without contestation. Quoting the anthropologist Lewis H. Morgan (*Ancient Society*, 1877), Service argues, "primitive society, Morgan had discovered, was basically communistic, lacking important commerce, private property, economic class, or despotic rulers" (Service 1975, 33). Thus, at one point in human pre-Neolithic history, democracy, that is, self-rule by the people, was a reality everywhere. This also implies that Athens was not the birthplace of democracy—it was merely the place where democratic institutions were written down and codified in such a way that we can still read about them today.

Relying on game theory, Carles Boix (2015) has demonstrated that inequality undermines cooperation. In his analysis of pre-Neolithic, as well as historical and contemporary hunter and gatherer societies and small stateless settlement communities, Boix finds that rational, self-interested individuals and groups will cooperate, without needing a state to coerce them to do so, as long as living conditions are broadly equal and technological advance is broadly shared. He concludes, "the price of growth is then inequality. And inequality brings about, in turn, the breakdown of cooperation that exists in the 'state of nature'" (Boix

2015, 9). A system of reciprocal sharing and cooperation is only disrupted, or ended, when some individuals or groups start accumulating more assets than everybody else. For Boix, "cooperation is only sustainable if there is some fundamental equality of income" (2015, 28). Accordingly, "primitive societies are societies without a State" (Clastres 1989, 189) and states emerged out of inequality, created either by the privileged or against them (Axelrod 2006; Olson 2000). Despite the at times problematic assumptions and inconclusive findings reached by all these authors, it seems clear that inequality, rule, and the state form an intimately connected triad. When thinking about democracy, we thus must consider their connection and the different ways they interact.

The State

There is no "around the state," or an autonomy outside of, or without, the state (Dinerstein 2014; Gibson-Graham 2006). The state, as an ontological reality, is constituted and reproduced by struggles over political power, dominance, control, and rule. Questions of security and bureaucracy cannot and should not be avoided when discussing autonomy and self-rule. As an analytical exercise, it might bode well to think outside of the state and, as John Holloway (2010) has argued, we might even think about changing the world without taking (state) power, but when doing so, we should rather try to think of the state in different ways instead of avoiding the questions that the conceptual model of the state allows us to ask.

As the work of many anarchist scholars, such as James Scott (2009), has shown, free association and free society in general are under threat from encroaching states and state power. Almost all historical examples of anarchism, council democracy, or Soviet rule show us that these experiments ended because they were created in situations of conflict and (civil) war. From a realist perspective, as movements more concerned with their internal dynamics, they were unable to stand up to the violent onslaught of the Bolsheviks, the Freikorps, the French Army, the fascists, or the socialists. Or as long as states are controlled by economic elites and corporations, the state will serve their interests—against those seeking to establish a more egalitarian order. This is, after all, how states emerged—at least if we follow Elman Service, who explains, "Here is the economic genesis of the state: From their *material* (economic) beginnings, classes become gradually social, and finally political as well when the rich erect a structure of permanent force to protect their class interests. The political state is thus a special means of repression by the propertied class" (1975, 34).

In fact, according to Pierre Clastres, "Primitive societies are societies without a State" (1989, 189). To this day, as James Scott (2009) has shown, many regions of the world have successfully escaped statehood and instead rely on local administrative bodies to organize their collective lives, selected or elected among community members. The history of the state is, after all, a history of organizing violence and cannot be understood outside of the history of warfare and hostile takeovers of territories. Once created, states tend to become even more powerful and dangerous to their neighbors, thus triggering the emergence of other states in response. European history provides ample examples of this intimate connection of state apparatuses with violence and external threat.

The other face of the state, clearly, is that of directing violence inwardly, toward the people it seeks to control. States, explains Clastres (1989), serve the purpose of extracting excess from people by forcing them to work more and harder, so that profits can be made. According to most accounts, most noncapitalist societies require no more than four hours of work to meet daily needs. Anything beyond that is extra and serves to make profit. According to Clastres, "In primitive society—an essentially egalitarian society—men control their activity, control the circulation of the products of the activity: they act only on their own behalf, even though the law of exchange mediates the direct relation of man to his product" (1989, 197ff.). When states rule over people's lives, egalitarianism and individual or even community control over production all come to an end.

Against the predominant conclusion that the state emerged out of societal inequality and represents an institutionalized form of political domination, I want to suggest a different reading of the scant historical and archaeological evidence available to us: It seems that in "primitive" societies the people *were* the state.[1] If the state is defined as institutionalized domination and rule, then those societies controlling and ruling themselves literally are the state. This reading of stateness as the expression and manifestation of citizenship has also been suggested by those who have studied Athenian direct democracy (Manville 1997). The historian John Pocock (1995), for example, suggests that what made Athenian democracy so special was precisely the fact that its citizens ruled and administered themselves. They were political beings and as such they did not delegate political power.

According to the research quoted above, most human societies moved from egalitarianism to inequality and hierarchy—most, but not all. Many indigenous societies were able to shield themselves from encroaching state power and the social hierarchies they sought to impose, retreating into mountains, forests and jungles, and other difficult territory, where they preserved their practice of self-rule (Scott 2009).

In most cases, however, political power and hence states were ripped away from communities and appropriated by specific groups to first construct and then defend their privileges. Doing so required monopolizing violence, concentrating it, and then legitimizing it. This is, apparently, how states separated from communities and became separate entities, institutionalized and made into apparatuses (Olson 2000).

If this is indeed how societal development writ large can be explained, then the path leading to equality, justice, and egalitarianism is not through civil society, citizen participation, or democratizing society, all of which, after all, occur in a sphere outside of the state proper. It is also not in democratizing the state—as long as the state remains controlled by the few who rule over the many. Instead, the path toward egalitarianism and true democracy is one of bringing the state back under societal control from where it was ripped out. Only when the state is truly controlled by its people can we start talking about measures to democratize it. As long as it remains controlled by an elite, no amount of democratization will be able to rein it in and subject it to the people's will. Popular sovereignty, in other words, is the precondition for democracy.

This might seem an overly utopian program. It is not. Indigenous communities everywhere have been following exactly this program ever since colonizers have started to take statehood away from them. Some of them can look back at a history of successful defense of their statehood, never taken away from them altogether by colonizers and their creole descendants. This is the case of the Mayans of southern Mexico, as well as the people described by James Scott (2009), living in the mountains of Zomia, in Southeast Asia. It is also true for some tribes who have found refuge in different forests and jungles—such as the BaMbuti, in contemporary Congo (Turnbull 1968), or some tribes deep inside the Amazon or high up on some mountaintops, such as the Wintukua of Colombia, to whom I return in more detail below.

Most indigenous groups, however, have been struggling to win their statehood back after it was taken away from them by colonizers and their modern successor states (Van Cott 2008; Yashar 2005). This is the story of most indigenous groups—whether in North or South America, Africa, or Asia. In North America, this struggle to regain political autonomy and wrest it away from white America and Canada can be traced back to the wars different tribes fought against the white invaders of their lands—ever since those invaders set foot on it. The great Ottawa leader Pontiac fought back the British in the 1770s, and many other tribes and tribal alliances achieved partial, if temporary, victories against the French, the British, the Spaniards, the Portuguese—and their creole successors. The aim of all these struggles was not only to repel the white invaders but to defend Indian statehood and self-rule. The Iroquois Confederacy is said to have been founded as early as 1570, and it successfully resisted the French in the sixteenth and seventeenth centuries (Deloria 1969). In the early 1800s, the Shawnee leader Tecumseh endeavored to forge a pan-Indian confederacy to fight against the Americans so that Indians could live apart and among themselves (Dowd 1992; Tucker, 1956).

The Stoney Indians of Canada finally achieved self-government in 1946—even though several agreements assuring their independence had been signed much earlier, in the mid-nineteenth century (Snow 1977). Almost all native tribes of the Americas can look back at agreements and treaties signed and broken—until they finally achieved land in the form of reservations and autonomy in the twentieth century. Vine Deloria (1933–2005), for many years director of the U.S. National Congress of American Indians, locates Indian nationalism in the 1960s. However, he also explains, "The idea of self-government for Indians began almost as soon as Indians had fairly continuous contact with non-Indians" (Deloria and Lytle 1984, 266). To some, self-government and land came very late, and in many cases the reservations they were able to secure for themselves are either too small or too barren to make a decent living on them—or both. Nunavut only became an autonomous territory of Canada in 1999. The Zapatistas of southern Mexico finally declared war on the Mexican government in 1994, issuing a declaration that started, "Ya Basta"—*Enough*. Since then, they have labored to construct their own political autonomy (Stahler-Sholk 2008, 2014).

Indigenous struggle everywhere has been, almost by definition, a struggle for autonomy and self-rule, and it almost always has a territorial dimension (Blaser et al. 2010; Dinerstein 2014). According to Vine Deloria, who discusses the situation of indigenous, or First People, in the United States, "In 1934 the Indian Reorganization Act was passed. Under the provisions of this act reservation people were enabled to organize for purposes of self-government" (1969, 16). Deloria finds that in general, "Tribes that can handle their reservation conflicts in traditional Indian fashion generally make more progress and have better programs than do tribes that continually make adaptations to the white value system" (1969, 21). He also asserts, "The awakening of the tribes is just beginning. Traditionalists see the movement as fulfilling the ancient Hopi and Iroquois religious predictions of the end of white domination of the continent" (Deloria 1969, 246). Echoing the demands of indigenous or First People everywhere in the world, Deloria sees the only solution to the problems of indigenous people in their territorial sovereignty, political autonomy, and self-rule: "What we need is a cultural leave-us-alone agreement, in spirit and in fact" (1969, 27).

Only Tribes Will Survive: Escaping Wétiko

The cornerstone of this very consistent Native American quest for political autonomy and territorial sovereignty (even if limited and circumscribed) is community or, in the language of Native Americans, the tribe. Political autonomy requires as its foundation a strong and functioning community. In the North American context, the quest for the renewal of tribes as the foundations of political self-rule took place in the form of Indian nativism.

According to Gregory Dowd (1992), Native American nativism emerged as a movement among different Native tribes in the eighteenth century. Its early proponents were the Ottawa warrior Pontiac and the Delaware prophet Neolin. In the early nineteenth century, Indian nativism advanced further under the guidance and leadership of the Shawnee brothers Tecumseh and Tenskwatawa (Dowd 1992).

Inspired by the then-emerging doctrine of polygenesis, these Native leaders argued that Indians and whites were not the same people and needed to live separately. Explains Gregory Dowd, who quotes from Governor Harrison's *Messages and Letters* (1810), "If, as the Shawnee Prophet said, Americans were inimical to Indians, if 'the Great Spirit did not mean that white and red people should live near each other [because the newcomers] poison'd the land,' and if all Indians came from a common creation different from others, then it made sense that only Indians should unite against the American threat" (Dowd 1992, 313).

Indeed, invading white "civilizers" never relented in seeking ways to physically annihilate Native American tribes and change their culture, thus leading them to their cultural death. According to Dowd (1992), who quotes from Philip Thomas's missionary account published in 1807 in the *Massachusetts Missionary Magazine*, "The Quakers, arguing against Indian tradition, claimed that women 'are less than Men, they are not as strong as Men, they are not as able to endure fatigue and toil as men.' Rather, women should 'be employed in our houses, to keep them clean, to sew, knit, and weave; to dress food for themselves and [their] families'" (Dowd 1992, 318).

Tecumseh and his younger brother Tenskwatawa, known as the Shawnee Prophet, opposed this civilizing mission and argued for political autonomy: "The Prophet's concern with the civilizing mission, and the gender revolution it would entail, grew out of both the very earthly grounds that it robbed from the Indians, their political independence and the cosmological proposition that robbed the Indians of their sacred powers" (Dowd 1992, 318). Tecumseh argued:

The annihilation of our race is at hand unless we unite in one common cause against a common foe. Think not, brave Choctaws and Chickasaws, that you can remain passive and indifferent to the common danger, and thus escape the common fate. Your people, too, will soon be as falling leaves and scattering clouds before their blighting breath. Will we not soon be driven from our respective countries and the graves of our ancestors? The white usurpation in our common country must be stopped or, we, its rightful owners, be forever destroyed and wiped out as a race of people. (Klinck, 92, quoted in Yadelski 1995, 74–75)

To many native Americans, white civilization is indeed a disease, sometimes referred to as wétiko. Jack Forbes (1934–2011), himself a member of the Powhatan-Renápe and Delaware-Lenápe and a professor of Native American studies, dedicated a whole book to the analysis of wétiko (*Columbus and Other Cannibals*): "*Wétiko* is a Cree term (*windigo* in Ojibway, *wintiko* in Powhatan) which refers to a cannibal or, more specifically, to an evil person or spirit who terrorizes other creatures by means of terrible evil acts, including cannibalism. . . . I have come to the conclusion that *imperialism and exploitation are forms of cannibalism and, in fact, are precisely those forms of cannibalism which are most diabolical and evil*" (Forbes 2008, 24).

To Forbes and many other Native American leaders, the only way to avoid infection by the wétiko disease is to avoid contact with white civilization and live separately. Indeed, William Denevan estimates the native population of the Americas to have been around 54 million in 1492. By 1650, it had declined to a hemispheric total of less than 6 million. The European conquest of the Americas thus was the worst genocide ever committed against any people (Denevan 1992). Following their physical annihilation, the surviving Native Americans were subject to continued land invasion, betrayal, mistreatment, and racism. Their rights were systematically disregarded, treaties previously signed ignored, and their legal status reduced by many American states to those of children. Many of the survivors were pushed onto reservations, far too small and barren for them to survive on, let alone prosper. In many contemporary countries of the Americas, *Indian* or *Indio* is still considered a curse word among those who deem themselves white and European. Natives have been transformed into despised minorities in their own countries.

It is this history of genocide, mistreatment, betrayal, and racism that explains the remedy of nationalism and separateness embraced by most Native people in the Western Hemisphere as the only way to escape the wétiko disease. Political autonomy and self-rule are perceived as concrete measures to ensure physical and cultural survival. Today, Latin America and the Caribbean have a total indigenous population of some 40 million (International Work Group of Indigenous Affairs). In the United States, the 2010 census reported 2.9 million people declaring themselves "American Indian or Alaska Native." In addition, 2.3 million reported as "American Indian or Alaska Native" in combination with "one or more other races" (U.S. Census Bureau 2010). In Canada, the native population in 2016 was 1.4 million (Statistics Canada 2016). The total native, aboriginal, indigenous, or Indian population of the Americas can be estimated to have reached between 40 and 50 million people—thus about the same number it was in 1492. Significant demographic recovery only started at the beginning of the twentieth century for Native Americans (Denevan 1992)—and it must be attributed to their successful mobilization and organization in defense of their reservations and their political autonomy. Securing their own territories and achieving political autonomy on them has been the central tool to survive for Native American people everywhere in the Western Hemisphere. To highlight the centrality and potential of this strategy, I will take a closer look at one specific indigenous group—the Wintukua of Colombia.

The Wintukua: Guardians of the Earth

The Wintukua are one of four indigenous groups living in the territory of the Sierra Nevada de Santa Marta, Colombia.[2] The Sierra Nevada reaches a height of 5,775 meters above the sea and extends to the edge of the Caribbean. The Wintukua are about 50,000 people and tend to live in small settlements consisting of only a few households, on farms and *fincas*. A minority live in larger agglomerates—especially in Nabusimake, the Wintukua capital and their holy city, which is about 2,000 meters above sea level in the heart of the Sierra. After many struggles, invasions by missionaries (whom they successfully repelled), settlers, guerilla fighters, and their paramilitary enemies, the Wintukua, together with the Wiwa, Kaggaba (Kogi), and Kankuamo peoples, were finally able to secure a reservation for themselves—even if its size reflects only a fraction of their ancestral lands. In 1980, the Colombian government officially recognized a reservation in the mountains of the Sierra Nevada de Santa Marta, now totaling 661,527 hectares.

Since the 1980s, the life of the indigenous people living on the reservation has started to improve, as they have been able to define, on their own terms, what sort of development they would like to achieve. Political autonomy and self-rule according to their own laws and traditions constitute a central element of their development. Concretely, the Wintukua practice direct, deliberative democracy and, by doing so, offer lessons in democratic procedure to the rest of the world. The rest of this chapter is dedicated to highlighting some features of Wintukua democracy.[3]

The 1991 Constitution of Colombia provides in its article 330 that "indigenous territories shall be governed by councils formed and regulated according to the customs of their communities." With this, the Colombian state recognized the customary laws of indigenous groups such as the Wintukua. In many cases, particularly among Andean native communities, this custom consists of the Cabildo, a municipal council organization of Spanish origin. According to the Colombian Ministry of Interior, "The Indigenous Council is a special public entity, whose members are members of the indigenous community, elected and recognized by it as a traditional sociopolitical organization whose function is to legally represent the community, to exercise authority and perform the activities attributed to it by the laws, their customs and internal rules of each community" (my translation).[4] According to Enrique Sánchez Gutiérrez and Hernán Molina Echeverri:

> In the Andean region political authority rests in the Cabildos. Each reserve (or reservation) has its own council, and council members are elected periodically by members of the community. The role of the council is to organize the work, divide the available communal lands, settle internal disputes, and represent the reservation to the white authorities. The council was an institution imposed by the Spanish on the indigenous communities in the seventeenth and eighteenth century, but it was adapted to our interests and traditions. It has been one of the main instruments for the defense of indigenous communities and is key to the defense of reservation lands and the recovery of land stolen by landowners. . . . Experience has shown—both in northern Cauca and throughout the country—that the Cabildos are our best weapon to organize, to recover the land that we have been deprived of and to maintain and develop our community life. (2010, 215, my translation)

Parallel to the Cabildo structure, the Wintukuas have another structure, internal, of sacred and wise people, who have great authority among the peoples of the Sierra: the Mamos. According to Romero Infante and Guzmán Barrios, the Wintukua "administer themselves through a dual system between traditional authorities or Mamos and civil authorities or Cabildos, secretaries, commissioners, prosecutors and counselors. The Cabildos are elected by the Mamos in special councils and decisions are made in assembly considering the advice and words of the same Mamos" (2007, 55, my translation).

This system of dual power was evident during my stay in Colombia. On May 17, 2014, the Wintukuas chose their new Cabildo governor, José María Arroyo. The process of choosing him followed the traditional model. First, the Mamos agreed on who should be the new governor. Seventy Wintukua Mamos, through numerous meetings and after several spiritual consultations, deliberated to the point where everyone agreed on the candidate. This process took several weeks. Then the selected candidate was presented to the general assembly. In the first phase there was no vote but a deliberative process that extended to the point where all seventy Mamos agreed. Then there was a general assembly meeting, open to all community members.

Margarita Moisés Villafaña, a Wintukua spokesperson, explains, "We live apart, in families, but weekly, or monthly, depending on the need, we meet to make decisions. In these meetings in the villages, everyone has a voice, including women, youth and children. When we need to take major decisions that affect everyone, we hold a general assembly, with all the people" (interview in Santa Marta, June 1, 2014, my translation).

Thus, among the Wintukua, two basic principles are of importance. The first is the deliberative process among leaders, in this case to choose a new Cabildo governor, which in 2014 lasted for fifteen days, until all Mamos came to an agreement. The second stage is the general public assembly of all the Wintukua people, where the decision of the seventy Mamos was presented to the people. On this occasion, some four hundred Wintukuas attending the general assembly decided whether to accept the candidate suggested by the Mamos. They also listened to the rendering of accounts given by the outgoing governor and to the proposals of the new governor to be.

Moisés Villafaña explains, "First, each village forms an assembly for discussion. Then, they communicate their decisions to the authorities. After that, all the Mamos meet, and finally the Mamos take their decision to the general assembly for discussion. That is when the final decision is made" (interview, 2014, my translation). To my question, "How many times does the general assembly meet?" the Wintukua representatives I interviewed explained, "As often as necessary—whenever there is a decision to take or a project to approve." They also explained that each investment and intervention project has to be approved by an internal deliberative process, followed by a process of discussion and approval at a general assembly.

As such, the Wintukua political system is best characterized as deliberative and direct democracy, where legislative decisions are reached in public assembly. Assemblies, it is worth noting, are held frequently, whenever needed. Public assemblies are open to all, men, women, youths, and children, and they are held at different levels: in villages or meeting places of the families residing in a region; between Mamos; and in general, mostly at the capital of Nabusimake, where all people attend. Thus, Wintukua democracy is deliberative and direct.

My research also demonstrated that the citizenship of the peoples living in the Sierra de Santa Marta is active and full of responsibilities that extend beyond their own groups, because, according to their worldview, they have a responsibility toward the world. Their culture thus contrasts sharply with the white and mestizo culture around them, because among them, citizenship is built not on responsibilities but on rights and entitlements. These rights come from the law and are not the result of communal or social pacts or contracts.

Political Leadership

According to Miguel Rocha Vivas, "The *mamus,* mamas or mamus, are priests, physicians, and community leaders who have different specializations and ranks depending on their place of origin, community, descent, training, religious prestige, etc. In that sense, the mamos are the ultimate bearers of the original words, major words that after having been written down in Latin characters have come to be called myths, stories, songs, and what we call traditional literatures and wisdom, or *oralituras,* in reference to their origin and preeminently oral transmission" (2010, 503ff., my translation). Explains Atí Saraí, a Wintukua, "A Mamo is already born Mamo. They come from Mamo families. Early on they are taught and their learning never ends. They must live a healthy lifestyle. They practice fasting. They have special regulations and food restrictions" (interview in Santa Marta, May 17, 2014, my translation).

The Mamos are the spiritual leaders of the Wintukua. They are their priests, guides, and counselors. They are leaders, but they are not representatives. They are counselors, but they have no political power. To become a Mamo, one has to be trained and prepared from youth. The future Mamos have to go through times of seclusion and meditation. Their lives must follow stringent behavioral and dietary codes. They do not eat meat or salt. The more prestigious a Mamo, the greater his responsibilities.

In general, the responsibilities of the Wintukua reach far beyond their own community, because, according to their beliefs, they are responsible for the world. In their view, the Sierra Nevada contains the whole world—it is the heart and navel of the world. The Mamo Vicencio Torres Marquez, in his complaint letter to the president of the republic on July 7, 1968, expressed a conviction that I often heard when talking to members of the four indigenous groups in the Sierra Nevada de Santa Marta: "This place is the heart of all human beings who exist everywhere in the world" (Sánchez Gutiérrez and Molina Echeverri 2010, 76, my translation).

In the same letter, this important Mamo writes, "Of this consist our laws, religion, and customs: those who belong to these tribes have to care for and assist all those mentioned sites and fulfill our duties in the work of our hidden and traditional science. That is our obligation. In this way, the highlands and mountains of the Sierra Nevada were made and from here the world spread to other places, before the daylight came. It was here that the mothers of the three kingdoms of nature resided, which are: the mineral kingdom, the plant kingdom, and the animal kingdom" (Sánchez Gutiérrez and Molina Echeverri 2010, 70, my translation).

The Mamos are, in the words of Margarita Moisés Villafaña, spiritual guides, counselors, astrologers, and wise men. They do not give orders—they give advice. They also serve as judges for civil and criminal cases that do not involve non-Indians. For the Wintukua, bad behavior, crime, and other antisocial behaviors are the result of a spiritual problem in the person who did it. It is part of the responsibility of a Mamo to identify the root of this problem and address it with the person. It is understood that the cause of a spiritual problem may be rooted in the past—including in previous generations. If a problem occurs in this way, a Mamo guides the healing process, which, over time, also includes the party affected by any misbehavior or crime. This usually consists of acts of restitution. Moisés Villafaña explains, "For us, the conflict comes from a spiritual disease and you have to heal this disease. If not repaired, it will follow us. For us, unlike the Western system, the emphasis is not on punishment, but on restoring. It may also involve community work or work for the victim" (interview, 2014, my translation).

In sum, the Wintukua Mamos are the spiritual leaders and judges of their people. They have many responsibilities and an obligation to lead exemplary lives. Their learning is perpetual. They are the translators of the law of nature and the conduits linking the physical to the spiritual life. Their main responsibility is to maintain the balance and harmony between the people and the spiritual world, where the spirit world is very closely connected to nature and the ancestors. They lead by example; they live in poverty; they wield no political power; they live by severe behavioral and dietary codes; they undergo lifelong training; they deliberate until they reach agreement. In short, they could not be more different from the leaders and political representatives of the so-called advanced democracies surrounding them.

A Culture of Responsibility

Similar to other native people, the Wintukua feel responsible for the world. The Dakota of North America have been described in similar ways. According to Dorothy Lee, "The Dakota were responsible for all things, because they were at one with all things. In one way, this meant that all behavior had to be responsible, since its effect always went beyond the individual. In another way, it meant that an individual had to, was responsible to, increase, intensify, spread, recognize, experience this relationship. To grow in manliness, in humanness, in holiness, meant to plunge purposefully deeper into the relatedness of all things. A Dakota never *assumed* responsibility, because responsibility was had, was there always" (1987, 61).

Leadership, among the Wintukua, similar to other native groups, is not a matter of rule. It is a matter of guidance and advice. Culture provides the framework under which Wintukua society unfolds, and culture, as well as nature, provides the rules and guidelines. The task of the holy men is not to enforce. It is to assist and help everybody else to interpret these rules and live by them. The responsibility is with everyone. As is the case with the Burmese and the Navahos, "the authority of the headman or the chief or the leader is in many ways like the authority of the dictionary, or of Einstein. There is no hint of coercion or command here; the people go to the leader with faith, as we go to a reference book, and the leader answers according to his greater knowledge, or clarifies an obscure point, or amplifies according to his greater experience and wisdom" (Lee 1987, 9).

Culture among many indigenous groups provides a framework in which obedience is not driven by individual authority, or the authority of a specific group, a political party, or the state. Instead, it is a broadly shared framework under which all support each other in their effort to act in conformity with its structure and the guidelines and taboos derived from it. As the research of cultural anthropologists shows, this has been achieved in many societies together with safeguarding individual autonomy and freedom. In fact, as Lee argues, "The concept of equality is irrelevant to this view of man. Here we have instead the full valuing of man in his uniqueness, enabling him to actualize himself, to use opportunity to the fully, undeterred by the standards of an outside authority, not forced to deviate, to meet the expectations of others" (Lee 1987, 46).

Individual autonomy and freedom are thus combinable with equality and equal opportunity if and when strong community ties bring people and families together in common pursuit, guided by a shared framework or values and guidelines, that is, a shared culture. If that is the case, then, according to Lee:

Here and among the Trobrianders, equality itself is present, I think; that is, we find the fact of equality, as a dimension in relationships, as an aspect of the opportunity to be, to function. But its existence is derivative; it is not a goal, but is incidental to some other basic concept. It derives from the recognition of the right to be different, noncommensurate, unique; from the valuing of sheer being. When it is being itself which is valued, then none can be inferior or superior; would it be nonsense to say this is because all being equally *is*? If absolute fullness of opportunity is afforded, if the culture facilitates and implements freedom, thus making it possible for the individual to avail himself of his opportunity, then equality of opportunity may be said to be present, since all have fullness of opportunity. (Lee 1987, 44)

A shared culture is able to provide the behavioral guidelines for a group in a strong sense—to the point where the task of formulating rules and enforcing them does not fall onto specific individuals or groups. Instead, rules are shared rules, anchored in a shared culture. Such a shared culture must be seen as the result of collective agreements about how to live—a loosely codified but highly institutionalized way to live the good and right life—different, in theory, in every specific group. In modern societies, cultural agreement has been replaced with a culture of law, which, according to some, is no longer specific to one particular culture, but able to do justice to all the different cultures living under it (Habermas 1996).

However, the failure to provide morally binding behavioral codes for the different individuals and groups living under one constitution sheds a critical light on the viability of having rule, let alone self-rule, without a strong cultural component, as only when the whole community feels invested in those rules can harmonious living together be achieved. Culture, thus, provides the glue that holds communities together and provides them with guidance and rules. In the absence of culture, authority must be exercised by specific individuals and groups—who, by definition, then become rulers over others. To avoid rule, in other words, a broadly and deeply shared culture must take its place. The indigenous experience in the Americas provides ample examples for this conclusion.

The First People of the Americas offer many other lessons as well: self-rule is possible—as long as political autonomy provides the background for it. Deliberative democracy can be a reality—as long as equality is protected. Responsible political leadership can be achieved—when leaders wield no economic or political power. When all of these components are present and a practiced reality, the state no longer is an externalized reality but a part of the community, and development takes on an entirely different meaning.

CONCLUSION

Politics in a democracy must be every citizen's business. If not, a democracy loses its most central component: self-rule. The liberal, representative alternative is no alternative at all, as all it can achieve is to hand over the business of rule to a select few, who then become rulers over others. Rule over others, however, can never be justified morally. It also cannot be combined with the core idea of democracy. All efforts to justify the combination of democracy with any sort of elite rule are, and must be, demagogy.

Elite rule was the condition that brought about the state, or maybe inequality and the wish to justify and defend privilege triggered the need to erect state apparatuses that are not of the people, but separate entities. In a true democracy, the people *are* the state. Any effort to strengthen civil society or to democratize the bureaucracy and the state apparatus are ultimately distractions from the real task ahead, if and when democracy is the goal: bringing the state back under the control of communities. While this might seem an overly utopian agenda, indigenous people of the Americas embarked on this path centuries ago and some have advanced considerably in establishing true democracy and self-rule. The Zapatistas of southern Mexico are but one among many examples. Given their shared history of genocide at the hands of European civilizers, indigenous people of the Americas have been able to recognize the character and content of Western civilization more clearly than most, labeling it a wétiko disease.

Their remedy is equally clear: territorial separation and political autonomy. Much can thus be learned about politics, democracy, and viable alternatives to Western, civilized, capitalist development from American native people. Of central importance in all of their approaches to organizing collective life is a strong and deeply shared culture. Culture, if shared in such a deep way, can take on the role of rulers in that it can provide the behavioral guidelines for all. Leaders can then become inspiring role models—instead of enforcers of authority. The responsibility of acting according to the rules of the community falls on all, and the rules and norms are broadly shared. Democratization then becomes the task of democratizing culture so as to avoid the exclusion of some (often women) and the concentration of political power in few hands (chiefs or kings). Cooperation critically relies on relative equality, and its defense is a sine qua non condition for true democracy. Here, too, much can be learned from American Indians, as many of them to this day practice communal land ownership, sometimes called *ejido*, yet distribute the right to use the land to individual families, according to their needs, for a lifetime. This practice, too, is anchored in culture, as all indigenous peoples of the hemisphere seem to share the religious understanding that the land is sacred and cannot be individually owned. The Wintukua provide an example of what politics can mean, how leadership can look, and how collective decisions can be made in a true democracy. The lessons from the First People are clear. The question is: will we listen?

NOTES

1. I use the term *primitive* very reluctantly here, as it makes no sense to me to refer to societies able to avoid social hierarchy and elite rule as primitive. I nevertheless apply the term here only because of its broad usage, allowing me to focus on exactly those societies I want to discuss.

2. An earlier version of this section on the Wintukua was published in *Anarchist Studies*, spring 2017.

3. This section is the result of empirical research with the Wintukuas, conducted between April and June 2014. In addition to consultations with the existing literature, I conducted open and semistructured interviews with some Wintukua and Wiwa representatives and tribal members. My main interest was to learn more about Wintukua political organization. Specifically, I sought to discover how collective decisions are made, how political rule is constituted, how political elites are selected, and what role these political elites play in Wintukua political and everyday life. I am not trained as an ethnographer, and the ethnographic theory informing this work is scant at best. This is justifiable, in my mind, by my rather narrow research interest, which is restricted to unveiling the institutional dimensions of Wintukua political life. The methodology I chose reflects this interest, as well as my own academic training and experience as a political scientist. I do not claim to be a specialist on the Wintukua people or on Colombian indigenous cultures—if such a specialization exists (which I would find odd, as the most qualified specialists on Wintukua life are the Wintukuas themselves).

4. Colombian Ministerio del Interior. Accessed November 10, 2017, http://www.mininterior.gov.co/content/cabildo-indigena.

REFERENCES

Anderson, Warwick. 2009. "From Subjugated Knowledge to Conjugated Subjects: Science and Globalization, or, Postcolonial Studies of Science?" *Postcolonial Studies* 12, no. 4: 389–400.

Anderson, Warwick, and Vincanne Adams. 2007. "Pramoedya's Chickens: Postcolonial Studies of Technoscience." In *The Handbook of Science and Technology Studies*, 3rd ed., edited by Edward J. Hackett, Olga Amsterdam, Michael E. Lynch, and Judy Wajcman, 181–207. Cambridge, MA: MIT Press.

Axelrod, Robert. 2006. *The Evolution of Cooperation*. New York: Basic Books.

Blaser, Mario, Ravi de Costa, Deborah McGregor, and William Coleman, eds. 2010. *Indigenous People and Autonomy*. Vancouver: UBC Press.

Boix, Carles. 2015. *Political Order and Inequality*. New York: Cambridge.

Castoriadis, Cornelius. 2001. "The Retreat from Autonomy: Post-modernism as Generalised Conformism." *Democracy and Nature* 7 (1): 17–26.

Clastres, Pierre. 1989. *Society against the State: Essays in Political Anthropology*. Brooklyn, NY: Zone Books.

Deloria, Vine. 1969. *Custer Died for Your Sins: An Indian Manifesto*. Norman: University of Oklahoma Press.

Deloria, Vine. 2007. *We Talk, You Listen*. Lincoln: University of Nebraska Press.

Deloria, Vine, and Clifford Lytle. 1984. *The Nations Within*. Austin: University of Texas Press.

Denevan, William, ed. 1992. *The Native Population of the Americas in 1492*. Madison: University of Wisconsin Press.

Dinerstein, Ana C. 2014. *The Politics of Autonomy in Latin America: The Art of Organizing Hope*. Edited by Jude Howell. Hampshire, UK: Palgrave Macmillan.

Dowd, Gregory. 1992. "Thinking and Believing: Nativism and Unity in the Ages of Pontiac and Tecumseh." *American Indian Quarterly* 16 (3): 309–35.

Forbes, Jack. 2008. *Columbus and Other Cannibals*. New York: Seven Stories.

Gibson-Graham, J. K. 2006. *The End of Capitalism (As We Knew It): A Feminist Critique of Political Economy*. Minneapolis: University of Minnesota Press.

Habermas, Jürgen. 1996. *Between Facts and Norms*. Cambridge, MA: MIT Press.

Hartsock, Nancy. 1983. "The Feminist Standpoint." In *Discovering Reality*, edited by Sandra Harding and Merrill Hintikka, 283–310. Alphen aan den Rijn, Netherlands: Kluwer.

Hess, David J. 2011. "Science in an Era of Globalization: Alternative Pathways." In *The Postcolonial Science and Technology Studies Reader*, edited by Sandra Harding, 419–38. Durham, NC: Duke University Press.

Hollinger, David. 1996. *Science, Jews, and Secular Culture*. Princeton, NJ: Princeton University Press.

Holloway, John. 2010. *Change the World without Taking Power*. London: Pluto Press.

International Work Group for Indigenous Affairs. https://www.iwgia.org/en/.

Jasanoff, Sheila, Gerald E. Markle, James C. Petersen, and Trevor Pinch, eds. 1995. *Handbook of Science and Technology Studies*. Thousand Oaks, CA: SAGE.

Lee, Dorothy. 1987. *Freedom and Culture*. Long Grove, IL: Waveland Press.

Manville, Philip Brook. 1997. *The Origins of Citizenship in Ancient Athens*. Princeton, NJ: Princeton University Press.

Mignolo, Walter D. 2000. *Local Histories/Global Designs: Coloniality, Subaltern Knowledges and Border Thinking*. Princeton, NJ: Princeton University Press.

Ministerio del Interior, Colombia. http://www.mininterior.gov.co/content/cabildo -indigena.

Morana, Mabel, Enrique Dussel, and Carlos A. Jauregui, eds. 2008. *Coloniality at Large: Latin America and the Postcolonial Debate*. Durham, NC: Duke University Press.

Olson, Mancur. 2000. *Power and Prosperity*. New York: Basic Books.

Pocock, J. G. A. 1995. "The Ideal of Citizenship since Classical Times." In *Theorizing Citizenship*, edited by Ronald Beiner, 29–52. Albany: State University of New York Press.

Reisch, George A. 2005. *How the Cold War Transformed Philosophy of Science: To the Icy Slopes of Logic.* Cambridge: Cambridge University Press.

Rocha Vivas, Miguel. 2010. *Antes el Amanecer: Antología de las Literaturas Indígenas de los Andes y la Sierra Nevada de Santa Marta.* Bogotá: Ministerio de Cultura.

Romero Infante, Jaime Alberto, and Joaquin Alberto Guzman Barrios. 2007. "Administración ambiental del pueblo Wintukua, un ejemplo de colaboración Universidad El Bosque—Resguardo Indígena." *Cuadernos Latinoamericanos de Administración* 2 (4): 50–64.

Rousseau, Jean Jacques. [1762] 2003. *The Social Contract.* Translated by Judith Masters and Roger Masters. New York: St. Martin's.

Sánchez Gutiérrez, Enrique, and Hernán Molina Echeverri, eds. 2010. *Documentos para la historia del movimiento indígena colombiano contemporáneo.* Bogotá: Ministerio de Cultura.

Scott, James. 2009. *The Art of Not Being Governed.* New Haven, CT: Yale University Press.

Selin, Helaine, ed. 2008. *Encyclopedia of the History of Science, Technology and Medicine in Non-Western Cultures.* 2nd ed. Dordrecht: Kluwer.

Service, Elman. 1975. *Origins of the State and Civilization.* New York: W. W. Norton.

Seth, Suman 2009. "Putting Knowledge in Its Place: Science, Colonialism, and the Postcolonial." *Postcolonial Studies* 12, no. 4: 373–88.

Smith, Dorothy. 1974. "Women's Perspective as a Radical Critique of Sociology." *Sociological Inquiry* 44 (1): 7–13.

Smith, Dorothy. 1990. *The Conceptual Practices of Power: A Feminist Sociology of Knowledge.* Toronto: University of Toronto Press.

Snow, Chief John. 1977. *The Mountains Are Our Sacred Places.* Toronto: Samuel Stevens.

Stahler-Sholk, Richard. 2008. "Resisting Neoliberal Homogenization: The Zapatista Autonomy Movement." In *Latin American Social Movements in the Twenty-First Century*, edited by Richard Stahler-Sholk, Harry Vanden, and Glen Kuecker, 113–30. Lanham, MD: Rowman and Littlefield.

Stahler-Sholk, Richard. 2014. "Mexico: Autonomy, Collective Identity, and the Zapatista Social Movement." In *Rethinking Latin American Social Movements*, edited by Richard Stahler-Sholk, Harry Vanden, and Marc Becker, 187–208. Lanham, MD: Rowman and Littlefield.

Statistics Canada. 2016. "Census Program." http://www12.statcan.gc.ca/census -recensement/index-eng.cfm.

Thomas, Philip. 1807. "Brief Account: Friends Committee for the Improvement of the Civilization of the Indians." *Massachusetts Missionary Magazine*, no. 5:267–70.

Tucker, Glenn. 1956. *Tecumseh: Vision of Glory.* Indianapolis: Bobbs-Merrill.

Turnbull, Colin. 1968. *The Forest People.* New York: Simon and Schuster.

U.S. Census Bureau. 2010. "2010 Census Data." http://www.census.gov/2010census/data/.

Van Cott, Donna Lee. 2008. *Radical Democracy in the Andes.* New York: Cambridge University Press.

Yadelski, Robert. 1995. "A Rhetoric of Contact: Tecumseh and the Native American Confederacy." *Rhetoric Review* 14 (1): 64–77.

Yashar, Deborah. 2005. *Contesting Democracy in Latin America.* New York: Cambridge University Press.

15 · Iran's Path toward Islamic Reformism

A Study of Religious Intellectual Discourse

The aim of this research is to examine and explore the emergence and development of an intellectual discourse that conceptually and ideologically transformed political Islam into a new, modern interpretation of Islam, namely Islamic reformism. This discourse, represented by a circle of religious intellectuals, emerged as an alternative interpretation of political Islam, one that seeks not necessarily to separate Islam from the political process but instead to reform what it sees as an increasingly intolerant and opportunistically motivated interpretation of the religion.

This chapter seeks to examine their ideas and ideals, which have mutated from their previous Islamic revolutionary ideology and specifically from their views on the Islamic state, democracy, and secularism. This study then argues that the discourse of Islamic reformism plays a key role in the development and consolidation of democracy in Iran by offering a new interpretation of religious norms and values with respect to the moral basis of legitimate political authority and individual rights. By examining this community of intellectuals, this research aims to fill a critical gap in the studies of postrevolutionary intellectuals. More specifically, this study focuses on the following research questions:

- What does religious intellectualism mean? What are the main elements of this reformist movement?
- How have Iranian religious intellectuals defined democracy and secularism? What are the main elements of democracy for them?

The emergence of religious intellectualism in the history of modern Iran has certainly been one of the most significant developments to take place over the country's intellectual and political course. From the nineteenth century onward, Iran has witnessed three major political movements in which religious thinkers have played an important role: first, the Iranian constitutional revolution of 1906–11, which has been seen as the expression of Iran's political awakening at the turn of the century and which aimed to remove the traditional authoritarianism of the Qajar dynasty and establish a modern democratic system of government able to overcome the country's social, political, and economic backwardness (Jahanbakhsh 2003). During the revolution, many religious thinkers defended the idea of liberty, of a political system responsible to the people, and of an autonomous judiciary (Khosrokhavar 2004). They voiced the long-standing aspiration of the people for institutionalized justice, self-determination, and political change. Second, the Islamic revolution of 1979, which was a response to the shah's autocratic rule, his strong policy of Westernization, and the failure of overly ambitious economic reform, replaced Iran's monarchy with an Islamic republic.

It was the work of Ali Shariati (1933–1977), the most prominent religious intellectual of his time, which provided the intellectual component required for mobilizing support for Khomeini's leadership and helped the clergy to justify its position as the only true interpreter and ideologue of revolutionary Islamic discourse (Jahanbakhsh 2003). It is no surprise that Shariati was called "the teacher of the revolution" after the establishment of the Islamic republic.

Borrowing the revolutionary and ideological jargon of Marxism, he articulated an ideological Islamic discourse that promoted social justice, political freedom, and social equality. Finally, the reform movement of the late 1990s, which challenged the theocratic political system, was established after the 1979 revolution in which Islam informed the official ideology of the state and supported President Khatami's plans to reform the system to include more freedom and democracy (Kamrava 2008). Religious intellectuals have not only criticized the dominant religious discourse, which is by its very nature exclusive, militant, and populist and demands absolute obedience and conformity to the clergy, but they have also provided an effective alternative to the official religious discourse that embraces religious pluralism and democratic values.

However, the journey from theological resources to liberal democracy is not a smooth one. Religious reformism is a relatively new political-cultural and social trend that has emerged in the past three decades in response to the failures and contradictions of the Islamic state. It refers to a departure from revolutionary ideological discourse to a reformist religious one, which became the gateway to democratic discourse. It has criticized the ideological understanding of religion as not only theoretically, but also practically, misleading and misled.

Religious reformists argued that discussion about the form of governance is nonjurisprudential by its very nature and belongs to the domain of political philosophy; what determines whether this topic should be tackled from within religion or outside it depends on our expectations and definitions of religion (Jahanbakhsh 2003). They therefore defined religion by its core element, namely religious experience, as the free pursuit of inner spiritual experience. In this way, methods of governance that deal with the administration of different aspects of public life are essentially nonreligious. To them, it is a mistake to try to find a religious plan for government. Accordingly, a necessary prerequisite to democratization of religious government is to make religious thought more flexible by elevating the role of reason in it. In the past decades, many extra-Islamic values and beliefs were adopted and incorporated into religious tradition; therefore, democracy, which is conceived of as an effective system of governance, can function in religious societies too. But the religious reformists did not advocate the privatization of Islam. They were careful not to equate secularism with the complete rejection of religiosity, but rather defined it as the restriction of religious authority in the political and social spheres.

The case of Iran has great significance because it has inspired the rise of Islamist movements of different kinds in the Middle East. And yet, all evidence points to the possibility that the first country that produced a religious state in modern times might also be the first in the region to liberate itself from the grip of an Islamic state. The failure of the Islamic republic in almost every political and social aspect has important lessons and consequences for the region. The example of Iran clearly shows that neither authoritarian secularist regimes nor Islamic dictatorial states can resolve the multifaceted problems of these societies. The only solution must be the establishment of a democratically accountable state, which guarantees political and social rights and freedoms. By challenging the underpinning of the religious-political establishment in Iran, religious intellectuals have played a key role in the development and consolidation of democracy in the country.

Theoretical and Historical Background

Given the focus of this research, I start out with a definition of *discourse*, because the concept of discourse seems suited to capturing religious intellectualism and the reformism trend in postrevolutionary Iran. The conceptualization of discourse in this study is based on Mehran Kamrava's work on Iran's intellectual revolution. For him, discourse is a general body of thought, based on a series of assumptions, about the nature of things as they are and as they ought to be (Kamrava 2008, 3). As such, discourse is meant to articulate a worldview and critically examine the present but also to show signposts to the future. Despite serving the same function and purpose as ideology—"a blueprint for political thought and action"—discourse goes beyond it and offers "the larger framework of ideas that inform ideology" (Kamrava, 2008, 3). In short, as a framework for ideas, discourse establishes the limits of discussion and defines the range of issues that can be tackled. The intellectual quest to define the very meaning and essence of Iranian identity and, more importantly, the contest over the path to be followed by Iranians have given rise to three broad discourses in contemporary Iran.

The Islamic revolution of 1979 led to the emergence of Islamist discourse, which has sought to theoretically justify the inseparability of religion and politics as well as the unlimited dominance of the clergy over Iran's political system and cultural life. It has sought to build "an ideological community," an Islamic state that implements Islamic laws and moral codes (Bayat 1996). It gives political leadership to the clergy—in the absence of the divinely inspired imam. This discourse imagines a maximalist understanding of Islam.

In reaction to this discourse, an alternative interpretation of Islam emerged in the late 1980s and the early 1990s that does not necessarily seek to separate Islam from politics but instead wants to reform what it sees as an ideological understanding of Islam. This discourse of Islamic reformism is an attempt to reconcile Islam with freedom, democracy, and modernity. It represents an endeavor to produce a nonideological, pluralistic understanding of Islam, which rejects the intervention of religion into politics on the basis of any kind of Islamic arguments and argues that politics should be run only by rational methods of administration. When it is translated into political discourse, this pluralist reading of Islam will only support democracy and political pluralism (Jahanbakhsh 2003).

Contrary to the dominant ideological discourse, which sees people as "duty-bound individuals, responsible for fulfilling their religious duties by participating in political and public affairs," the new discourse views people as "right-bound" individuals who are entitled to certain inalienable rights, including the right to decide how to govern their affairs (Jahanbakhsh 2003). This discourse has succeeded in developing a powerful and coherent theoretical critique from within the Iranian Islamic framework of the ruling clerics. This discourse of Islamic reformism is being put forward by a group of religious intellectuals who were once key figures themselves within the post-revolutionary establishment. Disappointed with the authoritarian and repressive character of the postrevolutionary government, they started to question the absolutist theology of the ruling clerics and attack totalitarian Islam. So it can be argued that the discourse is very much a product of the children of the 1979 revolution and can be seen as one of its unintended long-term consequences (Arjomand 2002).

In the last decade, in response to the state's perceived theoretical excesses and the political incompetence of the religious reformists, Iran has witnessed the rearticulation of secular discourse with its emphasis on modernity and the separation of religion and politics. However, the secular discourse has remained absolutely marginal, for several reasons. In the deeply religious society of Iran, the discourse is seen by many to be alien, Westernized, and anti-Islamic and therefore does not enjoy a strong following. But, more importantly, it has failed to provide a novel solution from within Iranian culture and has hardly gone beyond mere criticism of the current situation. Moreover, it has remained an exceptionally disorganized force (Jahanbakhsh 2003).

Theoretical Tension between Religion and Democracy

The tension between religion and democracy is as old as political philosophy itself. At first glance, this tension seems inherently insurmountable and contradictory because religion and democracy speak to different aspects of the human condition. While religion is a system of values and practices that is related to the sacred and the divine, democracy is decidedly mundane, this-worldly, and secular. Religion sets up boundaries between believers and nonbelievers in a society, whereas democracy, in particular in its liberal form, implies an equality of rights before the law for all citizens regardless of their gender, religious beliefs, or race. The rules of democracy, unlike religious commandments, can be adjusted, changed, and amended. To put it in a nutshell, it is the inclusive nature of democracy that differentiates it from any religiously based political system (Hashemi 2009).

One way of conceptualizing this theoretical friction is to imagine a horizontal and vertical axis. As figure 15.1 shows, religion in its most basic form is a relationship between an individual and God that does not necessarily affect or concern other members of society. Democracy, in contrast, is a political system that comes to regulate horizontal relationships among individuals in a society.

A point of high tension occurs when members of society bring their vertical relationship with God into the horizontal public sphere in order to regulate their social relationships, when the legitimacy of political authority no longer depends on popular sovereignty (the horizontal axis) but instead is based exclusively on divine rights (the vertical axis). In other words, the core tension between religion and democracy is rooted in the question of the moral basis of legitimate political authority.

From the perspective of liberal-democratic theory, the objection to religious interference in politics is justified on the following three grounds: first, while

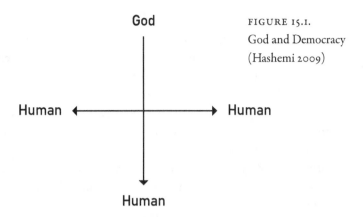

FIGURE 15.1.
God and Democracy
(Hashemi 2009)

religions may differ in their various manifestations, all religions and sects are infamous for their dogmatic claim to possess absolute and universal truth. The ideological rigidity that often comes with this religious belief undermines pluralism, compromise, and tolerance, which all are key features of democratic politics (Reichley 1986). Second, unlike religion, whose tendency is to exclude, democracy is egalitarian, inclusive, and nondiscriminatory; citizenship is based not on adherence to religious beliefs and principles but rather on membership in political society (Hashemi 2009). Religion also undermines the secular conviction of politics that it is necessary to maintain liberalism and sustain a democratic peace. It breaks the distinction between vertical and horizontal axes by bringing God into the center of public debate.

Secularism and Its Discontents in Iran

If there is one thing that can be affirmed with certainty about secularism, it is that the concept is deeply contested. It is not entirely clear what values secularism promotes and what problems it seeks to resolve. While secularism sometimes refers to the complete separation of religion from politics or the rejection of religious symbols in the public sphere, it is sometimes defined more narrowly as state neutrality and equidistance toward all religions or the separation of the institutions of the state from the control and influence of religion (Hashemi 2009). Keddie (2003) identifies three ways in which secularization is commonly understood today: as (1) "a decline of religious influence and control over major spheres of life," (2) "an increase in the number of people with secular beliefs and practices," and (3) "a growth in state separation from religion and in the secular regulation of formerly religious institutions and customs."

One way of thinking about the concept is in relation to three core disciplines in the social sciences: philosophy, sociology, and political science. Philosophically, secularism is defined as "a rejection of the transcendental and the metaphysical with a focus on the existential and the empirical" (Hashemi 2009). It refers to the rise of alternative belief systems and the eclipse of religious and metaphysical ideas. Sociologically, secularism is associated with modernization: a gradual process that leads to the retreat of religion from social institutions, communal life, and human relationships. This is the most common understanding of secularism in the popular discussion of the topic. Politically, it is about a separation of the private and public spheres and in particular the separation of church and state.

Investigating the roots of these different forms of secularism is beyond the aims and scope of this chapter, yet the recognition that political secularism has various models allows us to reconsider the prospect for secularism in Muslim society. It can be argued that Muslim-dominated societies might be able to develop their own version of secularism, one that would be compatible with their own historical, cultural, and religious traditions.

One important analytical error commonly made when discussing secularism and liberal democracy in Muslim societies is a false universalism which assumes that the Western experience with religio-political relations should be the universal norm for the rest of the world. From this perspective, any manifestation of religion in politics that challenges Western assumptions about secularism is regarded as a sign of religious fascism. It should be noted that, while the question of religion's relationship to democracy and its proper role in politics has been largely resolved in the West and a broad secular consensus has been reached, it is still an ongoing question for most Muslim societies.

In his insightful theoretical discussion of the relationship between Islam, secularism, and democracy, Nader Hashemi (2009) points to a seemingly irreconcilable paradox that confronts religious intellectuals: on the one hand, to sustain itself, liberal democracy requires a form of secularism, yet simultaneously secularism has a troubled legacy in most Muslim societies.

The crisis of secularism in the Muslim world is deeply connected to the failure of state-led projects of secularization. Typically, a secular conception of politics should emerge from within civil society through a democratic negotiation over the proper role of religion in politics, but for most Muslim societies secularism was first and foremost a top-down project led by the state and was not a product of socioeconomic, cultural change. For a generation of Muslims growing up in a postcolonial era, secularism is intimately connected to authoritarianism, dictatorship, and human rights abuses, having been introduced by colonial powers and then tied into the developmental failures and repressions of the autocratic state (Hashemi 2009).

As the case of Iran clearly shows, the sequence and process of democratic development in Muslim societies were the reverse of the European experience. While in Europe a religious reformation preceded and then led to secularization, in the Muslim world religious reformation has been a response to an authoritarian imposition of secularization by the state. This fact helps considerably to explain the weak intellectual roots of secular concepts of politics in Muslim societies (Filali-Ansary 2003).

Given the fact that secularism has had such a troubled legacy in Muslim societies and in order to let religious groups reconcile themselves with secularism, a religion-based theory of secularism is required. This chapter argues that in many Muslim societies with weak democratic traditions, including Iran, where large parts of the population are under the sway of an authoritarian religious doctrine, the reevaluation of religious ideas and values with respect to government instead of a categorical rejection of them is a prerequisite for liberal democratic development. It argues that in societies where religion is a marker of identity, the democratization process requires religious norms to be reinterpreted with respect to the moral basis of legitimate political authority and individual rights. By engaging in this interpretation, religious intellectuals and reformists have played a key role in the development and consolidation of liberal democracy in Iran, supplying an indigenous understanding and theory of Muslim democracy.

The Reformist Religious Discourse

The emergence of reformist religious intellectuals dates back to some decades after the establishment of the Islamic republic, when the internal contradictions and changing dynamics of the state made intellectual activism once again possible. Having been deeply disappointed with the pseudo-totalitarian theocratic regime established after the Islamic revolution and its radical ideology, the new generation of religious intellectuals, which is represented most compellingly by Abdolkarim Soroush, a Tehran-based university professor and Rumi scholar, articulated a nonideological, pluralistic understanding of Islam that rejects the intervention of religion into politics on the basis of any kind of Islamic argument and argues that politics must be run only by rational methods of administration. When it is translated into political discourse, this reading of Islam will only support democracy and political pluralism. Although all religious intellectuals agree that Islam does and should continue to play an important role in the overall life of Iranian society, including its politics, most of them maintain that Islam does not mandate a specific form of government. Accordingly, this reformist generation posed serious and substantial challenges to the ideological foundation of the ruling clerics in Iran.

The religious intellectuals strongly criticize their revolutionary predecessors for leading the country's intellectual tradition astray at a critical moment in the country's history and for providing ideological and theoretical legitimation for the clerics in power. They believe that their predecessors were more revolutionary ideologues than intellectuals, who in order to turn Islam into a revolutionary ideology simply compiled irrelevant arguments and ideas offered by others. They viewed their subjects of study through an ideological lens rather than thinking about them objectively. Their self-ascribed responsibility was to move people toward some supposedly revolutionary nirvana (Kamrava 2008).

Among the prominent features of the new discourse represented by the postrevolutionary religious intellectuals are some that stand out as contradicting the dominant ideological discourse advocated by the Iranian regime. While the new religious intellectuals define religion by its core element, namely religious experience, understood as the free pursuit of inner spiritual experience, the ideological understanding of Islam reduces religion to a set of laws regulating social and religious behavior.

On a practical level, by removing Sharia from the center of religion and replacing it with religious experience, the new discourse not only eliminates the need for the clergy to offer official interpretations but also recognizes the plurality at the heart of religion, since religious experience is plural by its nature. Unlike the dominant ideological discourse, which sees people as "duty-bound individuals responsible for fulfilling their religious duties by participating in political and public affairs," the new discourse views people as "right-bound" individuals who are entitled to certain inalienable rights, including the right to decide how to govern their affairs (Jahanbakhsh 2003). Moreover, the ideological discourse advocated by conservative Islamists has a maximalist understanding of religion. It claims that Islam provides answers and solutions to all social, economic, and political problems. In this view, Islam encompasses the specific form and type of government that should be established in Iran. The new religious intellectuals, however, have a minimalist understanding of religion and question the efficiency of religious laws in governing society. They reject the claim that Islam mandates a specific form of government and argue that the ideal political system differs according to the conditions of the time and a society's knowledge and understanding (Kamrava 2008).

At least three factors broadly contributed to the shift in ideological orientation of the postrevolutionary intellectuals from a revolutionary to a relatively moderate and liberal interpretation of Islam: first, the failures of Iran's Islamic regime to fulfill its populist promises and expectations, which led to a considerable erosion in the legitimacy of the current regime and entailed a rethinking of its revolutionary Islamic ideology; second, social changes within the country (urbanization, increasing literacy, and an economic shift) that created a new generation (an educated but impoverished middle class, urban youths, and women) who successfully resisted the socially and politically restrictive policies of the Islamic republic and asked for political change; and third, the global trend after the collapse of the Soviet Union and the triumph of liberalism, which made the languages of pluralism, democracy, and human rights the globally accepted norms and standards (Bayat 2007).

Abdulkarim Soroush and the De-ideologization of Religion

In the late 1980s, former professor Abdulkarim Soroush (1994) made a radical break with the ideological characterization of Islam in a series of talks and articles, which are collected in the book *Loftier Than Ideology*. Soroush criticized the articulation of ideological Islam as a narrow conception of religion, arguing that "Islam as a world religion is 'richer than ideology' because 'it allows for a variety of different interpretations.'" According to Soroush, the disadvantages and harmful aspects of an ideology, particularly in the case of religious ideology, are much greater than its benefits: while Islam as an ideology is a useful discursive tool against oppression, it prescribes the establishment of an ideological society that would hamper the development of a free society (Soroush 1994). He praised Ali Shariati's earlier theological intervention in articulating a socially engaged and dynamic public religion, but argued that it transformed Islam into a mere manifesto for social change. More importantly, it paved the way for the domination of the clergy and helped them to justify their position as the only true interpreters of Islam. In this way, the ideological reading of Islam led to another form of authoritarianism in Iran (Soroush 1995).

Rejecting the articulation of Islam as a state ideology, Soroush offered a minimalist interpretation of religion that sought to cut down the realm of religion and focus more on its spiritual dimension, as opposed to the maximalist discourse of ideological Islam. In his words, "the 'greatest pathology of religion I have noticed after the revolution is that it has become plump, even swollen. . . . It is neither possible nor desirable for religion, given its ultimate mission, to carry such a burden. This means purifying religion, making it lighter and more buoyant'" (cited in Mahdavi 2011). He then argued that, to survive, religion needs to be flexible and open to different interpretations, but in an ideological society where religion is enclosed within the fixed mold of an ideology, it is transformed into a rigid means for organizing a particular social order (Soroush 1994). Ideological societies become illusionary utopias where diversity is not tolerated; they are breeding grounds for the growth of authoritarian and dictatorial political systems.

Soroush (1995), in his book *The Theory of Expansion and Contraction of Religious Knowledge*, reinstated the core of Islam through a hermeneutic distinction between religion and religious knowledge. The former, according to Soroush, has a revelatory essence and as such might be perfect, true, and immutable. The latter, in contrast, is the result of human attempts to interpret and understand religion, which in the case of Islam includes the Qur'an and the Prophet's traditions. Like other human knowledge, it is changeable, relative, and time bound. More importantly, it is affected by and in constant exchange with other fields of human knowledge. Thus religious knowledge is not sacred.

By making a distinction between the changing, time-bound human understanding of religion and its immutable, eternal, and sacred essence, Soroush succeeds in resolving the problem that all his predecessors were faced with: reconciling a fixed religion with the changing nature of the modern world and those who want to preserve the immutability of religion with those who would render it compatible with a changing world. In fact, Soroush takes the problem to a different level, arguing that all the solutions provided hitherto lacked an epistemological approach. According to Soroush, meaning is given to religion rather than extracted from it. Religion, in this sense, is silent; it is given a voice by social agents and social contexts. Therefore, it is not religion that must be changed in order to become compatible with the dynamics of the changing world, but rather our understanding of it. This is what must be altered.

The Religious Democratic State

As already stated above, the journey from theological resources to liberal democracy is not a smooth one. Soroush's rejection of the characterization of Islam as the legitimizing factor in an Islamic state does not amount to a denial of the role of religion in politics. Rather, he sought to democratize the state without diminishing the public role of religion in the country. Soroush called for the establishment of a democratic state that would be compatible with a religious society—an idea that later came to be known as religious democracy.

The notion of a religious democratic state can probably be better understood in light of the distinction between two different readings of religion, each one yielding an alternative notion of what a religious state means. Depending on which aspect of Islam is highlighted, inner faith or outward practice, two different types of religious states will emerge. In a *fiqh*-based (jurisprudential) society, where the observance of all religious practices and ritual is given priority, executing religious orders and laws becomes the main task of the religious state, even if it has to appeal to force (Soroush 1995). Accordingly, the clergy serve as the custodians of jurisprudential Islam and enjoy a privileged and special position in politics. In this fiqh-based state, the methods of governance and its legitimacy are derived from religion. Soroush (1995), however, argues that the significance of Islam lies neither in imposing religious orders nor in rituals, but rather in its morality, ethics, and faith. Religious jurisprudence, according to him, is far from being the core of the religion. Contrary to what historically had been imposed on Muslim communities, he argues that the enforcement of religious laws or insisting on the observation of its rituals does not make a society and hence its government religious. If people are not truly free to choose their faith, the society cannot be called religious. This jurisprudential government is also not democratic because it imposes religious dictates on the people and seeks uniformity in the will and religious experience of all.

In a faith-based society, in contrast, where primacy is given to the inner religious experience, the main task of the state will be limited to providing an environment in which people can freely pursue their faith. In such a society, a government does not rule because of its religious right; its legitimacy is derived not from a divine source but rather from the will of the people. The beliefs and will of the majority determine the ideal of a religious democratic state (Soroush, Sadri, and Sadri 2002).

Soroush then argues that the discussion about the form of governance is nonjurisprudential by its very nature and belongs to the domain of political philosophy. According to him, what determines whether this topic should be tackled from within religion or outside it, in other words, whether it is a religious or jurisprudential matter, depends on our expectations and definitions of religion.

For Soroush, religion is defined by its core element, namely religious experience, as the free pursuit of inner spiritual experience. Understood in this way, methods of governance, which deal with the administration of different aspects of public life, are essentially nonreligious. Hence, following Soroush, it is a mistake to try to find a religious plan for government. He added that the idea of democratic government is grounded in the natural right of human beings to govern their own affairs. All people are inherently entitled to this right regardless of their gender, national origin, religion, culture, personal values, or belief systems. The clergy, therefore, cannot claim to have an a priori right to interpret this sovereignty. Accordingly, Soroush rejected the idea of *velāyat-e faqih'* (the guardianship of the Islamic jurist), which gives political leadership to the clergy, as an undemocratic and thus unacceptable form of government, vehemently arguing that the management of modern societies is possible only through scientific rationality in democratic structures (Soroush, Sadri, and Sadri 2002).

According to Soroush, "a necessary prerequisite to democratization of religious government is to make religious thought more flexible by elevating the role of reason in it" (1994). Although democracy is not compatible with a jurisprudential understanding of Islam, he argued, it can be reconciled with another reading of it in which human values such as freedom, justice, and reason are accorded a position of primacy. In other words, any attempt to reconcile Islam and democracy depends on one's theoretical success in reconciling reason and religion. He argued that in the past, many extra-Islamic values and beliefs were adopted and incorporated into religious tradition; therefore, democracy, which is conceived of as an effective system of governance, can function in religious societies too. Soroush, however, did not advocate the privatization of Islam. He was careful not to equate secularism with the complete rejection of religiosity, but rather defined it as the restriction of religious authority in the political and social spheres.

CONCLUSION

In examining the emergence and development of an intellectual discourse that conceptually and ideologically transformed political Islam into a modern interpretation of Islam, namely Islamic reformism in the late 1990s, this chapter argues that the reformist discourse plays a key role in the development of democracy by offering a new interpretation of religious norms and values with respect to the moral basis of legitimate political authority and individual rights, supplying an indigenous understanding and theory of the Muslim democracy. Synthesizing the ethics of Islam with various fields of political thought, this discourse not only criticized the dominant religious discourse, which is by its nature exclusive, militant, and demands absolute obedience to the clergy, but also provides an alternative to the official religious discourse that embraces religious pluralism and democratic values.

The case of Iran has great significance because it has inspired the rise of Islamist movements of different kinds in the Middle East. And yet, all evidence points to the possibility that the first country that produced a religious state in modern times might also be the first in the region to liberate itself from the grip of an Islamic state. The failure of the Islamic Republic in many political and social aspects has important lessons and consequences for the region. The example of Iran clearly shows that neither authoritarian secularist regimes nor Islamic dictatorial states can resolve the multifaceted problems of these societies. The only solution must be the establishment of a democratically accountable state that guarantees political and social rights and freedoms. By challenging the underpinning of the religious-political establishment in Iran, religious intellectuals have played a key role in the development and consolidation of democracy in the country.

Religious intellectuals argue for the possibility of multiple readings of Islam and the rationalization of religious discourse, while challenging the usefulness and legitimacy of the ideological understanding of Islam. Asserting that any reading of religion is historically and culturally contingent, they masterfully articulate the thesis that no understanding of religion is ever sacred, absolute, and final. Accordingly, the ideological reading of Islam is only one of its many possible readings, which has no particular advantage at all. This ideological understanding, which gained the upper hand after the revolution, has been undermined by a crisis of legitimacy in having ignored and violated people's democratic rights and justifying the totalitarian control of society by theocratic government. In short, Islam is not an ideology; it has not mandated a particular form of government. Yet Muslims can produce a rationalist interpretation of Islam that concurs with democracy.

REFERENCES

Arjomand, Said Amir. 2002. "The Reform Movement and the Debate on Modernity and Tradition in Contemporary Iran." *International Journal of Middle East Studies* 34 (4): 719–31.

Arjomand, Said Amir. 2009. *After Khomeini: Iran under His Successors.* Oxford: Oxford University Press.

Bayat, Asef. 1996. "The Coming of a Post-Islamist Society." *Critique: Journal for Critical Studies of the Middle East* 5 (9): 43–52.

Bayat, Asef. 2007. *Making Islam Democratic: Social Movements and the Post-Islamist Turn.* Palo Alto, CA: Stanford University Press.

Filali-Ansary, A., 1999. "Muslims and Democracy." *Journal of Democracy* 10 (3): 18–32.

Hashemi, Nader. 2009. *Islam, Secularism, and Liberal Democracy: Toward a Democratic Theory for Muslim Societies.* Oxford: Oxford University Press.

Jahanbakhsh, Forough. 1980. "Islam, Democracy and Religious Modernism in Iran." *Philosophy* 51:117.

Jahanbakhsh, Forough. 2003. "Religious and Political Discourse in Iran: Moving toward Post-fundamentalism." *Brown Journal of World Affairs* 9:243.

Kamrava, Mehran. 2008. *Iran's Intellectual Revolution*. Cambridge: Cambridge University Press.

Keddie, Nikki R. 2003. "Secularism and Its Discontents." *Daedalus* 132 (3): 14–30.

Khosrokhavar, Farhad. 2004. "The New Intellectuals in Iran." *Social Compass* 51 (2): 191–202.

Mahdavi, Mojtaba. 2011. "Post-Islamist Trends in Postrevolutionary Iran." *Comparative Studies of South Asia, Africa and the Middle East* 31 (1): 94–109.

Mirsepassi, Ali. 1994. "The Crisis of Secular Politics and the Rise of Political Islam in Iran." *Social Text* 38:51–84.

Mirsepassi, Ali. 2000. *Intellectual Discourse and the Politics of Modernization: Negotiating Modernity in Iran*. Cambridge: Cambridge University Press.

Reichley, A. James. 1986. "Democracy and Religion." *PS: Political Science and Politics* 19 (4): 801–6.

Soroush, Abdolkarim. 1994. *Loftier Than Ideology*. Tehran: Serat.

Soroush, Abdolkarim. 1995. *The Theory of Expansion and Contraction of Religion*. Tehran: Serat.

Soroush, Abdolkarim, Mahmoud Sadri, and Ahmad Sadri. 2002. *Reason, Freedom, and Democracy in Islam: Essential Writings of Abdolkarim Soroush*. Oxford: Oxford University Press.

Conclusion

Sandra Harding once wrote that we need to "reevaluate indigenous knowledge and traditional environmental knowledge not from the perspective of conventional Northern exceptionalist and triumphalist standards, but rather as projects which respond well, or not, to concerns of non-European societies and their peoples" (2008, 134). She calls us to "reevaluate and examine more thoroughly both the traditional environmental knowledge of other societies and their indigenous knowledge traditions more generally" (138).

In chapter 2 of this volume, Harding further stresses the need for standpoint methodologies that take context into account and produce knowledge that is situated, or grounded, by the specific historical, cultural, and environmental context under which it was produced. Such knowledge production must be limited and partial and hence escapes the universalist claims advanced by traditional, triumphalist Northern science, whose practitioners have claimed to be the sole retainers of neutral, objective, and disengaged knowledge production. Maybe ironically, as the contributions by Walter Mignolo, Arturo Escobar, and Aram Ziai highlight again, it is precisely this sort of supposedly neutral and objective science that has provided the script for the destruction of the environment and the expansion of Western consumerism as the sole model of development. For Harding, as well as for Raewyn Connell, the solution to this problem must grow out of feminist critique and a "feminist democracy of theory" (chapter 1).

The call to add the "voices and presences of peoples whose cultures have borne more of the costs and received fewer of the benefits of Northern research practices" and "stir" them (chapter 2) thus also is a call for help, as it seems that some of the problems created by Northern modernity cannot be solved with modern solutions, as Arturo Escobar argues in chapter 3, quoting Boaventura de Sousa Santos. Not that we should romantically assert that everything produced and done in the North is bad and all that emanates from the Global South good. Rather, the "stirring" Sandra Harding calls for is a deep engagement with contextualized knowledge production from the North and the South. Such a project also requires a conscious recognition of those productions and proposals that transport domination, consumerism, and individualism in the very fabric of their ontologies and epistemologies—and a courageous stripping away of these destructive components from the scientific endeavor.

This can be done, as Walter Mignolo suggests, by inhabiting the border, that is, by assuming a border positionality—one that allows a researcher to see and understand systems of oppression and domination by being exposed to and thus experiencing them. For Mignolo, "decoloniality starts with the transformations and liberations of subjectivities controlled by the promises of the state, the fantasies of the market, and the fears of armed forces, all tied together by the messages of mainstream media" (foreword). Mignolo's border positionality, which he takes from Gloria Anzaldúa, resembles the recognition, also advanced by Patricia Hill Collins, that black women's positionality as "outsiders within" allows them to recognize and see through systems of racial and gendered domination more clearly than white men, who, after all, live inside the symbolic worlds created for their benefit.

Most contributions written for this book emanate from such borders, or from outsiders who have nevertheless had access to Western institutions of knowledge production. Their positionalities as outsiders within allow them to "see with both eyes," as Sandra Harding suggests, and perceive the good and the bad in both, Western knowledge production as well as other knowledges produced outside of metropolitan centers.

However, as Arturo Escobar highlights in chapter 3, the destructive forces unleashed by modern Western science and their applications focused on developing the world have not only destroyed native, non-Western worlds. They are also threatening to erode the lifeworlds of many middle classes in Europe, as the Indignados, Podemos, and Ya Basta!, movement demonstrate. The project of development, as Aram Ziai explains (chapter 5), is one that not only speaks for others, thus undermining their autonomy. It is also one that reproduces hierarchy, violence, and behavioral structures that erode community everywhere, in the South as well as in the North. His call thus is for a un-developing of the North and free cooperation among different communities and peoples—if and as long as such cooperation is actually sought and demanded—and not imposed by those who think they know better. Ziai's call thus resonates strongly with Escobar's analysis of emerging transitional discourses. These discourses are, after all, emerging in the Global North and the Global South.

The positionalities and backgrounds of the authors assembled in this book reflect this multipolar emergence of transitional discourse, nurtured by discontent, fear, or at a minimum doubt of the benefits of Western models, both analytical and applied-developmental. Those who live in the Global South directly experience the effects of modernization, globalization, and Westernization in the erosion of local culture and community; those who live in the Global North witness similar trends as local communities in the North have long suffered from the onslaught of capitalist rationality on local communities but also on epistemic communities. However, Northerners are necessarily implicated in the project of global development and thus write from a position of moral coresponsibility. Southerners, on the other hand, had to learn and adopt the language of Western science, still perceived as objective and neutral, to make their voices heard and to survive the disciplinary power and mental policing instituted by the guardians of (Western) knowledge production: universities, publishing houses, and peers whose blind reviews decide who has a voice and who does not and, if so, what kind of language this voice is allowed to speak in. In short: none of the authors assembled here sits comfortably in their offices and homes. All inhabit, to some extent, borderlands—even if for some, these are more borderlands of the mind, whereas for others the borderlands affect their bodies along with their minds.

Inhabiting borderlands thus is, to some extent, the result of consciousness, critical awareness, and doubt as only the numb and the ruthless are able to overlook and find excuses for the continued and accelerated destruction of lifeworlds—real and symbolic—Northern development has brought us. Transition movements, as Escobar shows, are thus spreading everywhere, north and south, east and west.

As transition movements spread, they all seek to not simply protest the old; they all seek to propose the new—be this new the Ecozoic, Transition Town, degrowth, postdevelopment, or postextractivism, among others, as Escobar shows. The new, however, has not yet taken shape and, if we believe the verdict of such authors as Boaventura de Sousa Santos, Arturo Escobar, and Walter Mignolo, we should resist finding one solution to the different problems created by Western modernity, development, and progress. Instead, Walter Mignolo argues for pluriversality as a new universal, and Santos, quoted by Escobar, finds that we have arrived at the impossibility of general theory.

The alternative ontologies, epistemologies, and conceptualizations of democracy presented in this book thus cannot be brought together under one coherent umbrella. While they all depart from the same place, namely the critique of the Western civilizational model and the different dimensions this model transports, namely the idea of the individual as rational and profit maximizing and development as an expansion of destructive consumerism bought with the destruction of ecosystems and the erosion of local community life, the proposals aimed at overcoming this civilizational trap are manifold and multidimensional.

Whereas Burchardt seeks to rescue the writings of Norbert Elias and Baruch Spinoza in order to capture and operationalize nonrational and nonindividualistic human (inter)action (chapter 11), others, such as Kashfi, seek to introduce systems of thought that aim not at scholarly analysis but at different practices. Concretely, Kashfi's introduction of the work of Ali Shariati and Abdulkarim Soroush represents an effort to think about religion and democracy and the role religion can play in a democracy (chapter 15). This is, of course, an urgent task as the Western developmental model, with its focus on secularization and demystification, has caused much resentment and resistance from all those who refuse to live in the iron cage of modernity. It should not surprise us that some of the most ardent critiques of the Western civilizational model come from the Middle East, as it was there that Western colonialism first cast its net, as if rehearsing and refining its methods of destruction before it set out to conquer Africa, the Far East, and the Americas. It should not come as a surprise then that it was the Iranian intellectual Jalal al-e Ahmad who introduced the term *Westoxification*—a term later adopted by Ali Shariati.

The other groups that have produced a biting critique of the Western civilizational model are native peoples of the Americas—north and south. They have, after all, suffered through five hundred years of enslavement, colonization, exploitation, discrimination, and disrespect, all in the name of bringing progress and prosperity to them—even Christian salvation, if all else failed. As chapter 14 shows, some Native American intellectuals have thus associated Western civilization with disease—wétiko. The proposals to redirect development toward buen vivir, as explained by Escobar and discussed in more detail by Walsh, must be seen as a response to the bankruptcy of the Western model of capitalist development—even if buen vivir is still linked to the very idea of development, as Catherine Walsh explains (chapter 9).

Hence, while the diagnoses overlap, the proposals emerging from these accounts are as different as we expect the pluriverse to be, with one looking to Islam as a way to provide moral guidelines for good behavior in a moral society and another focusing on communal practices and tribalism as the only way to resist the erosive forces of capitalism and the kind of progress introduced forcefully into the world by Western agents and developers.

The overlap of the accounts of resistance elaborated by Native Americans and Muslim scholars with Gandhi's advocacy for swaraj, local self-rule and autonomy, is obvious, but it also differs in important aspects from those accounts, as Gandhi seeks to ground his autonomy from the colonial empire in spiritual autonomy, as Samnotra explains in chapter 8. For Gandhi, it is through the practices of satyagraha and ahimsa that self-rule, swaraj, can be achieved. Gandhi thus presents a constructivist argument par excellence—long before and different from Western intellectuals' ability to link individual consciousness and behavior to social structures. Much of Gandhi's understanding of individual consciousness and societal structure seems based in religion as well—as Venu Mehta indicates (chapter 13). As she explains, Jainism as a religious practice advocates and embraces very similar attitudes to those proposed by Gandhi, but also those espoused by feminist theorists and postcolonial authors. Here, too, a commitment to truthfulness, combined with an attitude of not forcing one's own truth onto others, grows out of spiritual knowledge—but ultimately informs political action via epistemology.

If we consider the critiques of Western civilization and the alternative epistemological, ontological, and political proposals emerging from this critique together, it appears that one of the facets of the Western wétiko disease is precisely its delinking of the spiritual from the political, as well as its decoupling of the individual from the communal and the epistemological from the ontological. The treatises presented here allow us to gauge that this is not simply a matter of an inevitable transition from the traditional to the modern, where *tradition* stands for superstitious and oppressive and *modern* for reasonable and free. Western civilization advanced by lying and making false promises, as can still best be read in Bartolomé de las Casas's *Short Account of the Destruction of the Indies* (1542). The Spanish conquerors dissociated what they knew from what they actually did. As they proceeded, they thus dissociated from their own spirituality, instrumentalizing religion, and spirituality into tools of destruction, oppression, and the erosion of community. Wétiko, seen from this angle, starts to appear as a sort of zombie disease, a hollowing-out of people and communities for the sake of profit, leaving behind dead people, dead communities, and dead ecosystems and spreading a corrosive virus. Any conquest and any act of enslavement, exploitation, and discrimination, carried out by different colonial agents at different times and in different places, ultimately undermines not just the integrity and viability of local cultures and knowledge systems; it also hollows out the moral bases upon which Western and Northern civilization is erected. You cannot have it both ways: domination and claiming the moral high ground are mutually exclusive.

As this virus has reached almost all corners of the planet, it has become clear that there is no effective hiding from it. Instead, the call of the hour is to actively construct and advance the pluriverse by recognizing the dangers transported inside the bellies of progress and development—and face them. As we said earlier: not everything within the Western tradition is destructive and not all Northern knowledge production nihilistic. Similarly, just because a system of knowledge emerged in the Global South does not make it better and more suitable to guide our actions than Northern-produced systems. Instead, we need to rescue difference, assess it, and apply it pragmatically where it fits. Instead of constructing new canons, we should aim at not allowing one tradition to claim for itself the status of a canon. Instead of intellectual policing, we should engage in more ahimsa and anekāntavāda and accept otherness, embrace logical contradictions, and seek out intellectual ruptures. Only if we do that can we hope to learn from Ibn Khaldun, the griots of West Africa, and from all those who have been able to relink individual spirituality, communal practice, epistemology, ontology, and political action.

REFERENCE
Harding, Sandra. 2008. *Sciences from Below*. Durham, NC: Duke University Press.

Contributors

ZAID AHMAD is currently a professor of philosophy and civilization studies at the Faculty of Human Ecology, Universiti Putra Malaysia. He obtained his first degree from the National University of Malaysia and received his MA and PhD from the Victoria University of Manchester. His major work, *The Epistemology of Ibn Khaldun* (2003), is now an important reference in contemporary Khaldunian studies. He has also published more than one hundred works in his field of expertise, including books, journals, chapters, and proceedings.

MANUELA BOATCĂ is professor of sociology and head of school of the Global Studies Programme at the Albert-Ludwigs-University Freiburg, Germany. Her work on world systems analysis, postcolonial and decolonial perspectives, gender in modernity and coloniality, and the geopolitics of knowledge in Eastern Europe and Latin America has appeared in the *Journal of World-Systems Research, Cultural Studies, South Atlantic Quarterly, Political Power and Social Theory, Berliner Journal für Soziologie, Österreichische Zeitschrift für Soziologie, Zeitschrift für Weltgeschichte, Theory, Culture and Society*, and *Current Sociology*. She is author of *Global Inequalities beyond Occidentalism* (2016) and coeditor (with E. Gutiérrez Rodríguez and S. Costa) of *Decolonizing European Sociology: Transdisciplinary Approaches* (2010).

HANS-JÜRGEN BURCHARDT, PhD, since 2005 has held the chair of international and intersocietal relations at the University of Kassel, is since 2017 director of the Maria Sibylla Merian Center of Latin American Advanced Studies (CALAS), and was from 2009 to 2015 director of the International Center for Development and Decent Work (ICCD) and director of the doctoral program in global social policies and governance. He studied sociology and economics at the universities of Freiburg, Havana, and Bremen and has published and edited about twenty books and numerous articles in four languages. His main areas of research are North-South relations; ecological, labor, and social policy regimes in international perspective; democracy and social inequality; theory of development; and development politics in Latin America.

RAEWYN CONNELL is professor emerita at the University of Sydney and a Life Member of the National Tertiary Education Union. Recent books are *Southern Theory* (2007), about social thought in the postcolonial world; *Confronting Equality* (2011), about social science and politics; *Gender: In World Perspective* (3rd ed., with Rebecca Pearse, 2015), and *El género en serio* [Gender for real] (2015). Raewyn's other books include *Schools and Social Justice*; *Ruling Class Ruling Culture*; *Gender and Power*; *Masculinities*; and *Making the Difference*. She was the 2017 recipient of the American Sociological Association's Jessie Bernard Award for feminist sociology. Details can be found at her website www.raewynconnell.net and on Twitter @raewynconnell.

ARTURO ESCOBAR is professor of anthropology at UNC, Chapel Hill, and research associate at Universidad del Valle, Cali, Colombia. His main interests are political ecology, design, and the anthropology of development, social movements, and technoscience. Over the past twenty-five years, he has worked closely with Afro-Colombian social movements in the Colombian Pacific, particularly the Process of Black Communities (PCN). His most well known book is *Encountering Development: The Making and Unmaking of the Third World* (1995, 2nd ed. 2011). His most recent books are *Territories of Difference: Place, Movements, Life, Redes* (2008; 2010 for the Spanish ed.); *Sentipensar con la Tierra: Nuevas lecturas sobre desarrollo, territorio y diferencia* (2014); and *Autonomía y diseño: la realización de lo comunal* (2016; English version in press).

SANDRA HARDING is a distinguished research professor in the Graduate School of Education and Information Studies at UCLA. She is the author or editor of seventeen books on topics in feminist and postcolonial epistemology, methodology, and philosophy of science. Her most recent books are *Objectivity and Diversity: Another Logic of Scientific Research* (2015) and *The Postcolonial Science and Technology Studies Reader* (ed., 2011). She coedited *Signs: Journal of Women in Culture and Society* 2000–2005, and was the 2013 recipient of the John Desmond Bernal Prize for lifetime achievement of the Society for the Social Studies of Science (4S).

EHSAN KASHFI is a PhD candidate and instructor at the USF School of Interdisciplinary Global Studies. He earned his master's degree in international relations of the Middle East from Durham University (UK) and his bachelor's degree from National University of Iran. His research interests include Middle Eastern politics, Iranian intellectual history, and narratives of national identity in Iran.

VENU MEHTA is a PhD student at the Department of Religion, University of Florida. Mehta completed her second MA degree in religious studies with a special focus on Jainism at Florida International University. She completed her first MA degree in English literature and a PhD in the field of multicultural education and literature. She was a Fulbright Fellow (FLTA) at Indiana University, Bloomington. Her current research is on Jainism and diaspora Jains in the United States. She is an author of two books: *Multiculturalism and Globalization: Society, Literature, Education* and *Learn Gujarati: A Resource Book for Global Gujaratis, Beginner's Level.*

WALTER D. MIGNOLO is William H. Wannamaker Professor and Director of the Center for Global Studies and the Humanities at Duke University. He has been an associate researcher at Universidad Andina Simón Bolívar, Quito, since 2002 and an honorary research associate for CISA (Center for Indian Studies in South Africa), Wits University at Johannesburg. He is a senior advisor of DOC (Dialogue of Civilizations) Research Institute, based in Berlin, and received a doctor honoris causa degree from the National University of Buenos Aires, Argentina. Among his books related to the topic are *The Darker Side of the Renaissance: Literacy, Territoriality and Colonization* (1995, Chinese and Spanish translation 2015); *Delinking: The Rhetoric of Modernity, the Logic of Coloniality and the Grammar of Decoloniality* (2007, translated into German, French, Swedish, Romanian, and Spanish); *Local Histories/Global Designs: Coloniality, Subaltern Knowledges and Border Thinking* (2000, translated into Spanish, Portuguese, and Korean); and *The Idea of Latin America* (2006, translated into Spanish, Korean, and Italian). Forthcoming: *On Decoloniality: Concepts, Analysis, Praxis,* coauthored with Catherine Walsh (2018) and *Decolonial Politics: Border Dwelling, Re-existence, Epistemic Disobedience* (2018).

ULRICH OSLENDER is associate professor of geography in the Department of Global and Sociocultural Studies at Florida International University in Miami, Florida. He has published over forty articles and book chapters in both English and Spanish, mostly in relation to social movement theory, political geography, and Afro-descendant populations in Latin America. He has authored two books, most recently *The Geographies of Social Movements: Afro-Colombian Mobilization and the Aquatic Space* (2016), and coedited, with Bernd Reiter, *Bridging Scholarship and Activism: Reflections from the Frontlines of Collaborative Research* (2015). He has also frequently worked with the media and produced, among others, programs on black cultural politics in Colombia for the BBC World Service.

ISSIAKA OUATTARA, PhD, was born and still resides in Abidjan, Republic of Côte d'Ivoire. Married and the father of two children, he was successively teacher, professor in the Center of Animation and Pedagogical Formation (CAFOP), and finally doctor of letters and specialist in traditional and African oral literature. He currently works as an instructor and researcher at Université Alassane Ouattara of Bouaké and serves as director in charge of personnel of preprimary and primary education of the national education system of Côte d'Ivoire. He is the author of several works on traditional African education.

BERND REITER is a professor of comparative politics at the University of South Florida. Before joining academia, he worked as a social worker and NGO consultant in Brazil and in Colombia. He earned his PhD in political science from the City University of New York's Graduate Center and has been a visiting scholar in Germany, Colombia, and Spain. His work focuses on democracy and citizenship. His publications include *The Dialectics of Citizenship* (2013); *Bridging Scholarship and Activism* (2014); and *The Crisis of Liberal Democracy and the Path Ahead* (2017).

MANU SAMNOTRA is an assistant professor of political theory at the University of South Florida. He received his BA in economics and politics from Ithaca College, his MA in politics from the New School for Social Research, and his PhD in political science from the University of Florida. His research interests are at the intersection of continental philosophy and postcolonial political thought. He is currently writing a book about Hannah Arendt and the political uses of shame.

CATHERINE WALSH is senior professor and director of the doctoral program in Latin America Cultural Studies at the Universidad Andina Simón Bolívar in Ecuador, where she has also coordinated the Afro-Andean Documentary Fund and is the chair in Afro-Andean Studies. She has been a visiting professor at a number of universities in Europe and the Americas, and is the author of more than 200 publications, including *On Decoloniality: Concepts, Analytics, Praxis* with Walter Mignolo (2018), which opens the Duke University Press series On Decoloniality (coedited by Mignolo and Walsh).

ARAM ZIAI is Heisenberg-Professor for Development and Postcolonial Studies at the University of Kassel. He has studied in Aachen and Dublin (TCD) (MA in sociology, minors in history and English literature) and received his PhD in political science in Hamburg and his habilitation in political science in Kassel.

Afterward he had research and teaching posts in the universities of Aachen, Magdeburg, Kassel, Amsterdam (UvA), Vienna (IE), Bonn (ZEF), and Accra (Legon). Furthermore, Ziai is cochair of the section on development theory and policy of the German Political Science Association (DVPW), member of the board of directors of the International Center for Development and Decent Work (ICDD), member of the editorial board of the journal *Peripherie*, and member of the BUKO (Bundeskoordination Internationalismus).

Index

civilization, x, 46, 50, 71, 74, 83–84, 154, 156,
168–69, 178–79, 184, 197, 199, 206, 232,
242–46, 248–50, 253, 255, 260, 286; crisis
of, 65–67, 78, 85n7; northern, 47, 317;
western, 79, 92, 97, 100–101, 103, 105, 175,
181, 294, 315
class (economic), 26, 41–42, 45, 63, 95–96, 119,
125, 128, 197, 221, 230, 252–53, 280–81,
307, 314
cognition, 11, 108, 111, 259–60, 262, 266, 271–72
Cold War, xiii–xiv, 93–94, 103–4
colonialism, 1, 3–5, 8, 10–11, 19, 22–23, 25–26,
50, 119, 169, 174, 197–98, 204, 316
coloniality of gender, 23–24, 26–27, 31; of knowledge, 2; of power, 2, 5, 8, 10, 24, 73, 97, 208
colonial matrix of power (CMP), xi, 97, 192
communal, the, 79–80, 108–11, 317; assemblies,
76; government, 75; engagement, 109;
knowledge, 109; lands, 29, 288, 294; life, 304;
logics, 66, 76, 79, 81; power, 75; praxis, 109,
316; systems, 79; form of democracy, 76;
form of politics, 79, 95. See also ejido
communism, 122, 280
community, 44, 57, 69, 74, 79–80, 108, 143–44,
151–52, 154–55, 161, 186, 279–80, 282, 285,
288–94, 298, 301, 314–15, 317
Congress: U.S., 42; Berlin, 102; China, 103; U.S.
National of American Indians, 284
constitution: of Bolivian, 12, 72; of Colombian,
137, 288; of Ecuador, 12, 72–73, 75, 184,
188–89, 191; of Iran, 298
consumerism, 8, 95, 253, 313, 315
cooperation, 11, 53, 56, 81, 104, 114, 144, 168,
200, 232, 280–81, 294; free, 126–31, 314
corporations, xii, 39, 48, 82, 95, 96, 105, 111, 281
cosmology, ix–x, xii, 5–6, 70, 138, 188. See also
cosmovision; cosmovivencia
cosmovision, 72–73, 187–88, 192
cosmovivencia, xii
councils, 281, 288
counterpublics, 32
creolization, 12, 198, 209, 215n6
crime, 249, 252–53, 291
crisis, 4, 29, 63, 65–67, 71, 78–79, 82, 104, 304, 311
culture, 2, 4, 9, 24, 30, 39–41, 43–55, 57, 65, 67,
71, 73, 74, 82, 90, 92, 94, 138, 140–41, 151–52,
154, 156, 162, 164–65, 176, 186, 188–90, 225,
227–28, 231, 240, 242, 244–45, 248–50, 252,

253, 255, 260, 279, 285, 290, 292–95, 302, 310,
313, 315, 317
Cusicanqui, Silvia Rivera, 5, 8, 86n14
customary law, 288

decentering, xiii, 76
decolonization, xii–xiv, 5, 8–9, 26, 50, 73,
78, 90, 92, 98, 104–5, 109, 197, 202, 205,
240–42, 255
degrowth, 66–67, 69, 126, 315
Deleuze, Gilles, 118–19, 148n2
delinking, x, xiv, 48–50, 93, 95, 103, 105–7,
110–13, 317
dependence, dependency, 23, 97, 128, 184–85,
208, 235n1, 240–41
design, ix–xi, xiii–xiv, 42–43, 56, 63, 83, 95, 99,
101, 103–5, 108, 162, 185, 190
dewesternization, xiii–xiv, 90, 92–94, 97, 99,
102–7, 109, 111–13
difference, cultural, 19, 28, 47; fundamental, 69;
gender, 73; territories of, 138
differentiation, 79, 199, 212, 228–34
dignity, 73, 80, 94, 161, 171
diversity (cultural, religious) of viewpoints,
ix–x, 6, 19, 26, 28, 30–31, 47, 51, 54, 65, 70,
76–77, 83, 95, 156, 169–70, 181, 185–88, 190,
192, 273, 308
domination, 1, 12–13, 27, 63, 100–101, 103, 107,
109, 124–25, 127–30, 184, 205, 232, 250, 282,
284, 307, 313–14, 317
Dussel, Enrique, ix, 4, 8, 206
duties, 175, 182, 291, 301, 306

East, Eastern, 91, 175, 199, 201, 203–7, 210, 244,
315–16
ecology, 65, 70, 73
ecozoic, 66–67, 69–70, 315
Ecuador, 72–75, 77–78, 96–97, 184, 188,
191–92
education, 19, 27, 31, 41, 56, 119, 151, 162, 175, 181,
186, 188–89, 240–42, 246, 250, 253
egalitarian, egalitarianism, 5, 53, 280–83, 303
Ejército Zapatista de Liberación Nacional
(EZLN)/Zapatistas, ix–x, 75–76, 110–11, 118,
121–22, 128, 260, 279, 284, 294
ejido, 295
elite(s), 3, 41–42, 44, 48, 52, 99, 230–31, 281,
283, 294

emancipation, 119, 123–31, 168, 190
emotions, xii, 12, 100, 125, 128, 143, 156, 221, 228
enlightenment, 43, 59n7, 99
epistemicide, 4, 8
epistemology, mosaic, 1–2, 11, 30
Esteva, Gustavo, 76, 80
European Commission, 26, 200, 210–11
European Union (EU), xiii, 99, 187, 200–201, 210–11, 214–15
exceptionalism, 40, 47
exclusion, 28, 71, 128, 159, 201–2, 229, 231, 294
extractivism, postextractivism, neoextractivism, 66–67, 77–78, 81, 315

femicide, 32
feminism, 3, 19–24, 26–32, 80
food sovereignty, xii, 71, 73
Foucault, Michel, 4, 9, 118–19, 128, 225
France, 4, 8, 101–2, 200–205, 210, 212
freedom, 64, 126–27, 180, 186–87, 208, 219, 222, 230, 292–93, 299, 300–301, 310–11
free trade, 117, 122
Freire, Paulo, 56
French Revolution, 204, 211–12
fuzzy logic, 5–6

genealogy, ix, 1, 11, 65, 160
globalism, 101–2, 107
globalization, 8, 10, 20, 26, 54, 63–64, 69, 71, 82, 84, 117–19, 121, 123, 187, 314
global political society, xii, 94–96, 106–7, 112
gnoseology, ix–x
governance, xiv, 100, 251–52, 254, 299, 300, 309–10
government, 56, 75–77, 96, 104, 188, 191, 246, 251, 284, 287, 299, 300–301, 305–6, 309–11
grassroots, 69, 181–82
Greece, ancient, 94, 175
Grosfoguel, Ramón, 4–5, 8
Gudynas, Eduardo, 72–74, 77–78, 189

Habermann, Friedrike, 122–23, 126
Habermas, Jürgen, 225, 293
Haraway, Donna, 3, 58, 226, 260–62
health, 44, 46, 49, 51, 56, 181, 186, 189, 251–53, 290
Hegel, Wilhelm Friedrich, xi–xii, 122, 205
hegemony, western, 1, 100, 260

hermeneutics, ix–x, 138, 157, 308
Hirschman, Albert, 221–23
Hountondji, Paulin, 1–2, 20–21, 24
humanities, 4, 8, 10, 113, 248

identity, 2, 11, 22, 27–28, 50, 71, 78, 139, 143, 154–56, 159, 161–62, 164–65, 199–202, 206–7, 213–14, 221, 223, 230, 240–41, 243, 254–55, 259, 264, 266, 301, 305
ideographic, 5, 9
ideology, 7–8, 119, 129–30, 250, 298–301, 305–8, 311
imperialism, x–xii, 5, 11, 20, 23, 25–26, 50, 52–53, 81, 94, 99–103, 124, 131, 138, 185, 197–98, 201, 203–5, 207, 211–13, 241, 286
indignados, 63, 314
individualism, 109, 221, 313
industrialization, 27, 126, 173, 204
inequality, 21, 30, 41, 125, 201, 212, 229, 252, 280–82, 294
insecurity, 219, 252
intellectuals, ix, 2–3, 10, 13, 21–22, 40, 65, 77–78, 95–97, 107, 112, 119, 152, 187, 241, 255, 298–301, 304–7, 311, 316–17
internationalism, 117–18, 121, 123–25
international law, 48, 101–2
International Monetary Fund (IMF), 39, 45, 105, 107, 117–18, 187

justice: gender, 28, 33; social, 31, 42–44, 50, 53–54, 73, 190, 299

labor, 20–21, 24, 26, 29, 40, 42, 46, 49, 79, 124–27, 130, 189, 208, 214, 226, 228
land: communal, 29, 288, 294; rights, 29; reform, 162
law, universal, 4, 48
liberalism, 76, 93–94, 128, 260, 280, 303, 307. See also neoliberalism; postliberalism
liberation, xiv, 21, 70, 113, 123–24, 261, 265, 314. See also liberation theology
liberation theology, 56, 97
lifeworld, 9, 147, 314–15
love, xiv, 11, 19, 108–11, 160, 172–73, 177, 190, 223, 233

mapping, 55, 65, 206, 213–14
markets, 10, 12, 48–49, 69